TExES 161 Special Education EC-12

Teacher Certification Exam

By: Sharon Wynne, M.S.

XAMonline, INC.

Boston

XAMonline, Inc.
21 Orient Avenue
Melrose, MA 02176
Toll Free 1-800-509-4128
Email: info@xamonline.com
Web www.xamonline.com
Fax: 1-617-583-5552

Library of Congress Cataloging-in-Publication Data

Wynne, Sharon A.
    Special Education EC-12 161: Teacher Certification / Sharon A. Wynne.
    ISBN 978-1-60787-391-4
        1. Special Education EC-12 161.   2. Study Guides.   3. TExES
        4. Teachers' Certification & Licensure.   5. Careers

Disclaimer:
The opinions expressed in this publication are the sole works of XAMonline and were created independently from the National Education Association, Educational Testing Service, or any State Department of Education, National Evaluation Systems or other testing affiliates.

Between the time of publication and printing, state specific standards as well as testing formats and website information may change that is not included in part or in whole within this product. Sample test questions are developed by XAMonline and reflect similar content as on real tests; however, they are not former tests. XAMonline assembles content that aligns with state standards but makes no claims nor guarantees teacher candidates a passing score. Numerical scores are determined by testing companies such as NES or ETS and then are compared with individual state standards. A passing score varies from state to state.

Printed in the United States of America   œ-1

TExES: Special Education EC-12 161
ISBN: 978-1-60787-391-4

ACKNOWLEDGEMENTS
Special Education

Recognizing the hard work in the production of our study guides we would like to thank those involved. The credentials and experience fulfilling the making of this study guide, aided by the professionalism and insight of those who expressed the subject mastery in specialized fields, is valued and appreciated by XAMonline. It results in a product that upholds the integrity and pride represented by modern educators who bear the name **TEACHER**.

Providers of foundational material

Founding authors 1996	Kathy Schinerman
	Roberta Ramsey
Pre-flight editorial review	Paul Sutliff
Pre-flight construction :	Brittany Good
Authors 2006	Paul Sutliff
	Beatrice Jordan
	Marisha Tapera
	Kathy Gibson
	Twya Lavender
	Carol Moore
	Christi Godard
Sample test rational	Sidney Findley

XAMonline Editorial and Production acknowledgements

Project Manager	Sharon Wynne
Project Coordinator	Twya Lavender
Series Editor	Mary Collins
Editorial Assistant	Virginia Finnerty
Copy Editor	Jeanette M. Ritch
Marketing Manager	John Wynne
Marketing support	Maria Ciampa
Cover design	Brian Messenger
Sales	Justin Dooley
Production Editor	David Aronson
Typist	Julian German
Manufacturing	Chris Morning/Midland Press
E-Books	Kristy Gipson/Lightningsource
Cover Administrator	Jenna Hamilton

About the Test

The TExES Special Education EC-12 is formulated for teachers who want to teach Special Education in the state of Texas. The test confirms your knowledge to teach Texas-state curriculum, known as the Texas Essential Knowledge and Skills. It is important to be familiar with the requirements for teaching this genre of students. Please refer to the Texas Examinations of Educator Standards.

The test is comprised of four content areas referred to as domains. The exam breakdown is as follows:

Domain I: Understanding Individuals with Disabilities and Evaluating Their Needs is approximately 13% of the test. This domain includes skills in competency areas one and two.

Domain II: Promoting Student Learning and Development is approximately 33% of the test. This domain which includes skill in competency areas three through seven.

Domain III: Promoting Student Achievement in English Language Arts and Reading and in Mathematics is approximately 33% of the test. This domain includes skills in competency areas eight and nine.

Domain IV: Foundations and Professional Roles and Responsibilities is approximately 20% of the test. This domain includes skills in competency areas ten through twelve.

Taking the TExES Test and Receiving Scores

Please refer to the current TExES registration bulletin for information on test dates, sites, fees, registration procedures, and policies at http://cms.texes-ets.org/registrationbulletin/

As of 2009, score reports are no longer mailed. Scores are available online, approximately four weeks after each test you take. Score reports for paper-based tests are posted by 5:00PM Central Time on the date indicated on the registration bulletin. The report will indicate whether you have passed the test and will include the following:

- A scaled score, which is reported to compare scores on the same content-area test taken on different test administration dates.

  For all TExES tests, the score scale is 100–300 with a scaled score of 240 as the minimum passing score. This score represents the minimum level of competency required to be an entry-level educator in Special Education in Texas public schools.

- The applicant's performance in the major content domains of the test and in the specific content competencies of the test.

  This information may be useful in identifying strengths and weaknesses in the applicant's content preparation and can be used for further study or for preparing to retake the test.

- General information to help the applicant understand the score scale and interpret the results.

TABLE OF CONTENTS

Great Study and Testing Tips!

What to study in order to prepare for the subject assessments is the focus of this study guide, but equally important is *how* you study.

You can increase your chances of truly mastering the information by taking some simple, but effective steps.

Study Tips:

1. Aid the learning process with food. Foods such as milk, nuts, seeds, rice, and oats help your study efforts by releasing natural memory enhancers called CCKs (*cholecystokinin*) composed of *tryptophan*, *choline*, and *phenylalanine*. All of these chemicals enhance the neurotransmitters associated with memory. Before studying, try a light, protein-rich meal of eggs, turkey, or fish. All of these foods release memory enhancing chemicals. The stronger the connections, the more you comprehend.

Likewise, before you take a test, stick to a light snack of energy boosting, yet relaxing foods. A glass of milk, a piece of fruit, or some peanuts all release various memory-boosting chemicals and help you to relax so you may readily focus on the subject at hand.

2. Learn to take great notes. A byproduct of our modern culture is that it has allowed society to grow accustomed to getting information in short doses (i.e. TV news sound bites or *USA Today* style newspaper articles.)

Consequently, we have subconsciously trained ourselves to assimilate information better in neat little packages. If your notes are scrawled in a disorganized manner all over the paper, then the flow of the information will appear fragmented. Therefore, you must strive for clarity. Newspapers use a standard format to achieve such clarity. Your notes can be much clearer through use of proper formatting. A very effective format is called the *"Cornell Method."*

Take a sheet of loose-leaf lined notebook paper and draw a line all the way down the paper about 1-2" from the left-hand edge.

Draw another line across the width of the paper about 1-2" up from the bottom. Repeat this process on the reverse side of the page.

Look at the highly effective result. You have ample room for notes, a left hand margin for special emphasis items or inserting supplementary data from the textbook, a large area at the bottom for a brief summary, and a little rectangular space for just about anything you want.

3. <u>Get the concept then the details.</u> Test-takers often focus on the textual or conceptual details, and forget to properly gather an understanding of the concept. However, if a test-taker is simply memorizing dates, places, or names, then he or she may miss the whole point of the subject.

A key way to understand over-arching ideas and main concepts is to put them in your own words. This paraphrasing technique will help you connect with the concepts at hand and personalize the information given. Also, If you are working from a textbook, automatically summarize each paragraph in your mind. This chunking technique prevents boredom due to the length of the text, but it also assesses knowledge gained as you are actively reading.

If you are outlining text, don't simply copy the author's words. Select meaningful portions of the text and mix them with your thoughts, reactions, and insights as well. You remember your own thoughts and words much better than someone else's, and subconsciously tend to associate the important details to the core concepts.

4. <u>Ask "Why?"</u> Pull apart written material paragraph by paragraph and don't forget the captions under the illustrations. For example, if the heading is "Stream Erosion", flip it around to read "Why do streams erode?" Then answer the question created. If you train your mind to think in a series of questions and answers, not only will you learn more, but it also helps to lessen the test anxiety because you are used to answering questions.

5. <u>Read for reinforcement and future needs.</u> Even if you only have ten minutes of free time to spare for studying one day, put your notes or a book in your hand. Your mind is similar to a computer; you have to input data in order to have it processed. *By reading, you are creating the neural connections for future retrieval.* The more times you read something, the more you reinforce the learning of ideas. Even if you don't fully understand something on the first pass, *your mind stores much of the material for later recall.*

6. <u>Relax to learn; go into exile.</u> Our bodies respond to an inner clock which controls cycles called biorhythms. Burning the midnight oil works well for some people, but not everyone. Your learning style dictates your preference for light, sound, or lack thereof when studying, so be sure to design an optimal space for studying while 'in exile.' Set aside a particular place to study that is free of distractions. Shut off the television, cell phone, all electronic devices, and ask your friends and family to let you focus during your study period.

If you really are bothered by silence, try background music. Light classical music at a low volume has been shown to aid in concentration over other types. Music that evokes pleasant emotions without lyrics are highly suggested.

7. Use arrows and underlining, not highlighters. At best, it is difficult to read a page full of yellow, pink, blue, and green streaks. These markers can also bleed through the page onto other text, and make it appear highlighted, which may confuse you. A quick note, a brief dash of color, an underline, and an arrow pointing to a particular passage is much clearer than a horde of highlighted words.

8. Budget your study time. Although you should not ignore any of the material, *allocate your available study time in the same ratio that topics may appear on the test.* For example, Domain II, "Promoting Student Learning and Development," accounts for one-third of the test. Therefore, devote one-third of your study time to this area.

Testing Tips:

1. Avoid assumptions. Try not to read into the question. Do not assume the test writer is looking for something else than what is asked. Stick to the question as written and answer it concretely.

2. Read the question and all the choices *twice* before answering the question. You may miss something critical by not carefully reading your first time through. If you have enough time to do so, please read and them re-read both the question and the answers. If you do not know the answer right away, feel free to leave it blank. Go on to the other questions, as they may provide a clue as to how to answer the skipped questions.

Later on, if you still cannot answer the skipped ones . . . *Guess.*
The only penalty for guessing is that you *might* get it wrong. Only one thing is certain; if you don't put anything down, you *will* get it wrong! Statistically, each question has four potential answers, so eliminating even one of the answers will increase your chances of choosing the correct answer by 25%.

3. Turn the question into a statement. Analyze the manner in which a question is worded. The syntax of the question usually provides a clue. Does it seem more familiar as a statement rather than as a question? By turning a question into a statement, you may be able to spot if a correct answer, and it may also trigger memories of material you have read.

4. Look for hidden clues. It is actually very difficult to create multiple-choice questions without giving away part of the answer in the options presented.

In most multiple-choice questions, you can readily eliminate one or two of the potential answers. This leaves you with only two real possibilities by virtue of process of elimination. The two remaining answers can be discerned by recalling text you have studied, life experiences you have had, or referring back to the question to see if there is an inherent, subtle connection between question wording and answer wording.

5. <u>**Trust your instincts.**</u> For every fact that you have read, you subconsciously retain at least a portion of that knowledge gained. On questions that you aren't really certain about, go with your initial instinct; your first impression is usually correct. Over analyzing answer choices can create a feeling of impending doom; read each choice lightly, but select the one that resonates with your reasoning most.

6. <u>**Mark your answers directly on the test booklet AND the scan sheet**</u>. Answer demarcation and 'bubbling in' is a stylistic preference; some test-takers prefer to circle answers in the test booklet, then transcribe all answers onto the scan sheet. Other like to strictly bubble in answers, and do not cross reference. *Be very careful not to mismark your answers when you eventually transcribe them to the scan sheet.*

7. <u>**Watch the clock**</u>! You have five hours to complete the test. Be sure to work steadily and methodically, attacking each question with ease. Do not be discouraged if you come across a question you do not know the answer to. You can always return to that question, so you can keep a steady pace. And a note regarding watches and electronic time pieces that make noise: make sure they are turned off before beginning the test.

Three full Practice Tests

Now with Adaptive Assessments!

Adaptive learning is an educational method which uses computers as interactive teaching devices. Computers adapt the presentation of educational material according to students' learning needs, as indicated by their responses to questions. The technology encompasses aspects derived from various fields of study including computer science, education, and psychology.

In Computer Adaptive Testing (CAT), the test subject is presented with questions that are selected based on their level of difficulty in relation to the presumed skill level of the subject. As the test proceeds, the computer adjusts the subject's score based on their answers, continuously fine-tuning the score by selecting questions from a narrower range of difficulty.

The results are available immediately, the amount of time students spend taking tests decreases, and the tests provided more reliable information about what students know—especially those at the very low and high ends of the spectrum. With Adaptive Assessments, the skills that need more study are immediately pinpointed and reported to the student.

Adaptive assessments provide a unique way to assess your preparation for high stakes exams. The questions are asked at the mid-level of difficulty and then, based on the response, the level of difficulty is either increased or decreased. Thus, the test adapts to the competency level of the learner. This is proven method which is also used by examinations such as SAT and GRE. The Adaptive Assessment Engine used for your online self-assessment is based on a robust adaptive assessment algorithm and has been validated by a large pool of test takers. Use this robust and precise assessment to prepare for your exams.

Our Adaptive Assessments can be accessed here:
xamonline.4dlspace.com/AAE
You will be presented with a short form to complete for your account registration. You will need an active email address to register.

DOMAIN I.   UNDERSTANDING INDIVIDUALS WITH DISABILITIES AND EVALUATING THEIR NEEDS

COMPETENCY 1.0   THE SPECIAL EDUCATION TEACHER UNDERSTANDS AND APPLIES KNOWLEDGE OF THE CHARACTERISTICS AND NEEDS OF STUDENTS WITH DISABILITIES

Skill 1.01   Knows the characteristics of individuals with disabilities including individuals with different levels of severity and multiple disabilities across eligibility categories.

This particular competency skill, 1.01, addresses the characteristics of individuals with disabilities. This skill answers the following questions:

- What is a disability?
- What causes a disability?
- What is an eligible disability category?
- What qualities do individuals with disabilities have?

The Term 'Disability'

A disability is a general impairment, but what is the definition of 'disability' as encountered by teachers? The Americans with Disabilities Act (ADA) utilizes a three-part definition of disability. According to the ADA, a person with a disability: (1) has a physical or mental impairment that substantially limits one or more major life activities; OR (2) has a record of such an impairment; OR (3) is regarded as having such an impairment.

The ADA considers a physical impairment to be "any physiological disorder or condition, cosmetic disfigurement, or anatomical loss affecting one or more of the following body systems: neurological, musculoskeletal, special sense organs, respiratory (including speech organs), cardiovascular, reproductive, digestive, genitourinary, hemic and lymphatic, skin, and endocrine."

Students in our classrooms may also have learning disabilities, that may or may not be comorbid (occurring in conjunction with) other disabilities. Some students are learning disabled or have multiple disabilities, but may not have physical manifestations of such disabilities. The IDEA (Individuals with Disabilities Education Act) creates definitions for specific disability terms to assist how States define disabilities and delegate special education services. There is a general list of disabilities created by the IDEA. A student's overall educational performance must be "adversely affected due to the disability" in order to receive special education services. The list is as follows:

Autism   Deaf-blindness   Deafness

Developmental delay

Emotional disturbance

Hearing Impairment

Intellectual disability

Multiple disabilities

Orthopedic impairment

Other health impairment

Specific Learning disability

Speech or language impairment

Traumatic brain injury

Visual impairment, including blindness

The Causation of a Disability

The precise cause of a disability is often unknown, due to a wide variation of factors which may contribute to the development of a disability. Potential causes can occur before, during, or after pregnancy. They include:

- **Complications in Fetal Brain Development** - Throughout pregnancy, brain development is vulnerable to potential disruptions. Such disruptions to fetal brain development may result in miscarriage, or the infant may be born with extensive disabilities. Maternal factors that can complicate fetal brain development can include folic acid intake, thyroid function, exposure to medication(s), substance abuse, and contact to toxins.

- **Problems During Delivery** - Complications during delivery can contribute to the development of disabilities. Delivery difficulties in which the infant oxygen deprivation for any period of time can impact a child's development can occur during an obstructed labor (the child does not fit through the mother's pelvis) or a prolonged labor.

- **Genetic Factors** - Learning disabilities can run in families, a genetic predisposition to inherit or carry specific genes associated with disabilities is a strong possibility based upon recent research findings. Although some disabilities, such as Down Syndrome and Williams Syndrome, are related to chromosomal defects and deletions, and are not necessarily inherited, others are in fact inherited. For example, Fragile X Syndrome is inherited, as well as DYX1C1, which is the gene associated with familial patterns of dyslexia.

- **Environment** - Environmental factors within the context of upbringing and the home surroundings can also contribute to the development of–disabilities. For example, a parent with an expressive language disorders may not verbally interact well with their child, or the child may mimic the parent's articulation errors. In this case, the lack of a sufficient language model at home can contribute to a speech or language delay. Studies show parents and guardians who expose children to reading and language from birth onward increase the vocabulary base. These children enter kindergarten with a larger vocabulary lexicon then other students who in turn, have limited vocabulary knowledge.

- **Exposure to Toxins** – Brain cells and critical neural connections are constantly being created and wired during fetal development. Certain environmental toxins, such as cadmium and lead, may contribute to the development of disabilities, learning disabilities in particular.

  Neurological research has focused on cadmium, found in metal production processes, and lead, often found in the paint in older homes, which may be significant factors in the development of disabilities in children. These elements can leach into the soil, groundwater, and ultimately into the food supply. Lead was once common in paint and gasoline, and is still present in some water pipes.

  Children with cancer who have been treated with chemotherapy or radiation at an early age can also develop learning disabilities. Radiation for the treatment of tumors carries a risk of the development of learning disabilities, as the radiation may damage brain cells. Doctors are particularly cautious with children under three years old. The likelihood of developing a learning disability is increased when both radiation and chemotherapy are used when the brain is targeted.

In order to prevent disabilities from occurring, information on the causes of disabilities should be widely available so that parents can take the necessary steps to safeguard their children from conception. While some of the causes of disability are unavoidable or incidental, there are many causes that can be limited or even prevented.

Identify Characteristics of Students with Behavioral Disorders

Children with behavioral disorders are not always easy to identify. The acting-out child who gets into physical altercations, or cannot stay on task for more than a few minutes, or who shouts obscenities when angry is readily identified. The child with a behavioral disorder may suffer from depression, shyness, or fears. Unless the problem becomes severe enough to impact school performance, the internalizing child may go for a long period of time without being identified or served.

Studies of children with behavioral disorders have identified general characteristics:

- **Lower Academic Performance:** While it is true that some children with emotional disturbance possess average or above average scores on intelligence (IQ) tests, many are behind their peers in measures of school achievement. A child with a behavioral disorder may also have a learning disability.

- **Social Skills Deficits:** Students behavioral disorders may be uncooperative, unacquainted with what to do in social situations, or—unaware of the consequences of their actions. As a result, a student may not be able to build strong relationships with peers, teachers, administrators, or even family members.

- **Classroom Behaviors**: Significant classroom behaviors frequently exhibited by the child with an emotional disturbance vary,. But may include: habitually getting out of his or her seat or running around the room, invading the personal space of classmates, acting aggressively, exhibiting nonverbal tendencies or inability to communicate effectively, and displaying other types of inappropriate behavior. The child with an behavioral disturbance may be defiant, delinquent, noncompliant, and/or verbally disruptive.

- **Withdrawn Behaviors:** Children who manifest withdrawn behaviors may act in an immature fashion or prefer to play with younger children. The withdrawn child may daydream, or complain of regular illness despite good health. The withdrawn child may also exhibit behaviors such as crying, clinging to the teacher, and ignoring those who attempt to interact with him or her. Phobias can also be prevalent, such as social phobia or social anxiety disorder, which prohibits a student from fully interacting with others due to a paralyzing, unreasonable, or excessive fear.

- **Schizophrenia and Psychotic Behaviors:** Schizophrenia typically manifests itself between the ages of 15 and 45, but symptoms can be noted in childhood. Children with schizophrenia or related disorders may have bizarre delusions, hallucinations, incoherent thoughts, and disconnected thinking. These behaviors usually require intensive treatment beyond the scope of the regular classroom setting, including counseling, therapeutic sessions with a psychologist, and prescriptive medication.

- **Gender:** Many more boys than girls are identified as having emotional and behavioral problems, particularly hyperactivity, attention deficit disorder, autism, and childhood psychosis. Boys typically are identified as having problems with control, such as aggression, more often than are girls. Girls, tend to exhibit more difficulty with behaviors such as withdrawal and phobias.

- **Age Characteristics:** When girls enter adolescence, emotional disorders such as anorexia, depression, bulimia, and anxiety occur at twice the rate of boys, which mirrors the adult prevalence pattern. Other disorders such as ADHD, report an average onset age of seven years old, although children with more severe cases of ADHD were diagnosed earlier.

- **Family Characteristics:** Having a child with an emotional or behavioral disorder does not allude to a dysfunctional home or family life. However, there are family factors that may contribute to the development of behavior disorders and emotional disturbances.

- Abuse and neglect
- Lack of appropriate supervision
- Lax, punitive, and/or lack of discipline
- High rates of negative types of interaction among family members

- Lack of parental concern and interest
- Negative adult role models
- Lack of proper health care and/or nutrition
- Disruption in the family, such as moving, divorce, ill family member(s), or traumatic event(s)

Identify Characteristics of Children with Intellectual Disabilities

An intellectual disability, according to AAIDD (American Association on Intellectual and Developmental Disabilities), is "characterized by significant limitations in both intellectual functioning and in adaptive behavior." It is diagnosed before age 18.

Intellectual functioning is a term for intelligence, which includes learning, reasoning, logic, and so forth. Intelligence is measured by IQ tests, such as the Stanford-Binet IQ test. In general, IQ scores that are less than 70 indicate intellectual limitations.

Significant limitations in adaptive behavior are observed from a mix of social and practical skills that students need to use in their everyday lives. This includes conceptual skills, such as language, reading, time, numeracy. It also includes limitations in social skills, such as following rules, self-esteem, and problem solving. Daily living skills are also impacted, such as personal hygiene, safety, and occupational skills.

Identify Characteristics of Students with Learning Disabilities

Learning disabilities can go unidentified; the identification of a learning disability requires psychological testing, such as psycho-educational evaluations. This testing confirms evidence and provides a platform for the diagnosis of a learning disability. According to NDCCD (National Dissemination Center for Children with Disabilities), learning disabilities include dyslexia, dysgraphia, and dyscalculia.
Characteristics of students with learning disabilities include:

- **Hyperactivity:** a rate of motor activity higher than normal
- **Perceptual difficulties:** visual, auditory, and perceptual problems
- **Perceptual-motor impairments:** poor integration of visual and motor systems, including fine motor coordination and evidence of dyspraxia
- **Disorders of memory and thinking:** memory deficits, trouble with problem-solving, weak concept formation and association, poor awareness of own metacognitive skills (learning strategies) and executive functioning (planning and organizing)
- **Impulsiveness:** acting out before considering consequences, poor impulse control.
- **Academic problems** in reading, math, writing or spelling; significant discrepancies in ability levels

- **Language-based impairments:** speech and language articulation, oral and expressive language difficulties

The severity of a learning disability widely varies. Learning disabilities are on a scaled continuum of moderate to severe. Early remediation and intervention efforts are critical to the lessening of severity, as the young brain is most receptive to rewiring new schemas for reading, writing, and mathematics. For example, a student with dyslexia should be taught specific spelling patterns through a prescriptive program such as Orton-Gillingham, and strategies for prosody and fluency when reading. Additionally, a student struggling with dysgraphia should encounter fine motor skills improvement programs, to increase legibility of handwriting, and ability to express written words fluidly. And a math student with dyscalculia could benefit from receiving small group and individualized instruction to strengthen concepts of arithmetic, sequencing, and pattern formation.

Identify Characteristics of Students with Autism

Autism appears very early in childhood and signs are often apparent by toddlerhood. If a child is not babbling or pointing by age 1, nor creating two word phrases by age 2, autism may be investigated. Poor eye contact and lack of social responsiveness are also early indicators of autism. Autism covers a broad spectrum of neurodevelopmental impairments, however, and entails communication problems, lack of sociability, and repetitive behaviors. This continuum starts with a milder form of autism, Asperger syndrome, as well as pervasive developmental disorder (PDD/PDD-NOS). It varies significantly in severity, and occurs across ethnicities, though males are four times as likely to have ASD then females. It is likely both genetics and environment play a role in this disorder, though scientists are not fully aware of its origins. Some studies suggest there are several irregularities in the brain; others indicate those with ASD have abnormal levels of serotonin and other neurotransmitters.

According to the National Institute for Neurological Disorders and Stroke, ASD symptoms may go unrecognized if a child is mildly affected, or when it is obscured by more apparent disabilities. ASD can co-occur with other disorders, such as Fragile X Syndrome, epileptic seizures, and learning disabilities. When assessing a child, expert evaluators look for ASD signs, including:

- no response to name
- lack of social skills
- loss of language
- reduced eye contact
- extremely repetitious or patterned behaviors, such as lining up objects
- no social responsiveness.
- inability to make friends or hold conversations with peers
- lack of imaginative play
- stereotyped, repetitive, or unusual use of language, such as echolalia
- fixation on very specific objects or subjects
- abnormal observance or lack of observance to specific routines and rituals

In accordance with the new DSM-5 (Diagnostic and Statistical Manual 5) released in May 2013, the diagnosis of autism has changed. The manual, last updated in 1994, is now modified because the 19 years of research the occurred. The diagnosis will be called Autism Spectrum Disorder (ASD). There are no longer subcategories (Autistic Disorder, Asperger Syndrome, Pervasive Developmental Disorder Not Otherwise Specified, Disintegrative Disorder). Additionally, Rett syndrome is now a discrete neurologic disorder and is not a subcategory under ASD. However, patients with Rett syndrome may have ASD as well.

The DSM-5 also includes a new category of Social Communication Disorder (SCD) which describes students with social and pragmatic language differences that impede upon verbal comprehension, speech production and social awareness in conversation. SCD is not caused by delayed cognition or other language delays.

Fetal Alcohol Spectrum Disorder

According to thearc.org, FASD (Fetal Alcohol Spectrum Disorder) is an umbrella term describing the range of effects that can occur in an individual whose mother drank alcohol during pregnancy. These effects can include physical, behavioral, mental and/or learning disabilities with possible lifelong implications. It is identified by abnormal facial features, central nervous system problems and slowness of growth, and occurs when pregnant women drink alcohol and pass the alcohol along to their unborn babies through the blood stream. FASD can cause physical and mental disabilities of varying levels of severity (including intellectual disability).

Individuals with Medical Conditions

Students afflicted with health conditions may be placed in the 'OHI' or Other Health Impairment disability category. This category of students is vast; it includes students who have a health impairment with adversely affects their educational performance, per the National Dissemination Center for Children with Disabilities. This umbrella term covers a large amount of conditions, such as diabetes, leukemia, nephritis, and Tourette syndrome.

These students may need medical and/or school nurse services in order to function in the school environment. Those with medical conditions may require these services for medication dispersal, disease management, and special feedings, to list a few.

Disabilities Vary: Every Student is Different

Students in all areas of disabilities may demonstrate difficulty in academic skills.
The creation of an IEP, or Individualized Education Plan, is essential to the success of each student. The IEP is a written plan specifically for a student, to meet their academic, social, and cognitive needs. It is a hallmark of the federal legislation, IDEA (Individuals with Disabilities Education Act. The IEP is a highly goal-oriented document which delineates all facets of learning for the student, and must be regularly updated.

Mastered goals are replaced with new challenges to be met. For example, a student with mental retardation will need special instruction across all areas of academics, so his or her IEP may include goals in every subject area, as well as occupational therapy, physical therapy, as well as speech and language services. On the other hand, a student with a learning disability, such as dyslexia, may need assistance in only one or two subject areas.

Special education teachers should be aware that although students across disabilities may demonstrate difficulties in similar ways, the causes may be drastically different. For example, some disabilities are due to specific sensory impairments (hearing or vision), some due to delayed cognitive ability (mental retardation), and some due to particular neurological impairments (autism or some learning disabilities). The reason for the difficulty should be an initial consideration when planning the program, or IEP, of special education intervention.

Additionally, special education teachers should be aware that each area of disability has a range of involvement. Some students may have a very minimal disability and therefore, will not require services. Others may need only a few accommodations. These students may not have a full-length IEP, but perhaps they have 504 Plans. According to the US Departments of Education, Office of Civil Rights, a 504 Section 504 is a civil rights law that does not tolerate discrimination against individuals with disabilities, and safeguards these individuals so they may have equal access to an education, with accommodations and modifications if necessary. Section 504 requires educators to meet the individual needs of all students, regardless of disability.

Some students may need extensive goals and objectives that outline a specific special education program, which would be delineated in an IEP. Implementation of the goals and objectives could be carried out in a variety of settings, including general education and special education programs. For example, a student with an attentional deficit may be able to participate in the regular education environment with accommodations that may include a checklist system to keep the student organized and a therapy or wiggle cushion, to allow the student to receive stimulation in order to focus while sitting for a lesson. Other students with attentional deficits may need different accommodations, such preferential seating near the teacher and away from windows or doorways, modified homework assignments, and extra time for testing.

Special educators should be knowledgeable of the causes and levels of severity of disabilities and characteristics when planning an appropriate special education program for each individual student. Because of the unique needs of each child, such programs must be discussed among team members, parents, administrators, and should be well documented in the child's Individualized Education Plan (IEP).

Skill 1.02   Knows how the developmental, academic, social, career, and functional characteristics of individuals with disabilities relate to levels of support needed, and applies knowledge of human development and disabilities to plan and implement appropriate curriculum.

Each child with a disability has unique needs that may not necessarily be applied to another child with the same or similar disability. In order to adequately assess a student's educational needs, the teacher must plan for each student on an individual basis. Collaboration with others, such as the general education teacher, parents, and service providers is essential to assure appropriate programming and instruction for students with disabilities.

Students with mild learning, intellectual, and behavior disabilities are identifiable by academic and social behaviors that deviate from those of their classmates. Generalities can be made about this population. Students with mild intellectual disabilities, learning disabilities, and behavior disorders are the largest subgroups of students receiving special education services. Students with mild disabilities are typically served by special education during their school year, but mild disabilities are often unrecognized before and after school years.

No nationally accepted criteria for identifying mild disabilities exist; therefore, the categories of intellectual disabilities, learning disabilities, and behavior disorders can vary from state to state. Each state has developed its own identification criteria; therefore, a student may be eligible for special education service delivery in one state and not necessarily in another. Effective collaboration between general and special education teachers is vital to the development of appropriate educational programming for students with disabilities, regardless of the state.

Human development knowledge is the underpinning of good service implementation. Human development addresses biological, cognitive, emotional, and social factors that shape the development of all students, including those in the special education realm. Being familiar the stages of development, such as Erikson's stages of psychosocial development, as well as the overall human development spectrum from birth to adulthood, gives insight into the appropriate times when communication, various emotions, sharing, and other behaviors are normally expressed.

Skill 1.03   Knows theoretical explanations for behavior disorders, and analyzes the varied characteristics of behavior disorders and their effect on learning.

Behavior disorders can range from mild to serious. A child is said to have a specific disorder when the behavior occurs frequently and to a degree that impacts the learning and safety of the child, as well as others.

One theoretical explanation for behavior disorders is developmental psychopathology. It is a premise for understanding disordered behavior when comparing it to normal human development. This framework explores the origins of behavior disorders, how individuals develop with this disorder, and how adaptations and successes of individuals unfold.

Social and Environmental Theory is based on the premise that specific social and environmental factors influence the decision to commit or even exacerbate certain behaviors. Factors such as dysfunctional family environments and gang participation are related to the development of behavior disorders in children. The environment heavily impacts children and their behaviors.

Interaction Theory attempts to explicitly define interactions between characteristics of the individual and features of the social environment that are considered integral to behavioral development. There are two main approaches within this perspective. Dynamic-behavior theory focuses on developmental aspects, while the functional analysis model offers an explanation for the maintenance of the behavior.

Instinct Theory focuses on the innate and evolutionary nature of humans; it states we are driven by underlying biological instincts. Freudian Theory supports this through his psychoanalysis theory. Psychic energy is always being created, requiring an outlet. The release of such energy or aggression is considered a catharsis. It is believed that the id, ego, and superego act as a system of checks and balances on behavior. The id is the pleasure seeking, impulsive force that is dominant in childhood. The superego is the conscience, which represents moral and ethical beliefs. The ego mediates between the id and the superego. The ego guides actions by taking into account the natural consequences of behavior. Students need to learn ways to decrease excessive or aggressive energy through appropriate means.

The **Biophysical Perspective** emphasizes the relationship between physical and biological factors, including body chemistry and genetics, and that of behavior. Genetic factors are more readily being identified, and scientists find genetic inheritance determines many aspects of childhood functioning and behavior. Drug therapy is often utilized in this approach.

The **Psychodynamic Approach** underscores the need to understand why students are disruptive. This approach emphasizes the connection between how a student feels and how a student acts. The Psychoeducational framework utilized with the Psychodynamic Approach integrates clinical insights in behavior with practical methods for managing the behavior. This type of approach resulted from the merging of behavior management with the psychodynamic theory.

The **Behaviorist** views observable behavior as the critical element. Treatment strategies are focused on modifying environmental factors that reinforce appropriate behavior. The key points of behavioral theory and practice are summarized as follows.

1. Behaviorists view inappropriate and appropriate behavior as learned. Behavior is a response to a person's interaction with the environment.

2. Learning occurs when environmental conditions reinforce a specific behavior. Reinforcement takes several forms, including imitation, modeling, and operant conditioning (i.e. consequences that shape behavior).
3. Inappropriate behavior is learned through environmental conditioning and new, appropriate behaviors can be learned with proper reinforcement.
4. Effective implementation of behavior treatments in classrooms requires observable descriptions of behavior to be changed, targeting of new behaviors, systematic application of reinforcers, and collection of pre- and post-data to determine treatment effectiveness. (Henley, Ramsey, & Algozzine, 1993, 125).

A synthesis of these models highlights the interactional nature of behavioral and emotional disorders. Typically, a combination of treatment approaches is used in many classrooms. For instance, one student may be taking medication to facilitate concentration and adequate attention span while another student may be participating in a token system designed to reinforce task completion.

The most common behavior disorders include the following:

Adjustment Disorders are demonstrated with emotional or behavioral symptoms that children display when they cannot adapt to stressful events that occur in their lives. The symptoms may occur within three months of a stressful event, and last no more than six months after the stressor has ended. A range of behaviors are associated with adjustment disorders including fear, anxiety, truancy, vandalism, and physical aggression.

Anxiety Disorders are a large family of disorders (School Phobia, Post-Traumatic Stress Disorder (PTSD), Avoidant Disorder, Obsessive-Compulsive Disorder (OCD), Panic Disorder, Panic Attack, etc.) where the primary feature is exaggerated anxiety. Anxiety disorders can result in expressed physical symptoms, disorders in conduct, or as inappropriate emotional responses such as excessive emotional outbursts or crying. Anxiety is also a brief normal reaction to stressful events. However, when the anxiety is intense, persistent and interferes with the child's functioning, it may then result in a diagnosis of anxiety disorder.

The primary feature of **Oppositional Defiant Disorder (ODD)** is a recurrent pattern of negative, disobedient and hostile behavior toward authority figures, which lasts for at least six months. Typical behaviors include arguing with adults, defying or refusing to follow adult directions, deliberately annoying people, blaming others, or being spiteful or vindictive. A stubborn or malicious attitude is noted.

A primary feature of a **Conduct Disorder** is a repetitive and persistent pattern of behavior in which the basic rights of others, or age-appropriate social norms, are violated. Children with conduct disorder may bully or threaten others, and can potentially be physically cruel to both animals and people.

Attention Deficit / Hyperactivity Disorder is a condition in which the child shows symptoms of inattention and hyperactivity that are not consistent with his/her developmental level. The key feature of **Attention Deficit Hyperactivity Disorder** is a persistent pattern of inattention and/or hyperactivity-impulsivity that is more frequent and severe than is typically observed in individuals at a similar level of development.

Post-Traumatic Stress Disorder (PTSD) can develop after exposure to an extremely traumatic event in a child's life, or witnessing or learning about a death or injury to someone close to the child. Victims of child abuse may also experience PTSD. The onset varies. Responses of PTSD in children include intense fear, helplessness, difficulty falling asleep, nightmares, persistent re-experiencing of the event, numbing of general responsiveness, or increased arousal. Young children that experience such stress may lose recently acquired skills, such as toilet training or expressive language skills.

> **Skill 1.04   Knows the different ways that students with and without disabilities learn.**

The special education teacher has traditionally taught students with disabilities exclusively. Today, however, special education teachers must be versed in the needs of students *with* and *without* disabilities. More special education teachers are needed in the mainstream education classroom, to provide inclusive, in-class, and/or co-teaching services, to support students in their least restrictive environments. They are no longer 'tucked away' in a resource room or office unit, although these settings are still least restrictive environments in many respects, and can provide an exceptional learning environment for the appropriate genre of students. Regardless of locale, a special education teacher must have a broad knowledge of the different ways students with and without disabilities obtain knowledge.

The dawn of multisensory teaching techniques has come at an ideal time. All students, with or without learning disabilities, thrive in a learning environment which provides many different modalities of absorbing content material. Modern learning theorists, such as Howard Gardner, have proposed the methods for reaching all students by using a variety of teaching methods. Engaging all of a student's senses enables information to be acquired in the brain through a multitude of pathways, whether a student has a disability or not.

Experiential and hands-on learning are both tactile and kinesthetic. In these manners, a student can derive information in a practical setting through centers, labs, field trips, reality-based projects, and other empirical learning experiences. Therefore, a student who has trouble reading or writing can still have the opportunity to learn important information through a diverse venue: experience. This is an excellent method for all students, regardless of learning ability.

This computer generation also responds to a visual means of teaching across the curriculum. Using technology, such as Smartboards, laptops, television clips, computer generated graphics, and pictorials, inundates students of all levels with imagery to assist their learning and retention of content. Visual learning methods should be employed regularly, as students with and without disabilities will respond positively. For example, providing a classroom of students with a simple graphic organizer prior to writing a draft for an essay gives all learners a spatial sense of where information is placed, the inherent coherence of a written framework, and most importantly, a visual representation of idea placement. Additionally, the use of flashcards is also a visual method and tool that can be stretched from Dolch sight word practice to organic chemistry formula memorization. Today's learners respond to visual stimulus, and a disability does not hinder this method of conveyance.

Tiered lesson planning is also crucial when addressing students with and without disabilities, especially when they are taught heterogeneously. Tiered instruction allows a concept to be taught, but may be slightly augmented or modified to meet the needs of all students. Perhaps a special education teacher is giving a classroom assessment on the week's science vocabulary words and definitions. His or her dyslexic students may have a modified test with a word bank for spelling pattern reference of multisyllabic words. The students with dysgraphia or graphomotor impairments may use a word processor or computer, or even an iPad, to type the words and definitions. The student with a marked processing disorder may be allowed to choose ten of the twenty words to work on. The students without disabilities may complete the general assessment as is. Providing such modifications can effectively help students with disabilities learn side-by-side with their peers who do not have disabilities.

Addressing the learning needs of both genres of students is not always easy, but is certainly necessary. Knowing the different ways students learn is essential to adhering to ethical teaching standards.

Skill 1.05   Applies knowledge of human development and the effects of various types of disabilities on developmental processes in order to identify the needs of individuals with and without disabilities.

Physical Development, Including Motor and Sensory

It is important for the teacher to be aware of the physical stages of development and how the child's physical growth and development affect his/her learning. Factors determined by the physical stage of development may include: ability to sit and attend, the need for activity, the relationship between physical skills and self-esteem, and the degree to which physical involvement in an activity (as opposed to being able to understand an abstract concept) impacts learning.

Physical impairments manifest in a variety of disabling conditions. Although there are significant differences among these conditions, similarities also exist. Some physical disabilities are congenital, others occur later due to injury (trauma), disease, or other factors.

In the state of Texas, physical disabilities typically fall under the disability categories of Orthopedic Impairment (OI), Other Health Impairment (OHI), or Traumatic Brain Injury (TBI).

Characteristics of individuals with OI, OHI, or TBI may include:

1. Lack of physical stamina; fatigue
2. Chronic illness; poor endurance
3. Deficient motor skills; normal movement may be prevented
4. Physical limitations or impeded motor development
5. Limited mobility
6. Limited self-care abilities
7. Progressive weakening and degeneration of muscles
8. May experience pain and discomfort throughout the body
9. May have effects from disease or treatment
10. May exhibit erratic or poor attendance patterns

Cognitive Development

Children go through patterns of learning beginning with pre-operational thought processes and move to concrete operational thoughts. Eventually, they begin to acquire the mental ability to think about and solve problems mentally, because they have developed the ability to symbolically manipulate objects. Children of most ages can use symbols such as words and numbers to represent objects and relations, but need concrete reference points.

The teacher of students with special needs must be knowledgeable about cognitive development. Although the cognitive development of children with special needs may be different than the cognitive development of other children, a teacher of students with special needs must be aware of characteristics of each stage of development in order to determine *what* should be taught and *when* it should be taught.

The following information about cognitive development was taken from the Cincinnati Children's Hospital Medical Center at www.cincinattichildrens.org. Some common features indicating a progression from more simple to more complex cognitive development include the following:

Children (ages 6-12)

- Begin to develop the ability to think in concrete ways. Concrete operations are operations performed in the presence of the object and events that are to be used.
- Examples: how to combine (addition), separate (subtract or divide), order (alphabetize and sort/categorize), and transform (change things such as 25 pennies=1 quarter) objects and actions

Adolescence (ages 12-18)

- Adolescence marks the beginning development of more complex thinking skills, including abstract thinking, the ability to reason from known principles (form own new ideas or questions), the ability to consider many points of view according to varying criteria (compare or debate ideas or opinions), and the ability to think about the process of thinking.

Cognitive Changes During Adolescence

During adolescence, particularly between 12 and 18 years of age, the developing teenager acquires the ability to think systematically about all logical relationships within a problem. The transition from concrete thinking to formal logical operations occurs over time. Every adolescent progresses at varying rates in developing his/her ability to think in more complex ways. Each adolescent develops his/her own view of the world. Some adolescents may be able to apply logical operations to school work long before they are able to apply them to personal dilemmas. When emotional issues arise, they often interfere with an adolescent's ability to think in more complex ways. The ability to consider possibilities, as well as facts, may influence decision making, in either positive or negative ways.

Early Adolescence

During early adolescence, the use of more complex thinking is focused on personal decision making in school and home environments, including the following:

- Demonstrating use of formal logical operations in school work.
- Questioning authority and society standards.
- Beginning to form and verbalize his/her own thoughts and views on a variety of topics and queries, usually more related to his her own life, such as:
  - Which sports are better to play?
  - Which groups are better to be included in?
  - What personal appearances are desirable or attractive?
  - What parental rules should be changed?

Middle Adolescence

With some experience in using more complex thinking processes, the focus of middle adolescence often expands to include more philosophical and futuristic concerns, including the following:

- Questioning more extensively
- Analyzing more extensively
- Pondering and forming his/her own code of ethics
- Thinking about different possibilities and developing own identity
- Systematically considering possible future goals
- Beginning to think long term
- Using systematic thinking to influence relationships with others

Late Adolescence

During late adolescence, complex thinking processes are used to focus on less self-centered concepts, as well as personal decision making, including the following:

- Developing idealistic views on specific topics or concerns
- Debating and developing intolerance of opposing views
- Beginning to focus thinking on making career decisions
- Considering his or her emerging role in adult society
- Tackling global concepts such as justice, history, politics, and patriotism

Encouraging Healthy Cognitive Development During Adolescence

The following seven suggestions will help to encourage positive and healthy cognitive development in the adolescent:

1. Include adolescents in discussions about a variety of topics, issues, and current events.
2. Encourage adolescents to share ideas and thoughts with adults.
3. Encourage adolescents to think independently and develop their own ideas.
4. Assist adolescents in setting their own goals.
5. Stimulate adolescents to think about possibilities of the future.
6. Compliment and praise adolescents for well thought-out decisions.
7. Assist adolescents in re-evaluating poorly made decisions for themselves.

Certain stages of child development have their own sets of problems, and it should be kept in mind that short-term, undesirable behaviors can and will occur during these stages. Child development is also a continuum, and children may manifest these problem behaviors somewhat earlier or later than their peers

About 15-20% of the school-aged population between 6 and 17 years old receive special education services. Students with disabilities are very much like their peers without disabilities. The main difference is that they have an intellectual, emotional, behavioral, or physical deficit that mildly or significantly interferes with their ability to benefit from education.

Skill 1.06   **Understands the effects of cultural and environmental influences (e.g. linguistic characteristics, socioeconomic issues, abuse/neglect, substance abuse) on the child and family.**

As cultures place varying value on education or on the role of genders, different views may be absorbed by individuals with disabilities. Cultural views vary regarding the special education student's appropriate education plans, career goals, and role(s) in society. The special educator must first become familiar with the cultural representations of his/her students and the community in which he/she teaches. Demonstrating respect for the individual student's culture will build the rapport necessary to work with the student, family, and community to prepare the student for the future, productive work, independence, and possible post-secondary education or training (IDEA 2004).

While society has progressed and many disabilities are more acceptable and more openly embraced today than they were yesterday, having a disability still carries a stigma. Historically, people with disabilities have been ostracized from their communities. Up until the 1970s, a large number of people with special needs were institutionalized at birth because the relatives either did not know what to do, they felt embarrassed to admit they had a child with a disability, or they gave into the cultural peer pressure to put their "problem" away. Sometimes this meant hiding a child's disability, which may even have meant locking a child in a room in the house. Perhaps the worst viewpoint society had expressed up to the 1970s, and one which still is evident today, is that the person with "special needs" is unable to contribute to society.

Today, American society has left the "must institutionalize" method for a "normalize" concept. Houses in local communities have been purchased for the purpose of providing supervision and/or nursing care that allows for people with disabilities to have "normal" social living arrangements. Congress has passed laws in which those with disabilities have easier access public facilities. American society has widened doorways, added special bathrooms, designated parking spots, and generally, has made the physical accommodations necessary for the mobility of those with disabilities. America's media now provides education and frequent exposure of people with special needs. The concept of acceptance appears to be occurring for those with physically noticeable disabilities.

The appearance of those with special needs in media, such as television and movies, generally are those who rise above their "label," perhaps because of an extraordinary skill. Most people in the community are portrayed as accepting the person with a disability when that special skill is noted. In addition, those who continue to express revulsion or prejudice toward the person with a disability often express remorse when the special skill is noted or peer pressure becomes too intense. This portrayal often ignores those with learning and emotional disabilities who seemed normal by appearance, but often feel and suffer from prejudices.

The most significant group any individual faces is their peers. Pressure to appear normal and not "needy" in any area is intense from early childhood to adulthood. During teen years, when young people are beginning to express their individuality, the very appearance of walking into a special education classroom often brings feelings of inadequacy, and labeling by peers that the student is "special" or "different." Being considered normal is the desire of all individuals with disabilities, regardless of the age or disability. Some people with disabilities today, as many years ago, still measure their successes by how their achievements mask/hide their disabilities.

The most difficult cultural/community outlook on those with disabilities comes in the adult work world where disabilities can become highly evident and may result in difficulty in finding and keeping a job. The world of work can be a particularly difficult place for those who have not learned to self-advocate or accommodate for their area(s) of special needs.

Skill 1.07   Understands normal, delayed, disordered communication patterns, including non-symbolic communication, and the impact of language development on the academic and social skills of individuals with disabilities.

Language is the means whereby people communicate their thoughts, make requests, and respond to others. Communication competence is an interaction of cognitive competence, social knowledge, and language competence.

Language consists of several components, each of which follows a sequence of development. Brown and colleagues were the first to describe language as a function of developmental stages rather than age (Reid, 1988, p 44). He developed a formula to group the mean length of utterances (sentences) into stages. Counting the number of morphemes per 100 utterances, one can calculate a Mean Length of Utterance (MLU). Total number of morphemes / 100 = MLU e.g. 180/100 = 1.8

A summary of Brown's findings about MLU and language development:

Stage	MLU	Developmental Features
I	1.0-2.0	• 12-26 months • 14 basic morphemes (e.g. in, on, articles, possessives)
II	2.0-2.5	• 27-30 months • Beginning of pronoun use, auxiliary verbs
III	2.5-3.0	• 31-34 months • Using questions and negative statements
IV	3.0-3.75	• 35-40 months • Use of complex (embedded) sentences
V	3.75-4.5	• 41-46 months • Use of compound sentences
V+	4.6+	• 47+ months • Strong command of language

Components of Language
Language learning is composed of five components. Children progress in developmental stages through each component.

Phonology
Phonology is the system of rules about sounds and sound combinations for a language. A phoneme is the smallest unit of sound that combines with other sounds to make words. A phoneme, by itself, does not have a meaning; it must be combined with other phonemes to have significance. Problems in phonology may be manifested as developmental delays in acquiring consonants, or reception problems, such as misinterpreting words because a different consonant was substituted.

Morphology
Morphemes are the smallest units of language that convey meaning. Morphemes are root words, or free morphemes that can stand alone (e.g. walk), and affixes (e.g. ed, s, ing). Content words carry the meaning in a sentence, and functional words join phrases and sentences. Generally, students with problems in this area may not use inflectional endings in their words, may not be consistent in their use of certain morphemes, or may be delayed in learning morphemes such as irregular past tenses.

Syntax
Syntax rules, commonly known as grammar, govern how morphemes and words are correctly combined. Wood, (1976) describes six stages of syntax acquisition (Mercer, p 347).

- **Stages 1 and 2-** Birth to about 2 years: Child is learning the semantic system.
- **Stage 3 –** Ages 2 – 3 years: Simple sentences contain subject and predicate.
- **Stage 4-** Ages 2 ½ to 4 years: Elements such as question words are added to basic sentences (e.g. where), word order is changed to ask questions. The child begins to use "and" to combine simple sentences, and the child begins to embed words within the basic sentence.
- **Stage 5-** About 31/2 to 7 years: The child uses complete sentences that include word classes of adult language. The child is becoming aware of appropriate semantic functions of words and differences within the same grammatical class.
- **Stage 6-** About 5 to 20 years: The child begins to learn complex sentences and sentences that imply commands, requests and promises.

Syntactic deficits are manifested by the child using sentences that lack length or complexity for a child that age. The child may have problems understanding or creating complex sentences and embedded sentences.

Semantics
Semantics is language content: objects, actions, and relations between objects. As with syntax, Wood (1976) outlines stages of semantic development:

- **Stage 1**- Birth to about 2 years: The child is learning meaning while learning his first words. Sentences are one-word in length, but the meaning varies according to the context. Therefore, "doggie" may mean, "This is my dog," or, "There is a dog," or "The dog is barking."
- **Stage 2**- About 2 to 8 years: The child progresses to two-word sentences about concrete actions. As more words are learned, the child forms longer sentences, until about age 7; things are defined in terms of visible actions. The child begins to respond to prompts (e.g. pretty/flower), and at or before age 8, the child can respond to a prompt with an opposite (e.g. pretty/ugly).
- **Stage 3**- Begins at about age 8: The child's word meanings relate directly to experiences, operations and processes. Vocabulary is defined by the child's experiences, not the adult's. At about age 12, the child begins to give "dictionary" definitions, and the semantic level approaches that of adults.

Semantic problems take the form of:

- Limited vocabulary
- Inability to understand figurative language or idioms; interprets literally
- Failure to perceive multiple meanings of words, changes in word meaning from changes in context, resulting in incomplete understanding of what is read
- Difficulty understanding linguistic concepts (e.g. before/after), verbal analogies, and logical relationships such as possessives
- Misuse of transitional words such as "although" and "regardless"

Pragmatics

Commonly known as the speaker's intent, pragmatics is used to influence or control actions or attitudes of others. Communicative competence depends on how well one understands the rules of language, as well as the social rules of communication such as taking turns and using the correct tone of voice.

Pragmatic deficits are manifested by failures to respond properly to indirect requests after age eight. Children with pragmatic language deficits have trouble reading cues. For example, when the listener expresses he or she does not understand what the child is saying, the child may not know how to repeat or reword themselves.

Pragmatic deficits can also be characterized by inappropriate social behaviors, such as interrupting others or monopolizing conversations. Children with pragmatic language deficits may use immature speech and have trouble sticking to a topic. These problems can persist into adulthood, affecting academic, vocational, and social interactions.

Within the school setting, a child with speech/language deficits may exhibit certain characteristics at different age/grade levels. Characteristics that may be observed in a child with a speech/language deficit include the following:

Preschool and Kindergarten: The child's speech may sound immature, he or she may not be able to follow simple directions, and often cannot name things such as the days of the week and colors. The child may not be able to discriminate between sounds and the letters associated with the sounds. The child might substitute sounds and have trouble responding accurately to certain types of questions. The child may play less with his peers or participate in non-play or parallel play.

Elementary School: Problems with sound discrimination persist, and the child may have problems with temporal and spatial concepts (e.g. before/after). As the child progresses through school, he/she may have problems making the transition from narrative to expository writing. Word retrieval problems may not be very evident because the child begins to devise strategies, such as talking around a word not readily recalled, or using fillers and descriptors. The child might speak slowly, have problems sounding out words, and/or get confused with multiple-meaning words. Pragmatic problems show up in social situations as well, such as failure to correctly interpret social cues and adjust to appropriate language, inability to predict consequences, and inability to formulate requests to obtain new information.

Secondary School: At this level, difficulties become more subtle. The child lacks the ability to use and understand higher-level syntax, semantics, and pragmatics. If the child has problems with auditory language and, he or she may also have problems with short-term memory. Receptive and/or expressive language delays impair the child's ability to learn effectively. The child often lacks the ability to organize or categorize the information received in school. Problems associated with pragmatic deficiencies persist but because the child is aware of them, he or she may become inattentive, withdrawn, or frustrated.

Skill 1.08   **Knows aspects of medical conditions affecting individuals with disabilities, including the effects of various medications on behavior and functioning and the implications of medical complications for student support needs (e.g., seizure management, tube feeding, catheterization, cardiopulmonary resuscitation [CPR]).**

Students with disabilities who take medications may experience side effects that can impact behavior and educational development. Some medications may impair concentration, which can lead to poor processing ability, lower alertness, and even cause drowsiness or hyperactivity. Students who take several medications may have an increased risk of behavioral and cognitive side effects.

The student's parents should inform school personnel when a child is beginning or changing a medication, so school personnel can note any side effects. Good communication between the home and school is essential in monitoring the effects of medication(s) on a student.

Antidepressants
Antidepressants prescribed to school age children typically fall into three types. One type is selective serotonin-reuptake inhibitors (SSRIs). SSRIs block certain receptors from absorbing serotonin. Over time, SSRIs may cause changes in brain chemistry. The

side effects of SSRIs include dry mouth, insomnia or restless sleep, increased sweating, and nausea. Mood swings have also been associated with antidepressant use.

A second type of antidepressant is the tricyclic antidepressant. Tricyclic antidepressants are generally prescribed for treating depression and obsessive-compulsive behavior. They cause similar side effects to the SSRIs such as sedation, tremor, seizures, dry mouth, light sensitivity, and mood swings.

A third type of antidepressant is the monoamine oxidase inhibitor (MAOI). MAOIs are not as widely used as the other two types due to unpleasant and life-threatening interactions with many other drugs, including common over-the-counter medications. People taking MAOIs must also follow a special diet, because these medications interact with many foods. The list of foods to avoid includes chocolate, aged cheeses, and more.

Stimulants are often prescribed to help with attention deficit disorder and attention deficit hyperactivity disorder. Common medications include various monitored doses of Adderall, Ritalin and Concerta. The drugs can have many side effects including agitation, restlessness, aggressive behavior, dizziness, insomnia, lac of appetite, headache, or tremor.

In severe cases of anxiety, an anti-anxiety medication (tranquilizer) may be prescribed. Most tranquilizers have a potential for addiction and abuse. Tranquilizers tend to be sedating, and can cause a variety of unpleasant side effects, including blurred vision, confusion, sleepiness, and tremors.

If educators are aware of the types of medication that students are taking along with the myriad of possible side effects, they will be able to respond proactively to changes in behavior, response rate, and attention span as a result of medication side effects.

Medical complications must be considered when developing schedules and curricular plans. Students may miss school due to medical conditions that require extensive rest or hospital-based intervention. Cooperative programs with home and hospital teachers can decrease the impact of such absences. For example, a student receiving a new kidney may be out of school for nine weeks, and will require homeschooling and tutoring through district cooperation with the hospital.

For students with medical needs, routine interruptions for suctioning, medication dispersion, or other medical interventions should not be disruptive to the classroom and learning atmosphere. The focus should be on maximizing opportunities for educational success and social interaction, not on limitations and isolation. For example, class parties can include food treats that meet a student's dietary restrictions, or medical intervention can be completed during individual work times rather than during group learning activity periods.

Students with seizures may require medical support apart from nursing services for medications. A seizure is an abnormal electrical discharge in the brain. While there are several types of seizures, three major types of seizures are more commonly observed.

With a **petit-mal seizure**, the student may appear to be frozen in space for a brief period of time. From the French work "petit", meaning small, a petit-mal seizure may not be noticed and a child may have multiple petit-mal seizures throughout the day.

Psychomotor seizures involve moving about, which may involve continuing a task. Psychomotor seizures may often go unnoticed as the child may continue with motor movement, but is cognitively "absent" for a brief moment.

The **grand-mal seizure** is the most easily recognized, while the other two may require a trained observer to note. A grand mal seizure involves jerking and spasms throughout the body. The individual may experience altered consciousness, loss of consciousness, muscle control, or bladder control.

It is generally believed that some seizures can be triggered by repetitive sounds, flashing lights, video games, certain drugs, low blood sugar levels, or low oxygen levels in the blood. However, most seizures appear to have no causative factor.

School personnel should be trained to handle the different types of seizures that may be encountered in the classroom to assure the safety of the student having the seizure as well as the other students. In the case of a grand-mal seizure, furniture and other objects should be moved from the area so as not to injure the child. Adults should be cautious to avoid injury, as the student may thrash and flail. Other students should be removed from the area to avoid injury. The school nurse should be notified as soon as possible. After a seizure, the child is typically physically exhausted and will usually fall asleep.

Some students may require tube feeding. Tube feeding is a method of providing nutrition to people who cannot sufficiently obtain calories by eating or to those who cannot eat because they have difficulty swallowing. Tubes which transport nutritional formulas can be inserted into the stomach (G-tubes), through the nose and into the stomach (NG-tubes), or through the nose and into the small intestine (NJ tubes). The NG and NJ tubes are considered to be temporary and the G tube is considered more permanent, but it can be removed. Tube feeding is common with those students with dysphagia, a condition that hampers swallowing.

Some students may require a catheter to assist with bladder function. A catheter is a thin, flexible, hollow plastic tube that can be used to perform various diagnostic and/or therapeutic procedures. They are designed to gain access to the body with as little trauma as possible.

Close communication between the teacher, school nurse, parent and the parents' physician are imperative in developing and implementing appropriate school programming for students with intense medical needs. In some cases, paraprofessional staff can be trained to perform certain procedures, such as tube feeding, in the classroom. However, all medical procedures conducted within the school setting must be under the supervision of a licensed medical professional, such as a school nurse, and recommended by a physician. Before any medical procedure is conducted in a classroom setting, a physician must approve the treatment plan. Close and continued monitoring is also needed to ensure that proper medical protocol is followed.

Skill 1.09   **Understands ways in which physical disabilities and health impairments relate to development and behavior, and knows the etiologies and effects of sensory disabilities and other conditions affecting individuals with disabilities.**

Some physical disabilities are congenital while other physical disabilities occur later due to injury (trauma), disease, or other factors. In addition to motor disorders, individuals with physical disabilities may have multi-disabling conditions such as concomitant hearing impairments, visual impairments, perceptual disorders, speech defects, behavior disorders, or mental disabilities.

In 1981, autism was moved from the exceptionality category of Emotional Disturbance to that of Other Health Impairment by virtue of a change in language in the original definitions under Public Law 94-142 ("Education of Handicapped Children." Federal Register, 1977). With IDEA, in 1990, autism was made into a separate exceptionality category.

COMPETENCY 002	THE SPECIAL EDUCATION TEACHER UNDERSTANDS FORMAL AND INFORMAL ASSESSMENT AND EVALUATION PROCEDURES AND KNOWS HOW TO EVALUATE STUDENT COMPETENCIES TO MAKE INSTRUCTIONAL DECISIONS

Skill 2.01	Applies knowledge of basic terminology used in assessment and evaluation, the uses and limitations of various types of instruments and techniques, and methods for monitoring the progress of individuals with disabilities.

Assessments and evaluations are given to special education students, as well as regular education students, in various ways for several reasons. Assessments guide the decisions an educator makes regarding content and material to be presented. Assessing before, during, and after a lesson provides an understanding of what information the student is absorbing and recalling. Gathering accurate information can be difficult and potentially stressful at times, so the assessment must be reliable, valid, and fair, and administered in a comfortable environment. Assessments can improve the quality of educational programs, and directly benefit the student's academic growth.

Recognizing Basic Concepts and Terminology of Assessments

The following terms are frequently used in behavioral as well as academic testing and assessment.

Baseline - In establishing a baseline, data is collected about a target behavior or performance of a skill before certain interventions or teaching procedures are implemented. Comparison of the baseline information to the data collected after the intervention or teaching procedure has been implemented will indicate whether or not progress has been made in regard to the target behavior or skill.

Criterion-Referenced Test - A test in which the individual's performance is measured against mastery of curriculum criteria rather than comparison to the performance of other students. Criterion-referenced tests may be commercially or teacher made, and include formal data collection. Since these tests measure what a student can or cannot do, results are especially useful for identifying goals and objectives for IEPs and lesson plans.

Curriculum-Based Assessment - Assessment of an individual's performance of objectives of a curriculum, such as a reading or math program. The individual's performance is measured in terms of what objectives were mastered.

Duration recording - Measuring the length of time a behavior or academic task (i.e. reading passage) lasts.

Error Analysis -The mistakes on an individual's assessment are noted and categorized by type. For example, an error analysis in a reading test could categorize mistakes by miscues, substituting words, omitted words or phrases, and miscues that are self-corrected.

Event recording - The number of times a target behavior occurs during an observation period.

Formal Assessment - Standardized tests, such as state, intelligence or achievement tests, that have specific procedures for administration, norming, scoring and interpretation.

Frequency - The number of times a behavior occurs in a time interval.

Frequency Distribution - Plotting the scores received on a test and tallying how many individuals received those scores. A frequency distribution is used to visually determine how the group of individuals performed on a test, illustrate extreme scores, and compare the distribution to the mean or other criterion.

Informal Assessment - Non-standardized tests, such as criterion-referenced tests and teacher-prepared tests. There are no required, rigid rules or procedures for administration or scoring. Examples of data collection can include observation, interviews, and hands-on tasks.

Intensity - The degree of a behavior as measured by its frequency and duration.

Interval recording - Breaking an observation into an equal number of time intervals, such as ten second intervals during a five minute period. At the end of each interval, the observer notes the presence or absence of the target behavior. The observer can then calculate a percentage by dividing the number of intervals in which the target behavior occurred by the total number of intervals in the observation period. This type of recording works well for behaviors which occur with high frequency or for long periods of time, such as on or off-task behavior, pencil tapping, or stereotyped behaviors. The observer does not have to constantly monitor the student, yet can gather enough data to get an accurate idea of the extent of the behavior.

Latency - The length of time that elapses between the presentation of a stimulus (i.e. the question), and the response (i.e. the student's answer).

Mean - The arithmetic average of a set of scores, calculated by adding the set of scores and dividing the sum by the number of scores. For example, if the sum of a set of 35 scores is 2935, dividing that sum by 35, (the number of scores), yields a mean of 83.9, or the "average" score.

Median - The middle score: 50% of the scores are above this number and 50% of the scores are below this number. In the example above, a middle score of 72 would yield 17 students with scores less than 72, and 17 students would have scored more than 72.

Mode - The score occurring most often in a frequency distribution. In the example above, the most frequently occurring score might be 78. It is possible for a set of scores to have more than one mode.

Momentary Time Sampling - Used for measuring behaviors of a group of individuals or several behaviors from the same individual. Time samples are usually brief, and may be conducted at fixed or variable intervals. The advantage of using variable intervals is increased reliability, as the students will not be able to predict when the time sample will be taken.

Multiple Baseline Design - Used to test the effectiveness of an intervention in a skill performance or to determine if the intervention accounted for the observed changes in a target behavior. First, the initial baseline data is collected, followed by the data during the intervention period. To get the second baseline, the intervention is removed for a period of time and data is collected again. The intervention is then reapplied, and data collected on the target behavior. An example of a multiple baseline design might be ignoring a child who calls out in class without raising his hand. Initially, the baseline could involve counting the number of times the child calls out before applying interventions. During the time the teacher ignores the child's call-outs, data is collected. For the second baseline, the teacher would resume the response to the child's call-outs in the way that was done before implementing planned ignoring. The child's call-outs would probably increase again, if ignoring actually accounted for the decrease. If the teacher reapplies the ignoring strategy, the child's call-outs would probably decrease again.

Norm-Referenced Test - An individual's performance is compared to the group that was used to calculate the performance standards in this standardized test. Examples of norm-referenced tests include standardized intelligence tests such as the Wechsler Intelligence Test for Children or the Stanford-Binet Intelligence Test. Common norm-reference achievement tests include the Woodcock-Johnson Tests of Achievement and Wechsler Individual Achievement Tests.

Operational Definition - The description of a behavior and its measurable components. In behavioral observations, in order to maintain reliability, the description must be specific and measurable so that the observer will know exactly what constitutes instances and non-instances of the target behavior.

Percentile – A ranking scale which ranges from 1 to 99, with a middle or median score of 50. A percentile score can be used as a reference point when comparing a student's scores to those of a norm group. The percentile score is often confused with percentage of questions answered correctly; the percentile is simply the student's relation to the norm group of test takers.

Pinpoint - Specifying and describing the target behavior for change in measurable and precise terms. "On time for class" may be interpreted as arriving physically in the classroom when the tardy bell has finished ringing, or it may mean being in one's in seat and ready to begin work when the bell has finished ringing. Pinpointing the exact behavior makes it possible to accurately measure the behavior.

Profile - Plotting an individual's behavioral data on a graph.

Rate - The frequency of a behavior over a specified time period, such as five talk-outs during a 30-minute period, or typing 85 WPM (words per minute).

Raw Score - The number of correct responses on a test before they have been converted to standard scores. Raw scores have no basis of comparison to the performance of other individuals.

Reliability -The consistency (stability) of a test over time to measure what it is supposed to measure. Reliability is commonly measured in four ways:

- Test-retest method — The test is administered to the same group or individual after a short period of time and the results are compared.
- Alternate form (equivalent form) — Measures reliability by using alternative forms of the same test to measure the same skills. If both forms are administered to the same group within a relatively short period of time, there should be a high correlation between the two sets of scores if the test has a high degree of reliability.
- Inter-rater Reliability — Refers to the degree of agreement between two or more individuals observing the same behaviors or scoring the same tests.
- Internal Reliability — Determined by statistical procedures or by correlating one-half of the test with the other half of the test.

Standard Deviation - The Standard Deviation (SD) is a statistical measure of the amount a set of scores varies from the mean.

Standard Error of Measure - Measures the amount of possible error in a score. If the Standard Error of Measure (SEM) for a test is + or -3, and the individual's score is 35, then, the actual score may range from 32 to 38.

Standard Score - A derived score that is used to compare the performance of one student to another on a standardized test. The Standard Score indicates how far from average a score falls. Common Standard Scores include:

Z-Scores—Scaled on -4 to 4 scale, with zero as average
T-Scores—Scaled from 10-90 in intervals of 10, with 50 as average
Stanine—Range from 1-9, with 5 as average.

Some test publishers establish their own Standard Scores for a particular test, such as the SAT (score scale 200-800 per category) and ACT (scale score 0-36 per category) exams.

Task Analysis - Breaking an academic or behavioral task down into its sequence of steps. Task analysis is necessary when preparing criterion-referenced tests and performing error analysis.

Validity - The degree to which a test measures what it claims to measure. A test may be highly reliable, but it will be useless if it is not valid. There are several types of validity to examine when selecting, or constructing, an assessment instrument.

- **Concurrent Validity** - Refers to how well the test relates to a criterion measure given at the same time. For example, a new test, which probably measures reading achievement, may be given to a group, which also takes the WJIII, which has established validity. The test results are compared using statistical measures.
- **Construct Validity** - Refers to the ability of the test to measure a theoretical construct, such as intelligence, self-concept, and other non-observable behaviors. Factor analysis and correlation studies with other instruments that measure the same construct are ways to determine construct validity.
- **Content Validity** - Examines the question of whether the types of tasks in the test measure the skill or construct the test claims to measure. For example, a test that claims to measure mastery in algebra would probably not be valid if the majority of the items involved basic operations with fractions and decimals.
- **Criterion–Referenced Validity** - Involves comparing the test results with a valid criterion. For example, a doctoral student preparing a test to measure reading and spelling skills may check the test against an established test such as the Woodcock-Johnson Tests of Achievement (WJIII), or another valid criterion such as school grades.
- **Predictive Validity** - Refers to how well a test will relate to a future criterion level, such as the ability of a reading test administered to a first-grader to predict that student's performance at third or fifth grade.

Limitations of Various Types of Assessment

Achievement tests are instruments that directly assess students' skill development in academic content areas. This type of test measures the extent to which a student has profited from educational and/or life experiences compared to others of like age or grade level. Emphasis needs to be placed upon the kinds of behaviors each tests samples, the adequacy of its norms, the test reliability, and its validity.

An achievement test may be classified as a diagnostic test if strengths and weaknesses in skill development can be delineated. Typically, when used as a diagnostic tool, an achievement test measures one basic skill and its related components. For example, a reading test may measure reading recognition, reading comprehension, reading fluency, decoding skills, and sound discrimination. Each skill measured is reported in sub-classifications.

In order to render pertinent information, achievement tests must reflect the content of the curriculum. Some achievement tests assess skill development in many subject areas, while others focus upon single content areas. Within similar content areas, the particular skills assessed and how they are measured, differ from test to test. The more prominent areas assessed by achievement tests include math, reading, and spelling.

Achievement test usages include screening, placement, progress evaluation, and curricula effectiveness. As screening tests, these instruments provide a wide index of academic skill development and may be used to pinpoint students for whom educational interventions may be necessary for purposes of remediation or enrichment. They offer a general idea of where to begin additional diagnostic assessment.

Placement decisions in special education include significant progress, or lack thereof, in academic achievement. It is essential that data from individually administered achievement tests allow the examiner to observe quantitative (i.e. scores) performance as well as to denote specific strengths and weaknesses inherent in qualitative (e.g. attitude, motivation, problem-solving) performance. Knowing how an individual reacts or produces answers during a testing situation is equally relevant to measured skill levels when making placement decisions.

Achievement tests are routinely given in school districts across the nation as a means of evaluating progress. Scores of students can be compared locally, statewide, and with national norms. Accountability and quality controls can be kept in check through the reporting of scores. The Texas Education Agency has a list of approved group-administered achievement tests on www.tea.state.tx.us, posted in 2013. Several approved tests are listed by company name/publisher, including those of CTB/McGraw-Hill, Pearson Educational Measurement, and Riverside Publishing.

Achievement tests may be norm-referenced or criterion-referenced, and administered individually or within groups. Results of norm-referenced achievements tests may not provide information needed for individual program planning. Criterion-referenced achievement tests contain items that correspond with stated objectives, thus enabling identification of cognitive deficiencies. Knowledge of specific skill deficits is needed for developing Individualized Education Plans (IEPs).

Teachers can also be provided with measures showing the effectiveness of their instruction. Progress reflected by student scores should be used to review, and often revise, instructional techniques and content. The Texas Education Agency will overhaul teacher evaluations in 2013 and 2014, as the evaluations have not been refined rigorously since 1997. Many school districts use the Professional Development and Assessment System. The system ranks teachers in eight categories, on a four-point scale. There is usually a 45-minute classroom observation. There are several pilots being explored, including one designed by Charlotte Danielson, entitled *Framework for Teaching*.

Skill 2.02 **Understands ethical concerns related to assessment and evaluation, including legal provisions, regulations, and guidelines regarding unbiased evaluation and the use of psychometric instruments and instructional assessment measures with individuals with disabilities.**

If instructional modifications in the regular classroom have not proven successful, a student may be referred for multidisciplinary evaluation. The evaluation is comprehensive and includes norm and criterion-referenced tests, such as IQ and diagnostic tests, curriculum-based assessments, systematic teacher observation, samples of student work, and parent interviews. The results of the evaluation are twofold: to determine eligibility for special education services and to identify a student's strengths and weaknesses in order to plan an individual education program (IEP).

The wording in federal law is very explicit in regard to the manner in which evaluations must be conducted, and about the existence of due process procedures that protect against bias and discrimination. Provisions in the law include the following:

1. The testing of children in their native or primary language unless it is clearly not feasible to do so.
2. The use of evaluation procedures selected and administered to prevent cultural or ethnic discrimination.
3. The use of assessment tools validated for the purpose for which they are being used (e.g. achievement levels, IQ scores, adaptive skills).
4. Assessment by a multidisciplinary team utilizing several pieces of information to formulate a placement decision.

Furthermore, parental involvement must occur in the development of the child's educational program.

According to the law, parents must:

1. Be notified before initial evaluation or any change in placement by a written notice in their primary language describing the proposed school action, the reasons for it, and the available educational opportunities.
2. Consent, in writing, before the child is initially evaluated.

Parents may:

1. Request an independent educational evaluation if they feel the school's evaluation is inappropriate.
2. Request an evaluation at public expense if a due process hearing decision is that the public agency's evaluation was inappropriate.

3. Participate on the committee that considers the evaluation, placement, and programming of the student.

All students referred for evaluation for special education should have the results of a relatively current vision and hearing screening on file. This will determine the adequacy of sensory acuity and ensure that learning problems are not due to a vision and/or hearing problem.

All portions of the special education process from assessment to placement are strictly confidential to parties outside of the people who will directly be servicing the student. Under no circumstances should information be shared outside of the realm of parent/guardian and those providing educational and/or related services without the consent of the parent/guardian.

Skill 2.03   Identifies appropriate evaluation strategies for individual students with diverse characteristics and needs (e.g., related to culture, language, personal beliefs, nature, severity of disabilities).

The term multicultural encompasses the idea that all students, regardless of their gender, social class, ethnic, racial, or cultural characteristics, should have an equal opportunity (Banks & Banks, 1993). This is as true in the evaluation of students when learning knowledge in school, and performing tasks on a work site.

The issue of fair assessment for individuals from minority groups has a long history of philosophical changes in educational thought that have brought about reforms in law. Slavia and Ysseldyke, in 1995, pointed out three aspects of this issue that are particularly relevant to the assessment of students.

1. **Representation**
   Individuals from diverse backgrounds need to be represented in assessment materials. It is essential that persons from different cultures be fairly represented. The presentation of individuals from differing genders in non-stereotypical roles and situations is of equal importance.

2. **Acculturation**
   It is important that individuals from different backgrounds receive opportunities to acquire the tested skills, information, and values. When students are tested with standardization instruments, they are compared to a set of norms in order to gain an index of their relative standing, and to make comparisons. It can be assumed that the students tested are similar to those on whom the test was standardized. The assumption is that their acculturation is comparable. Acculturation is a matter of educational, socioeconomic, and experiential background rather than of gender, race, or ethnic background. When it is said that a child's acculturation differs from that of the group used as a norm, what is really meant is that the experiential background differed, not simply that the child, is of a different ethnic

origin (Slavia & Ysseldyke, 1991). Differences in experiential backgrounds should therefore be accounted for when administering tests.

3. **Language**
   The language and concepts that comprise test items should be unbiased. Students should be familiar with terminology and references to which the language is being made when they are administered tests, especially when the results of the tests are going to be used for decision making purposes. Many tests given in regular grades relate to decisions about promotion and grouping of students for instructional purposes. Tests and other assessment instruments that relate to special education are generally concerned with two types of decisions: (1) eligibility, and (2) program planning for individualized education.

When selecting a test, many factors are considered, and perhaps the most important consideration is the purpose for testing. The teacher may be screening a large group of students to determine which students would benefit from further assessment of skills, performing a progress check, diagnosing capabilities or deficiencies, or perhaps evaluating special placement qualifications. The decision to use a criterion-referenced rather than a norm-referenced test, an informal versus a formal type of test, or an individual rather than a group administered test may be decided based upon one's reason for testing. Scope and content, as well as the form in which scores are reported, are related to purpose and should be given primary consideration. Additional evaluative criteria might include:

1. **Restrictions.** Are there special limitations (e.g. hearing, sight, and physical) present? Are there test norms covering these limitations, or will special adaptations or accommodations be necessary? If norm-referenced measures are used, are the student's characteristics or acculturation similar to those with whom the test was normed? Is the test age or grade appropriate?
2. **Number.** Is individual testing required, or will an entire class or small group of students be tested at one time?
3. **Training.** Has the teacher been fully trained to administer the test, or does the test require administration, scoring, and interpretation of results by a person trained in another specialty area (e.g. speech pathologist, psychologist, educational diagnostician)?
4. **Presentation-Response Modes.** How are the test items presented to the student? Likewise, what method of response is required of the student? Will enough information be provided by student responses to determine capability versus chance factors?
5. **Format.** Depending on the types of question-response selected, what format does the teacher want to use? For example, if written answers are desired for written queries, will true-false, multiple choice, or essay type questions be used?
6. **Time.** Are there specific and required time constraints, or can testing be flexible and open-ended?
7. **Cost.** Is the price of the test and supplementary materials reasonable in relation to desired results? Are the test items current and of sufficient match to the

curriculum to be worth the investment? How expensive will it be to replace consumable items (e.g. test booklets, answer forms)?

8. **Physical Facility.** Are the physical attributes of the room, such as lighting, ventilation, sound reduction, and well-fitting, comfortable furniture, conducive to good testing?
9. **Space Considerations.** Is there adequate space for administering the test to a group of students? Does the amount of available room allow for proper spacing of test takers? If one student is to be tested, can suitable provisions be made for any other students for whom the teacher is responsible during that period?
10. **Professional Resources.** Are descriptive materials provided by publishing companies (e.g. test manuals, catalogs)?

Prior to making final decisions, the teacher or assessment professional should investigate professional reference sources for specific information about potential tests. Has the test administrator reviewed the *Standards for Educational and Psychological Tests*, a resource cooperatively prepared by The American Psychological Association, the American Educational Research Association, and the National Council on Measurement in Education?

Skill 2.04   Applies knowledge of procedures for screening, pre-referral intervention, referral, and determining eligibility, including criteria used to determine eligibility.

Referral

Referral is the process by which a teacher, parent, or other person formally requests an evaluation of a student to determine eligibility for special education services. The decision to refer a student may be influenced by: (1) student characteristics, such as the abilities, behaviors, or skills that students exhibit (or lack of), (2) individual differences among teachers, in their beliefs, expectations, or skills in dealing with specific kinds of problems, (3) expectations for assistance with a student who is exhibiting academic or behavioral learning problems, (4) availability of specific kinds of strategies and materials, (5) parents' demand for referral or opposition to referral, and (6) institutional factors which may facilitate or constrain teachers in making referral decisions.

It is important that referral procedures are clearly understood and coordinated among all school personnel. All educators need to be able to identify characteristics typically exhibited by special needs students involved in the referral process. The Legal Framework for the Child-Centered Special Education Process can be found online, on http://framework.esc18.net/display/Webforms/ESC18-FW-Summary.aspx?FID=202&DT=G&LID=en

In Texas, the student suspected of having a disability is referred to a multidisciplinary team called the Admission, Review and Dismissal (ARD) committee. This multidisciplinary committee determines if a student is eligible for special education services. Members of this committee generally include: school members involved in the education of the student, the educational diagnostician, a special educator, parents, and sometimes the student themselves. This committee also develops and reviews the Individual Education Program (IEP). From the initial referral, schools districts have sixty calendar days to complete an individual evaluation and then an addition thirty calendar days to complete an ARD meeting. Reevaluations occur every three years, with updates to the IEP occurring on an annual basis, often at the end of the school year.

Evaluation

The evaluation is comprehensive and includes norm and criterion-referenced tests (e.g. IQ and diagnostic tests), curriculum-based assessments, systematic teacher observations (e.g. behavior frequency checklist), samples of student work, and parent interviews. The results of the evaluation are twofold: to determined eligibility for special education services and to identify a student's strengths and weaknesses in order to plan an individual education program.

Eligibility

Eligibility is based on criteria defined in federal law and state regulations, which vary from state to state. Evaluation methods correspond with eligibility criteria for the special education classifications. For example, a multidisciplinary evaluation for a student being evaluated for intellectual disabilities would include the individual's intellectual functioning, adaptive behavior, and achievement levels. Other tests are based on developmental characteristics exhibited (e.g. social, language, and motor).

Disability Criteria for Disability Areas in the State of Texas

According to IDEA, a **Learning Disability (LD)** is a disorder in one or more of the basic psychological process involved in understanding or in using language, spoken or written, which may manifest itself in an imperfect ability to listen, think speak, read, write, spell, or do mathematical calculations. The term includes such conditions as perceptual handicaps, brain injury, minimal brain dysfunction, dyslexia, and developmental aphasia.

The **State of Texas** adds additional guidelines to the eligibility criteria for **Learning Disability** to include:

- Student does not achieve adequately for the his or her age, or meet state-approved grade-level standards in oral expression, listening comprehension, written expression, basic reading skill, reading fluency skills, reading comprehension, mathematics calculation, or mathematics problem solving when provided appropriate instruction, as indicated by performance on multiple measures such as in-class tests; grade average over time (e.g. six weeks, semester); norm-or criterion-referenced tests; statewide assessments; or a process based on the child's response to scientific, research-based intervention;

AND

- Student does not make sufficient progress when provided a process based on the child's response to scientific, research-based intervention, as indicated by the child's performance relative to the performance or the child's peers on repeated, curriculum-based assessment of achievement at reasonable intervals, reflecting student progress during classroom instruction; **OR**

- Student exhibits a pattern of strengths and weaknesses in performance, achievement, or both relative to age, grade-level standards, or intellectual ability, as indicated by significant variance among specific areas of cognitive function, such as working memory and verbal comprehension, or between specific areas of cognitive function and academic performance.

In the state of Texas, Pervasive Developmental Disorders (PDD) are included in the eligibility criteria for autism. In Texas, the written report of evaluation for autism must include recommendations for behavioral interventions and strategies.

Autism, according to the IDEA, is a developmental disability significantly affecting verbal and nonverbal communication and social interaction, generally evident before age three, that adversely affects a child's educational performance. It does not apply if a child's educational performance is affected mainly due to a child's emotional disturbance.

Deaf-Blindness, as defined by IDEA, means concomitant hearing and visual impairments, the combination of which causes such severe communication and other developmental and educational needs that they cannot be accommodated in special education programs solely for children with deafness or children with blindness. Additional information regarding services for this genre of students can be retrieved at: http://www.dars.state.tx.us/dbs/deafblind.shtml

Texas adds additional criteria for Deaf-Blindness:

A. Meets the eligibility criteria for auditory impairment and visual impairment as specified in IDEA.
B. Meets the eligibility criteria for a student with a visual impairment and has a suspected hearing loss that cannot be demonstrated conclusively, but a speech/language pathologist indicates there is no speech at an age when speech would normally be expected.
C. Has documented hearing and visual losses that, if considered individually, may not meet the requirements for auditory impairment or visual impairment, but the combination of such losses adversely affects the student's educational performance; **OR**
D. Has a documented medical diagnosis of a progressive medical condition that will result in concomitant hearing and visual losses that, without special education intervention, will adversely affect the student's educational performance.

Auditory Impairment (AI) is an impairment in hearing, whether permanent or fluctuating, that adversely affects a child's educational performance. Additional Texas requirements for Auditory Impairment state that the data reviewed by the multidisciplinary team must include an otological examination performed by an licensed otologist (physician), and an audiological evaluation by a licensed audiologist. The evaluation data must also include a description of the implications of the hearing loss in a variety of circumstances with or without recommended amplification.

For eligibility under the condition of **Emotional Disturbance (ED),** IDEA specifies that the student must exhibit one or more of the following characteristics over a long period of time and to a marked degree that adversely affects a child's educational performance:

A. An inability to learn that cannot be explained by intellectual, sensory, or health factors.

B. An inability to build or maintain satisfactory interpersonal relationships with peers and teachers.

C. Inappropriate types of behavior or feelings under normal circumstances.

D. A general pervasive mood of unhappiness or depression.

E. A tendency to develop physical symptoms or fears associated with personal or school problems.

Schizophrenia is included in the definition of Emotional Disturbance. The term does not apply to children who are Socially Maladjusted, unless they meet the criteria for Emotional Disturbance. Texas requires that the written evaluation report should include specific recommendations for behavioral support and interventions.

Mental Retardation (MR), by IDEA definition, means a student has significantly sub-average general intellectual functioning, existing concurrently with deficits in adaptive behavior and manifested during the developmental period, that adversely affects a child's educational performance.

Texas defines Mental Retardation as a student who:

A. Has been determined to have significantly sub-average intellectual functioning as measure by a standardized, individually administered test of cognitive ability in which the overall test score is at least two standard deviations below the mean, when taking into consideration the standard error of measurement of the test; **and**

B. Concurrently exhibits deficits in at least two of the following areas of adaptive behavior: communication, self-care, home living, social/interpersonal skills, use of community resources, self-direction, functional academic skills, work, leisure, health, and safety.

Multiple Disabilities (MD), by IDEA definition, means concomitant impairments (such as mental retardation-blindness or mental retardation-orthopedic impairment), the combination of which causes such severe educational needs that they cannot be accommodated in special education programs solely for one of the impairments. Multiple disabilities do not include deaf-blindness.

Texas adds the following to the definition of Multiple Disabilities:

A. The student's disability is expected to continue indefinitely; **and**

B. The disabilities severely impair performance in two or more of the following areas: psychomotor skills, self-care skills, communication, social and emotional development, or cognition.

The IDEA definition of **Orthopedic Impairment (OI)** means a severe orthopedic impairment that adversely affects a child's educational performance. The term includes impairments caused by a congenital anomaly, impairments caused by disease (e.g., poliomyelitis, bone tuberculosis), and impairments from other causes (e.g., cerebral palsy, amputations, and fractures or burns that cause contractures). Texas criteria for OI states that information regarding the disability from a licensed physician must be included in the evaluation data.

Other Health Impairment (OHI) means having limited strength, vitality, or alertness, including a heightened alertness to environmental stimuli, that results in limited alertness with respect to the educational environment, that:

A. Is due to chronic or acute health problems such as asthma, attention deficit disorder or attention deficit hyperactivity disorder, diabetes, epilepsy, a heart condition, hemophilia, lead poisoning, leukemia, nephritis, rheumatic fever, sickle cell anemia, and Tourette syndrome; **AND**

B. Adversely affects a child's educational performance.

Texas requires information from a licensed physician to be included in the evaluation data for appropriate review.

Speech Impairment (SI), according to IDEA, means a communication disorder, such as stuttering, impaired articulation, a language impairment, or a voice impairment, that adversely affects a child's educational performance. In Texas, the multidisciplinary team must include a certified speech and hearing therapist, a certified speech and language therapist, or a licensed speech/language pathologist.

Traumatic Brain Injury (TBI), by IDEA definition, means an acquired injury to the brain caused by an external physical force, resulting in total or partial functional disability or psychosocial impairment, or both, that adversely affects a child's educational performance. Traumatic brain injury applies to open or closed head injuries resulting in impairments in one or more areas, such as cognition; language; memory; attention; reasoning; abstract thinking; judgment; problem-solving; sensory, perceptual, and motor abilities; psychosocial behavior; physical functions; information processing; and speech. Traumatic brain injury does not apply to brain injuries that are congenital or degenerative, or to brain injuries induced by birth trauma. In Texas, evaluation data for TBI must include information from a licensed physician.

Visual Impairment (VI), as defined by IDEA, *means* an impairment in vision that, even with correction, adversely affects a child's educational performance. The term includes both partial sight and blindness.

In Texas, as student with a Visual Impairment is one who:

A. Has been determined by a licensed ophthalmologist or optometrist to have no vision or to have a serious visual loss after correction, **or** to have a progressive medical condition that will result in no vision or a serious loss after correction.

B. Has received the following evaluations to determine the need for special education services:

    a. Functional Vision Evaluation: conducted by a professional certified in the education of students with visual impairments or a certified orientation and mobility instructor. The evaluation must include the performance of tasks in a variety of environments and recommendations regarding the need for a clinical low vision evaluation as well as an orientation and mobility evaluation.

    b. Learning Media Assessment: conducted by a professional certified in the education of students with visual impairments. Assessment must include recommendations concerning which specific visual, tactual, and/or auditory learning media are appropriate and whether there is a need for ongoing evaluation in this area.

Noncategorical (NCEC), refers to students between the ages of three and five, who may meet eligibility requirements under the disability areas of MR, ED, LD, or AU. This is a temporary diagnosis; it cannot be used after age five.

Skill 2.05 **Knows how to gather background information regarding academic, medical, and family history, collaborate with parents/guardians and with other professionals to conduct assessments and evaluations, document ongoing student assessment, and maintain accurate records.**

Relevant background information regarding the student's academic, medical, and family history should be used to identify students with disabilities and evaluate progress.

In order to properly identify students with disabilities and evaluate their progress, the evaluator should include background information regarding academic, medical, cultural, and family history when making an evaluation. The evaluation should include a developmental history, relevant medical history including current medications, academic history including results of prior standardized testing, reports of classroom performance, relevant family history, including primary language of the home, and the student's current level of fluency in English. Additional pertinent information may include relevant psychosocial history, and information regarding any previously diagnosed disability condition.

By utilizing all possible background information in the assessment, the evaluator can rule out alternative explanations for academic problems such as poor education, poor motivation and study skills, emotional problems, and cultural and language differences. If the student's entire background and history is not taken into account, it is not always possible to institute the most appropriate educational program for the student with disabilities.

Strategies for Collaboration

The assessment process is an essential part of developing an individualized program for students. The needs of the whole child must be considered. Information should be gathered by using various sources.

A vital person in the assessment process is the parent or guardian. The parent can provide needed background information on the child, such as medical, physical, and developmental history. Paraprofessionals, doctors, and other professionals are also very helpful in providing necessary information about the child.

Methods of Gathering Information

Interview: Interviews can be conducted in person or on paper. The related parties can be invited to a meeting to conduct the interview. If the parent does not respond after several attempts, a paper interview may be sent or mailed home.

Questionnaires: Questionnaires are also a good way of gathering information. Some questionnaires may contain open-ended questions and some may be several questions to be answered using a rating scale.

Conference/Meeting: An informal meeting with related persons involved with the child may prove to be beneficial; relatives may be able to offer any information about the child, the child's academic progress, physical development, social skills, behavior, or medical history.

Skill 2.06	Knows how to interpret and apply information from formal and informal assessment and evaluation instruments and procedures, including interpreting various types of scores (e.g., standard scores, percentile ranks, age/grade equivalents).

Having the knowledge of interpreting and applying formal and informal assessment data is very important to the development of IEPs. An individualized educational program is designed around the child's strengths and weaknesses. The special educator must be able to interpret formal and informal assessment data.

Informal Assessments
Information about the student's achievement is gathered various ways, including formal assessments such as standardized intelligence or achievement tests. Information is gathered through methods such as observations, performance-based assessments, interviews, and student portfolios as well.

Observations
Observations can be informal and based upon anecdotal reports by the student's parents, teachers, or others involved with the child. Formal observations are those in which someone other than the child's teacher observes the student in a variety of settings and notes his/her performance and participation in relation to other students within those settings.

Performance-Based Assessments
A performance-based assessment requires students to perform a task rather than select an answer from a ready-made list. The teacher then judges the quality of the student's work based on a predetermined set of criteria or a rubric.

Portfolios
Portfolios are selected collections of a variety of the student's work. Portfolios should include work samples that demonstrate the student's strengths and weaknesses. They are ideal assessments for parent-teacher conferences as well, to show progression and growth, or lack thereof.

Formal Assessments
Results of formal assessments are reported in derived scores, which compare the student's raw score to the performance of a specified group of subjects. Criteria for the selection of the group may be based on characteristics such as age, sex, or geographic area. The test results of formal assessments must always be interpreted in light of what type of tasks the individual was required to perform. The most commonly used scores are as follows:

Age and Grade Equivalent scores are considered developmental scores because they attempt to convert the student's raw score into an average performance indicative of a particular age or grade group.

Quartiles, Deciles, and Percentiles are statistical values. **Quartiles** divide scores into four equal parts, each containing 25% of the scores of the sample population. **Deciles** divide the distribution into ten equal parts; the seventh decile would mark the point below which 70% of the scores fall. **Percentiles** are the most commonly used and are based on a scale from 1-99.

Standard Scores indicate how far a particular score is from the average or mean score for that particular test. The unit that tells the distance from the average is the standard deviation (sd) for that test. Standard scores are useful because they allow for direct comparison of raw scores from different individuals. In interpreting scores, it is important to note what type of standard score is being used.

Criterion Referenced Tests and Curriculum-based Assessments are interpreted on the basis of the individual's performance on the objectives being measured. These types of assessments are designed by selecting objectives, analyzing those objectives, and selecting measures to test the skills necessary to meet those tasks. Results are calculated for each objective, e.g. "Cindy was able to divide 2-digit numbers by 1-digit numbers 85% of the time and was able to divide 2-digit numbers by 2-digit numbers 45% of the time". These results are useful for writing IEPs as well as deciding what to teach.

Skill 2.07	Knows how to communicate assessment and evaluation results appropriately to individuals with disabilities, parents/guardians, administrators, and other professionals

The special educator must be able to communicate assessment results into understandable language for a variety of individuals. These individuals may include parents or guardians, paraprofessionals, professionals in general education, members of the administration, and even the student. An overall picture of the student with a disability, including his or her assessment results, and knowledge of the continuum of services provided are important to communicate to the ARD committee members.

When communicating with parents, it is important to build trust. The promotion of student-centered communication is the basis for a sustained, positive teacher-parent relationship. The child is the focus of the conversation; all parties involved have the child's best interest in mind.

Skill 2.08   **Understands the reciprocal nature of assessment and instruction; applies skills for developing individualized assessment strategies to evaluate the results of instruction; and knows how to use assessment and evaluation results to design, monitor, and modify instruction for individuals with disabilities.**

The correct assessment of academic achievement is an essential component of a psychoeducational evaluation. Achievement tests are instruments that directly assess students' skill development in academic content areas. This type of test measures the extent to which a student has profited from educational and/or life experiences compared to others of like age or grade level. Emphasis needs to be placed upon the kinds of behaviors each tests samples, the adequacy of its norms, the test reliability, and its validity.

An achievement test may be classified as a diagnostic test if strengths and weaknesses in skill development can be delineated. Typically, when used as a diagnostic tool, an achievement test measures one basic skill and its related components. For example, a reading test may measure reading recognition, reading comprehension, reading fluency, decoding skills, and sound discrimination. Each skill measured is reported in sub-classifications. In order to render pertinent information, achievement tests must reflect the content of the curriculum. The more prominent areas assessed by achievement tests include math, reading, and spelling.

Achievement test usages include screening, placement, progress evaluation, and curricula effectiveness. As screening tests, these instruments provide a wide index of academic skill development and may be used to pinpoint students for whom educational interventions may be necessary for purposes of remediation or enrichment.

Placement decisions in special education include significant progress, or lack thereof, in academic achievement. It is essential that data from individually administered achievement tests allow the examiner to observe quantitative (e.g. scores) performance as well as to denote specific strengths and weaknesses inherent in qualitative (e.g. attitude, motivation, problem-solving) performance.

Achievement tests are routinely given in school districts across the nation as a means of evaluating progress. Scores of students can be compared locally, statewide, and with national norms. Achievement tests may be norm-referenced or criterion-referenced, and administered individually or within groups. Results of norm-referenced achievements tests though important in making comparisons, may not provide information needed for individual program planning. Criterion-referenced achievement tests contain items that correspond with stated objectives, thus enabling identification of academic deficiencies. Knowledge of specific skill deficits is needed for developing individualized education plans.

Teachers can be provided with data showing the effectiveness of their instruction. Progress reflected by student scores should be used to review, and revise instructional techniques, content, and instructional delivery methods.

Assessment information, which is gathered from various sources, is key to identifying the strengths and the weaknesses of the student. Each test offer insight about the child, therefore increasing the possibility of creating a well-developed plan to assist in the success of the student. The special education and general education teacher, along with other professionals, will use the assessment data to make appropriate instructional decisions and to modify the learning environment so that it is conducive to learning.

The information gathered can be used to make some of the following instructional decisions:

Classroom Organization: The teacher can vary grouping arrangements (e.g. large group, small group, peer tutoring, or learning centers) and methods of instruction (teacher directed, student directed).

Classroom Management: The teacher can vary grading systems, reinforcement systems, and the rules (differentiate for some students).

Methods of Presentation:
   A. Content: Amount to be learned, time to learn, and concept level
   B. General Structure: Advance organizers, immediate feed-back, memory devices, and active involvement of students
   C. Type of presentation: Verbal or written, transparencies, audiovisual

Methods of Practice:
   A. General Structure: Amount to be practiced, time to finish, group, individual or teacher-directed, and, varied level of difficulty
   B. Level of response: Copying, recognition, or recall with and without cues
     C. Types of materials: Worksheets, audiovisual, texts

Methods of Testing:
   A Type: Verbal, written, or demonstration
   B. General Structure: Time to complete, amount to complete, group or individual testing
   C. Level of response: Multiple choice, essay, recall of facts

Presentation of Subject Matter
Subject matter should be presented in a fashion that helps students organize, understand, and remember important information. Advance organizers and other instructional devices can help students to:

- Connect information to what is already known
- Make abstract ideas more concrete

- Capture students' interest in the material
- Help students to organize the information and visualize the relationships

Organizers can be visual aids such as diagrams, tables, charts, guides, or verbal cues that alert students to the nature and content of the lesson. Organizers may be used:

- **Before the lesson** to alert the student to the main point of the lesson, establish a rationale for learning, and activate background information.
- **During the lesson** to help students organize information, keep focused on important points, and aid comprehension.
- **At the close of the lesson** to summarize and remember important points.

Examples of organizers include:

- Question and graphic-oriented study guide.
- Concept diagramming: students brainstorm a concept and organize information into lists.
- Semantic feature analysis: students construct a table with examples of the concept in one column and important features or characteristics in the other column opposite.
- Semantic webbing: The concept is placed in the middle of the chart or chalkboard and relevant information is placed around it. Lines show the relationships.
- Memory (mnemonic) devices. Diagrams, charts, and tables.

Instructional modifications are tried in an attempt to accommodate the student in the regular classroom. Effective instruction is geared toward individual needs and recognizes differences in how students learn. Modifications are tailored to individual student needs. Many strategies for modifying regular classroom instruction shown in Table 1-1 are effective with students with disabilities and students without learning or behavior problems.

Table 1-1 Strategies for Modifying Classroom Instruction

Strategy 1   Provide active learning experiences to teach concepts. Student motivation is increased when students can manipulate, weigh, measure, read, or write using materials and skills that relate to their daily lives.

Strategy 2   Provide ample opportunities for guided practice of new skills. Frequent feedback on performance is essential to overcome student feelings of inadequacy. Peer tutoring and cooperative projects provide non-threatening practice opportunities. Individual student conferences, curriculum-based tests, and small group discussions are three useful methods for checking progress.

Strategy 3   Provide multisensory learning experiences. Students with learning problems sometimes have sensory processing difficulties. Lessons and directions that include visual, auditory, tactile, and kinesthetic modes are preferable to a single sensory approach.

Strategy 4   Present information in a manner that is relevant to the student. Particular attention to this strategy is needed when there is a cultural or economic gap between the lives of teachers and students. Relate instruction to a youngster's daily experience and interests.

Strategy 5   Provide students with concrete illustrations of their progress. Students with learning problems need frequent reinforcement for their efforts. Charts, graphs, and check sheets provide tangible markers of student achievement.

Skill 2.09   **Knows how to design and use ecological assessments, portfolio assessments, task analyses, and functional assessments (e.g. behavioral, social, communication) to accommodate the unique abilities and needs of individuals with disabilities.**

Ecological Assessments

Ecological assessments entail assessing students in real-life contexts and environments. This would involve comparing the performance of a student with disabilities with a student who does not have disabilities, but more importantly, this assessment allows the child to be observed and assessed in different environments to see how he or she functions in these difference places. For example, a student may be well behaved during math class, but may often exhibit inappropriate behaviors during social studies. Therefore, these assessments can assist teachers in identifying the student's needs. Teachers use discrepancies between the performance of a student with disabilities and that of a student without disabilities as a point of reference for identifying potential instruction and support strategies.

There are numerous types of ecological assessments. These include the following:

- **Authentic Assessment:** Demonstration of a skill or behavior in a real life context.
- **Curriculum-Based Assessment:** A broad approach to linking assessment to instruction.
- **Dynamic Assessment:** A technique in which the assessor actively engages the student in learning. Interactions between the evaluator and the student reflect upon the world of the student by focusing on the student and giving immediate feedback.
- **Performance Assessment:** Demonstration of the behavior that has been outlined by the assessor.
- **Product Assessment:** Analysis of the product of the student's performance.

Portfolio Assessments

The use of student portfolios for some aspect of assessment has become quite common. The purpose, nature, and policies of portfolio assessment vary greatly from one setting to another. In general, a student's portfolio contains samples of work collected over an extended period of time. In some cases, the student and teacher make joint decisions as to which work samples go into the student's portfolios. A collection of work compiled over an extended time period allows a teacher, a student, and parents to view the student's progress from a unique perspective. Qualitative changes over time can be readily apparent from work samples. Such changes are difficult to establish with strictly quantitative records typical of the scores recorded in the teacher's grade book.

Task Analysis

A teacher can use the set of behavioral specifications that are the result of the task analysis to prepare tests that will measure the student's ability to meet those specifications. These tests are referred to as criterion measurements. If task analysis identifies which skills will be needed to perform a task successfully, then the criterion measurements will further identify whether the student possesses the necessary skills or knowledge for that task. The level of performance that is acceptable is the "criterion level."

Criterion measurements must be developed along certain guidelines if they are to accurately measure a task and its sub-skills. Johnson and Morasky (1977) give the following guidelines for establishing criterion measurement:

1. Criterion measurement must directly evaluate a student's ability to perform a task.
2. Criterion measurements should cover the range of possible situations in order to be considered an adequate measure.
3. Criterion measurements should measure whether or not a student can perform the task without additional or outside assistance.
4. All responses in the criterion measurement should be relevant to the task being measured.

Behavioral objectives offer descriptive statements defining the task that the student will perform, state the conditions under which the task will occur, and show the criterion measurement required for mastery. The criterion measurement is the process for evaluating what the student can do. For the instruction to be meaningful, there must be a precise correspondence between the capabilities determined in a criterion measurement and the behavioral demands of the objective.

Functional Assessments

A **Functional Behavioral Assessment (FBA)** is a procedure which tries to identify the problem behavior a student may show in school, to determine the function or purpose of the behavior, and to develop interventions to teach satisfactory alternatives to the behavior. The first step in carrying out an FBA is for the school team to identify and agree upon the primary behavior that needs to be changed. The next step is to gather data on the occurrence of the target behavior, identifying frequency, intensity, and where, when and how the behavior takes place. The third step is to develop a hypothesis about the function or purpose of the student's behavior and to develop an intervention. The last step is to evaluate the effectiveness of the proposed intervention. FBAs have been utilized for students with severe disabilities, to help parents and teachers understand the function of inappropriate behavior, and to plan effective interventions. FBAs are also a helpful approach to evaluating the reason for inappropriate behaviors for students who have milder disabilities, when their behaviors do not improve with the use of typical school interventions.

Skill 2.10	**Applies skills for using assessment and evaluation information from various sources (e.g., teachers, other professionals, parents/guardians, individuals with disabilities) to make instructional decisions, plan effective programs for individuals with disabilities, including those from culturally and/or linguistically diverse backgrounds, and identify supports needed for integration into various program placements.**

Please refer to Skill 2.07 and Skill 5.04 for more information that pertains to this skill.

Review of Student Needs with Inclusion Teacher and Support Staff

It may be determined at a student's ARD meeting that some time in the general education setting is appropriate. The student's IEP should specify which classes and activities are appropriate and the amount of time that the student will be with general education peers. The IEP should also list any modifications or accommodations that will be needed.

Accommodations are changes to the school environment, or the use of necessary equipment to overcome a disability. An accommodation for a student with a hearing impairment, for example, might include the use of an auditory trainer or asking another student to serve as a note taker.

Prior to the student starting in a general education placement, the general education teacher and support staff should be provided with training with regard to the student's disability and his needs according to his IEP.

Student Expectations in the Inclusion Setting

The student with a disability should be well aware of his or her responsibilities in the general education setting ahead of time. These expectations should be a combination of behavior and task performance. Although the student should be aware of needed accommodations and modifications and should be a self-advocate for such, he or she should not be allowed to use the disability as an excuse for not fulfilling the expectations.

Once the student is in the general education setting for the time and activities listed on the IEP, the special education teacher will need to monitor student progress. This can be done through verbal follow up with the general education teacher or by asking the teacher to periodically complete a progress form. Grades, progress reports, and the student's ability to restate learned information or answer questions are also indicators of the level success the student is experiencing in the inclusive setting.

Evaluation of Student's Future Placement in the Inclusion Setting

If the student is successful in the general education activities and classes listed on the IEP, the special education teacher may consider easing back on modifications and accommodations on the next IEP. He or she may also consider adding minutes or classes for to the student's general education inclusion.

If the student had difficulty, the special educator may consider adding more modifications or accommodations on the next IEP. If the student had significant difficulty, the student may need to receive more services in the special education classroom.

INSTRUCTIONAL PLANNING FOR A VARIETY OF INCLUSIVE MODELS

According to IDEA 2004, students with disabilities are to participate in the general education program to the extent that it is beneficial for them. As these students are included into a variety of general education activities and classes, the need for collaboration among teachers grows.

Co-Teaching

One model that is used for general education and special education teacher collaboration is co-teaching. In this model, both teachers actively teach in the general education classroom. Both teachers are in the classroom for the entire class period and share the teaching responsibilities, resources, and accountability for the students, both with and without disabilities, in the classroom.

In-Class Support or Support Facilitation

In the In-Class Support or Support Facilitation model, the general education teacher is responsible for the instruction and the special education teacher works with the students with disabilities within that setting to provide modifications. In this model, the special education teacher may not be in the classroom for the entire class period, but may come into the classroom to provide assistance for the students with disabilities. In this model, the special education teacher may work with a small group of students to reinforce concepts, re-teach, or work on prerequisite skills. The special education teacher may modify the content or presentation of materials to meet the needs of the students with disabilities.

Consultant Teaching

In the consultant teaching model, the general education teacher conducts the class after planning with the special educator about how to differentiate activities so that the needs of the student with a disability are met. The special education teacher may not directly work with the student with disabilities, but does provide support for the general education teacher regarding appropriate modifications, teaching strategies, and needs of the students.

Programming and Support Considerations for the Special Education Student from a Culturally Diverse

Although special education placement is not made because of a delay due to cultural diversity, if both a disability and a language difference exist, both should be considered when making placement and programming decisions. In some instances, a Bilingual or English as a Second Language (ESL) teacher may be a part of the ARD committee and may provide consultation or direct instruction to the Special Education teacher.

Community/Family Support

Each cultural has its own values. For example, students with disabilities from diverse cultural backgrounds may come from cultures where education is not valued or where females do not work outside of the home. They may come from cultures that question the importance of special education itself.

Awareness of cultural diversity and beliefs will help the special educator understand how best to communicate school goals with the students' families. As understanding and communication grow, family support will help the student become more successful in academics.

Language Considerations

If the student with a disability does not speak English as a native language, or if English is not used primarily by the student's family, language considerations will be important in the classroom. For example, key words and concepts may need to presented in a parallel fashion, in both languages, explaining in the student's native tongue, as well as in English.

COMPETENCY 003   **THE SPECIAL EDUCATION TEACHER UNDERSTANDS AND APPLIES KNOWLEDGE OF PROCEDURES FOR PLANNING INSTRUCTION FOR INDIVIDUALS WITH DISABILITIES**

Skill 3.01   **Knows how to select, develop, and apply instructional content, materials, resources, and strategies that are responsive to cultural and other factors (e.g., language, religion, gender, personal beliefs, nature and severity of disability).**

Teachers establish a classroom climate that is culturally respectful and engaging for students. In a culturally sensitive classroom, teachers maintain equity and fairness in student interactions and curriculum implementation. Assessments include cultural responses and perspectives that become further learning opportunities for students. Artifacts that reflect teacher/student sensitivity to diversity might consist of the following:

- Student portfolios reflecting multicultural/multiethnic perspectives
- Journals and reflections from field trips/ guest speakers from diverse cultural backgrounds
- Printed materials and wall displays from multicultural angles
- Projects that include cultural history and diverse inclusions
- Disaggregated student data reflecting cultural groups

The target of diversity allows teachers a variety of opportunities to expand their experiences with students, staff, community members and parents from culturally diverse backgrounds, so that their experiences can be proactively applied in promoting cultural diversity inclusion in the classroom. Teachers are able to engage and challenge students to develop and incorporate their own diversity skills to build character and relationships with cultures beyond their own. In changing the thinking patterns of students to become more cultural inclusive in the 21st century, teachers are addressing the globalization of our world.

Skill 3.02   **Knows curricula for developing cognitive, academic, social, language, affective, motor, functional, transition, and career life skills for individuals with disabilities.**

The Texas Education code requires school districts to provide instruction in the essential knowledge and skills at the appropriate grade levels. The TEKS (Texas Essential Knowledge and Skills) form the basis for the curriculum in the state of Texas. The Division of Curriculum oversees the development and implementation of the TEKS in public schools. The Division provides curriculum and professional development information and guidance in the ten curriculum and program unit areas. The TEKS became effective in all content areas in 1998, and has been recently revised in October, 2013.

One popular curriculum for students receiving special education services is the Functional Academic Curriculum for Exceptional Students (FACES). The primary purpose of the curriculum is to teach functional age-appropriate skills within integrated school and non-school settings and to base instruction on the systematic evaluation of students' progress. It is also designed to serve as a guide for teachers to utilize as they prepare students with disabilities to lead successful and personally fulfilling lives. Helpful FACES websites and resources are available for each region.

FACES is made up of six modules. These include: Personal Health, Science, Social Studies, Functional Math, Vocational, and Language Arts. Each module is made up of content areas and each objective is associated with the Texas Essential Knowledge and Skills (TEKS). More than one teaching activity is usually suggested for each component. The curriculum is utilized as a continuum of skills from early childhood through high school. The curriculum is designed to help in the development of skills that increase independence and encourage cooperation and mutual problem solving in a variety of environments such as home, school, and community.

There is a necessary overlapping of objectives for skill development across areas. Modules have been cross-referenced throughout the curriculum. Areas are coded according to school-age levels for organizational purposes. The levels are developed along a developmental continuum and are a general guideline and not a requirement. They provide a structure and format from which a creative teacher can design and implement additional learning activities.

Skill 3.03   Knows the role of the Texas Essential Knowledge and Skills (TEKS) in developing Individual Education Programs (IEPs) for students with disabilities, and applies skills for sequencing, implementing, and evaluating individual learning objectives.

The Texas Essential Knowledge and Skills (TEKS) provide information on what Texas students should know and be able to achieve at every grade and in every course in the required curriculum. The TEKS are the framework for the Texas Assessment of Knowledge and Skills (TAKS) assessment objectives. A thorough understanding of the TEKS is essential for student success in the classroom, on state assessments, and as reflected in the state accountability system.

The teacher works collaboratively with parents, students, and school as well as community personnel in the development of clear, measurable Individual Educational Plan (IEP) goals and objectives that are aligned with the TEKS. The IEP objectives for any given student should reflect the TEKS as closely as possible. The state has mandated that all IEPS be TEKS based.

Students in grades 3 through 11 take the Texas Assessment of Knowledge and Skills (TAKS) examinations. These tests indicate how much the students have learned and help to indicate how well the district's instructional program is functioning. Students receiving special education services are required to take some form of TAKS. Testing decisions for students receiving special education services are made by each student's ARD committee.

Options for TAKS testing for students in special education include:

- **TAKS:** A student may take the standard TAKS test.
- **TAKS-Accommodated (TAKS-A):** Covers the grade level TEKS, but has format accommodations, such as larger font, fewer items per page, and no embedded field test questions.
- **TAKS-Modified (TAKS-M):** Covers the grade level TEKS, has more format accommodations then the TAKS-A, such as fewer test items, reduced number of answer choices, larger font with more white space, and simplified sentence structure, vocabulary, and graphics.
- **TAKS-Alternate (TAKS-Alt):** Performance based assessment linked to TEKS, developed on an individual basis according to student functioning level. TAKS-Alt is designed for students with significant cognitive deficits.

Teachers are responsible for sequencing the skills that the students will be learning so that a progression of skills and abilities is attained. In addition, teachers should implement the objectives outlined in the IEP with the ultimate goal of evaluating the learning objectives and ensuring students are mastering the objectives, which will in turn allow them to demonstrate mastery on the TAKS.

Skill 3.04   Applies procedures for developing and using Individual Education Program (IEP) objectives to plan instruction for individuals with disabilities.

No Child Left Behind, Public Law 107-110, was signed on January 8, 2002. It addresses accountability of school personnel for student achievement with the expectation that every child will demonstrate proficiency in reading, math, and many areas of academics.

The general education curriculum should reflect state learning standards. Because special educators are responsible for teaching students to a level of comparable proficiency as their non-disabled peers, this curriculum should also be followed closely in the special education program.

Developing an IEP

Texas Project First has an informative website which delineates the basics of IEPs and why they are a critical component to student learning. The following is the web address: http://www.texasprojectfirst.org/DevelopingAnIEP.html

Some helpful pointers from the site can be derived by a parent, but also a special educator as well. Essentially, the IEP is developed by the ARD committee during an ARD meeting. Many special educators and school personnel may draft IEP goals for the ARD committee to consider. The goals are to be measurable, so progress can be tracked easily. Parents should be a part of goal creation process, and they have the right to question or object to a goal. Some parents also may ask for a pre-ARD meeting, so they may be a part of the drafting of the goals. Regardless of whether a special educator is in the formal and/or informal ARD meeting, he or she should be positive and honest, and utilize the time to make a strong connection with the team. The overarching goal is always to maximize a student's learning and optimize his or her school experience.

Naturally, certain modifications and accommodations will be necessary to meet learning standards. IEP goals and objectives are based on the unique needs of the child with a disability in meeting the curriculum expectations of the school (and the state/nation). Consider the following modification scenarios:

1. Teachers in grades K-3 are mandated to teach reading to all students using scientifically-based methods with measurable outcomes. Some students (including some with disabilities) will not learn to read successfully unless taught with a phonics approach. It is the responsibility of the general education teacher and special education teacher to incorporate phonics into the reading program.

2. Students are expected to learn mathematics. While some students will quickly grasp the mathematical concept of groupings of tens (and further skills of adding and subtracting large numbers), others will need additional practice. Research shows that many students with disabilities need a hands-on, tactile or kinesthetic approach. Perhaps those students will need additional instruction and practice using snap-together cubes or base-ten blocks to grasp the grouping-by-tens concept.

In the first scenario, a notation of the use of phonics-based reading instruction should be notated in the IEP. In the second scenario, the use of manipulatives and tactile, didactic tools for math lessons would be indicated in the IEP.

School districts, individual general education classrooms, and special education classrooms are not functioning independently; in fact, they are a cohesive unit. Learning standards set forth by the government now hold all facets of education to the same standards and is evidenced in curriculum and related IEP goals and objectives.

Skill 3.05 **Prepares, adapts, and organizes materials to implement developmentally appropriate and age-appropriate lesson plans based on Individual Education Program (IEP) objectives for individuals with disabilities.**

It is essential to use the school system's course of study and the student's IEP to prepare and organize materials to implement daily lesson plans. IEPs have to demonstrate that the student is working on goals as close to their general education peers as possible. Therefore, the school system's course of study should be a formatted document used to create the annual goals of the IEP. Schools often adopt a computerized program to help special educators and other teachers implement goal and data into a common system. The materials and didactic teaching tools necessary to meet the IEP goals should be either adapted to fit the needs of each student, or specially designed materials should be purchased or perhaps teacher-made.

The IEP must also include any assistive technology that maybe needed for the student to be successful. The teacher must gather the necessary technology before planning a lesson. Please refer to skill 8.6 to learn about different kinds of assistive technology.

Skill 3.06 **Applies knowledge of issues, resources, and appropriate strategies for teaching students with disabilities in specialized settings (e.g., alternative schools, special centers, hospitals, residential facilities), including transitions to and from school- and community-based settings**

Please refer to skill 2.09

The ARD committee convenes to discuss the child's current functional level along with assessment results and other information gathered by the committee. From that information, the ARD Committee agrees upon the goals the child should be working toward. The ARD Committee then discusses the supports and services, as well as the modifications the child needs to reach those goals. Finally, the ARD Committee determines where those special education services will be provided (location and placement). The location where services will be provided and the student's placement must be in the student's least restrictive environment.

Special education services occur at a variety of levels, some more restrictive than others. The largest number of special education students (i.e. mild disabilities) is served in settings closest to normal educational placements. Service delivery in more restrictive settings is limited to students with severe or profound disabilities, who comprise a smaller population within special education. The exception is correctional facilities, which serve a limited and restricted populace.

Options for placement of special education students are given on a "cascade of services," the term coined by Deno (1970). In Texas, the term "continuum of services" is often used. The multidisciplinary team must be able to match the needs of the student with an appropriate placement in the continuum of services.

According to Polloway, et al. (1994), two assumptions are made when we place students using the cascade (continuum) of services as a guide. First, a child should be placed in an educational setting as close to the regular classroom as possible, and placed only as far away from this least restrictive environment as necessary to provide an appropriate education.

Second, program exit should be a goal. A student's placement may change when the team obtains data suggesting the advisability of an alternative educational setting. As adaptive, social, cognitive, motor, and language skills are developed, the student may be placed in a lesser restrictive environment. The multidisciplinary team is responsible for monitoring and recommending placement changes when appropriate.

Cascade (Continuum) System of Special Education Services

Level 1   Regular Classroom, including students with disabilities able to learn with regular class accommodations, with or without medical and counseling services.

Level 2   Regular Classroom with supportive services (i.e. consultation, inclusion).

Level 3   Regular Class with part-time special class (i.e. itinerant services, resource room).

Level 4   Full-time Special Class (i.e. self-contained).

Level 5   Special Stations (i.e. special schools).

Level 6   Homebound

Level 7   Residential (i.e. hospital, institution)

Adapted from 1. Deno, "Special Education as Developmental Capital." Exceptional Children 1970, 37, 239, 237 Copyright 1970 by The Council for Exceptional Children Reprinted with permission from The Council for Exceptional Children.

TRANSITION SERVICES

By age sixteen, a statement of required transition services should be included in every IEP in the areas of instruction, related services, development of employment, community experiences, activities of daily living and functional vocational evaluation. Because transition is a process, the planning required to help students reach their desired post-school outcomes must become a part of the IEP in time for skills and knowledge to be gained and for goals to be reached to be successful in chosen life endeavors.

Transition services will be different for each student. Transition services must take into account the student's interests and preferences. Evaluation of career interests, aptitudes, skills and training must be considered.

The transition activities that must be addressed, unless the ARD Committee finds it uncalled for, are: (a) instruction, (b) related services, (c) community experiences, (d) the development of objectives related to employment and other post-school areas, and (e) daily living skills.

a) **Instruction:** The instruction part of the transition plan deals with school instruction. The student should have a portfolio and/or resumé completed upon graduation, preferably earlier. They should research and plan for further education and/or training after high school. Education can be in a college setting (two-year or four-year), technical school, or vocational center. Goals and objectives created for this transition domain depend upon the nature and severity of the student's disability, the student's interests in further education, plans made for accommodations needed in future education and training, and identification of post-secondary institutions that offer the requested training or education. College-bound students with disabilities must seek schools in which there are strong academic services, writing centers, and tutors easy accessible and available upon request.

b) **Related Services:** Along with planning for instruction, any needed related services (e.g. Speech Therapy, Occupational Therapy), must be taken into consideration when developing a transition plan.

c) **Community Experiences:** This part of the transition plan investigates how the student utilizes community resources. Resources entail places for recreation, transportation services, agencies, and advocacy services. It is essential for students to deal with the following areas:

- Recreation and Leisure - examples: movies, YMCA, religious activities.
- Personal and Social Skills - examples: calling friends, religious groups, going out to eat.
- Mobility and Transportation - examples: passing a driver's license test or using public transportation.
- Agency Access - examples: utilizing a phone book, navigating email, and making calls.
- System Advocacy- examples: have a list of advocacy groups to contact, attending weekly support groups, or maintaining appointments with specialists.
- Citizenship and Legal Issues - examples: registering to vote or obtaining a passport for travel.

d) **Development of Employment:** This segment of the transition plan investigates becoming employed. Students are recommended to complete a career interest inventory. They need chances to investigate different career paths. Many work skill activities can take place within the classroom, home, and community. Classroom activities may concentrate on employability skills, community skills, mobility, and vocational training. Home and neighborhood activities may concentrate on personal responsibility and daily chores. Community based activities may focus on part-time work after school and in the summer, cooperative education or work-study, individualized vocational training, and volunteer work.

e) **Daily Living Skills:** This segment of the transition plan is also important to the IEP. Living away from home can be an enormous undertaking for people with disabilities. Numerous skills are needed to live and function as an adult. In order to live as independently as possible, a person should have an income, know how to cook, clean, shop, pay bills, get to a job, and have a social life. Some living situations may entail independent living, shared living with a roommate, supported living, or group homes. Areas that may need to be addressed include: personal and social skills; living options; income and finances; medical needs; community resources and transportation.

Specialized Settings

On some occasions, placement of a student in a specialized setting outside the public school system is needed. Reasons for placement in a specialized setting such as a residential placement, hospital, alternate school, or other special education center are varied.

Programming Considerations in the Specialized Setting

In addition to staffing considerations, students in specialized educational settings are somewhat isolated from the general population. While this may offer a better opportunity to focus on the needs of students with a specific disability, effort should be made to include students in the general population. This may be done through field trips and activities in the community or by bringing the public into the specialized setting for programs, open houses, or as volunteers. In some instances, students from the specialized setting may take classes in the local public school.

There are, however, some instances when a special education student must be homebound or in a hospital due to an illness or surgery, and may have to be out of the regular education environment temporarily or indefinitely. Making an effort to have general education students reach out to students who are homebound or in a hospital setting would deeply and positively impact such students.

Skill 3.07   **Knows how to collaborate with other professionals to interpret and use sensory, mobility, reflex, and perceptual information to create appropriate learning plans (e.g., sensory stimulation, physical positioning, lifting).**

One of the primary requirements of the special education teacher is to work together with other professionals to create appropriate learning plans for students. In serving the needs of students with disabilities, special education teachers work together with occupational therapists (OT), physical therapists (PT), general education teachers, and other specialists.

The role of the occupational therapist is to work with a team, including the student, family, teacher, and other professionals to develop an intervention program. When OTs, families, and other team members collaborate, they can facilitate success in a number of performance areas. The OT can link specific interventions to specific daily, academic or wider social objectives for increased overall positive impact.

An OT may recommend a number of techniques such as making changes or modifications to the individual's physical environment or routine, and improving skills and coordination through activities designed to enhance certain aspects of the skill to make improvements in the individual's functioning.

In addition to motor delays, OTs can help treat sensory impairments. Sensory processing impairments are associated with an inefficient nervous system that cannot effectively integrate stimuli. As a result, a person with sensory integration dysfunction may shutdown, withdraw, become irritable or seek out intense sensory experiences by committing actions such as mouthing toys, spinning, or banging.

The role of the physical therapist is similar to the OT in working as a part of a collaborative team to ensure that specific aspects of the physical therapy requirements are implemented in the home and school setting. The PT can assist students with the development of transfer skills, e.g., getting back into a wheelchair from the floor, manual wheelchair skills, and gait training with or without assistive devices.

The goal of both occupational therapy and physical therapy is to enable students with disabilities to achieve functional independence in the school environment. The OT and PT can recommend strategies, modifications, and adaptive aids that can help improve school performance, enhance fine and gross motor skills, and allow students with disabilities to participate in school activities. School OT and PT interventions are intended to provide the services necessary to allow the student to benefit from the individualized educational program. With collaboration from the OT and PT the teacher and parents can also implement the procedures and help in the procurement of skills.

Skill 3.08   Knows how to collaborate with other professionals to plan, adapt, and implement effective instruction in the least restrictive setting for individuals with disabilities.

Support and Professional Services

When making eligibility, program, and placement decisions about a student, the special education teacher serves as a member of a multidisciplinary team. Since special education teachers are involved in every aspect regarding the education of individual students, they need to be knowledgeable not only about teaching and instructional techniques, but also about support services. These services will need to be coordinated, and teachers must be able to work in a collaborative manner.

The concept of mainstreaming special needs students, integrating them with their classmates in as many living and learning environments as possible, caught hold about the time that provisions for the Individuals with Disabilities Education Act (IDEA) were formulated in the early to mid-70s. Even though mainstreaming is not specifically addressed in this legislation, the education of all children and youth with disabilities in their least restrictive environment is mandated. In addition, this important legislation defines special education, identifies related services that may be required if special education is to be effective, and requires the participation of parents and other persons involved in the education of children and youth with disabilities.

Close contact and communication must be established and maintained between the school district staff, school staff, and the various specialists (or consultants) providing related services. These specialists often serve special needs students in auxiliary (i.e., providing help) and supplementary (i.e., in addition to) ways. The principles and methods of special education must be shared with regular educators, and tenets and practices of regular education must be conveyed to special educators. Job roles and unique responsibilities and duties of support specialists like speech/language therapists, physical and occupational therapists, school psychologists, educational diagnosticians, nurses, and others need to be known by all teachers.

The services that can be provided by community resources, and the support that can be given by parents and professional organizations, must be maintained in order for maximum educational benefit for students with disabilities to occur. Professional services are offered on a local, state, and national level for most areas of disability. Teachers are able to stay abreast of most current practices and changes by reading professional journals, attending professional conferences, and maintaining memberships with professional organizations.

Skill 3.09 **Knows how the general or special classroom and other learning environments (e.g., home, job site, cafeteria, transportation, community) impact student learning and behavior, and applies strategies for planning educational environments that promote students' learning, active participation, communication, self-advocacy, increased independence, and generalization of skills.**

Please refer to skill 5.08 regarding generalization of skills

Inclusion of the Student with Disabilities in General Education

It may be determined at a student's ARD meeting that some time in the general education setting is appropriate. The IEP will specify which classes and activities and the amount of time that the student will be with general education peers. The IEP will also list any modifications or accommodations that will be needed.

Modifications which may be considered for the general education classroom include adjustments to the amount of work or type of task required. Modifications for a student with a learning disability, for example, might include a reduced number of spelling words or writing the vocabulary word that goes with a given definition instead of writing the definition that goes with a given word. The impact of modifications varies from student to student, but generally, modifications are highly beneficial and promote a better understanding of content at hand. On occasion, a student may refuse a modification, for fear of social unacceptance. This behavior is not common, but not unheard of. The special education teacher should discreetly make changes to such a student's curriculum in order to respect the student's need for privacy, and to casually weave modifications into the content assignments without imposing on the child's self-esteem or perception of him or herself among general education classmates.

Accommodations are changes to the school environment or the use of necessary equipment to overcome a disability. An accommodation for a student with a hearing impairment might include the use of an auditory trainer or asking another student to serve as a note taker.

Prior to the student with a disability starting in a general education placement, the general education teacher and support staff (if any) should be provided information regarding the student's disability and his needs according to his or her IEP. Special education teachers must be particularly well-versed in their students' IEP goals.

Monitoring student progress in the inclusion setting

Once the student is in the general education setting for the time and activities listed on the IEP, the special education teacher will need to monitor student progress. This can be done through verbal follow up with the general education teacher or by asking him or her to periodically complete a progress form. Setting up informal meetings may also be helpful, or communicating via email or Skype can assist teacher time constraints. Numerical and performance based assessments, achieved grades and the student's ability to restate learned information or answer questions are indicators of the level of success the student is experiencing in the inclusive setting.

Evaluation of student's future placement in the inclusion setting

If the student is successful in the general education activities and classes listed on the IEP, the special education teacher may consider easing back on modifications and accommodations on the next IEP. The teacher may also consider adding minutes or classes for student's general education inclusion. The IEP is a living, legal document that can be altered at any time to fit a student's most current academic needs.

If the student had difficulty with a particular unit or content area, the special educator may consider adding more modifications or accommodations on the next IEP. If the student had significant difficulty, he or she may need to receive more services in the special education classroom.

Self-Advocacy

Learning about one's self involves the identification of learning styles, strengths and weakness, interests, and preferences. For students with mild disabilities, developing an awareness of the accommodations they need will help them ask for necessary accommodations on a job and in postsecondary education. Students can also help identify alternative ways they can learn. Self-advocacy involves the ability to effectively communicate one's own rights, needs, and desires and to take responsibility for making decisions that impact one's life.

The Learning Disabilities Association of America explains a student should be able to identify his or her strengths, recognize how the disability may impact performance, and determine which strategies work best. Being familiar with the law, including ADA and Section 504, also empowers students with disabilities so they may progressively advocate for themselves outside of the school building, in the "real world."

The role of the teacher in promoting a student's self-advocacy skills should include encouraging the student to participate in the IEP process as well as other key parts of his or her educational development. Self-advocacy lessons are effective when they are incorporated into the student's daily life. Teachers should listen to the student's problems and ask the student for input on possible changes that may need to be implemented. The teacher should talk with the student about possible solutions, discussing the pros and cons of doing something. A student who self-advocates should feel supported and encouraged. Good self-advocates know how to ask questions and get help from other people. They do not let other people do everything for them. Self-advocates can vocalize on behalf of themselves, and do not feel timid when asking for assistance. These students should know how to confidently request modifications, extended time, clarified directions, preferential seating, and/or other accommodations which may are defined in the IEP. Outside of the confines of school, these students must also be able to articulate themselves and explain how they learn best.

Students need to practice newly acquired self-advocacy skills. Teachers should have student's role play various situations, such as setting up a high school or college class schedule, moving out of the home, and asking for accommodations needed for a course. Role playing will help students exercise required dialogue needed to converse with others as they learn to define their needs.

The impact of transition planning on a student with a disability is very great. The student should be an active member of the transition team, as well as the focus of all activities. Unfortunately, some students think being passive and relying on others to take care of them is the way to get things done. Students should be encouraged to express their opinions openly throughout the transition process. They need to learn how to express themselves so that others listen closely and take them seriously. These skills should be practiced, as they are essential for a student's personal growth and feelings of self-efficacy.

Skill 3.10   Identifies ways in which technology can assist in planning and managing instruction for individuals with disabilities.

The Internet has provided a whole new world of assistance in planning and managing instruction. The Internet can provide grade book programs as well as vast resources of lesson plans and creative activities for various learning styles. Innovative, technology-infused classroom management is essential to being an efficient teacher. In addition to offering ideas, the Internet provides free materials such as seating charts, worksheets, and substitute teacher plans.

Students with disabilities often experience insufficient access to and a lack of success in the general education curriculum. To promote improved access to the general curriculum for all learners, information should be presented in various formats using a variety of media forms; students should be given numerous methods to express and demonstrate what they have learned; and students should be provided with multiple entry points to engage their interest and motivate their learning. Multisensory methods provide different venues for students to receive information. Using current Internet technology, such as network video clips, live camera streams, podcasts, and "webquests" will enhance visual and auditory leaners alike.

There are many current operating systems, such as Moodle, or e-Chalk, which allow teachers to have an interactive calendar and class website online via their district. Posting assignments and resources on the classroom website is also giving students a learning tool, which is also helpful for developing executive functioning and organization skills. Students can view what homework is due for the following day, when the upcoming tests and quizzes are, and access study materials such as PDF files of handouts, examples of past student projects, and rubrics for assignments.

Additional practice can be accessed online and skills can readily be reinforced. There are internet sites such as iXL and Digits, which allow students to practice math content by grade and concept. There are also several websites with educational games, where students can essentially play 'academic video games' in essence, to develop and reinforce learned knowledge.

New interactive whiteboards, such as SmartBoards, provide teachers with software in the classroom to take to the traditional projector screen to the next level. SmartBoards and interactive whiteboards present material in various formats for students. Touchscreen technology on such a large board enables students to get out of their seats and come up to the front of the classroom to take part in a lesson.

Some districts are even providing students with laptops or small, portable, multifunctional devices for school. Such learning devices can interactively meet a student's daily academic and even social needs, such as word processing, research and information retrieval (searching, textbooks, accessing school learning systems and sites) and communication (email, collaboration on sites such as Google docs. Laptops and devices also may have software installed to assist students, particularly those with special needs. Such software may enhance print, vocalize and read passages, or take notes from voice input. Historically, theorists from Dewey to Vygotsky saw learning as a personal process, in the social context. Technology is certainly pushing our students to new frontiers of learning, and perhaps special education students in particular.

Skill 3.11   Knows how to use local, state, and federal resources to assist in programming for individuals with disabilities.

The Texas Education Agency (TEA) is a state resource with goals of providing leadership, guidance, and resources to assist schools in meeting the educational requirements of its students.

TEA handles the textbook adoption process, manages development of the statewide curriculum, administers the statewide assessment program, administers a data collection system on public school students, staff, and finances, rates school districts under the statewide accountability system, operates research and information programs, monitors for compliance with federal guidelines, and serves as a fiscal agent for the distribution of state and federal funds.

Other key state resources are the twenty Regional Education Service Centers throughout the state. Regional Education Service Centers were originally created to work with school districts as media distribution centers, but the purpose of the centers have been expanded to include three main objectives that are outlined in the TEC§8.002. These objectives include: assisting school districts in improving student performance, aiding school districts in their maintaining efficient operations, and implementing the mandates of the Texas Education Agency and the Texas Legislature.

The Special Education Departments of Regional Education Service Centers focus on improving student performance and program effectiveness for students with disabilities ages 3 through 21 as indicated in the Individuals with Disabilities Improvement Education Act of 2004 (IDEA 2004). Staff from the Regional Education Service Centers support school districts and charter schools in meeting the requirements of law and service effectiveness through training and technical assistance for teachers, paraprofessionals, parents, support staff and administration.

A key federal legislation and resource that helps ensure that individuals with disabilities receive the services to which they are entitled is the Individuals with Disabilities Improvement Education Act of 2004 (IDEA 2004). IDEA ensures that each public agency shall ensure to the maximum extent appropriate that students with disabilities are educated with children who are do not have disabilities. Students with disabilities must be assured access to the general curriculum that applies to all students.

COMPETENCY 004   THE SPECIAL EDUCATION TEACHER UNDERSTANDS AND APPLIES KNOWLEDGE OF PROCEDURES FOR MANAGING THE TEACHING AND LEARNING ENVIRONMENT, INCLUDING PROCEDURES RELATED TO THE USE OF ASSISTIVE TECHNOLOGY.

Skill 4.01   Applies procedures for ensuring a safe, positive, and supportive learning environment in which diversities are valued, and knows how to address common environmental and personal barriers that hinder accessibility for and acceptance of individuals with disabilities.

Learning styles refer to the ways in which individuals learn best. Physical settings, instructional arrangements, materials available, techniques, and individual preferences are all factors in the teacher's choice of instructional strategies and materials. Information about the student's preference can be done through a direct interview or a Likert-style checklist where the student rates his preferences. Such questionnaires may allow students to self-report how they learn best, and in what conditions they prefer. Newer learning style surveys and inventories give students access to their personalized learning preferences, including environmental factors that impact their learning (light, noise level, group settings).

Physical Environment

The physical setting of the classroom contributes a great deal toward the propensity for students to learn. An adequate, well-built, and well-equipped classroom will invite students to learn. This has been called "invitational learning." Among the important factors to consider in the physical setting of the classroom are the following:

a) Adequate physical space
b) Repair status
c) Lighting adequacy
d) Adequate entry/exit access (including accessibility)
e) Ventilation/Climate control
f) Coloration
g) Cleanliness
h) Organization and Accessibility of Resources

A classroom must have adequate physical space so students can comfortably conduct themselves. Some students are distracted by windows, pencil sharpeners, doors, etc. Some students prefer the front, middle, or back rows. Some special education students have notations in their IEPs regarding preferential seating.

The teacher has the responsibility to report any items of classroom disrepair to maintenance staff. Broken windows, falling plaster, exposed sharp surfaces, leaks in ceiling or walls, and other items of disrepair present hazards to students. Cleanliness is equally as important, and the teacher should also enlist the help of building maintenance in the event the room is not adequately clean. Mold and water discoloration should be immediately reported, as they could be indicators of health hazards.

Another factor which must be considered is adequate lighting. Report any inadequacies in classroom illumination. Florescent lights placed at acute angles often burn out faster. Students prefer various levels of lighting, depending on their learning style preferences, and multiple dimmers and light sources may be available, including natural and artificial light sources.

Local fire and safety codes dictate entry and exit standards. In addition, all corridors and classrooms should be wheelchair accessible for students and others who use them. Proper placement of fire alarms, loudspeakers, and emergency telephones are also placed according to proper building codes, in the event of an emergency.

Another consideration is adequate ventilation and climate control. Specialty classes such as science require specialized hoods for ventilation. Physical education classes have the added responsibility for shower areas and specialized environments that must be heated, such as pools or athletic training rooms.

Classrooms with warmer subdued colors contribute to students' concentration. Neutral hues for coloration of walls, ceiling, and carpet or tile are generally used in classrooms so distraction due to classroom coloration may be minimized. Such neutral tones are aesthetically pleasing to the eye, but also minimize distraction.

In the modern classroom, there is a great deal of furniture, equipment, supplies, appliances, and learning tools to help the teacher teach and to help students learn. The classroom should be provided with furnishings that fit the purpose of the classroom. The kindergarten classroom may have a reading center, a playhouse, a puzzle table, student work desks/tables, a sandbox, and any other relevant learning/interest areas. The furniture is intended to fit the needs of the grade level and the learners within the space.

Whatever the arrangement of furniture and equipment may be, the teacher must provide for adequate traffic flow. Rows of desks must have adequate space between them for students to move and for the teacher to circulate. All areas must be open to line-of-sight supervision by the teacher. This is critical for both safety and instructional reasons. No equipment, materials, boxes, etc. should be placed where there is danger of falling over. Doors must have entry and exit accessibility at all times.

Noise level should also be considered as part of the physical environment. Students vary in the degree of quiet they need and the amount of background noise or talking they can tolerate without getting distracted or frustrated. A teacher must maintain an environment that is conducive to the learning of each child.

The major emergency responses include two categories for student movement: tornado warning response; and building evacuation, which includes most other emergencies (fire, bomb threat, etc.). For tornadoes, the prescribed response is to evacuate all students and personnel to the first floor of multi-story buildings, and to place students along walls away from windows. These are standard procedures for severe weather, particularly tornadoes. Other emergency situations may require evacuation of the school building. Teachers should be thoroughly familiar with evacuation routes established for each classroom in which they teach. Teachers should accompany and supervise students throughout the evacuation procedure, and check to see that all students under their supervision are accounted for. Teachers should then continue to supervise students until the building may be reoccupied (upon proper school or community authority notification), or until other procedures are followed for students to officially leave the school area and cease to be the supervisory responsibility of the school. Elementary students evacuated to another school can wear nametags and parents or guardians should sign them out at a central location.

Skill 4.02   Knows how to use instructional time efficiently and effectively for individuals with disabilities.

Schedule development depends upon the type of class (elementary or secondary) and the setting (regular classroom or special education classroom). There are, however, general rules of thumb that apply to both types and settings:

1. Allow time for transitions, planning, and setups.
2. Aim for maximum instructional time by pacing the instruction quickly and allotting time for practice of the new skills.
3. Proceed from short assignments to long ones, breaking up long lessons or complex tasks into short sessions or step-by-step instruction.
4. Follow a less preferred academic or activity with a highly preferred academic or activity.
5. In settings where students are working on individualized plans, do not schedule all the students at one time in activities that require a great deal of teacher assistance. For example, have some students work on math or spelling while the teacher works with the students in reading, which usually requires more teacher involvement.
6. Utilize scaffolding and instructional techniques to maximize time allotted to pre-teaching, teaching, and re-teaching content.

Special Considerations for Elementary Classrooms

1. Determine the amount of time that is needed for activities such as P.E., lunch, art, music, or recess.
2. Allow about 15 to 20 minutes for each opening and closing exercise. Spend time on "housekeeping" activities such as collecting lunch money, going over the schedule, cleaning up, reviewing the day's activities, getting ready to go home.

3. Schedule academics for periods when the students are more alert and motivated, usually in the early afternoon.
4. Build in time for slower-paced students to finish their work; others may work at learning centers or other activities of interest. Allowing extra time gives the teacher time to give more attention where it is needed, conduct assessments, or for students to complete or correct work.

Special Considerations for Secondary Classrooms

Secondary school days are usually divided into five, six, or seven periods of about forty to fifty minutes each, with time for homeroom and lunch. Students cannot stay behind and finish their work, since they have to leave to attend a different room. Special education support time should be scheduled so that the student does not miss academic instruction in his or her classroom or miss desirable nonacademic activities. In schools where special education teachers also co-teach or work with students in the regular classroom, the regular teacher will have to coordinate lesson plans with those of the special education teacher. Consultation time will also have to be budgeted into the schedule. Planning periods and even lunch periods may be ideal, depending on the schedules of all parties involved in instructional planning.

Instructional Time is Maximized by Collaboration Time

Effective collaboration among teachers and other professionals allows them to feel supported by other teachers in their mission to better meet the needs of their students. When collaboration is done successfully, teachers feel comfortable admitting what they do not know without feeling embarrassed or guarded, as it is assumed that everyone is faced with challenges and has knowledge to bring to the situation. When teachers are able to share challenges and difficulties, as well as successful teaching strategies, teachers can effectively evaluate teaching practices in schools and provide a variety of resources for fellow teachers to use in their classroom.

In collaborating, teachers can discuss effective techniques in dealing with transition time so that what is done effectively in one class can be shared and tried in other settings.

When teachers are sharing ideas for successful teaching practices with one another, they will have a wider base of knowledge to bring to the classroom. A variety of pedagogical approaches will be available, and the teacher will have a resource to rely on when they need additional input or advice in effectively teaching students. Additionally, if a teacher is part of a community of sharing, that teacher is more likely to value the benefits of the support and knowledge that is created in such a community. The teacher who places importance on collaboration, sharing, and peer-oriented learning will attempt to create a similar community in the classroom. A community of sharing within the classroom permits students to feel safe sharing ideas, challenges, and achievements with peers.

Depending on a student's disability and the school setting, special education teachers need to work with speech pathologists, educational diagnosticians, school psychologists, occupational therapists, physical therapists, general education teachers, and community workers to plan the most optimal education program for each student.

Special education teachers who work in inclusive settings or who co-teach or team-teach with general education teachers must spend enough time to sufficiently plan, develop, and put into practice an educational situation that is stimulating and suitable for all the students in the class. There are six modes of teaching in the co-teach model:

1. *One Teach, One Observe* is when one co-teacher directs a lesson while the other co-teacher makes detailed observations of students during the learning process.

2. *One Teach, One Drift* is when one co-teacher takes the main responsibility of leading the lesson while the other co-teacher walks or drifts around the room helping students as needed.

3. *Station Teaching* is when both students are divided among stations, and students move from one co-teacher's station to another. The content covered is different at each station.

4. *Parallel Teaching* is when both co-teachers teach the same information, but they split the class into two groups and give the lessons at the same time.

5. *Alternative Teaching* is when one co-teacher conducts a lesson with a large group while the other co-teacher conducts an alternate lesson or the same lesson but at a different, differentiation level.

6. *Team Teaching* is when both co-teachers deliver instruction simultaneously, and instruction is not turn-taking; the teachers fluidly teach side-by-side.

Parents are a significant part of the collaboration team. The parents are the experts on their child. Both parents and teachers have a lot to give in the educational planning for students with disabilities. If they work together, they can be a strong team. Such collaboration and teamwork efforts will maximize and tighten instruction.

Collaboration and working together requires time, which is in short supply in the educational setting. Educators never have enough time to do everything that they want to do. In order to work effectively, special education teachers need the time to work and plan with parents and other professionals.

Skill 4.03 **Knows how to design, structure, and manage daily routines, including transition time, for students in a variety of educational settings, and applies procedures for monitoring behavior changes across activities and settings.**

Managing daily routines is an executive functioning skill. Some teachers are stronger than others in this area, but nevertheless, all teachers an use tools necessary to increase timeliness. Prioritizing the day's lessons and embedding extracurricular activities, such as art, lunch, music, and P.E., can be done in a lesson book, agenda, or simply displayed on the board. Noting the beginning and ending time of each planned activity or lesson gives a visual cue to the reader; he or she can denote when to get ready to start or end a planned experience.

The daily routine is critical for students; predictability gives students a sense of stability. Students with behavioral disorders may also benefit from such structured time intervals, so they may anticipate and know what is to come. This is true for those with learning disabilities as well. Overall, functioning with a plan in any educational setting is beneficial to teachers and students.

Monitoring student behavioral changes across activities and settings can also be done easily with the help of a structured schedule. For example, a teacher may have a notebook in which the schedule is written on one side of the page, and notes can be taken on the opposite side, to indicate a time period when behaviors occur. Perhaps a student with dyslexia raises his or her hand to exit the room or use the bathroom every time reading instruction is planned. This is a type of avoidance behavior a teacher can record and see patterns in data collected. Both genders express avoidance behaviors (Larkin & Pines, 2003), although learning disabilities are more prevalent in boys.

Skill 4.04 **Applies knowledge of basic classroom management theories, methods, and techniques for individuals with disabilities, research-based best practices for effective management of teaching and learning, and management procedures that are appropriate to individual needs.**

Classroom Management Techniques

Classroom management plans should be in place when the school year begins. Developing a management plan takes a proactive approach; the teacher must decide what behaviors will be expected of the class as a whole, anticipate possible problems, and teach the behaviors early in the school year. Many teacher post classroom rules and expectation sin a highly visible area, so students are visually reminded of behavioral parameters in their environment. It is common practice to set the rules the very first day of school, to avoid any lapsed time or ambiguity, should a behavioral situation arise.

Some teachers even have their students volunteer rule ideas, and take their contributions into account, subconsciously promoting mutual respect and appreciation. Involving the students in the development of the classroom rules lets the students know the rationale for the rules, and allows them to assume responsibility in the rules because they had a part in developing them. When students get involved in helping establish the rules, they will be more likely to assume responsibility for following them. Once the rules are established, enforcement and reinforcement for following the rules should begin right away.

Consequences should be introduced when the rules are introduced, and they are to be clearly stated, and understood by all of the students. The severity of the consequence should match the severity of the offense and must be enforceable. The teacher must apply the consequence consistently and fairly and therefore, the students will know what to expect when they choose to break a rule.

About four to six classroom rules should be posted. These rules should be stated positively. Certain rules may also be tailored to meet target goals and IEP requirements of individual students. For example, a new student who has had problems with leaving the classroom may need an individual behavior contract to assist with adjusting to the class rule about remaining in the assigned area. As the students demonstrate the behaviors, the teacher should provide reinforcement and corrective feedback. Periodic "refresher" practice can be done as needed, for example, after a long holiday or if students begin to "slack off."

Like consequences, students should understand what rewards to expect for following the rules. The teacher should never promise a reward that cannot be delivered, and follow through with the reward as soon as possible. Consistency and fairness is also necessary for rewards to be effective. Students will become frustrated and give up if they see that rewards and consequences are not delivered fairly and in a timely manner.

The system of rewards and consequences is also known as a token economy. In a token economy, students are rewarded because of their good behaviors. This extrinsic motivation may be reinforced with stickers, small items, and extra credit points. The notion of having a token economy is also heavily used with students who have behavioral disorders and/or autism, particularly in Applied Behavior Analysis practices. Providing immediate positive feedback for completing tasks required, or for exhibiting desired behavior strengthens and increases the frequency of positive actions.

The teacher should always clarify and model the expected behavior for the students. In addition to the classroom management plan or rules, a management plan should be developed for special situations, (i.e., fire drills) and transitions (i.e., going to and from the cafeteria).

Procedures that use social humiliation, withholding of basic needs, pain, or extreme discomfort should never be used in a behavior management plan. Emergency intervention procedures used when the student is a danger to himself or others are not considered behavior management procedures. Throughout the year, the teacher should periodically review the types of interventions being used, assess the effectiveness of the interventions used in the management plan, and make revisions as needed for the best interests of the child.

Classroom Behavioral Interventions

Classroom interventions anticipate student disruptions and nullify potential discipline problems. Every student is different and each situation is unique, therefore, student behavior cannot be matched to specific interventions. Good classroom management requires the ability to select appropriate intervention strategies from an array of alternatives. The following non-verbal and verbal interventions were explained in Henley, Ramsey, and Algonzzine (1993).

Nonverbal Intervention - The use of nonverbal interventions allows classroom activities to proceed without interruption. These interventions also enable students to avoid "power struggles" with students.

Body Language - Teachers can convey authority and command respect through body language. Posture, eye contact, facial expressions, and gestures are examples of body components that signal leadership to students.

Planned Ignoring - Many minor classroom disturbances are best handled through planned ignoring. When teachers ignore attention-seeking behaviors, often students do likewise.

Signal Interference - There are numerous non-verbal signals that teachers can use to quiet a class. Some of these are eye contact, snapping fingers, a frown, shaking the head, or making a quieting gesture with the hand. Other non-verbal signals involve flicking the classroom lights on and off, raising a finger to the lips, or winking at a selective student.

Proximity Control - Teachers who move around the room merely need to stand near a student or small group of students, to exhibit authority in a passive but effective manner. Teachers who stand or sit as if rooted are compelled to issue verbal directions in order to deal with student disruptions.

Removal of Seductive Objects - Some students become distracted by objects. Removing seductive objects eliminates the need some students have to handle, grab, or touch objects that distract their attention. Be careful of removing objects *needed* to sustain attention, as certain ADHD students may require a small item in their hands or other object to actually *maintain* attention.

Verbal Interventions - Because non-verbal interventions are the least intrusive, they are generally preferred. Verbal Interventions are useful after it is clear that nonverbal interventions have been unsuccessful in preventing or stopping disruptive behavior.

Humor - Some teachers have been successful in dispelling discipline problems with a quip or an easy comment that produces smiles or gentle laughter from students. This does not include sarcasm, cynicism, or teasing, which increase tension and often creates resentment.

Sane Messages - Sane messages are descriptive and model appropriate behavior. They help students understand how their behavior affects others. "Carole, when you talk during silent reading, you disturb everyone in your group," is an example of a sane message.

Restructuring - When confronted with student disinterest, the teacher makes the decision to change activities. This is an example of an occasion when restructuring could be used by the teacher to regenerate student interest.

Hypodermic Affection - Sometimes students get frustrated, discouraged, and anxious in school. Hypodermic affection lets students know they are valued. Saying a kind word, giving a smile, or just showing interest in a child can give the encouragement that is needed.

Praise and Encouragement - Effective praise is directed at student behavior rather than at the student personally. "Catching a child being good," is an example of an effective use of praise that reinforces positive classroom behavior. Comments like, "You are really trying hard," encourage student effort.

Alerting - Making abrupt changes from one activity to another can bring on behavior problems. Alerting helps students to make smooth transitions by giving them time to make emotional adjustments to change. Such alerts serve as warnings so students can prepare for the change or transition prior to it occurring.

Accepting Student Feelings - Providing opportunities for students to express their feelings, even those that are distressful, helps them to learn to do so in appropriate ways. Role playing, class meetings or discussions, life space interviews, journal writings, and other creative modes help students to channel difficult feelings expressively into constructive outlets.

Transitional Time

Effective teachers efficiently use class time. This results in higher subject engagement and will likely result in more subject matter retention. One way teachers use class time efficiently is through a smooth transition from one activity to another; this is also known as "management transition." Management transition is defined as "teacher shifts from one activity to another in a systemic, academically oriented way." One factor that contributes to efficient management transition is the teacher's management of instructional material. Effective teachers gather their materials during the planning stage of instruction. Doing this, a teacher avoids flipping through books and notes, looking for the items necessary for the current lesson. Momentum is lost and student concentration is broken when this occurs.

Additionally, teachers who keep students informed of the sequencing of instructional activities maintain systematic transitions because the students are adequately prepared to move on to the next activity. For example, if a teacher says, "When we finish with this guided practice together, we will turn to page twenty-three and each student will do the exercises. I will then circulate throughout the classroom helping on an individual basis. Okay, let's begin." Following an example such as this will lead to systematic smooth transitions between activities because the students will be turning to page twenty-three when the class finishes the practice without a break in concentration. Writing this plan on the board is also helpful, particularly for students with sequencing and processing deficits, so they can refer to the steps visually, and not have to recall all of the verbalized directions.

Another method that leads to smooth transitions is to move students in groups and clusters, rather than one by one. This is called "group fragmentation." For example, if some students do seat work while other students gather for a reading group, the teacher moves the students in pre-determined groups. Instead of calling the individual names of the reading group, which would be time consuming and laborious, the teacher simply says, "Will the blue reading group please assemble at the reading station. The red and yellow groups will quietly do the vocabulary assignment I am now handing out." As a result of this activity, the classroom is ready to move on in a matter of seconds rather than minutes.

Additionally, the teacher may employ academic transition signals. For example, the teacher may say, "That completes our description of clouds, now we will examine weather fronts." Like the sequencing of instructional materials, this keeps the student informed on what is coming next so they will move to the next activity with little or no break in concentration.

Effective teachers manage transitions from one activity to another in a systematically oriented way through efficient management of instructional matter, sequencing of instructional activities, moving students in groups, and by employing academic transition signals. Through an efficient use of class time, achievement is increased because students spend more class time engaged in on-task behavior.

Transition refers to changes in class activities that involve movement. Examples are:

(a) Breaking up from large group instruction into small groups for learning centers and small-group instruction.
(b) Classroom to lunch, to the playground, or to elective classes.
(c) Finishing reading at the end of one period and getting ready for math the next period.

(d) Emergency situations such as fire drills.

Successful transitions are achieved by using proactive strategies. Early in the year, the teacher pinpoints the transition periods in the day and anticipates possible behavior problems, such as students habitually returning late from lunch. After identifying possible problems with the environment or the schedule, the teacher plans proactive strategies to minimize or eliminate those problems. Proactive planning also gives the teacher the advantage of being prepared, addressing behaviors before they become problems, and incorporating strategies into the classroom management plan right away. Transition plans can be developed for each type of transition and the expected behaviors for each situation taught directly to the students.

Students with autistic spectrum disorders may exhibit a particularly tough time with transitions. Transitions may make an autistic student feel disoriented, startled, uneasy, or angered. There are a multitude of strategies that may be used to handle such transitional times with these students. Picture schedules, social stories, and PECs (Picture Communication Exchange systems) are effective. Such systems allow students, particularly those who are nonverbal, those who are limited verbally, or those who have an expressive language deficit, to communicate what they desire through pictures. They can also identify feelings based on pictorial representations of emotions. The pictures help bridge communication between the autistic spectrum student and the teacher. It is a communication tool that can be used by all professionals on the child's team, as well as the parents at home.

Skill 4.05 Identifies ways in which technology can assist in managing the teaching and learning environment to meet the needs of individual students.

As we have transferred into the twenty-first century, technology has become an integral part of our day to day lives. In the classroom, technology levels vary greatly from state to state, district to district, and even building to building. There are, however, a variety of teaching tools available in today's market that truly help the educator meet the needs of all students in the classroom.

There are a large number of software programs and Internet based programs, which offer individualized instruction. These series allow the teacher to set instructional levels, monitor ongoing progress of the student, as well as provide the individual students with a continuum of skills at their own pace and level. Additionally, some of these programs have incentive natures to encourage children. Accelerated Reader and Math© through Renaissance Learning by Capstone, are programs that provide students with quizzes for completing work and are tied into incentives within the school building.

Other uses of technology allow students to access material they may otherwise be unable to utilize. Students, who are unable to speak, may use technology devices to communicate. These augmentative communication systems are crucial to the participation and success of these learners. In other incidences, there are programs that will read text to students unable to see or read the text independently. Programs are available that will allow the student to dictate written assignments and then the program will translate the spoken words into a word processing document which can be edited.

Smart boards, similar to white boards that are connected to a computer, provide a more interactive nature to oral presentations within the classroom. Students are able to use special markers/pointers or their hands to activate the display, allowing them to be more active participants in lectures.

Digital cameras and digital video recorders can be wonderful enhancements to the instructional process. They allow students to add pictures to their assignments making them more personal and real. Another use is to provide the students with authenticity to daily routines. For example, a student who is in need of appropriate behavioral reminders could be photographed completing the proper task. This picture reminder can be used within the classroom to provide the student with a visual cue to the behavior the child should be exhibiting.

E-Readers and the use of electronic reading devices, such as Kindle, are also commonly used by students. Rather than using a printed book or textbook, students may access various texts and textbooks on their iPads, tablets, or even their phones. Some e-readers will highlights text for students, or read text aloud to the student.

Whether the technology is digital clocks, computers, digital cameras, or the more complex Smart Boards, it is imperative that educators take full advantage of the resources available to them. Teachers today are preparing twenty-first century learners, and must utilize a variety of technological advances in education in order to keep students abreast of modern trends in communication and learning. Technology is a part of our daily lives and in order to prepare students, they need to feel comfortable using technology. The flexibility of the inherent nature of technology allows teachers to meet the needs of more students on an individual level than ever before.

Computers and Software

Computers are valuable teaching tools. Software programs and adaptations enable learners with disabilities (i.e., physical, cognitive, and sensory) to profit from instruction in the classroom that they might not otherwise be able to receive. For example, tutorial software programs simulate the teaching function of presentations, questions, and feedback. In this didactic manner, children are provided learning exercises on an appropriate level of difficulty, and in an interesting style. Other programs can be used which allow drill and practice (with correct answers shown) over previously learned material. Games are effective as motivators and reinforcers. In addition, use of computer software provides a way of testing students that is more appealing to many than a written test. The novelty of the interactive game format is often more inviting, and less threatening as well as less anxiety producing, then more formal testing layouts.

Interactive essay writing, note-taking, and homework completion is often conducted on Google docs, or Google drive now. Students and teachers can access documents simultaneously from remote locations, to compose and revise/edit works of writing. Such 'freeware' or free software, is essentially a web-based classroom or office in which students and teachers have access to documents at any time, and can interact with one another via computer interface.

Textbooks, such as those by Prentice Hall, often come with direct website access and CD-ROMs, so students may access online notes, interactive demo videos, photo galleries, quizzes, assessments, and numerous study materials. Students may easily peruse older units on the publisher's website when preparing for a cumulative exam, such as a midterm or final. Likewise, publishers give teacher's access to such tools as well, and teachers often have access to potential exams and test questions as well as rationales, and also teaching tools, like printable worksheets, video clips, and sound bites.

Teachers can acquire the skills needed to program the computer so that tasks provided by software correspond with students' individualized education programs. Teaching students to program will develop problem-solving and discovery skills, and also foster reasoning comprehension skills.

Computer Assisted Instruction

Stages of Learning

Suggestions about selecting and using software were given by Male (1994). These stages still apply to current technology, though students may process at an accelerated pace compared to the timeframe of this study, because technology today is much more abundant in the home and public settings (i.e., library, study centers). There is also an abundance of downloadable and free software available on the Internet, and teachers are not bound to traditional CD-ROMs as they were only a decade ago.

However, boundaries must be in place, for correct usage of software, maximization of student learning, and proper assessment. First, make sure there is a curriculum correspondence between what students are working on at their desks and what they do at the computers. This should follow what he calls stages of learning. Then, make certain the students proceed through the five stages of learning. Software should be selected with these stages in mind:

Acquisition:	Introduction of a new skill.
Proficiency:	Practice under supervision to achieve accuracy and speed.
Maintenance:	Continued practice without further instruction.
Generalization:	Application of the new skills in new settings and situations.
Adaptation:	Modifications of the task to meet new needs and demands of varying situations.

Learning Environment

Computers are used to provide a safe, stimulating learning environment for many students. The computer does not evaluate or offer subjective opinions about the student's work, unless the software the student is using is being used for assessment purposes, or is 'quizzing' a student in a facet of the program. The computer merely provides feedback about the correctness or incorrectness of each answer in a series. Some Internet games and websites may provide students with positive feedback, such as positive phrases, i.e., "Way to Go!" or "Great Work!" The computer is like an effective teacher by the way in which it:

1. Provides immediate attention and feedback.
2. Individualizes to the particular skill level.
3. Allows students to work at their own pace.
4. Makes corrections quickly.
5. Produces a professional looking product.
6. Keeps accurate records on correct and error rates.
7. Ignores inappropriate behavior.
8. Focuses on the particular response.
9. Is nonjudgmental. (Smith & Luckasson, 1992)

Computers are useful in teaching traditional academic subjects like math, reading, spelling, geography, and science. Effective teachers allow for drill and practice on the computer, monitor student progress, and reinforce appropriately. When students have mastered a particular level, these teachers help them to progress to another level. Reasoning and problem-solving are other skill areas which can be taught using computers.

Helpful note-taking software, particularly for students with dysgraphia, includes the Pulse SmartPen and the Echo SmartPen, from www.livescribe.com. They are audio recording devices which combine handwritten notes with audio recording capability. These SmartPens can be used in a traditional manner by tapping on a section of handwritten notes to activate the same portion of an audio presentation. In addition, SmartPens can be employed in a nontraditional manner, where students are instructed to listen for and jot down main ideas while recording the audio. After, students can listen to the audio recording and use a word processor, or even speech-recognition software, to record in the details under the mean ideas (Lacey-Castelot, 2013).

Computer games, software, and technological devices can enhance learning skills and provide a highly desired reinforcement opportunity in the learning environment. When played alone, the games may serve as leisure activities for the individual or individualized, prescriptive content reinforcement. When played with classmates, the games can help develop interpersonal relationships. This is particularly applicable to youngsters with behavioral disorders, and learning and intellectual disabilities, as well as those without any identified disability.

Word Processors, Programs and Typing Devices

Word processors and computers are used to assist students with written composition. Students with learning disabilities often have difficulty organizing thoughts. Problems with writing are compounded by handwriting difficulties. Many teachers report that use of a word processor or computer has enabled them to motivate students to write. Most are less resistant to rewriting texts when they can do it on a word processing program, such as Microsoft Word, that erases and replaces text quickly. Printed texts in typewritten form are easier to read. Spelling checkers, built into many word processing programs, assist those who may not be able to spell words correctly. Another option is a thesaurus which provides synonyms and helps to build vocabulary. The overall quantity and quality of written work improves when word processing programs are used in conjunction with computers.

Typing devices which can help students transcribe material electronically now go beyond the traditional computer and laptop technology, into the world of tablets and handheld devices. Typing devices also include touch-screen capabilities, in which students can tap keyboards directly on the face/screen of a tablet, such as the iPad. Students may also use a stylus, which is a pen that can used to tap on such screens with finer accuracy than the human index fingers.

When working on the word processor, each student needs a or storage device so that the student's work can be saved and evaluated over time. Having a portfolio of printouts, projects and files enables students to take work home to show parents.

Process Approach to Writing

The process approach to writing is encouraged, especially when using a word processor (Male,1994). This process consists of stages include planning/ prewriting, drafting, revising/editing, and sharing/publication. Progressing through these stages is particularly helpful to developing writers. Writing instruction is imperative to communication is today's society, whether students are writing exam essays, emails, resumes, or science lab reports. Each genre of writing can be taught to all learners by using the process approach. Writing is readily available for review and evaluation (Graham, MacArthur, & Fitzgerald, 2013).

The **planning stage** is characterized by written outlines, brainstorming, clustering or mind mapping, and lists of ideas, themes, or key words. The planning stage may also mean the student will use a graphic organizers, such as a flow chart or diagram, a timeline, a KWL chart (What I **K**now- What I **W**ant to Know-What I **L**earned), or another type of visual framework that may depict organization, such as a set of three boxes signaling before-during-after, or begging-middle-ending. For comparison of two themes, books, topics, or ideas, students may use a graphic organizer as well, such as a T-chart or a Venn diagram. These planning activities are ideally suited to a classroom that has a large television monitor, Smart Board, overhead projector, or a computer projection device that will allow the teacher to list, group, revise, and expand ideas as students share them. The modeling of the planning stage promotes student understanding directly by example. Producing printed copies of what was generated by the group can be distributed at the end of the class session, and used as a concrete example for future brainstorming and planning the students may be asked to do on their own for an assignment.

In the **drafting stage**, individuals can do draft work at a computer by themselves, or they can collaborate as a group on the work. Some students may choose to use pencil and paper to do initial draft work, or they may want to dictate stories to the teacher or another student who writes it down for them. Students with dysgraphia or expressive language disorders may need a typing device, scribe, or recorder for notes. They can also use software such as Wynn Literacy Software or Dragon Naturally Speaking, to record their orally spoken words and transfer them into a typed document on the computer.

Students share their work during the **revising/editing stage**. Students read their stories aloud to a partner, a small group, or the whole class. Classmates are instructed to ask questions and give feedback that will help the writer make revisions to his work. This type of revising may be referred to as peer editing, where students collaborate together and edit papers, provide constructive criticism, and note areas of strength, or weakness. After the assignment or story content has been completed, attention is given to mechanics and writing conventions.

The **sharing/publication stage** enables students to experience being authors responding to an audience. Students are encouraged to share their work by reading it aloud and in printed form. They can do this with or without graphics or illustrations. Teachers with class webpages may post work online with parent and student permission, for the class to access, or even the general public. Teachers may also want to display written work in hallway billboards, or around the room, particularly during conference or observation times, so examples of writing are evident in the classroom as a montage of collective work in a common theme. Posting student work will also instill pride in their finished products, and that very confidence is truly always our aim as teachers.

If there is a school publication, such as a magazine for poetry, or a school newspaper, encourage students to submit work. Ask the members in charge of the school publications if they are reviewing submissions, and find out upcoming themes. Students will be excited by the prospect of publication, and it will build their portfolios and resumes, especially if their work is chosen to be published. Many online magazines or webzines for students seek student work. Some magazines, such as *New Moon* or *Amazing Kids!*, enjoy receiving submissions from specific genders and age groups. These publications are for various age groups, and look forward to receiving work from our students.

Older students may be working on journalism pieces, and can submit small articles and editorials to the local newspaper. They may also want to submit works for scholarships, contests, and recognition.

Skill 4.06 **Knows how to make informed decisions about types and levels of assistive technologies, devices, and services for students with various needs, collect and analyze information about a student's environment and curriculum to identify and monitor assistive technology needs, and support the use of assistive technologies, devices, and services.**

Technology has helped individuals with physical and health impairments to gain access to and control the environment around them, communicate with others, and take advantage of health care. There are high-tech devices such as computers, but also low-tech devices like built-up spoons and crutches. Electric typewriters, computer keyboards, tablets and touchpads, as well as automated language boards provide means for communication to occur.

Consideration of Student Need

What are the expectations of the student in the classroom? Some expectations that may be best address with technology include:

- Basic communication of wants and needs
- Fluency with books on tape
- Use of Braille typewriters
- Effective note taking
- Completion of writing assignments
- Automaticity of math calculations
- Strong spelling and grammar skills
- Movement between locations
- Auditory input or processing

Consideration of Existing Technology

At times, the technology used by all students will meet the needs of the student with a disability. An example would be the student with a physical disability who is researching and writing a report about Texas. Like his classmates, the child can use the school computers to accomplish this task. However, the student with a physical disability may need the keyboard to be adjusted to a certain angle to accommodate his physical needs. Or he or she may need to use a touchscreen to type.

In other cases, existing general population technology does not meet student needs.

Determination of Student Need for Assistive Technology

Often the special educator will identify the need for consultation or testing in an area in which a student is having difficulty. Testing or other professional evaluations may result in the trial or ongoing use of some form of assistive technology as listed on the student's IEP.

Development of Student Skill Using Specific Assistive Technology

Students who have been identified as needing assistive technology require training in the use of the equipment. Sometimes a therapist or consultant will "push in" to the classroom providing training for the student in the classroom setting. Other times the student will practice using the assistive technology in a separate setting until a level of experience/expertise is reached. Then the assistive technology may be used in the special education or inclusion classroom.

Communication of Expected Skill Level in Classroom

As students begin to use assistive technology in the classroom, the desired use (including activity, location, and time) should be outlined for the special educator so that misunderstanding does not result in a student misusing or under using the technology. The student, then, will have a level of accountability and be functioning to the best of his abilities.

Training of School Personnel on Use of Assistive Technology

Although special educators are often trained in using a variety of assistive devices, advances in technology make it necessary for professionals to participate in ongoing training for new or unfamiliar equipment. This training may be conducted by a knowledgeable therapist or consultant in the school district, or school personnel may need to attend a workshop off campus. There are online training modules available for some software and assistive technology as well.

Evaluation of Student Independent Management of Assistive Technology in Various Settings

Ongoing evaluation of the student's use of the equipment is vital. This may be monitored through observation by the therapist or consultant, anecdotal records of the special educator, or some type of checklist. Often an IEP goal will address how the use and evaluation of the student's performance with the equipment will be implemented.

Visual and Auditory Impairments

Visual Aids

For those with visual disorders, the Laser Cane and Sonicguide are two examples of electronic devices that have been in use for some time. These devices operate on the principle that people can learn to locate objects by hearing their echoes. For instance, the Laser Cane emits three beams of infrared light (one up, one down, and one straight ahead) that are converted into sound when they strike objects in the path of the person. The Sonicguide functions as an ultrasonic aid that helps youngsters born blind to gain an awareness of their environment and objects in it. The device looks similar to a pair of glasses, emits ultrasound, and converts reflections from objects into audible sounds.

Advances in computer technology are providing access to printed information for many people with visual impairments. Books are now available in digital format, allowing for a variety of outputs: voice, enlarged print, and Braille. Today, simple programs, such as Duxbury and Megadots, allow simple translation programs to easily convert English to Braille and Braille to English. By attaching a specially designed Braille printer to a computer, standard text can be converted into readable Braille, allowing teachers to produce copies of handouts, worksheets, tests, maps, charts, and other class materials in Braille.

Closed-circuit television (CCTV) and digital magnifiers can be used to enlarge the print found in printed texts and books. By using a small television camera with a zoom lens and a sliding reading stand upon which the printed materials are placed, the greatly enlarged printed material can be viewed on a television monitor. All types of printed materials can be enlarged, such as magazines, textbooks, and photocopied handouts. Maggie Pro Portable Electronic Magnifiers are handheld and small enough for a student to keep in their desks or in their pockets.

Telecommunications and alerting devices are two types of assistive devices that use sight and touch. Captions are subtitles that appear at the bottom of a television screen that can be read. Open captions appear on the screen for all viewers to see (e.g., foreign films translations). Many televisions today come with the feature built in, and with the advent of DVD and Blue-Ray format for movies closed-captions can be easily selected for viewing.

Computers with word processing programs can produce large print displays that enable persons to adjust the size of the print with their visual capabilities. Not only can different size print be selected for individual students on the viewing monitor, but hard copy printouts can be printed in different sizes for individual uses. A student with visual or tactile-related disorders may require an enlarged keyboard (Bigkeys LX) or a keyboard with ABC-order keys rather than QWERTY.

Audio Aids

Talking books have been available through the Library of Congress since 1934, using specially designed record players and tape cassette machines developed by the American Printing House for the Blind. Regional resource and materials centers disseminate these records, tapes, and machines. Audiotape versions of many classic books and current best-sellers are available in most bookstores. Many audiobooks also are available for downloading as "apps" through iTunes on the iPad and related devices. Cross Forward Consulting offers many audiobook apps.

Newly devised systems that allow printed materials to be synthesized into speech are available. They can be purchased at a much lesser cost and with higher quality sound than older devices such as the Kurzwell Reader. One of these newer systems uses a small sensor attached to a computer. When the sensor is moved along a line of type, information is passed to the computer, which in turn translates the print to speech. The person listening can select how fast they want the speech to be delivered (rate), the pitch, and the gender of the voice/sound the computer generates. This enables students with auditory impairments to use the same books and materials as their regular classmates. They do not have to wait for orders to be prepared or mailed to them.

Hearing aids and other equipment that help people make better use of their residual hearing are referred to as assistive listening devices (ALDs). For those with hearing impairments, the hearing aid is the most commonly used electronic device. Other types of ALDs help individuals with hearing impairments use their residual hearing. Hearing aids differ in size, cost, and efficiency. Types range from wearable hearing aids to group auditory training units that can be used by several children at the same time. Wearable hearing aids can be inserted into the external auditory canal, built into glasses, and worn behind glasses, behind the ear, and on clothing.

FM (frequency-modulated) transmission devices (auditory trainers) are used in some classrooms by teachers and students. To use an auditory trainer, the teacher speaks into a microphone, and the sound is received directly by each student's receiver or hearing aid. This system reduces background noise, allows a teacher to move freely around the room, and help students benefit more from lectures.

The audio loop is an ALD that directs sound from its source directly to the listener's ear through a specially equipped hearing aid or earphone. Sound travels through a wire connection or by radio waves. Audio loops can be built into the walls of a classroom or some smaller area like a conference room. It is important for the teacher to remember that when wearing an FM microphone to be aware of where they are and what they are saying when using this device.

The TDD (Telecommunication Device for the Deaf) enables persons who have hearing impairments to make and receive telephone calls. A teletypewriter connected to the telephone prints out a voice message. The teletypewriter can also print out messages, but the receiver must have a teletypewriter as well in order to do this. A TDD can be used in a relay system, where the operator places the call on a voice line and reads the typed message to the non-TDD user. A full conversation can be made using a relay system (Smith & Luckasson, 1992).

Email and chat rooms, which were a mode of communication in the past for those with hearing impairments, are now a standard form of communication among everyone, with or without hearing impairments

Physical and Health Impairments

Technology has helped individuals with physical and health impairments to gain access to and control the environment around them, communicate with others, and take advantage of health care for decades. There are high-tech devices such as computers, but also low-tech devices like built-up spoons and crutches.

Mobility has been assisted by use of lightweight or electric specialized wheelchairs. These include motorized chairs, computerized chairs, chairs in which it is possible to rise, wilderness sports chairs, and racing chairs (Smith & Luckasson, 1992). Electronic switches allow persons with only partial movement (e.g., head, neck, fingers, toes) to be more mobile. Even driving a car is possible.

Mobility is also enhanced by use of artificial limbs, personalized equipped vans, and electrical walking machines. Myoelectric (or bionic) limbs contain a sensor that picks up electric signals transmitted from the person's brain through the limb. Robotic arms can manipulate objects by at least three directional movements: extension/retraction, swinging/rotating, and elevation/depression.

Speech/Communication

A communication board is a flat surface on which words, pictures, or both can be placed. The student is encouraged to point to the symbol of what is intended to be communicated. Simple boards can be made from magazine or newspaper pictures. Others can be written on to display messages. More sophisticated boards incorporate an attachment that synthesizes a "voice." Communication books function like a board and assist communication.

Skill 4.07   Knows how to make informed decisions about types and levels of assistive technologies, devices, and services for students with various needs, collect and analyze information about a student's environment and curriculum to identify and monitor assistive technology needs, and support the use of assistive technologies, devices, and services.

Please refer to Skill 4.06

Skill 4.08   **Applies procedures for participating in the selection and implementation of assistive technologies, devices, and services for students with various needs.**

Please refer to Skill 4.06

Skill 4.09   **Applies procedures for coordinating activities of related services personnel and directing the activities of paraprofessionals, aides, volunteers, and peer tutors.**

It is imperative to emphasize the need for a positive, working relationship teachers should have with those they work with in the classroom environment. There are six basic steps to having a rewarding collaborative relationship with those whom you share a working environment, whether they are para-professionals, aides, volunteers, or tutors.

While it is understood that there are many titles to those who may be assisting in a classroom, this section will summarize their titles as "Classroom Assistant."

Get to Know Each Other

The best way to start a relationship with anyone is to find time alone to get to know each other. Give your new classroom assistant the utmost respect and look at this as an opportunity to share your talents and learn those of your co-worker. Remember that this is your opportunity to find places you agree and disagree, which can help maintain and build your working relationship. Good working relationships require the knowledge of where each other's strengths and weaknesses are. Share what your strengths and weaknesses are, and listen to theirs. This knowledge may create one of one of the best working relationships you have ever had.

Remember Communication is a Two Way Street

As a professional educator, it is important to remember that you must actively communicate with others. Pay attention and make sure that your classroom assistant sees that you care what he or she thinks; express your appreciation for their camaraderie. When you ask for clarification of what a student said, you are also displaying interest and active listening. Remember that asking your classroom assistant for details and insights may help you further meet the needs of your students.

Remove and Prevent Communication Barriers

As professionals, teachers must avoid giving negative criticism or put downs. Do not "read" motivations into the actions of your classroom assistant. Learn about them through openly communicating. Negative attitudes and predetermined assumptions are unnecessary. Students can perceive teacher expectations and attitudes, so it is important to remain positive in front of and around the children. Any communication barriers should be remediated quickly. Do not hesitate to ask the principal, director of special education, or the school psychologist for assistance.

Establish Clear Roles and Responsibilities

The Access Center for Improving Outcomes of All Students K-8, has defined these roles in the following graph.

	Teacher Role	Classroom Assistant Role	Areas of Communication
Instruction	▪ Plan all instruction, including what your goals/objectives that you expect in your small groups. ▪ Provide instruction in whole-class settings.	▪ Work with small groups of students on specific tasks, including review or re-teaching of content ▪ Work with one student at a time to provide intensive instruction or remediation on a concept or skill	▪ Teachers provide specific content and guidance about curriculum, students, and instructional materials ▪ Classroom Assistants note student progress and give feedback to teachers
Curriculum & Lesson Plan Development	▪ Develop all lesson plans and instructional materials ▪ Ensure alignment with standards, student needs, and IEPs	▪ Provide assistance in development of classroom activities, retrieval of materials, and coordination of activities	▪ Mutual review of lesson plan components prior to class ▪ Teachers provide guidance about specific instructional methods
Classroom Management	▪ Develop and guide class-wide management plans for behavior and classroom structures ▪ Develop and monitor individual behavior management plans	▪ Assist with the implementation of class-wide and individual behavior management plans ▪ Monitor hallways, study hall, & other activities outside normal class	▪ Teachers provide guidance about specific behavior management strategies & student characteristics ▪ Classroom Assistants note student progress & activities and give feedback to teachers

("Working Together: Teacher-Paraeducator Collaboration" The Access Center for Improving Outcomes of All Students K-8, http://www.k8accesscenter.org/documents/RESOURCELIST3-1.doc)

It is often helpful to write out what roles and expectations you have for your classroom assistant together in a contract type fashion.

Plan Together

Planning together lets your classroom assistant know you consider him or her valuable and provides a timeline of expectations that will assist both of you in your classroom delivery to your students. This also gives the impression to your students that you are on the same page and that you both know what is going to happen next. This cooperative planning and organizing is beneficial for all parties involved, particularly the students. Cohesiveness enhances lessons and allows classroom activities to run smoothly.

Show a United Front

It is essential to let your students know that both adults in the room deserve the same amount of respect. Have a plan in place on how you should address negative behaviors both individually and together. Do not make a statement in front of your students that your classroom assistant is wrong. Take time to address issues you may have regarding class time privately, not in front of the class.

Reevaluate your Relationship

Feedback is wonderful! Stop every now and then to discuss how you are working as a team. Be willing to listen to suggestions and to take constructive criticism. Taking this time may be your opportunity to improve your working relationship, and even your own teaching habits.

Skill 4.10	Under the direction of related services personnel, applies knowledge of appropriate body mechanics to ensure student and teacher safety in transfer, lifting, positioning, and seating.

Rationale for Student Transfer

Students with physical disabilities range from mild impairments, such as having a minor wrist disfiguration, to more evident impairments, such as having to use an electronic wheelchair. There are times that the physical transfer of a student is necessary. Common reasons for student transfer:

- Movement to another chair, therapy table, or swing
- Assistance with toileting skills
- Transfer of student to bus seat
- Emergency evacuation of bus or school building

On rare occasions, students with visual impairments or other disabilities may need to be physically transported (e.g. emergency evacuations). Additionally, any student may need to be transported if injured temporarily.

Safety Considerations in Student Transfer

When transferring a student, safety must always be the primary consideration. Proper training by a nurse or physical therapist ensures that this is done correctly. On occasion, a specific building personnel may be 'in charge' of helping a student during a fire alarm, and 'assigned; a particular student.

Staff safety should also be a consideration. Again, proper training will address this issue. Staff may also be directed to wear a lifting and back belt. It is crucial that a special educator or other staff member does not attempt to lift someone who is heavier than they are. Staff should not use a Hoyer lift without training.

General Positioning for Student Transfer

In general, the lifter's knees should be bent in preparation to lift. The back should be straight, and the weight of the person to be carried should be close to the body. The lifting movement should be from the legs not the back. Occasionally, two people will be needed to transfer a student, such as one bound to a wheelchair.

Respect for Student Dignity

The personal dignity of the special needs student should be considered in all transfers and transports.

Common Methods of Student Transfer

- **Single person transport** is a means of lifting the student by one person.
- **Two person transfer** is generally a safe mode of transfer for those students who are too heavy to lift alone. Again, training in the proper technique is crucial.
- **The seat-carry method** can be used if two people are moving a student from one point to another point (not just transferring from a wheelchair to a toilet or another chair). In this method, each of the individuals places an arm behind the back and one under the thighs of the student being transported. With their hands clasping at the wrists, a type of seat is formed.
- **Transfer to another seat** can be accomplished by giving support under the arm pits with the adult's forearms while the student places his arms around the adult's neck.

COMPETENCY 005	THE SPECIAL EDUCATION TEACHER KNOWS HOW TO PROMOTE STUDENTS' EDUCATIONAL PERFORMANCE IN ALL CONTENT AREAS BY FACILITATING THEIR ACHIEVEMENT IN A VARIETY OF SETTINGS AND SITUATIONS.

Skill 5.01   Analyzes cultural factors and perspectives that affect relationships among students, parents/guardians, schools, and communities with regard to providing instruction for individuals with disabilities.

Please refer to Skill 1.06 for more information that pertains to this skill.

The mobile nature of society today provides a broader mixture of cultures around the country. Students moving from school to school may experience different curricula and different school cultural factors. As educators expect the students to adapt, they must also remember that the schools themselves must also consider the student's individual cultural influences. The class and school community is a microcosm of the broader community in the town/city.

Cultural relationships, moral principles, and values are not unique to students with disabilities. However, it is important to keep in mind that in certain cultures, individual differences may be thought of very differently than perhaps the current school views them. Many cultures now accept disabilities and realize the value and capability of students with special needs. However, there are still some families within cultures, as well as sects of cultures which unfortunately still harbor beliefs that shield and hide those who are different in any way. When discussing a child's disabilities with parents/guardians, it is important to keep in mind their views on disabilities.

Moreover, acculturation is not something that occurs overnight. It takes years for students to become acculturated, because acculturation is both a cultural and a psychological change. Students who move from a foreign country and do not speak English may require several years to become proficient in English. This notion may be similar for other aspects of culture. When considering the identification of students who are not succeeding in school, one must take into account these types of cultural factors. There are a number of acculturation surveys that can be used to help guide the teacher in examining the role of culture in the academic performance of the student.

Community agencies can often help schools bridge cultural gaps. Reaching out to families by including appropriate translators/translations, encouraging parents to share their heritage and traditions with the school, and respecting differences in what is considered acceptable exist, will help foster understanding. Beyond language, it is important to respect and provide accommodations for other cultural factors such as holidays or types of food.

The general issues that surround multiculturalism within schools are often exacerbated when dealing with disabilities. Identification of a disability naturally increases the stress level and can potentially damage or radically alter–relationships; therefore, it is more important to extend any possible method to secure positive interactions.

Skill 5.02   Knows how to serve as a resource person for families, general education teachers, administrators, and other personnel in recognizing the characteristics of and meeting the needs of individuals with learning differences in the general education classroom.

Current research and reauthorizations of the laws regarding special education are looking at different criteria for the identification of some disabilities. Some districts are adopting a Response to Intervention (RTI) model. In this model, the special educator becomes a critical component of the pre-referral process, instead of just providing service to children with already identified needs.

According to the National Center on Response to Intervention, RTI is essentially a combination of high quality, culturally and linguistically responsive instruction; assessment; and evidence-based intervention. Comprehensive RTI implementation contributes to the identification of learning and behavioral problems, improves instruction, provides all students with the best opportunities doe school success, and assists with the documentation of learning disabilities and other disabilities.

Here is a helpful diagram from their website to visually describe the overlapping of services which occur in the RTI model, from the center's articulate website, http://www.rti4success.org/whatisrti

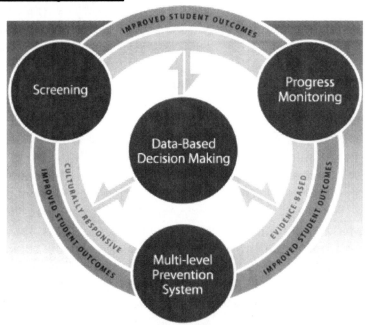

As always, it is important for the special educator to be open and available to other school personnel and families to help them work through the process of meeting individual needs. If a school adopts the RTI model, there will be numerous meetings on students and their individual data. The special educator should be very comfortable with looking at curriculum-based data and drawing out generalizations about student strengths and weaknesses.

Using these strengths and deficits, the special educator guides the general education teacher and/or parents through a myriad of strategies and suggestions that may help the student better reach the necessary curricular skills. Often times, the special educator is more familiar with data interpretation than is the regular educator. Sharing this knowledge allows both professionals to grow and more students' needs to be met.

Administrators can begin to rely on a team of intervention specialists who can meet regularly to address the needs of the students in the school setting. This team of specialists will usually include special educators, reading specialists, literacy coaches, math coaches, guidance counselors, etc.

Additionally, special educators often deal with agencies outside of the school setting, due to the needs of the students they serve. It is important to be familiar with counseling agencies, local pediatricians, local psychologists, social services, and mental health services available. This becomes a valuable resource for the special educator to access when asked by parents, regular education teachers, administrators, or others. Special educators should have names available for those that do not know where to begin to look for help. Special educators are points of resource in this manner.

Skill 5.03 **Knows how to use assessment results to design, monitor, and adapt and using effective, research-based instructional strategies, practices, and materials that are developmentally appropriate and age appropriate and that meet individual needs.**

Special educators need to be able to look at assessment results provided from regular classroom teachers, school psychologists, outside evaluators or other qualified personnel and plan appropriate instruction. Often times, this will be the first line of information received on a student. Many times, the special educator is given a set of assessment results and asked to write an Individualized Education Plan (IEP) from that information. Therefore, it is imperative that the assessment results are clearly interrupted.

The interpretation and understanding of psychological reports and various assessments is a critical point in instructional planning and IEP design. When possible, attend a lecture, class, or seek online support for proper interpretation of results. Educators will face WISC, Stanford-Binet, Bender-Gestault, Beery-VMI, and a multitude of other norm-referenced scores, in their careers. Do not hesitate to sit with your school psychologist, counselor, or even principal, when first tackling such reports. At the very least, refer to an online source, such as Dr. Joseph Gutting's helpful report interpretation hand-out (2002), easily accessed on: http://www.udel.edu/educ/gottfredson/451/Glutting-guide.htm

When first looking at assessment results, it is most beneficial to look at those skill areas that are at grade level. These scores represent skills that have adequate mastery for the age and grade level, and are not necessarily included in an IEP, but a good frames of references. The knowledge of student adequacies and strengths are pertinent information when conversing in IEP meetings, with parents, colleagues, and the students themselves. Of course, it is always critical to accentuate the positive and identify what the student can do in comparison to age and grade level peers. It is good to know these areas of student intellect, particularly when one wants to differentiate instruction in other areas. For example, if a student is reading at or above grade level in terms of comprehension, but has a pocket of phonological deficits, the special education teacher knows to choose high-interest texts when practicing phonics, to accentuate interest and complement the existent comprehension skill.

Then, scan the skills which were performed closest to grade level expectations. If the student is demonstrating skills which are very close to grade level, the special educator needs to think of what simple adaptations can be made to the regular curriculum to allow the student to achieve immediate, impactful success. There are numerous adaptations and modifications available that could be implemented easily to provide success, from providing an outline of the information to allowing extra time to complete written assignments. One may access the PsychCentral library collection online to see what types of accommodations and adaptations can be made in the classroom environment. For ADHD students, teachers can access the following website for tips: http://psychcentral.com/lib/classroom-adaptations-for-adhdstudents/0003545#.Ur ufJZAo5Ow

Once all of the possible adaptations have been made, then it is time to look deeper. Skills that are significantly below grade level require more than simple adaptations. The special educator needs to consider what strategy can be implemented that will help the student maximize learning time. It is not enough for the student to simply progress; the goal is to catch the student up to grade level in the shortest amount of time possible. There are very few exceptions, such as if the student's IQ is well below normal; it is then possible for the student to hit a 'ceiling' and not progress in a certain goal past a particular grade level point. It is imperative to look carefully at the assessment data and through the available research based materials/skills to determine what will help the student reach this goal of maximization. For some students, this may be achieved via curriculum program supplements or changes (i.e. a different reading program or methodology). For other students, it may be a time of relaxation before a test or perhaps stress-reduction strategies. Assessment results drive what instructional practices the special educator puts in place, to meet the individual needs of the students.

After the plan has been made, the special educator continually and systematically monitors the progress the student is making. Without this piece, the student could continue down a path far away from the goal of returning to grade level expectations. Using regular weekly or bi-weekly monitoring and assessments, the special educator can make appropriate adjustments to the student's individual plan with the end goal of helping the child reach grade level curriculum in the shortest, most effective time period possible.

Skill 5.04   **Knows instructional, compensatory, enrichment, and remedial methods, techniques, and curriculum materials, and applies strategies for modifying instruction based on the differing learning styles and needs of students.**

No two students are alike. Each student possesses a unique set of talents, likes, dislikes, strengths and deficits. Each student has an individual learning profile; some students prefer tactile learning modalities, some need low light to study, others need to raise their hands and verbalize, etc. To apply a one dimensional instructional approach and a strict tunnel vision perspective of testing and teaching is to impose learning limits on students. All students have the right to an education, but there cannot be a singular path to that education. A teacher must acknowledge the variety of learning styles and abilities among students within a class and the varieties from class to class and apply multiple instructional and assessment processes to ensure that every child has appropriate opportunities to master the subject matter, demonstrate such mastery, and improve and enhance learning skills with each lesson.

Multisensory teaching enhances student learning because it accesses multiple pathways to the brain. Students learn best in various ways, including visually, tactilily, kinesthetically, and auditorally, among many other modes. Access a Multisensory Teaching article, 5-11, written by Jeanette Moore in 2009, on the following website for helpful strategies, and for a general understanding of multi-sensory teaching: http://www.teachingideas.co.uk/more/management/contents.htm

It has been traditionally assumed that a teacher will use direct instruction in the classroom. The amount of time devoted to direct instruction will vary according to the age of the class as well as other factors. Lecturing can be very valuable because it is possibly the quickest way for a teacher to disseminate knowledge to students; note-taking and information-organizing skills be incorporated into this teaching strategy. There are many cautions to using an excessive amount of lecturing in a class of any age. Attention span, regardless of disability, even of senior high-school students, is noticeably shorter when students are using only one sense: the sense of hearing. Teachers should limit how much lecturing they do as compared to other methods and take note as to how long the lectures last.

Most teachers find students enjoy the learning process when lecturing is limited and the students themselves become active in and responsible for their own learning. Students' attitudes and perceptions about learning are the most powerful factors influencing academic focus and success. When instructional objectives center on students' interests and are relevant to their lives, effective learning occurs. Learners must believe that the tasks they are asked to perform have some value and that they have the ability and resources to perform them. If a student thinks a task is unimportant, he or she will not put forth much effort. If a student thinks that he or she lacks the ability or resources to successfully complete a task, even attempting the task becomes too great a risk. A teacher must understand the students' abilities and interests, and must also help students develop positive attitudes about tasks and learning.

Differentiated Instruction

The effective teacher will seek to connect all students to the subject matter through multiple techniques, with the goal that each student, through their own abilities, will relate to one or more techniques and excel in the learning process. Differentiated instruction encompasses several areas:

- **Content:** What is the teacher going to teach? Or, perhaps better put, what does the teacher want the students to learn? Differentiating content means that students will have access to content that piques their interests in a topic, with a complexity that provides an appropriate challenge to their intellectual development.

- **Process:** A classroom management technique where instructional organization and delivery is maximized for the diverse student group accentuates a strong processing of information. These techniques should include dynamic, flexible grouping activities, where instruction and learning occur both as whole-class, teacher-led activities, as well peer learning and teaching (while teacher observes and coaches) within small groups or pairs.

- **Product:** The expectations and requirements placed upon students to demonstrate their knowledge or understanding shape product. The type of product expected from each student should reflect each student's personal capabilities.

Alternative Assessments

Alternative assessment is an assessment where students create an answer or a response to a question or task, as opposed to traditional, inflexible assessments where students choose a prepared response from among a selection of responses, such as matching, multiple-choice or true/false types.

When implemented effectively, an alternative assessment approach will exhibit these characteristics, among others:

- Requires higher-order thinking and problem-solving.
- Provides opportunities for student self-reflection and self-assessment.
- Uses real world applications to connect students to the subject.
- Provides opportunities for students to learn and examine subjects on their own as well as to collaborate with their peers.
- Encourages students to continuing learning beyond the requirements of the assignment.
- Clearly defines objective and performance goals.

Teachers understand the value of giving assignments that meet the individual abilities and needs of students. After instruction, discussion, questioning, and practice have been provided, rather than assigning one task to all students, teachers are now asking students to generate tasks that will show their knowledge of the information presented. Students are given choices and thereby have the opportunity to demonstrate more effectively the skills, concepts, or topics that they as individuals have learned. It has been established that student choice increases student originality, intrinsic motivation, and higher mental processes.

Grouping Arrangements

A. Large Group with Teacher

Examples of appropriate activities include show and tell, discussions, watching plays or movies, brainstorming ideas, and playing games. The advantage of large-group instruction is that it is time-efficient and prepares students for higher levels of secondary and post-secondary education settings. However, with large groups, instruction cannot be as easily tailored to high or low levels of students, who may become bored or frustrated. Mercer and Mercer recommend guidelines for effective large-group instruction:

- Keep instruction short, ranging from five to fifteen minutes for first grade to seventh grade, five to forty minutes for grades eight through twelve.
- Use questions to involve all students, use lecture-pause routines, and encourage active participation among the lower-performing students.
- Incorporate visual aids to promote understanding, and maintain a lively pace
- Break up the presentation with different rates of speaking, giving students a "stretch" break", varying voice volume, etc.
- Establish rules of conduct for large groups and praise students who follow the rules.

B. Small Group Instruction

Small group instruction usually includes five to seven students and is recommended for teaching basic academic skills, such as math facts or reading. This model is especially effective for students with learning problems. Composition of the groups should be flexible to accommodate different rates of progress through instruction. The advantages of teaching in small groups is that the teacher is better able to provide feedback, monitor student progress, and give more instruction, praise, and feedback. With small groups, the teacher will need to make sure to provide a steady pace for the lesson, provide questions and activities that allow all to participate, and include lots of positive praise.

C. One Student with Teacher

One–to-one tutorial teaching can be used to provide extra assistance to individual students. Such tutoring may be scheduled at set times during the day or provided as the need arises. This type of teaching modality is difficult to accomplish on a daily, perhaps even weekly basis, but it is also a mode of instruction that may be provided also by the school tutors, paraprofessionals, teaching assistants, and resource personnel, as well as special educators. Students benefit greatly from one-to-one teaching, and should have the opportunity to experience it as often as possible.

D. Peer Tutoring

In an effective peer tutoring arrangement, the teacher trains the peer tutors and matches them with students who need extra practice and assistance. In addition to academic skills, the arrangement can help both students work on social skills such as cooperation and self-esteem. Both students may be working on the same material or the student being tutored may be working to strengthen areas of weakness. The teacher determines the target goals, selects the material, sets up the guidelines, trains the student tutors in the rules and methods of the sessions, and monitors and evaluates the sessions.

E. Cooperative Learning

Cooperative learning differs from peer tutoring in that students are grouped in teams or small groups and the methods are based on teamwork, individual accountability, and team reward. Individual students are responsible for their own learning and share of the work, as well as the group's success. As with peer tutoring, the goals, target skills, materials, and guidelines, are developed by the teacher. Teamwork skills may need to be taught, too. By focusing on team goals, all members of the team are encouraged to help each other as well as improve their individual performance.

Curriculum Design

Effective curriculum design assists the teacher from demonstration to independent practice. Components of curriculum design include:

- Quizzes or reviews of the previous lesson.
- Step-by-step presentations with multiple examples.
- Guided practice and feedback.
- Independent practice that requires the student to produce faster responses.

The chosen curriculum should introduce information in a cumulative sequence without introducing too much new information at a time, review difficult material, and provide practice to aid retention. New vocabulary and symbols should be introduced one at a time, and the relationships of components to the whole lesson/theme should be stressed. Students' background information should be recalled to connect new information to the old.

Course objectives may be obtained from the department head at the local school. The special education department chair or coordinator may have copies of objectives for functional courses or applied special education courses. District program specialists also have lists of objectives for each course provided in the local school system. Additionally, publishers of textbooks will have scope and sequence lists in the teacher's manual.

Addressing Students' Needs

There are a number of procedures teachers can use to address the varying needs of the students. Some of the more common procedures are:

1. Vary assignments
A variety of assignments on the same content allows students to match learning styles and preferences with the assignment. If all assignments are written types of assignments, for example, students who are hands-on or visual learners are at a potential disadvantage.

2. Structure the environment
Students benefit from a clear structure that defines the expectations and goals of the teacher. The students know what is expected and can work or plan accordingly. Posting lists for the sequence of steps to a problem is an example of structure in its simplest form. Structure helps students perform tasks sequentially, methodically, and with confidence.

3. Clearly stated assignments
Assignments should be clearly stated along with the expectation and criteria for completion. Clarified language and diction choice should be used properly according to grade level. Directions are concise and do not seem ambiguous or vague.

4. Independent practice
Independent practice involving application and repetition is necessary for thorough learning. Students become independent learners by practicing independent learning. These activities should always be within the students' abilities to perform successfully without or with minimal assistance.

5. Repetition
A student is not often successful with a single exposure to curriculum content. Learners generally require multiple exposures to the same information in order for learning, retention and recall to take place. However, this repetition does not have to be dull and monotonous. In conjunction with #1 above, varied multisensory assignments provide repetition of content without repetition of specific activities. This helps keep learning fresh and exciting for the student.

6. Overlearning
As a principle of effective learning, overlearning is when students continue to study and review after they have achieved initial mastery. The use of repetition in the context of varied assignments offers the means to help students pursue and achieve overlearning.

Skill 5.05   Applies knowledge of techniques for motivating students, including the effects of high teacher expectations on student motivation.

Motivation

Before the teacher begins instruction, he or she should choose activities that are at the appropriate level of student difficulty, are meaningful as well as relevant. In order for a teacher to motivate students, one must:

- Maintain expectations for success through teaching, goal setting, establishing connections between effort and outcome, and self-appraisal and reinforcement.
- Have a supply of extrinsic incentives such as rewards (for younger students or students who seek novelty) and appropriate competition, if any, between students.
- Focus on students' intrinsic motivation through adapting the tasks to students' interests, providing opportunities for active response, including a variety of tasks, providing rapid feedback, incorporating games into the lesson, allowing students the opportunity to make choices, create, and interact with peers.
- Stimulate students' learning by modeling positive expectations and attributions. Project enthusiasm and personalize abstract concepts. Students will be better motivated if they know what they will be learning about. The teacher should also model problem-solving and task-related thinking so students can see how the process is done.

Motivation may be achieved through extrinsic reinforcers or intrinsic reinforcers. This is accomplished by allowing the student a degree of choice in what is being taught or how it will be taught. The teacher will, if possible, obtain a commitment either through a verbal or written contract between the student and the teacher. Adolescents also respond to regular feedback, especially when that feedback shows that they are making progress.

Dr. Glasser originally coined the term "Choice Theory" in 1998. It is an effective theory to use when teaching students and wanting them to achieve intrinsic motivation when learning. This concept can be further researched on the following website: http://www.wglasser.com/

Rewards for adolescents often include free time for listening to music, recreation, or games. They may like extra time for a break or exemption from a homework assignment. They may receive rewards at home for satisfactory performance at school. Other rewards include self-charting progress, and tangible reinforcers. Motivational activities may be used for goal setting, self-recording of academic progress, self-evaluation, and self-reinforcement.

Skill 5.06 **Knows life-skills and self-help curricula and strategies for providing students with life-skills instruction relevant to independent or assisted living and employment.**

Adaptive life skills refer to the skills that people need to function independently at home, school, and in the community. Adaptive behavior skills include communication and social skills (intermingling and communicating with other people); independent living skills (shopping, budgeting, and cleaning); personal care skills (eating, dressing, and grooming); employment/work skills (following directions, completing assignments, and being punctual for work); and functional academics (reading, solving math problems, and telling time).

Teaching adaptive life/behavior skills is part of the special education program for students with disabilities. Parent input is a critical part of the assessment process since there are many daily living skills that are observed primarily at home and are not prevalent in the educational setting.

The measurement of adaptive behavior should consist of surveys of the child's behavior and skills in a diverse number of settings including his class, school, home, neighborhood or community. Since it is not possible for one person to observe a child in all of the primary environments, measurement of adaptive behavior depends on the feedback from a number of people. Because parents have many opportunities to observe their child in an assortment of settings, they are normally the best source of information about adaptive behavior. The most prevalent method for collecting information about a child's adaptive behavior skills in the home environment is to have an educational diagnostician, school psychologist, or counselor interview the parents using a formal adaptive behavior assessment rating scale. These individuals may interview the parents at home, or hold a meeting at the school to talk with the parent about their child's behavior. Adaptive behavior information is also procured from school personnel who work with the student, in order to understand how the child functions in the school environment.

There are a variety of strategies for teaching adaptive life skills including incorporating choice, which entails allowing students to select the assignment, and allowing students to select the order that they complete tasks. In addition, pre-teaching, or pre-practice "priming" is an effective classroom intervention for students with disabilities. Pre-teaching entails previewing information or activities that a student is likely to have problems with before they begin working on that activity.

Partial participation or multi-level instruction is another strategy that allows a student with a disability to take part in the same projects as the rest of their class, with specific adaptations to the activity so that it suits a student's specific abilities and requirements. Additional instructional practices include self-management, which requires teaching the student to function independently without relying on a teacher or a one-on-one aid. This strategy allows the student to become more involved in the intervention process and it improves autonomy.

Cooperative groups are an effective instructional technique for teaching social skills. Cooperative grouping has been known to result in increased frequency, duration, and quality of social interactions.

A functional curriculum approach focuses upon what students need to learn to prepare them for functioning in society as adults. With this approach, concepts and skills needed for personal-social, daily living, and occupational readiness are taught students. The specific curriculum contents needs to be identified in a student's individualized educational program (IEP), and be considered appropriate for his chronological age and current intellectual, academic, or behavioral performance levels (Clark, 1994).

The need for a functional curriculum has been heightened by the focus upon transition, or movement from one level to another (ACT, 2012), until the individual is prepared to live a life in a self-sufficient manner. The simplest form includes movement from school to the world of work. But like career education, life preparation includes not only occupational readiness, but also personal-social and daily living skills.

Halpern (1992) contends that special education curricula tend to focus too much on remedial academics and not enough on functional skills. A functional curriculum includes like skills and teaches them in the classroom and in the community. When using this approach, basic academic skills are reinforced in an applied manner. For instance, math skills may be taught in budgeting, balancing checkbooks, and/or computing interest payments for major purchases.

The Texas Adult Education standards are often noted and adapted for secondary level students in special education in a number of school districts in Texas. M. J. Ochoa wrote a comprehensive summary of Texas Adult Education standards, revised in 2009, available on: http://www-tcall.tamu.edu/taesp/westsum/index.html

Functional competence is conceptualized as two-dimensional. Major skill areas are integrated into general content/knowledge domains. The major skills that have been identified by this curriculum model as requisite for success are reading, writing, speaking, listening, problem solving, and computation.

Skill 5.07   Knows how to select and use appropriate technologies to accomplish instructional objectives, and applies skills for appropriately integrating technology into the instructional process.

Please refer to Skills 4.05 and Skill 4.06 regarding technology.

Once teachers have thus developed a clear picture of the goals and needs of their students with learning differences, they can seek resources for best practices, including school district-based support, the federal and state departments of education, teacher training programs, and educational literature, as well as professional development.

Ultimately, skilled teachers will layer creativity and keen observation with their professional skills to decide how best to individualize instruction and facilitate student achievement. Examples include:

- Varying learning modalities (visual, kinesthetic, tactile, aural).
- Integrating technology (calculators, computers, game consoles).
- Providing tools and manipulatives (Cuisinart rods, beans, protractors).
- Developing a range of engaging activities (games, music, storytelling).
- Using real world problem solving (fundraising, school-wide projects, shopping, cooking, budgeting).
- Adopting a cross-curricular approach (studying historical events strongly influenced by math, music theory).
- Developing basic skills (guided practice, pencil-and-paper computation, journaling and discussing problem solving strategies).
- Adaptations (extended wait time, recorded lessons, concept videos, ergonomic work areas, mixed-ability learning groups).

All modes listed can be enhanced with modern technology. For example, using computerized equipment, such as PowerPoint presentations and SmartBoards, can create a technological platform for teaching visually and aurally.

Skill 5.08   Applies strategies for integrating affective, social, and career/vocational skills with academic curricula, teaching students with disabilities to solve problems and use other cognitive strategies to meet their individual needs, and facilitating maintenance and generalization of skills across learning environments.

Strategies for Integrating Affective, Social, and Career/Vocational Skills with Academic Curricula

A major focus of special education is to prepare students to become working, independent members of society. IDEA 2004 (Individuals with Disabilities Education Act) also includes preparing students for *further education*. Certain skills beyond academics are needed to attain this level of functioning.

Affective and social skills transcend to all areas of life. When an individual is unable to acquire information on expectations and reactions of others or misinterprets those cues, that person is missing an important element needed for success as an adult in the workplace and community in general. Such pragmatic and expressive language skills are the underpinnings of communication, as well as articulation and even (gesticulation gesturing).

Special education should incorporate a level of instruction in the affective/social area as many students will not develop these skills without instruction, modeling, practice, and feedback.

Social skills taught throughout the school setting might include social greetings, eye contact with a speaker, interpretation of facial expression, body language, and personal space, ability to put feelings and questions into words, and ability to use words to acquire additional information as needed.

Career/vocational skills of responsibility for actions, a good work ethic, and independence should be incorporated into the academic setting. If students are able to regulate their overall work habits with school tasks, it is likely that the same skills will carry over into the work force. Accountability and reliability are high-quality characteristics in a student. The special education teacher may assess the student's level of career/vocational readiness by using the following list.

The student show signs of:

- Being prepared by showing responsibility for materials/school tools such as books, assignments, study packets, pencils, pens, assignment notebook.
- Knowing expectations by keeping an assignment notebook completed. Asking questions when unsure of the expectations.
- Using additional checklists as needed.
- Utilizing needed assistive devices.
- Completing assignments on time to the best of his/her ability.

An additional responsibility of the special educator when teaching career/ vocational skills is recognition that a variety of vocations and skills are present in the community. If academics are not an area in which students excel, other exploratory or training opportunities should be provided. Such opportunities might include art, music, culinary arts, childcare, technical, or building instruction. These skills can often be included (although not to the exclusion of additional programs) within the academic setting. For example, a student with strong vocation interest in art may be asked to create a poster to show learned information in a science or social studies unit. While addressing a career/ vocational interest and skill this way, the teacher would also be establishing a program of differentiated instruction.

Transfer of Learning

Transfer of learning occurs when experience with one task influences performance on another task. Positive transfer occurs when the required responses are about the same and the stimuli are similar, such as moving from baseball, handball, to racquetball, or field hockey to soccer. Negative transfer occurs when the stimuli remain similar, but the required responses change, such as shifting from soccer to football, tennis to racquetball, and boxing to sports karate. Instructional procedures should stress the similar features between the activities and the dimensions that are transferable. Specific information should emphasize when stimuli in the old and new situations are the same as or similar, and when responses used in the old situation apply to the new.

To facilitate learning, instructional objectives should be arranged in order according to their patterns of similarity. Objectives involving similar responses should be closely sequenced, thus, the possibility for positive transfer is stressed. Likewise, learning objectives that involve different responses should be programmed within instructional procedures in the most appropriate way possible. For example, students should have little difficulty transferring handwriting instruction to writing in other areas, however, there might be some negative transfer when moving from manuscript to cursive writing. By using transitional methods and focusing upon the similarities between manuscript and cursive writing, negative transfer can be reduced.

Generalization

Generalization is the occurrence of a learned behavior in the presence of a stimulus other than the one that produced the initial response (e.g. novel stimulus). It is the expansion of a student's performance beyond conditions initially anticipated. Students must be able to generalize what is learned to other settings (e.g. reading to math, word problems; resource room to regular classroom).

Generalization training is a procedure in which a behavior is reinforced in each of a series of situations until it generalizes to other members of the same stimulus class. Stimulus generalization occurs when responses, which have been reinforced in the presence of a specific stimulus, the discriminative stimulus (SD), occur in the presence of related stimuli (e.g. bathrooms labeled women, ladies, dames). In fact, the more similar the stimuli, the more likely it is that stimulus generalization will occur. This concept applies to identify task similarity, in that the more one task resembles another; the greater the probability the student will be able to master it. For example, if James has learned the initial consonant sounds of "b" and "d," and he has been taught to read the word "dad," it is likely that when he is shown the word "bad," he will be able to pronounce this formerly unknown word upon presentation.

Generalization may be enhanced by doing the following:

1. Use many examples in teaching to deepen application of learned skills.
2. Use consistency in initial teaching situations, and later introduce variety in format, procedure, and use of examples.
3. Have the same information presented by different teachers, in different settings, and under varying conditions.
4. Include a continuous reinforcement schedule at first, later changing to delayed, and intermittent schedules as instruction progresses.
5. Teach students to record instances of generalization and to reward themselves at that time.
6. Associate naturally occurring stimuli when possible.

Skill 5.09   Knows how to adapt lessons to maximize the physical abilities of individuals with specialized needs.

Just as no two snowflakes are the same, no two children demonstrate exactly the same skills. School systems need to consider the strengths of all students. Finding the strengths of students is something that all educators need to address.

When we look at the physical abilities of students with special needs, we must take into considerations ways to adapt the instruction and settings to maximize their ability to access the same information as other students who do not possess physical differences.

Keeping in mind there can be numerous physical conditions which could prevent a student from accessing the regular curriculum, it is important to be flexible in thinking and problem solving. Students may simply need items enlarged or put on tape if they have visual or auditory difficulties. In some cases, in room audio systems can be utilized to address auditory discrimination issues and also have a research base for helping students with Attention Deficit Disorder.

Other times, it may be necessary to rearrange the physical layout of the room to allow enough space for walkers or wheelchairs to be maneuvered. Some children may require special pencils, pencil grips or even regular access to an augmentative communication device to be able to participate. There are special chairs and additive seating devices that can be used to help position the students correctly.

Finding equipment is only half the battle. Sometimes discussions with the nondisabled peers are critical components overlooked by schools. Helping others to understand how to provide what is necessary without enabling is a daunting task, but one well worth undertaking. It is when everyone understands and has the opportunity to ask appropriate questions, that they can truly accept others into their world without unnecessary stigma.

The many adaptations are available from a variety of sources. Schools contract with or hire their own speech therapists, occupational therapists, physical therapists, hearing and vision specialists. Accessing the knowledge these professionals can provide can be the missing critical element to finding the appropriate needs for students to become integral members of the learning community.

Skill 5.10   Knows how to integrate related services into all types of educational settings.

Students with identified special education needs often times have additional services that are provided by someone other than a special educator. All services must be delivered as seamlessly as possible to provide the most effective education for the student.

Some services and therapies that might be involved with the students include: occupational therapy, physical therapy, speech therapy, vision, hearing, audiological, and counseling. While a specialist in the field will deliver these services, the areas addressed by these professionals are explained in the student's IEP and are part of the overall, comprehensive program.

The special educator must know how to tap into the knowledge of the professionals when available to help address issues that may be affecting the students at times the specialists are not available. Keeping a notebook or index card for each child with related services where the teacher can jot down issues and concerns as they arise is a strategy to help manage what questions to ask when the other service providers are available. This will help the teacher keep track and also maximize the time for the itinerant personnel.

Talking to other staff who are working with the student to get feedback into areas of strength and weakness are greatly appreciated by service providers. Since their time is usually very limited, it is unlikely they will have time to, for example, talk to the music teacher to see if the augmentative communication device has the appropriate choices to allow the student to respond. Or the physical therapist may not have time to keep track of the units in physical education to provide ideas for helping a student participate that may have physical limitations. It is part of the role of the special educator to facilitate and share this information across all instructional settings.

The issues being attended to by the related service provider are pervasive across all areas of the day; therefore, it is important to share the necessary information and tools with the other educators involved with the student. If there is adaptive equipment or materials, a plan should be worked out for how these items will transition from one setting to another.

It is equally important to remember to include the related service goals and objectives within the Individualized Education Plan (IEP). In writing academic goals and objectives, the impact of the related services interventions should be considered. Also, it is important to consider what adaptations and modifications might need to be in place for the student in order to ensure success. Service providers often write and suggest goals in their realm of therapy, and add them to sections of the IEP designated for their particular provided service.

Skill 5.11   Knows how to provide community-referenced and community- based instruction as appropriate.

Field Trips and Community Involvement

Students with special needs should be a part of a larger group, outside of the school setting. The school can facilitate or act as a liaison to other organizations, such as the YMCA or a local NAMI support group, to broaden a student's understanding of their impairment and to foster a friendly support system.

Community involvement for students, as well as teachers, can also include field trips and field work. Special education teachers and classroom teachers can plan field trips and outings to various points in the community, such as the communal garden, town court house, local museum, firehouse, police station, zoo, movie theater, famous historical point, or beach. Community reference points bring students together, and allow them to understand their place within the context of their hometown or city. Teachers can skew lessons and content material to meet the curriculum while visiting a particular site. Consider field trips to be living aspects of text books, as they are certainly multisensory modes of learning.

Volunteering and community service experiences are also inherent to community-based instruction. Children may learn important values, cooperative learning skills, and communication when working toward a common goal. Baking for fundraisers, donating goods and services, uniting to fundraise through a carwash, and other venues of communal bonding can bring children together, regardless of whether they have special needs or not.

Development of Employment Skills

Students should complete a career interest inventory while in high school, to assess their direction beyond the confines of the school building. They should have chances to investigate different careers. Many work skill activities can take place within the classroom, home, and community. Classroom activities may concentrate on employability skills, community skills, mobility, and vocational training. Home and neighborhood activities may concentrate on personal responsibility and daily chores. Community based activities may focus on part-time work after school and in the summer, cooperative education or work-study, individualized vocational training, and volunteer work.

Skill 5.12 **Knows how to design and implement instruction in independent living skills, vocational skills, and career education for students with physical and health disabilities and how to promote the use of medical self-management procedures for students with specialized health care needs.**

Developmental Issues to Consider when Designing Instruction

To effectively assess and plan for the developmental needs of individuals with disabilities, special education teachers should first be familiar with the development of the typically developing child. Developmental areas of speech and language, fine and gross motor skills, cognitive abilities, emotional development, and social skills should be considered.

To illustrate the consideration of child development, consider a second grade student who may have difficulty buttoning clothing. Because that is a skill that is typically mastered around age four, a developmental delay in fine motor skills may be present. It is appropriate for the special educator to request consultation and possibly formal evaluation of the child's needs.

In addition to being aware of the ages of typical developmental milestones, the special education teacher should consider the sequence in which the skills are acquired. While not all children go through every step of development, most follow the typical sequence. In an example of language development, children name objects with single words long before they form phrases or sentences. In other words, David cannot understand how to form the sentence *I see a cat on the fence* before he can accurately voice *cat* when he sees a cat or a picture of one.

Sometimes the disability itself will hinder or prevent a child from accomplishing a developmental task. A child with visual-spatial difficulty may not be able to see the components of a certain letter in print. Given a handwriting program that shows the parts of a letter made with wooden pieces may provide the link to the child mastering that letter formation.

Key to understanding the role of development and the needs of the special education student is being knowledgeable of typical development and seeing such skills in a number of typically developing students. This is another benefit of the inclusive classroom. Given a foundation of developmental understanding and knowledge of the specific child's disability [refer to Skill 1.01]; the special education teacher can better assess and implement an appropriate education program to meet the unique needs of the child.

Monitoring Medical Needs

With medical advances and educational legislation such as IDEA 2004, students with a variety of medical needs attend public school programs. Many of these students are eligible for special education services as *Other Health Impaired.* Some may not have a learning disability per se, rather, their medical condition requires attention during the school day so they are able to participate in classes.

Goals and objectives may include the student communicating changes in health to his teacher or the school nurse. Self-monitoring may also be followed by some type of medical procedure done by the student or a school staff member.

In some instances, students have individual care assistants who help with routine services such as tube feeding or care for urine bags. In other instances, the school health care provider is responsible for services. In still other cases, the student, with the supervision of an adult, can perform the needed medical task.

The *who* and *what* of medical treatment should be discussed by the ARD committee and written into the student's IEP. The following are considerations for review.

1. How will the student monitor his/her own progress?

Will the child use a checklist or possibly come into the school office or nurse's office at a designated time (before lunch, after recess, etc.) to use monitoring equipment?

2. Who will oversee the monitoring?

Depending on the situation, this may be done by a teacher or assistant in the classroom or by the school nurse.

3. What equipment/medication will be housed at school?

Some common types of equipment to keep at school would be:

- Auditory training equipment (including batteries and chargers)
- Feeding tubes
- Kits for testing diabetes and administering needed substances (insulin, etc.)
- Medication for ADHD, ADD, epilepsy, etc. if it will be taken at school
- Inhalers for asthma
- Catheters

4. Where will the equipment be kept?

Again, the equipment may be kept in the classroom, school office, or in nurse's office. Occasionally, a student may keep items in their lockers, backpacks, or even in their pockets, such as a rescue-type of asthma inhaler.

5. Can the student independently complete the needed task?

If the student will be completing the needed procedure (for example, a diabetic student giving an insulin shot or a student with spina bifida doing self-catheterization), parental permission should be acquired. In some instances depending on the condition and procedure, an additional form may be required.

6. What type of medical authorization should be obtained?

Many kinds of medical procedures will require a doctor's authorization. Some kinds (such as self-management of an FM auditory training devices) will not.

An example of a written medical care plan in which the student is largely responsible can be found at the American Diabetes Association website by accessing http://www.diabetes.org/living-with-diabetes/parents-andkids/diabetes-care-at-school/written-care-plans/

COMPETENCY 006   **THE SPECIAL EDUCATION TEACHER UNDERSTANDS AND APPLIES KNOWLEDGE OF ISSUES AND PROCEDURES FOR TEACHING APPROPRIATE STUDENT BEHAVIOR AND SOCIAL SKILLS**

Skill 6.01   **Applies knowledge of how culturally and/or linguistically diverse backgrounds of students impact behavior management and social skills instruction.**

According to the College Board, Latinos comprise a large sector of the United States; in fact, as of 2010, over 78% of the U.S. Hispanic population reside in ten states, and this includes the state of Texas. Other states include Arizona, California, Colorado, Florida, Georgia, Illinois, New Jersey, New Mexico, and New York. Many are at risk for having limited English language, and may be deemed as having Limited English Proficiency (LEP). This impacts instruction tremendously, from a linguistic standpoint, and an ESL teacher may be a part of their education team, alongside the special education teacher, if the student also has special needs.

Additionally, culturally diverse students may speak a dialect of a language such as Spanish, which has its own system of pronunciation and rules. It should be stressed that speaking a dialect does not in itself mean that the child has a language problem. Certain English sounds and grammar structures may not have equivalents in some languages, and failure to produce these elements may be a function of inexperience with English, rather than a language delay.

When minority or culturally diverse children are being screened for language problems, learning disabilities, or other exceptional student programs, the tests and assessment procedures must be non-discriminatory. Furthermore, testing should be done in the child's native language; however, if school instruction has not been in the native language, there may appear to be a problem because assessments typically measure school language. Even with native English-speaking children, there are differences between the language that is functional at home and community, and the language requirements of school.

Normality in child behavior is influenced by society's attitudes and cultural beliefs about what is normal for children (e.g., the motto for the Victorian era was "Children should be seen and not heard"). However, criteria for what is "normal" involves consideration of cultural and societal attitudes towards gender change over time. While attitudes towards younger boys playing with dolls or girls preferring sports to dolls have relaxed, children eventually are expected as adults to conform to the expected behaviors for males and females.

Skill 6.02   Recognizes ways in which teacher attitudes and behaviors and personal cultural biases influence the behavior of students.

Influence of Teacher Attitudes

The attitude of the teacher can have a positive or negative impact on student performance. A teacher's attitude can impact the expectations that the teacher may have toward the student's potential performance, as well as how the teacher behaves toward the student. This attitude, combined with expectations, can impact the students' self-image as well as their academic performance.

The phenomenon of a self-fulfilling prophecy is based on the attitude of the teacher. A self-fulfilling prophecy means that what one expects to happen is usually what ends up happening. In the context of education, this can mean that the predictions of a teacher about the ability of a student to achieve or not to achieve educational objectives are always proven to be correct. In subtle ways, teachers communicate their expectations of individual students and sub-consciously add or detract from a student's feeling of self-efficacy. In turn, the student may adjust their behavior to match the teacher's expectations. Based upon this, the teacher's expectations of what will happen comes true, which is a self-fulfilling prophecy.

Researchers in psychology and education have investigated this occurrence and discovered that many people are sensitive to verbal and nonverbal cues from others regarding how they expect to be treated. As a result, they may consciously and subconsciously change their behavior and attitudes to conform to another person's hopes. Depending on the expectation, this can be either advantageous or detrimental.

The teacher has a responsibility of not allowing personal negative attitudes toward the student to impact on interactions with the child. If the teacher is able to communicate to all of her students that they all have great potential and is optimistic regarding this, then the student should excel in some aspect of his educational endeavors, as long as the teacher is able to make the student believe in his/her potential.

The teacher's attitude toward a student can be shaped by a number of variables including race, ethnicity, disability, behavior, appearance, and social class. All of these variables can impact the teacher's attitude toward the student and how the student will achieve academically. Negative teacher attitudes toward students with disabilities are detrimental to the students with disabilities who are included in general education classrooms.

It can be hard for teacher's to maintain a positive attitude at all times with all students, but it is important to be encouraging to all students at all times as every student has the potential to be successful in school. Consistent encouragement can help turn a 'C' student into a 'B' or even 'A' student. Negative feedback can lead to failure and loss of self-esteem.

Teachers should utilize their verbal communication skills to ensure that the things they communicate to students are said in the most positive manner possible. For example, instead of saying, "You talk too much" it would be more positive to state, "You have strong verbal communication skills and are sociable."

Teachers have a major influence on what happens in the classrooms because they are the primary decision makers and they set the tone for how the information they distribute is absorbed. In order for teachers to rise above their prejudices and preset attitudes, it is important that teachers are given training and support services to enable them to deal with students who come from challenging backgrounds or present challenging behaviors.

Skill 6.03 **Applies knowledge of ethics, laws, rules, and procedural safeguards related to planning and implementing behavior management and discipline for individuals with and without disabilities.**

Free Appropriate Public Education (FAPE)

Special education and related services which are provided at public expense, meet the standards of the state educational agency, include preschool, elementary, and/or secondary education in the state involved, are provided in conformity with each student's individualized education program, constitute a Free Appropriate Public Education, or FAPE.

Notification and Procedural Safeguards for Parents.

Procedural safeguards for parent include:

- Right to examine records and obtain independent evaluations.
- Right to receive a clearly written notice that states the results of the school's evaluation of their child and whether the child meets eligibility requirements for placement or continuation of special services.
- Parents who disagree with the school's decision may request a due process hearing and a judicial hearing if they do not receive satisfaction through due process.

Identification and Services to All Children

States must conduct public outreach programs to seek out and identify children who may need services. Developmental, corrective, and other support services that make it possible for a student to benefit from special education services must be provided. These may include speech, recreation, or physical therapy, among others.

Planning and Implementing Behavior Management

Behavior Management Plans or Behavior Support Plans are plans used to promote positive behaviors for students to exhibit in a variety of social settings. School personnel involved in the creation include similar members of the IEP or ARD committee, and some schools call upon outside members, such as behavior interventionists, to contribute to the BMP or BSP.

A helpful Functional Behavior Management Plan protocol form (Word document) can be accessed on Positive Behavioral Interventions and Supports website (2013):
http://www.pbis.org/pbis_resource_detail_page.aspx?Type=4&PBIS_ResourceID=247

Management is a team effort. Members first identify the behavior that is to be changed, or the target behavior. For example, perhaps a student with Fragile X Syndrome (genetic disorder) attends school but has a difficult time getting off of the bus in the morning. This transition needs to be remediated. He may flail or barricade himself in the doorway of the bus. The behavior management team then identifies what behavior they need to have happen: they want the child to be cooperative and get off of the bus successfully, in order to transition into the school building in the morning safely, and happily. The team may then debate a plausible reason why this negative behavior is occurring and develop a plan for change. They can also interview the student and find out the underpinnings of the behavior, and discuss the changes in behavior that need to occur. Behavior management is very systematic, and should occur in regular intervals, with routine assessment provided.

Principles of Behavior Management

Contingency, or systematically planned, management incorporates the methodical use of reinforcement and punishment to develop, maintain, or change behavior. The following guidelines may be used in developing a contingency management plan. They are very similar and summative of the Horner and Crone (2005) document posted on the PBIS website noted above (2013).

1. *Decide what to measure.* A desired target behavior is specified and defined.
2. *Select a measurement strategy.* The behavior must be observable and measurable as in frequency, and duration.
3. *Establish a baseline.* The level of the behavior prior to implementing a treatment plan or an intervention must be established.
4. *Design a contingency plan.* Reinforcers or punishers are selected that correspond with behavioral consequences.
5. *Implement the contingency plan.* Collect data, provide reinforcement or punishment for the behavioral occurrences in accordance with the schedule selected for use and record behavioral measurements on a graph.
6. *Evaluate the program.* Modify the contingency management plan as needed. Modifications can be achieved by (1) a reversal to baseline to determine effect of

treatment on behavior, (2) changing the reinforcer or punisher if needed, or (3) implementing a new treatment.

A contingency management plan can be very useful in the classroom setting. In most classrooms, teachers specify what behaviors are expected and the contingencies for performing those behaviors. Contingencies are stated in the form of "If...then..." statements. Contingency management may take the form of various treatment techniques, such as token economies, contingency contracting, and precision teaching.

Students may be involved in the process of designing, implementing, and evaluating a contingency management plan. They can decide on behaviors that are in need of modification, select their reinforcers, assist in data collection, record the data on graphs, and evaluate the effectiveness of the contingency or treatment plan. The ultimate goal in allowing students to participate in contingency management is to encourage them to use the procedures that they have been taught to manage their own behavior. As with self-recording, the transition from teacher-managed to student-managed programs must be gradual, and students should be explicitly taught how to use self-reinforcement or self-punishment.

Skill 6.04 **Knows theories relating to student problem behavior (e.g., noncompliance, self-stimulation, self-injury, withdrawal, aggression, defiance) and the theoretical basis of behavior management techniques (e.g., positive behavioral support, reinforcement, proactive strategies, reductive strategies that decrease negative behaviors).**

Please refer to Skill 1.01 about causations of prevention of disabilities
Please refer to Skill 4.04 about classroom management
Please refer to Skill 6.03 for student behavior management plans

Backward Chaining

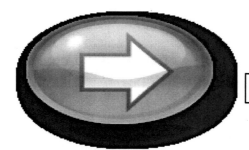

Last behavior or behavioral outcome is introduced first; break the task into steps, or view the entire process first.

First step is reviewed.

Behavioral chaining, or backward chaining is a procedure where individual responses are reinforced for occurring in sequence to form a complex behavior. Each link is subsequently paired with its preceding one, thus, each link serves as a conditioned reinforcer for the link immediately preceding it. Behavior chains can be acquired by having each step in the chain verbally prompted or demonstrated. The prompts can then be faded and the links combined with reinforcement occurring after the last link has been performed.

In backward chaining, the components of the chain are acquired by reversing the order of the steps like sub-skills necessary to complete successfully the target task. The task is modeled in the correct order by the teacher, and then each sub-skill is modeled in reverse order from beginning to end. The student practices the modeled sub-skill, and upon mastery of it, reverses back to the correct order until the task is completed. In this way, the final link or target behavior is consistently reinforced, and preceding links are built on, one at a time.

An example of backward chaining would be teaching a child to dress himself. The child is given the instruction, "Jimmy, take your jacket off," and his jacket is unzipped and lifted off the shoulders and down the arms until only the cuffs remain on Jimmy's wrists. If he does not pull the jacket the rest of the way off, he is physically guided to do so. He is given a reinforcer following removal of the garment. During the next session, the procedure is repeated, but the sleeve is left on his arms. In subsequent sessions, both arms are left in the sleeves, and then the jacket is left zipped. The instruction, "Jimmy, take your jacket off" is always presented, and a reinforcer is given only when the task is completed. The removal of each part of the garment is taught in this manner; and the component steps are combined until as instruction such as, "Jimmy, take your jacket off" has acquired stimulus.

Backward chaining may be used to teach other self-help skills such as toileting, grooming, and eating. Many academic and pre-academic readiness skills could be effectively taught using this procedure as well. Steps until the final one are provided, with prompting occurring on the last step, and reinforcements delivered following the behavior. Each step in the program is prompted until the student can perform the entire sequence independently. The backward chaining procedure may be of greatest assistance when a student exhibits limited receptive abilities or imitative behavior.

Bill Brandon (2013) wrote a descriptive article in the online Learning Solutions Magazine regarding on backward chaining, accessible on: http://www.learningsolutionsmag.com/articles/325/last-things-first-the-power-of-backward-chaining

Skill 6.05   Develops and/or selects social skills and behavioral curricula and strategies that promote socially appropriate behavior, and prepares individuals to live cooperatively and productively in society.

Developing Social Skills

Not all students with learning disabilities experience difficulties with social skills. Some kids are more likely to be accepted regardless of his or her learning issues because they are recognized for other skills, talents, or characteristics. Some children develop social awareness early in life and have strong interpersonal skills naturally, such as a sense of humor, an optimistic personality, and empathy toward others, which are qualities guaranteed to gain friends (Osman, 2008).

However, some children with learning disabilities and other issues, may lack the skills needed to be sociable. Computers and calculators can help children with writing and arithmetic, but there is no similar technology to help them handle a lonely recess at school, a family outing, or ordering at a restaurant. These require social competence, which encompasses the skills necessary for effective interpersonal functioning, including verbal and nonverbal behaviors likely to prompt a positive response from peers and adults (Osman, 2008).

It is essential to understand how a student's social shortcomings relate to his or her disabilities. Communication skills, both verbal and nonverbal, also have social implications. Children who don't "read" body language and facial expressions well are likely to miss important signals in life that are apparent to others (Osman, 2008).

To help children and adolescents develop social skills and promote social acceptance

- Teach how to initiate, maintain, and end a conversation
- Discuss how to give and receive compliments
- Practice how respond to teasing by peers
- Talk about how to accept constructive criticism

Not all students with learning disabilities struggle socially but those who do require special social skills training to help their current functioning, and allow them to become the fulfilled people they are capable of being. Students all want a feeling of acceptance and belonging.

Preparing Students to Live Cooperatively in a Diverse Society

Effective teaching and learning for students begins with teachers who can demonstrate sensitivity for diversity in teaching and relationships within school communities. Student portfolios include work that has a multicultural perspective and inclusion where students share cultural and ethnic life experiences in their learning. Teachers are responsive to including cultural and diverse resources in their curriculum and instructional practices. Exposing students to culturally sensitive room decorations and posters that show positive and inclusive messages is one way to demonstrate inclusion of multiple cultures. Teachers should also continuously make cultural connections that are relevant and empowering for all students and communicate academic and behavioral expectations. Cultural sensitivity is communicated beyond the classroom with parents and community members to establish and maintain relationships.

Diversity can be further defined as the following:

- Differences among learners, classroom settings and academic outcomes.
- Biological, sociological, ethnicity, and socioeconomic status.
- Psychological needs, learning modalities and styles among learners.
- Differences in classroom settings that promote learning opportunities such as collaborative, participatory, and individualized learning groupings.
- Expected learning outcomes that are theoretical, affective and cognitive for students.

Teachers establish a classroom climate that is culturally respectful and engaging for students. In a culturally sensitive classroom, teachers maintain equity and fairness in student interactions and curriculum implementation. Assessments include cultural responses and perspectives that become further learning opportunities for students. Other artifacts that could reflect teacher/student sensitivity to diversity might consist of the following:

- Student portfolios reflecting multicultural/multiethnic perspectives.
- Journals and reflections from field trips/ guest speakers from diverse cultural backgrounds.
- Printed materials and wall displays from multicultural perspectives.
- Parent/guardian letters in a variety of languages reflecting cultural diversity.
- Projects that include cultural history and diverse inclusions.
- Disaggregated student data reflecting cultural groups.
- Classroom climate of professionalism that fosters diversity and cultural inclusion.

The target of diversity allows teachers a variety of opportunities to expand their experiences with students, staff, community members and parents from culturally diverse backgrounds, so that their experiences can be proactively applied in promoting cultural diversity inclusion in the classroom. Teachers are able to engage and challenge students to develop and incorporate their own diversity skills in building character and relationships with cultures beyond their own. In changing the thinking patterns of students to become more culturally inclusive in the 21st century, teachers are addressing the globalization of our world.

Skill 6.06   Incorporates social skills instruction across settings and curricula and knows how to design, implement, and evaluate instructional programs that enhance an individual's social participation in family, school, and community activities.

Adaptive life skills refer to the skills that people need to function independently at home, school, and in the community. Adaptive behavior skills include communication and social skills (intermingling and communicating with other people), independent living skills (shopping, budgeting, and cleaning), personal care skills (eating, dressing, and grooming), employment/work skills (following directions, completing assignments, and being punctual for work), and functional academics (reading, solving math problems, and telling time).

Teaching adaptive behavior skills is part of the special education program for students with disabilities. The measurement of adaptive behavior should consist of surveys of the child's behavior and skills in a diverse number of settings including his class, school, home, neighborhood, or community. Since it is not possible for one person to observe a child in all of the primary environments, measurement of adaptive behavior depends on the feedback from a number of people. Because parents have many opportunities to observe their child in an assortment of settings, they are normally the best source of information about adaptive behavior. The most prevalent method for collecting information about a child's adaptive behavior skills in the home environment is to have school psychologist or LSSP, educational diagnostician, or guidance counselor interview the parents using a formal adaptive behavior assessment rating scale. Adaptive behavior information is also procured from school personnel who work with the student, in order to understand how the child functions in the school environment.

Cooperative groups are an effective instructional technique for teaching social skills. Cooperative grouping has been known to result in increased frequency, duration, and quality of social interactions. Students in need of improved social skills thrive best in small groups of peers, and are provided directly with age-appropriate verbal and nonverbal communication.

Social Skills Training

Social skills' training is an essential part of working with students who exhibit academic and social problems. Often these two problem areas, academic and social deficits, appear together. This issue presents a "chicken-and-egg" situation: Does the learning problem cause the behavior problem, or does the behavior problem cause the learning problem?

Typically, social skills are taught within the academic setting in special education. This is accomplished through classroom rules and contingency point systems that focus upon both areas at the same time. Rules, few in number, written in a positive direction, and designed jointly with students, help to set standards for acceptable behavior within the classroom. Contingency point systems are established to reinforce the occurrence of these behaviors, as well as other academic and social behaviors that are considered appropriate. Reinforcement contingencies are an important means of encouraging appropriate behaviors.

It is important to arrange the physical environment so that preventive discipline can occur. By this means, the teacher assumes responsibility for creating and maintaining an environment in which the needs of his/her charges are met. The teacher may modify the physical aspects of the room to create a warm, motivating atmosphere, adapt instructional materials to the respective functioning levels of the students, and deliver specialized services through the use of systematic, reinforcing methods and techniques. When instructional environments, materials, and techniques are implemented that respond to the academic needs of students, often the personal needs of the student are met as well, with a parallel effect of increased learning and appropriate social behaviors.

According to Henley, Ramsey, and Algozzine (1993, 1995), positive student behavior is facilitated by the teacher through techniques such as the following:

1. Provide students with cues about expected behavior. Both verbal and non-verbal signals may become a part of the general classroom routine. The teacher provides cues about acceptable and unacceptable behavior in a consistent manner.
2. Provide appropriate and necessary structure. Based upon individual differences and needs, structure should be built into the environment. Children with aggressive and anxious traits may need a high degree of structure, while others with less significant conditions will require lesser, but varied, amounts of structure. Structure is related to teacher direction, physical arrangement of environment, routine and scheduling, and classroom rules.
3. Involve each student in the learning process. Allow them to manipulate things, to explore surroundings, to experiment with alternative solutions, to compare findings with those of classmates, and to pose questions and seek answers. This approach helps to instill an internal focus of control while meaningfully involving the child in the learning process.
4. Enable the student to experience success. If the student is not provided tasks or activities in which success can be experienced, the teacher can expect misbehavior or withdrawal.
5. Having successful experiences are vital in developing feelings of self-worth and confidence in attempting new activities. (Jones & Jones, 1986).
6. Use interest boosting. If signs of disinterest or restlessness occur, the teacher quickly shows interest in the student. Conversing with the student may stimulate renewed interest or enthusiasm.
7. Diffuse tension through humor. A humorous comment may bring forth laughter that lessens the tension in a stressful situation.
8. Help the student hurdle lessons that produce difficulty. The teacher can get a student back on track by assisting in the answering of difficult problems. Thus, the hurdle is removed and the student is back on task.

9. Use signal interference. Cue the student with signals so that a potential problem can be extinguished. Individualized signals may be designed and directed toward specific students.

10. Incorporate antiseptic bouncing when it is obvious that a student needs to be temporarily removed from the classroom situation. This technique is useful in dispelling uncontrollable laughter or hiccups and in helping the student get over feelings of anger, or disappointment. This approach involves no punishment, and removal may be in the form of delivering a message, getting a drink of water, or other chores that appear routine.

11. Use teacher reinforcing. The teacher "catches the child engaged in appropriate behavior" and reinforces him at that time. For example, the teacher praises the student's task-oriented behavior in an effort to keep him from getting off task.

12. Employ planned ignoring. Unless the behavior is of a severe, harmful, or self-injurious nature, the teacher purposefully ignores the child. This strategy helps to extinguish inappropriate behavior by removing a viable reinforcer, that of teacher attention. The key is to deliver substantial reinforcement for appropriate behavior.

13. Use teacher commanding. The teacher uses direct verbal commands in an effort to stop the misbehavior. This technique should not be continued, however, if the student does not stop the inappropriate behavior upon the first instance his is told to do so. Inappropriate behavior will probably worsen upon repeated verbal commands.

14. Try teacher focusing. The teacher expresses empathy or understanding about the student's feelings, situation, or plight. The teacher uses inquiry to obtain information from the student, and then offers reasons or possible solutions to the problem.

Skill 6.07 **Identifies realistic expectations for personal and social behavior in various settings, and applies procedures for increasing an individual's self-awareness, self-control, self-management, self-reliance, and self-confidence.**

Self-Concept

Self-concept may be defined as the collective attitudes or feelings that one holds about oneself. Children with disabilities often perceive early in life that they are deficient in skills that seem easier for their peers without disabilities. They may also encounter expressions of surprise or even disgust from both adults and children in response to their differing appearances and actions, resulting in damage to the self-concept. The special education teacher will want to direct special and continuing effort to improve each child's own perception of himself.

1. The poor self-concept of a child with disabilities may cause that student at times to exhibit aggression or rage over inappropriate things. The teacher can ignore this behavior unless it is dangerous to others or too distracting to the total group, thereby reducing the amount of negative conditioning in the child's life. Further, the teacher can praise this child quickly and frequently for the correct responses that are given, remembering that these responses may require special effort on

the student's part to produce. Correction, when needed, can be done tactfully, and in private.

2. The child whose poor self-concept manifests itself in withdrawn behavior should be pulled gently into as many social situations as possible by the teacher, or even by sensitive, empathic peers. This child might be encouraged to share experiences with the class, to serve as teacher helper for projects, or to be part of small groups for tasks. Praise for performing these group and public acts is most effective if done immediately.

3. The teacher can plan, in advance, to structure the classroom experiences so that aversive situations will be avoided. Thus, settings that stimulate the aggressive child to act out can be redesigned and situations that stimulate group participation can be set up in advance for the child who acts in a withdrawn manner.

4. Frequent, positive, and immediate are the best terms to describe the teacher feedback required by children with disabilities. Praise for very small correct acts should be given immediately, and repeated when each correct act is repeated. Constructive criticism or correction should be done, whenever possible, in private. The teacher should review the total day's interactions with students to ensure that the number and qualitative content of verbal stimuli is heavily on the positive side. While this trait is desirable in all good teaching, it is fundamental and utterly necessary to build the fragile self-concept of youngsters with disabilities.

Skill 6.08   Knows strategies for modifying learning environments (e.g., schedule, physical and instructional arrangements) to promote appropriate behaviors.

Please refer to Skill 1.01 about environmental considerations
Please refer to Skill 4.04 for additional classroom management techniques.

Supporting the healthy learning environments to promote socially acceptable behavior is a priority of general education and special education teachers alike.. Positive learning environments may share these principles (Ottowa, 2000):

*   A positive learning environment is respectful and caring of all members.
*   An inclusive curriculum, recognizing diversity and promoting respect, is needed to help students resolve conflicts peacefully, learn about the law and acquire social and decision-making skills that contribute to the safety of their schools and communities.
*   Fair and consistently implemented class and school policies of behavior contribute to positive environments and reduce racism, bullying and other forms of harassment.
*   Decisions are guided by a problem solving, not punitive, approach as well as by supporting and enabling all members of the community to participate and contribute.

- Three levels of action are effective in maintaining positive learning environments. Prevention of all forms of violence should be universal, involving all members of the community. When intervention is requested, it should be progressive, constructive, supportive and transparent. Follow-up services should be utilized to ensure rehabilitation and to victims recover from critical incidents and crises.

Skill 6.09   Knows the impact of language on an individual's behavior and learning and knows how the communication skills of nonspeaking/nonverbal individuals affect their behavior.

Receptive – Input   Expressive - Output

Language development begins from the moment of birth, and some professional would argue, in the womb.   Children develop receptive language skills, the ability to understand language, first. When something interferes with that naturally developing skill, children often become frustrated because they misunderstand what someone is saying or they don't understand instructions. This type of misunderstanding often leads to a correction, with the child not understanding why he is being corrected, leading to further frustration for the child. Receptive language disorders present a significant communication barrier for students.   They simply cannot process what is being said to them.

Additionally, receptive language skills develop to include the ability to process and follow more than one direction at a time. Sometimes, students with receptive language deficits are unable to do this task. They need directions broken down into one step at a time in order to be successful. These misunderstandings lead to behavioral issues that can be usually be addressed through improving the receptive language skills of the child or by using different vocabulary or less oral language when communicating with the student.

After receptive language develops, expressive language (oral language) begins to advance. Difficulties here can be just as frustrating for the student. For these students, they are trying their best to communicate and get their point across, but no one seems able to understand what they are saying. Sometimes the misunderstanding is due to an articulation issue. Other times, it is due the child's inability to put feelings or thoughts into the appropriate words.

Everyone has occasionally been at the loss to recall a word. Phrases like "it's on the tip of my tongue" have become clichés because it is an occurrence that afflicts everyone on occasion.   For children with expressive language difficulties, the inability to recall a word happens much more frequently. The frustration at being unable to express one's self can lead to irritation and anger simply because no one understands what the child is trying to communicate.

Expressive language is important because it is how one expresses his or her wants and needs. This includes words and the grammar rules which govern how words are combined into phrases, sentences and paragraphs; expression also encompasses gestures and facial expressions. There is a subtle difference between expressive language and speech production. Speech production relates to the formulation of individual speech sounds using one's lips, teeth, and tongue. (Olson, 2012). This is different from one's ability to formulate thoughts, communicated by using a suitable combination of words.

Both expressive and receptive language are integral parts of the learning process. Numerous research studies have been completed indicating that lecture is still the most used method of delivering information in classrooms. If a child struggles with language, that method is not going to work well for them. Speech and language pathologists and professionals in the fields of strengthening receptive and expressive language are needed in the IEP development for the student.

Skill 6.10   Understands Functional Behavior Assessments (FBAs) and evaluations and their role in developing Behavior Intervention Plans (BIPs).

Please refer to Skill 2.09 for additional information on FBAs
Please refer to Skill 6.03 for detailed information on BIPs

Functional Behavior Assessment (FBA)

A Functional Behavior Assessment (FBA) is a method of gathering information. The information collected is utilized to assess why problem behaviors occur. The data also helps pinpoint strategies to employ to help alleviate the behaviors. The data from an FBA is used to create a positive behavioral intervention plan.

The Individuals with Disabilities Education Act (IDEA) specifically calls for a functional behavior assessment when a child with a disability has their present placement modified for disciplinary reasons. IDEA does not elaborate on how an FBA should be conducted as the procedures may vary dependent on the specific child.

Essential Elements of the Behavioral Intervention Plan (BIP)

A Behavior Intervention Plan (BIP) is utilized to reinforce or teach positive behavior skills. It is also known as a behavior support plan or a positive intervention plan. The child's team normally develops the BIP. The essential elements of a BIP are as follows:

- Skills training to increase the likelihood of appropriate behavior.

- Modifications that will be made in classrooms or other environments to decrease or remove problem behaviors.
- Strategies to take the place of problem behaviors and institute appropriate behaviors that serve the same function for the child support mechanisms for the child to utilize the most appropriate behaviors.

The ARD committee determines whether the school discipline procedures need to be modified for a child, or whether the penalties need to be different from those written into the school's code of conduct. This decision should be based on an assessment and a review of the records, including the discipline records or any manifestation determination review(s) (MDR) that have been concluded by the school.

Behavior Intervention Plans should concentrate on the student exhibiting acceptable behavior, changed behavior, which might mean teaching new skills. The end goal of the BIP is that the child will begin to display appropriate behavior.

It is difficult to defend punishment, by itself, as effective in changing problem behaviors. One of the most useful questions parents can ask when they have concerns about the discipline recommendations for their child, is "Where is the data that support the recommendations?" Special education decisions are based on data. If school staff wants to use a specific discipline procedure, they should check for data that support the use of the procedure.

Skill 6.11   Knows strategies for crisis prevention, intervention, and post-intervention; applies procedures for developing, implementing, and evaluating individual behavior crisis-management plans in educational settings; and implements the least intensive intervention consistent with individual needs.

Crisis Prevention

According to the Center for Effective Collaboration and Practice, most schools are safe, but the violence from the surrounding communities has begun to make their way into the schools. Fortunately, there are ways to intervene and prevent crisis in our schools.

Administrators, teachers, families, students, support staff, and community leaders must be trained and/or informed regarding early warning signs that indicate a student may be in crisis. It should also be emphasized not to use these warning signs to inappropriately label or stigmatize individual students.

Early Warning Signs

Early warning signs of a student in crisis include:

- Social withdrawal
- Excessive feelings of isolation and being alone

- Excessive feelings of rejection
- Being a victim of violence
- Feelings of being picked on and persecuted
- Low school interest and poor academic performance
- Expression of violence in writings and drawings
- Uncontrolled anger
- Patterns of impulsive and chronic hitting, intimidating, and bullying   behaviors
- History of discipline problems
- Past history of violent and aggressive behavior
- Intolerance for differences and prejudicial attitudes
- Drug use and alcohol use
- Affiliation with gangs

Imminent Warning Signs

Early warning signs and imminent warning signs differ because imminent warning signs require an immediate response. Imminent warning signs indicate that a student is very close to behaving in a way that is potentially dangerous to self and/or to others.

Imminent warning signs may include:

- Inappropriate access to, possession of, and use of firearms
- Serious threats of violence
- Serious physical fighting with peers or family members.
- Severe destruction of property.
- Severe rage for seemingly minor reasons.
- Detailed threats of lethal violence.
- Possession and/or use of firearms and other weapons.
- Other self-injurious behaviors or threats of suicide.

When imminent signs are seen school staff must follow the school board policies in place, which typically includes reporting it to a designated person or persons before handling anything on your own.

Intervention and Prevention Plan

Every school system's plans maybe different but the plan should be derived from some of the following suggestions:

- **Share responsibility by establishing a partnership with the child, school, home, and community.** Schools should coordinate with community agencies to coordinate the plan, in addition to rendering services to students who made need assistance. The community involvement should include child and family service agencies, law enforcement and juvenile justice systems, mental health agencies, businesses, faith and ethnic leaders, and other community agencies.

- **Inform parents and listen to them when early warning signs are observed.** Effective and safe schools make persistent efforts to involve parents by: informing them routinely about school discipline policies, procedures, and rules, and about their children's behavior (both good and bad); involving them in making decisions concerning school wide disciplinary policies and procedures; and encouraging them to participate in prevention

- **Maintain confidentiality and parents' rights to privacy.** Parental involvement and consent is required before personally identifiable information is shared with other agencies, except in the case of emergencies or suspicion of abuse.

- **Develop the capacity of staff, students, and families to intervene.** Schools should provide the entire school community including teachers, students, parents, and support staff with training and support in responding to imminent warning signs, preventing violence, and intervening safely and effectively. Interventions must be monitored by professionals who are competent in the approach.

- **Support students in being responsible for their actions.** Schools and members of the community should encourage students to see themselves as responsible for their actions and actively engage them in planning, implementing, and evaluating violence prevention initiatives.

- **Simplify staff requests for urgent assistance.** Many school systems and community agencies have complex legalistic referral systems with timelines and waiting lists. This should be a simple process that does not prevent someone from requesting assistance.

Drill and Practice

Most schools are required to have drills and provide practice to ensure that everyone is informed of proper procedure to follow if emergencies occur. In addition to violence caused by a student, the emergency can also be an intruder in the building, a bomb threat, a severe weather alert, or a fire.

COMPETENCY 007 **THE SPECIAL EDUCATION TEACHER UNDERSTANDS AND APPLIES KNOWLEDGE OF TRANSITION ISSUES AND PROCEDURES ACROSS THE LIFE SPAN**

Skill 7.01 **Knows how to plan, facilitate and implement transition activities as documented in Individualized Family Services Plans (IFSPs) and Individual Education Programs (IEPs).**

Refer to Skills 3.04 and 3.05 for more information on IEPs

Federal, State and local requirements for transition planning services are broken down into the Individualized Family Service Plan (IFSP) and Individualized Education Program (IEP). The IFSP, which provides early intervention services planning and documentation for an infant or toddler from birth to three years of age with a disability and her/his family, prepares for the IEP process, which provides special education services planning and documentation for school aged students with exceptionalities aged three to twenty-one years.

The purpose and function of the IFSP and IEP are considered similar in nature. Both plans provide communication between active participants, written resources, services management and progress monitors. The IFSP and IEP both require a written plan developed by a multidisciplinary team to include parents input and participation based on assessments of unique needs. All early intervention services address identified needs of an infant or toddler, including the involved family in the IFSP, just as all special education and related services must be reflected in an IEP. Communication and collaboration are frequently quoted as the most significant challenges from people involved in the transition process.

The participants in the transition process include children and their families, service coordinators, early intervention practitioners involved in a child's future/ pending/current IFSP program, IFSP teams and preschool teachers, early childhood special educators, related services practitioners, administrators and future/pending/current IEP teams. In order to facilitate transition success among these diverse groups of participants, skilled cross-agency communication with achievement based collaboration is required.

According to the National Early Childhood Transition Center (NECTC), individuals with disabilities experience the same difficulties with transitions as individuals who develop typically and often to an even higher degree. Clearly, transition involves more than a child moving from one program to another. Goals should be written that will support important aspects in proactive transitioning from one program of development to another for the individual and their families as suggested in the following quotes (Bredekamp & Copple, 1997; Hanson, 2005; Shotts et al, 1994; Rosenkoetter, 1995):

- Procedural supports should be developed to enhance successful transitions.
- Program decisions should meet individual needs.

- Services should be uninterrupted; appropriate services, equipment, and trained staff should be available in new settings
- Transition is actually a complex and gradual process rather than a specific event or product; this process begins long before the child moves to another setting or service program and it extends well after the child has engaged in the new services and activities
- Transition planning should prepare children, families and professionals.
- Transition practices should reduce stress for children, families and service providers.
- Transition should avoid any duplication in assessment and goal planning.
- Transition should be marked by ongoing communication and collaborative partnerships.
- Transition should be viewed as a process.
- Transition should meet legal requirements and make decisions in a timely manner.
- Transition should model non-confrontational and effective advocacy that families can emulate throughout their children's lives.
- Transition should orient the child to promote a joyful move to the new setting and encourage success .

The NECTC scrutinizes and authenticates strategies involved in both early and latent childhood transitioning. The organization supports positive school outcomes for individuals with disabilities. The NECTC has highlighted current and ongoing considerations listed here in bullets.

- A conceptual model for transition shared by all stakeholders should be enacted at the state level and if already enacted, it should be recognized and followed by participants in the transition process.
- A regular routine/schedule will help promote successful transitioning and will provide the individual with a sense of predictability and routine.
- Broad community support results in the highest quality services for ongoing education and transitioning of individuals.
- Contact with the individual's family and teacher before a transition is essential; meetings should involve time for listening to parents and should maintain a stress-free environment for all parties involved in the process.
- Family involvement in the child's program and education makes a difference, such as the family taking the individual to visit their new program.
- Following federal and state agency transition models and regulations provides a foundation with instruction for transitioning at the local level.
- Processes and procedures involved in transitioning must be collaborative between and among community agencies; to include who will be responsible for implementing procedures.
- Staff from sending and receiving programs must communicate with one another and the family regarding the individual's classroom experiences and their impending or ongoing needs.

- Staff from sending and receiving programs must visit each other's programs and settings to gain insight into the whole transition process.
- Transition strategies should be tailored to meet individual needs rather than implementing a cross-functional program as a simple remedy and these strategies should be offered to families with their reactions and suggestions denoted in follow-up planning.

The comprehensive Bruns and Fowler's (2001) review of conceptual and empirical transition policies, published as a technical report for The Early Childhood Research Institute on Culturally and Linguistically Appropriate Services (CLAS), offered five critical factors to meet transition needs of children with disabilities and their families from culturally and linguistically diverse groups, as follows:

- **Collaboration** - An understanding of cultural traditions concerning education and interaction with professionals will assist in formulating realistic options for collaboration in transition planning, implementation and evaluation.
- **Communication** - Communication with families is critical during times of transition; pre-service and in service training efforts must support the understanding of inter and intra-group differences in communication styles.
- **Community Context** - An awareness and understanding of the community context is needed for planning, implementing and evaluating transition.
- **Continuity** - Continuity between home and program must be incorporated throughout the transition process.
- **Family Concerns** - Service providers, administrators, and policymakers must be responsive to family concerns when planning, implementing, and evaluating transitions.

The renewed portion of IDEA for IFSP and IEP plans regarding transition presents quite a few updates to Federal policies, such as the following:

- Develop a plan to prepare for the transition from early intervention services to preschool special education or other services, when appropriate.
- Parents must give informed written consent before services may begin. If there is not agreement on all services, only agreed upon services will be provided.
- Services must be initiated "as soon as possible" after the IFSP meeting.
- The IFSP must be reviewed at least every six months and evaluated at least annually at an IFSP meeting. Additionally, the parents may request a review of the IFSP at any time.

Close communication and collaboration among all participants in the transition process reduces the risk of fragmentation, duplication or discontinuity of services as well as unmet family needs. Effective relationships are necessary in successful transitions and this includes intra-agency, inter-agency and family-professional relationships (Rosenkoetter et al, 1994). Even at the IDEA federal level, the acknowledgement of the need to recognize and support all of the relationships associated with transition is agreed upon in resounding affirmation. There is a cyclical bond between relationships and communication, where communication builds and strengthens strong, positive relationships in support of that effective communication. Even in the event of family goal and service provider conflicts, prevention can be achieved through the establishment of respectful working relationships that follow federal, state and local mandates.

Skill 7.02   Knows how to plan for and link students' current and previous developmental and learning experiences, including teaching strategies, with those of subsequent settings.

Transition planning is mandated in the Individuals with Disabilities Education Act (IDEA). The transition planning requirements ensure that planning is begun at age sixteen and continued through high school. Transition planning and services focus on a coordinated set of student-centered activities designed to facilitate the student's progression from school to post-school activities. Transition planning should be flexible and emphasize the developmental and educational requirements of the student at different grades and times.

Transition planning is a student-centered event that necessitates a collaborative endeavor. In reference to secondary students, the responsibilities are shared by the student, parents, secondary personnel, and postsecondary personnel, who are all members of the transition team.

According to the U.S. Department of Education, beginning when the child is age 14 (or younger, if appropriate), the IEP must address (within the applicable parts of the IEP) the courses he or she needs to take to reach his or her post-school goals. A statement of transition services needs must also be included in each of the child's subsequent IEPs.
In most cases when transition is mentioned, it is referring to a child fourteen or over, but in some cases children younger than fourteen may need transition planning and assistance. Depending on the child's disability and its severity, a child may need assistance with transitioning to school from home, or to school from a hospital or institution, or any other particular setting. In those cases, the members of the transition team may also include others such as doctors or nurses, social workers, speech therapists, and physical therapists.

It is important that the student play a key role in transition planning. This will entail asking the student to identify preferences and interests and to attend meetings on transition planning. The degree of success experienced by the student in postsecondary educational settings depends on the student's degree of motivation, independence, self-direction, self-advocacy, and academic abilities developed in high school.

In order to contribute to the transition planning process, the student should:

- Understand his/her disability and the impact it has on learning and work;
- Implement achievable goals;

- Present a positive self-image by emphasizing strengths, while understanding the impact of the disability;
- Know how and when to discuss and ask for needed accommodations;
- Be able to seek instructors and learning environments that are supportive; and
- Establish an ongoing personal file that consists of school and medical records, individualized education program (IEP), resume, and samples of academic work.

Transition planning involves input from four groups: the student, parents, secondary education professionals, and postsecondary education professionals. The primary function of parents during transition planning is to encourage and assist students in planning and achieving their educational goals. Parents also should encourage students to cultivate independent decision-making and self-advocacy skills.

The result of effective transition from a secondary to a postsecondary education program is a student with a disability who is confident, independent, self-motivated, and striving to achieve career goals. This effective transition can be achieved if the team consisting of the student, parents, and professional personnel work as a group to create and implement effective transition plans.

The transition team of a student entering the workforce may also include community members, organizations, company representatives, vocational education instructors, and job coaches.

Transition services will be different for each student. Transition services must take into account the student's interests and preferences. Evaluation of career interests, aptitudes, skills and training may be considered.

The transition activities that have to be addressed, unless the IEP team finds it uncalled for, are: (a) instruction (b) community experiences, (c) the development of objectives related to employment skill and other post-school areas, and (d) daily living skills.

a. Instruction – The instruction part of the transition plan deals with school instruction. The student should have a portfolio completed upon graduation. They should research and plan for further education and/or training after high school. Education can be in a college setting, technical school, or vocational center. Goals and objectives created for this transition domain depend upon the nature and severity of the student's disability, the students interests in further education, plans made for accommodations needed in future education and training, identification of post-secondary institutions that offer the requested training or education.

b. Community Experiences – this part of the transition plan investigates how the student utilizes community resources. Resources entail places for recreation, transportation services, agencies, and advocacy services. It is essential for students to deal with the following areas:

- Recreation and leisure - examples: movies, YMCA, religious activities.

- Personal and social skills - examples: calling friends, religious groups, going out to eat.
- Mobility and transportation - examples: passing a driver's license test or using public transportation.
- Agency access - examples: utilizing a phone book and making calls.
- System advocacy- example: have a list of advocacy groups to contact.
- Citizenship and legal issues - example: registering to vote.

c. Development of Employment - This segment of the transition investigates becoming employed. Students should complete a career interest inventory and have the opportunity to investigate different careers. Many work-skill activities can take place within the classroom, home, and community. Classroom activities may concentrate on employability skills, community skills, mobility, and vocational training. Home and neighbor-hood activities may concentrate on personal responsibility and daily chores. Community based activities may focus on part-time work after school and in the summer, cooperative education or work-study, individualized vocational training, and volunteer work.

d. Daily Living Skills – This segment of the transition plan is also important, although not essential to the IEP. Living away from home can be an enormous undertaking for people with disabilities. Numerous skills are needed to live and function as an adult. In order to live as independently as possible, a person should have an income, know how to cook, clean, shop, pay bills, get to a job, and have a social life. Some living situations may entail independent living, shared living with a roommate, supported living or group homes. Areas that may need to be looked into include: personal and social skills; living options; income and finances; medical needs; community resources and transportation.

Skill 7.03   Knows programs and services available at various levels and how to assist students and families in planning for transition.

Please refer to Skill 7.02

The Texas Education Agency (TEA) provides unique programs and services for students and families begin to plan for the transition process from school to work. TEA has a coordinated statewide High School Transition Network, which provide contacts across the Educational Service Center (ESC) Regions of the state. These transitions specialists can be contacted through email to provide additional support to schools in preparing for the transition process. A list of the email addresses for the entire state can be found at www.transitionintexas.org

This network of professionals is responsible for looking at state and federal initiatives and programs and helping school districts appropriately respond. The network is charged with the responsibility of ensuring that all students with disabilities have an appropriate plan for reaching the post school outcomes. They also provide professional development to educators to ensure they completely understand the transition process.

This planning process begins early in the child's education program, at the age of sixteen in Texas. The planning process includes both parental and student involvement and becomes an integral part of the IEP. The transition plan addresses postsecondary school options, vocational school options, as well as employment goals and objectives.

For students, TEA has provided a few detailed web sites explaining what the transition process involves. These sites use plain, young adult friendly language to help students better understands the transition process.

These sites include:
http://www.transitionintexas.org/Page/90

http://www2.ed.gov/about/offices/list/ocr/transition.html

http://fcsn.org/pti/topics/transition/

Additionally, TEA has launched a campaign to encourage students to strive for a post-secondary education through their *Education – Go Get It* program. This is an incentive program used to encourage students, parents, educators, communities, and colleges to embrace secondary learning as an option for students.

Finally, there are many career resources available to all interested parties. Career Development Resources, found at www.cdr.state.tx.us is a link to specific ways Texans can make career choices. It provides support for both employers and job seekers, using the latest Internet based software to encourage the improvement of the Texas workforce.

Skill 7.04   Knows how to teach students skills for coping with and managing transitions.

Any transition in life can be overwhelming and difficult, for both adults and children. For students with special needs, making transitions can be more than overwhelming. Specific tools and strategies need to be taught to students so they are better able to understand the issues facing them and then deal with those issues.

The coping skills for transitioning are similar in some respects to the same skills necessary to deal with life's stressors. One of the biggest factors that can help a student prepare to make the transition from school to work includes planning. Students that understand goal setting and the fundamentals of building a plan that can be used to reach these goals, have a leg up on students who are not taught to look into the future. Students as young as elementary aged can be taught goal setting. It may begin with setting a goal to complete a project. Taking the students through this process several times throughout their school careers will encourage them to better be able to make generalize the process at transition time.

Students need to understand how their own voices work in the process. Being a self-advocate is a critical factor in finding a successful path. Self-advocacy requires well developed communication skills. Students need to use both oral and written means to express their individual hopes and dreams. Once the school personnel understand clearly the hopes and ambitions of the student, they can build a framework to help the student reach his/her goals.

This framework may include helping to provide additional course work or specific skill knowledge or to provide opportunities for the students to participate in a work-study program where they can experience different work related experiences.

Outside agencies may also be a critical part of the transitioning process and should be included in all meetings and discussions. The schools do not have to be the only participants in helping students manage transitions. When all parties work together, they have a better opportunity to provide the smoothest school to work experience.

The impact of transition planning on a student with a disability is tremendous. The student should be an active member of the transition team, as well as the focus of all activities. Students often think that being passive and relying on others to take care of them is the way to get things done. Students should be encouraged to express their opinions throughout the transition process. They need to learn how to express themselves so that others listen and take them seriously. These skills should be practiced within a supportive and caring environment.

Managing Transitions in General: Children on the Autism Spectrum, and Students with Time Management Problems

Children with Autism, or related disorder, have difficulty managing their time efficiently. Routines and knowing what will come next in the schedule is soothing, and predictable, thus manages potential outbursts or changes in behavior. There are many tools are available to help students and young adults organize their time. Here are helpful skills from The Autism Transition Handbook, accessible on http://autismhandbook.org/index.php/Time_Management

1. Break each day up into chunks: Assign various tasks for each time period. For example, your child may be in school from 8 a.m.–3 p.m. From 3–4 p.m., he may work on homework; from 4–5 p.m., update his schedule for the next day; from 5–6 p.m., help with dinner, and so on. By chunking the tasks, it will help your child stay organized and not get overwhelmed.
2. Create an individualized activity schedule: You can help your child put together a "To Do" list of items, including homework, chores, and appointments or leisure/recreation activities. Over time, allow your young adult to do this on his own and check his progress (self-monitoring).
3. Use an organizer: – Simple paper organizer: These organizers can be divided by tabs and include sections for "To Do" lists, homework assignments, and a schedule of activities. Again, help your young adult establish a routine to check and update the organizer.

4. Electronic organizer (PDA): If your young adult likes technology, this could be a fun way to learn about organization. Most organizers have calendars and places to create "To Do" lists with pop-up reminders when a task should start. Help your child learn how to use these organizers. Create a routine to update the list and schedule every night.

Identify Ways of Developing Interpersonal Skills

Many youngsters with disabilities have difficulty in developing social behaviors that follow accepted norms. While non-disabled children learn most social behaviors from family and peers, children with disabilities are the product of a wide, complex range of different social experiences. When coupled with one or more disabilities, this experience adds up to a collective deficit in interpersonal relationships. In order to embrace a transition in the day, or furthermore, in life, a student must be equipped with interpersonal skills to cope with changes.

There is an irreducible philosophical issue underlying the realm of social behavior among children with disabilities. To some extent, the disability itself causes maladaptive behaviors to develop. Regardless of whether social skill deficits are seminal or secondary among youth with disabilities, it is the task of the special education professional to help each child develop as normally as possible in the social-interpersonal realm.

Children with disabilities can be taught social-interpersonal skills through developing sensitivity to other people, through making behavioral choices in social situations, and through developing social maturity.

Sensitivity to Others

Central to the human communication process is the nonverbal domain. Children with disabilities may perceive facial expressions and gestures differently than their nondisabled peers. There are several kinds of activities to use in developing a child's sensitivity to other people. Examples of these activities follow:

1. Offer a selection of pictures with many kinds of faces to the child. Ask the child to identify or classify the faces according to the emotion that appears in the picture. Allow the child to compare his reactions to those of the other students.
2. Compare common gestures through a mixture of acting and discussion. The teacher can demonstrate shaking her head in the negative, and then ask the students for the meaning of the gesture. Reactions can be compared, and then a game can be started in which each student performs a gesture while others tell what it means.
3. Videotapes, and movies are available in which famous people and cartoon characters utilize gestures. Children can be asked what a particular gesture means.

4. Digital recording devices with playback can be used to present social sounds. Again, a game is possible here, and the activity focuses the student's attention on one narrow issue - the sound and its precise social meaning.
5. Pairs of students can be formed for exercises in reading each other's gestures and nonverbal communications. Friendships of a lasting nature are encouraged by this activity.

Social Situations

Inherent differences in appearances and actions among children with disabilities cause some of them to develop behavior problems in social situations.

Here are some activities that strengthen a child's skills in social situations:

1. Anticipate the consequence of social actions. Have the students act out roles, tell stories, and discuss the consequences that flow from their actions.
2. Gain appropriate independence. Students can be given exercises in going places alone. For the very young and for those with developmental issues, this might consist of finding a location within the room. Go on a field trip into the city. Allow older students to make purchases on their own. Using play money in the classroom for younger children would be beneficial.
3. Make ethical and/or moral judgments. Utilize an unfinished story, requiring the pupil to finish it at the point where a judgment is required or make an independent critique of the choices made by the characters in a play.
4. Plan and execute. Children with disabilities can be allowed to plan an outing, a game, a party, or an exercise.

Having the teacher set an example is always a good way to teach social maturation. There are also various social skills books available for teachers to use with students, including:

Have You Filled Your Bucket Today? A Guide to Daily Happiness for Kids
Carole McCloud (2006)

The Social Skills Picture Book: For High School and Beyond
Jed Baker (2006)

Leonardo, The Terrible Monster
Mo Willems (2005)

Messages: The Communication Skills Book
Matthew McKay (1995)

Raise Your Child's Social IQ: Stepping Stones to People Skills for Kids
Cathi Cohen (2000)

The New Social Story Book: Over 150 Social Stories that Teach Everyday Social Skills to Children with Autism or Asperger's Syndrome and Their Peers
Carol Grey (1997)

Skill 7.05 **Knows sources of unique services, networks, and organizations for individuals with disabilities, including career, vocational, and transition support.**

As previously discussed, the Texas Education Agency (TEA) provides a statewide initiative and support network for helping students make the transition from school to work through their Statewide High School Transition Network. This network provides career, vocational and transitional support to all students with identified special needs across the state of Texas.

The Texas Health and Human Services System, in coordination with the Texas Department of Mental Health and Mental Retardation, have worked hard to provide a self-determination program, wherein, students with disabilities can better take an active role in deciding their own fates. This program ties community-based organizations and family service organizations with the school-based services.

There are many agencies available throughout Texas that provides support to students and families that may need additional assistance. Some include:

Advocacy, Inc – Provides legal support to persons with disabilities.

The Arc – Provide support groups, training, social, and leisure and respite services for individuals with intellectual and developmental disabilities.

ASK – Advocating Solutions for Kids – Provides help for students experiencing difficulty in school by connecting them with community organizations that can help provide solutions.

F.O.C.U.S. Initiative – Provides advocacy to ARD meetings, parental support, and offers classes in life skills for children with Autism Spectrum Disorders and other social cognitive disorders.

Imagine Enterprises – Provides transition, employment training, and helps to provide or find the support necessary to encourage and foster independence in Texas.

North Texas SNAP, Inc. – Coordinated system of supports to help cognitively impaired people live as independently as possible.

The above list is in no way complete, but provides some examples of services and networks available. There are numerous agencies that help provide the necessary supports and services for students to be successful.

Skill 7.06 **Applies knowledge of procedures and supports needed to facilitate transitions across programs and placements.**

In the state of Texas, transition planning begins when the child reaches the age of sixteen, or as early as fourteen, according to the U.S. Department of Education. From this point forward, the Admission, Review and Dismissal Committee (ARD) must consider what procedures and supports may be needed to allow for appropriate transition. These procedures must go across all programs and placements affecting the student.

The school is responsible for including the student, parents, and any involved community agencies in writing and developing the transition services. This plan then becomes a long-range goal to ensure the post-secondary outcomes the student hopes to achieve can be achieved. This may involve specific course selection, which would then need to be coordinated through the IEP. Finding the courses and enrolling the student becomes the school's responsibility, as is providing the necessary modifications and adaptations for the student to be successful.

External supports may be needed. Throughout the process, from age sixteen until graduation, or earlier, the level and frequency of these external supports may vary. It is also important that the services available at post-secondary institutions be explored completely. These services might include disability services, job placement services, written language support services, computer access services, or other such services.

When choosing a post-secondary institution, it is necessary to find a balance between curriculum and course offerings and the necessary services. Be sure to research if the university or college has a strong student support center, writing center, and learning specialists on hand, as well as tutors and peer tutors. Understand the degree offerings, or certification offerings, of each school, to deem what is appropriate for the student. Consider the class sizes, number of students on campus, and the living quarters.

Students need to have met the necessary requirements for graduation and any other prerequisites. Some post-secondary agencies have additional requirements, which must be completed for students with identified needs. It is the responsibility of the ARD committee to review and incorporate these into the transition plan.

In addition, functional vocational evaluations, employment goals and objectives, independent living goals and objectives, community experiences, acquisition of daily living skills, and governmental agency involvement should also be considered and discussed as appropriate.

Skill 7.07   Knows how to collaborate with the student, the family, and others to design and implement transition plans that meet identified student needs and ensure successful transitions.

Collaboration is vital for a transition plan to be successful. On the surface, it would seem that this undeniable fact would make collaboration an easily accomplished task; however, sometimes collaborating can be quite challenging.

There are numerous outside agencies and institutions that can be involved in the transition planning of students. Additionally, no one person can understand and be an expert at all of the available options for students with disabilities in the community. It is for this reason that collaboration is of the utmost importance.

One strategy for collaboration that works effectively is for each team member to complete a brief rough draft of the transition plan and ideas they may have for this student. Having a document like this from each person with vested interest in the process allows for better use of time when all parties are brought together. As case manager, the special educator can then compile the results of these documents. Then, bringing all players to the same table to hash out any further issues and discrepancies can be a much more efficient use of time and energy for all parties. It will also lesson the amount of time spent at the table.

Good collaborative strategies rely on a strong desire to keep the needs of the student at the center of the discussion, putting aside any individual agendas should they exist. Open communication and flexibility are also fundamental skills required for effective collaboration.

Skill 7.08   Applies skills for communicating with families about issues related to transition and strategies for helping their children make successful transitions.

In all of education, communication between school and home is paramount to providing the appropriate instruction. This is even truer when discussing students with special needs. There are often many home related factors involved with students with disabilities that it requires a coordinated effort to address the needs.

One crucial aspect of home to school communication is highlighted at times of transition. Whether the transition is from early childhood education experiences to school age or from secondary school to post-secondary educational options, it is imperative for the special educator to have the skills to assist the child and family in the transition process.

The most useful skill is to be a good listener. Often times, the issues and needs will be articulated through an open dialogue between the school and parents. It is important for the special educator to be able to pull out the key components from the information shared in order to develop an appropriate transition plan.

After listening, the special educator has the responsibility to look at what services or strategies may need to be incorporated to ensure a successful transition. Having a solid understanding of all facets of transitioning and the availability of services is important, but it is just as important to know where to go to obtain the accurate information. One person cannot be expected to know and understand every contingency available in a community, therefore, developing a resource folder on community resources is a useful tool.

Taking the time to sit and explain in common everyday language the steps the student and family members need to take as part of the transition process is key. Scheduling enough time to allow for questions and provide a relaxed atmosphere will be important for all parties. It is also at this juncture that any outside agencies which may need to be involved should be included to help clarify issues as they arise.

Including parents and the student, while required by law, also helps build the ownership of the plan. After all, it is the child's plan for their entire future. It is not the school's plan or the family's plan, but the student's plan for achieving life goals. The student has the most invested and his/her feelings and suggestions should be considered and not easily discounted. Open, caring communication is always the key to success.

DOMAIN III.   PROMOTING STUDENT ACHIEVEMENT IN ENGLISH LANGUAGE ARTS AND READING AND IN MATHEMATICS

COMPETENCY 008   THE SPECIAL EDUCATION TEACHER PROMOTES STUDENTS' PERFORMANCE IN ENGLISH LANGUAGE ARTS AND READING

Skill 8.01   Applies knowledge of developmental processes associated with communication systems (e.g., listening, speaking, writing), including emergent and preliteracy skills, and knows how to provide a variety of opportunities for students with disabilities to learn communication skills.

Please refer to Skill 1.07 for detailed information regarding speaking.

Language is the means whereby people communicate their thoughts, make requests and respond to others. Communication competence is an interaction of cognitive competence, social knowledge, and language competence. Communication problems may result from in any or all of these areas, which directly impact the student's ability to interact with others. Language consists of several components, each of which follows a sequence of development.

The following table describes the language, speech, and listening skills components of early childhood and childhood development. It is derived from the John Tracy Clinic (2012), located in Los Angeles, California. The full table can be accessed at: http://www.jtc.org/parents/ideas-advice-blog-comments/stages-of-listening-language-speech-development

From 3 to 4 years these skills may occur and be used in many situations		
Listening	**Language**	**Speech†**
• Initiates singing familiar songs • Participates in group story time • Includes actions in songs • Easily locates sound sources • Talks about sounds heard	**Receptive:** • Can follow three-step directions • Recognizes object functions • Understands 1000-2000 words **Expressive:** • Begins to use multi phrase sentences • Starts using numbers • Names letters of the alphabet • Uses words for feelings	• Tries different voices during play **May begin using:** • /j/ (from 3 – 7 years) • /v/ (from 3 – 8 years) • /th/ (from 3/5 – 7 years) **Continues to learn:** • /r/, /l/ (from 2 – 5 years) • /a/ (from 2 - 8 years)

	Includes prepositions (on, under) • Uses verbs is, are, am correctly • Takes turns in conversations • Uses 800-1500 words	• /sh/ and /ch/ (from 2.5 - 5.5 years) • /z/ (from 2.5 years - 8 years) • /t/, /ng/ (from 18 months to 5 years)

From 4 to 5 years these skills may occur and become more complex

Listening	Language	Speech†
• Concentrates in small school groups • Watches media and discusses it • Names environmental sounds • Knows he is expected to listen • Enjoys playing with words and word sounds	**Receptive:** • Understands same and different • Recognizes how objects are related • Comprehends most of what is said at home and in school **Expressive:** • Speaks in four to eight –word simple sentences • Includes verbs and adjectives • Sustains a topic in conversation • Applies possessives (mine, yours) • Uses pronouns correctly • Exchanges information	• Includes rhyming words • Speaks differently to adults than children • Speech is generally understandable **Continues to learn:** • /t/, /ng/ (from 18 months to 5 years) • /j/ (from 3 – 7 years) • /v/ (from 3 – 8 years) • /th/ (from 3.5 – 7 years) • /s/ (from 2 - 8 years) • /sh/ and /ch/ (from 2.5 - 5.5 years) • /z/ (from 2.5 years - 8 years) • /r/, /l/ (from 2 – 5 years)

From 5 to 6 years these skills may occur and be seen in school tasks

Listening	Language	Speech†
• Sounds out words in print • Attends to longer stories and activities	**Receptive:** • Follows multi-step directions • Understand some idioms • Recognizes synonyms and specialized vocabulary	• Uses different voice levels • Pronunciation is generally correct **Continues to learn:** • /j/ (from 3 – 7 years)

	Expressive:	• /v/ (from 3 – 8 years)
	• Initiates conversations and stays on topic	• /th/ (from 3.5 – 7 years)
	• Speaks in complex sentences	• /s/ (from 2 - 8 years)
	• Uses "if" statements	• /sh/ and /ch/ (from 2.5 - 5.5 years)
	• Applies past and future tenses	• /z/ (from 2.5 years - 8 years)
	• Accurately tells a story	

† The speech examples in this chart are based on American English. There are vowels and consonants listed here that do not occur in other languages. For example, Spanish does not have a short /a/, /i/, /u/ or a /j/, /v/, /z/. The production of some sounds may also vary in certain geographic areas and in different languages. Families can ask speech language therapists for lists of phonemes for their home language and ages they are typically acquired.

Skill 8.02   Knows how to use a variety of assessment practices and procedures to plan and implement instruction in English language arts and reading that is responsive to the strengths and needs of individuals with disabilities.

Most reading programs conceptually separate the reading process into three major categories: sight word vocabulary, word attack skills, and reading comprehension. These three areas constitute the basic questions that the teacher should ask when assessing a student's current level of functioning. From answers obtained, the pertinent questions are:

1. How large is the student's sight word vocabulary?
2. What kinds of word attack skills does the student employ?
3. How well developed are the student's reading comprehension skills?

Sight words are high-frequency words that are easily identified by the learner. The selection of words to be learned will rely to some extent on the age and abilities of the student. Primary age students will use word lists composed of high-frequency words such as the Dolch Sight Word List, which are available by grade level, starting with pre-primer or pre-kindergarten word lists.

Word attack skills are those techniques that enable a student to decode an unknown word so it is possible for the child to pronounce and understand a word in the right context. Word attack skills are included in the areas of phonics, structural analysis, contextual and configuration clues, and decoding.

Comprehension skills are categorized into levels of difficulty. The teacher should consider the following factors when analyzing a student's reading comprehension level (Schloss & Sedlak, 1986):

1. The past experience of the reader.
2. The content of the written passage.
3. The syntax of the written passage.
4. The vocabulary used in the written passage.
5. The oral language comprehension of the student.
6. The questions being asked to assess comprehension.

Comprehension involves understanding what is read regardless of purpose or thinking skills employed. Comprehension can be delineated into categories of differentiated skills. Thomas Barrett suggests that comprehension categories be classified as: literal meaning, reorganization, inference, evaluation, and appreciation. Strategies that might prove beneficial in strengthening a student's comprehension involve:

1. Asking questions of the student before he or she reads a passage. This type of directed reading activity assists the student in focusing attention on the information in the text that will help him or her to answer the questions.
2. Using teacher questions to assist the student in developing self-questioning skills covering all levels of comprehension.

Silent and Oral Reading Skills

Silent reading refers to the inaudible reading of words or passages. The accuracy of the silent reading process can only be inferred through questions or activities required of the student following reading. What may be observed is attention given to the printed material, the eye movements indicating a relative pace, and body language signifying frustration, or ease of reading. Strategies that might assist the child in reading silently are:

1. Preparing activities or questions pertaining to the printed passage. Vary the activities so that some are asking specific comprehension questions and others are geared toward creative expression like art and written composition.
2. Allowing time for pleasurable reading, such as through an activity such as sustained silent reading.

Skill 8.03   Knows the nature and stages of literacy development, and various contexts and methods for promoting students' literacy development.

Beginning Reading Approaches

Methods of teaching beginning reading skills may be divided into two major approaches: code emphasis and meaning emphasis. They may be referred to as the phonetic approach and the whole-word approach. Both approaches have supporters and critics. Advocates of code emphasis instruction point out that reading fluency depends on accurate and automatic decoding skills, while advocates of meaning emphasis favor this approach for reading comprehension. Teachers may decide to blend aspects of both approaches to meet the individual needs of their students. This integrative approach is the most widely used because it covers both phonics-based rules, and whole-word language functions. Readers who are intuitively identifying text with little phonics instruction may naturally thrive in whole-word approaches, though their spelling and word identification may benefit from the use of a phonetic approach as well, to delineate the spelling of the sounds of particular words. For example, the digraph /ph/ does not automatically look as if it would be pronounced /f/ and therefore, phonics instruction for reading is imperative.

Phonetic, or Code-Emphasis, Approach

1. Letter-sound regularity is stressed.
2. Reading instruction begins with words that consist of letter or letter combinations that have the same sound in different words. Component letter-sound relationships are taught and mastered before introducing new words.
3. Examples: phonics, linguistic, modified alphabet, and programmed reading series such as the Merrill Linguistic Reading Program, P.A.F. (Preventing Academic Failure), SPIRE, Orton-Gillingham, Wilson, and DISTAR Reading.

While Word, or Meaning Emphasis, Model

1. Reading for meaning is emphasized from the first stages of instruction.
2. Programs begin with words that appear frequently, which are assumed to be familiar and easy to learn. Words are identified by examining meaning and position in context and are decoded by techniques such as context, pictures, initial letters and word configurations.
3. Examples: whole language, language experience, and individualized reading programs, such as Dolch-based texts and the Edmark Reading Programs.

Other approaches that follow beginning reading instruction are available to help teachers design reading programs. Choice of approach will depend on the student's strengths and weaknesses. No matter what approach or combination of approaches is used, the teacher should encourage independent reading and build activities into the reading program that stimulate students to practice skills through independent reading.

Developmental Reading Approach

Developmental reading programs emphasize daily, sequential instruction. Instructional materials usually feature a series of books, often basal readers, as the core of the program.

Basal Reading

Basal reader series form the core of many widely used school-district and state-approved reading programs, from pre-primers to eighth grade readers. Depending on the series, basal readers may be meaning-emphasis or code-emphasis, or an integration of the two. Teacher manuals provide a highly structured and comprehensive scope and sequence, lesson plans, and objectives. Vocabulary is controlled from level to level and reading skills cover word recognition, word attack skills, fluency, prosody, and comprehension.

Stories in basal readers are chosen purposefully to develop specific reading skills, and are to be taught in a successive manner. Advantages of basal readers are the structured, sequential manner in which reading is taught. The teacher manuals have teaching strategies, controlled vocabulary, assessment materials and objectives readily available to use at very particular points in the series. Reading instruction is in a systematic, sequential, and comprehension-oriented manner.

Many notable companies offer basal series, such as Houghton Mifflin, Harcourt-Brace, and Scott Foresman (*Dick and Jane* series). Scholastic also offers such readers.

Many basal reading programs recommend the directed reading activity procedure for lesson presentation. Students proceed through the steps of motivation preparation for the new concepts and vocabulary, guided reading, and answering questions that give a purpose or goal for the reading. Strengths are developed through drills or workbook activities, followed by application of skills and evaluation.

A variation of the directed reading method is the direct reading-thinking activity (DRTA), where the student must generate the purposes for reading the selection, form questions, and read the selection. Students can make predictions about a story. After reading, the teacher asks questions designed to get the group to think of answers and justify their answers, and refute or prove their initial predications.

Disadvantages of basal readers are the emphasis on teaching to a group rather than the individual. Critics of basal readers claim that the structure may limit creativity and not provide enough instruction on organizational skills and reading for secondary content levels. Basal readers, however, offer the advantage of a prepared comprehensive program, and may be supplemented with other materials to meet individual needs.

Phonics Approach

Word recognition is taught through grapheme-phoneme associations, with the goal of teaching the student to independently apply these skills to new words. Phonics instruction may be synthetic or analytic. In the synthetic method, letter sounds are learned before the student goes on to blend the sounds to form words. The analytic method teaches letter sounds as integral parts of words. The sounds are usually taught in the sequence: vowels, consonants, consonant blends at the beginning of words (e.g. bl- and dr-), consonant blends at the end of words (e.g. -ld and -mp), consonant and vowel digraphs (e.g., /ph/ and /oa/), and diphthongs (e.g., /ow/ and /oy/).

Critics of the phonics approach point out that the emphasis on pronunciation may lead to the student focusing more on decoding than comprehension. Some students may have trouble blending sounds to form words, and others may become confused with words that do not conform to the phonetic "rules," such as the sight word 'was.' However, advocates of phonics say that the programs are useful with remedial reading and developmental reading. Examples of phonics series are *Science Research Associates, Merrill Phonics* and DML's *Cove School Reading Program.*

Linguistic Approach

In many programs, the whole-word approach is used. Words are taught in families as a whole (e.g., cat, hat, pat, and rat). The focus is on words instead of isolated sounds. Words are chosen on the basis of similar spelling patterns and irregular spelling words are taught as sight words. Examples of programs using this approach are *SRA Basic Reading Series* and *Miami Linguistic Readers* by D.C. Heath.

Some advantages of this approach are that the student learns that reading is talk written down, and develops a sense of sentence structure. The consistent visual patterns of the lessons guide students from familiar words to less familiar words to irregular words. Reading is taught by associating with the student's natural knowledge of his own language. Disadvantages are the extremely controlled vocabulary, in which word-by-word reading is encouraged. Others criticize the programs for the emphasis on auditory memory skills and the use of nonsense words in the practice exercises.

Whole Language Approach

In the whole language approach, reading is taught as a holistic, meaning-oriented activity and is not broken down into a collection of skills. This approach relies heavily on literature or printed matter selected for a particular purpose. Reading is taught as part of a total language arts program, and the curriculum seeks to develop instruction in real problems and ideas. Two examples of whole language programs are *Learning through Literature* (Dodds and Goodfellow) and *Victory!* (Brigance).

Students are assumed to develop their phonetic awareness through exposure to print. Writing is taught as a complement to reading. Writing centers are often part of this program as students learn to write their own stories and read them back, or follow along an audiotape of a book while reading along with it. Phonics is not taught in a structured, systematic way.

While the integration of reading with writing is an advantage of the whole language approach, the approach has been criticized for the lack of direct instruction in specific skill sets and strategies. When working with students with learning problems, instruction that is more direct may be needed to learn the word-recognition skills necessary for achieving comprehension of the text.

Language Experience Approach

The language experience approach is similar to the whole language, because literature is emphasized, and students are encouraged to write about their own life experiences. The major difference is that written language is considered a secondary system to oral language, while whole language treats the two as parts of the same structure. The language experience approach is used primarily with beginner readers, but can also be used with older elementary and with other older students for corrective, remediation-based instruction. Reading skills are developed along with listening, speaking and writing skills. The materials consist, for the most part, of the student's skills and writings. The philosophy of language experience was first developed in New Zealand among the Maori-speaking people in the 1960s, and includes:

1   What students think about, they can talk about.
2   What students say, they can write, or have someone write.
3   What students write or have someone write for them, they can read.

Students dictate a story to a teacher as a group activity. Ideas for stories can originate from student artwork, news items, personal experiences, or they may be creative. Topic lists, word cards, or idea lists can also be used to generate topics or ideas for a class story. The teacher writes down the story in a first draft and the students read them back. The language patterns come from the students and they read their own written thoughts. The teacher provides guidance on word choice, sentence structure and the sounds of the letters and words. The students edit and revise the story on an experience chart. Then, the teacher provides specific instruction in grammar, sentence structure, and spelling, if the need arises, rather than using a specified schedule. As the students progress, they create their individual storybooks, adding illustrations if they wish. The storybooks are placed in folders to share with others. Progress is evaluated in terms of the changes in the oral and written expression as well as in mechanics.

One disadvantage of the language experience approach is there is no set method of evaluating student progress. Materials are learner-generated, and thus, the learner him or herself provides the best assessment via reflection and perhaps personally-tailored checklists. However, the emphasis on student experience and creativity stimulates interest and motivates the students.

Individualized Reading Approach

Students select their own reading materials from a variety of sources, according to interest and ability, and they are able to progress at their own individual rates. Word recognition and comprehension are taught, as needed by the student. The teacher's role is to diagnose errors and prescribe materials, although the final choice is made by the students. Individual work may be supplemented by group activities with basal readers and workbooks for specific reading skills. The lack of systematic checking of a developmental skills and emphasis on self-learning may be a disadvantage for students with learning problems. Children may become frustrated or lose interest and motivation.

Skill 8.04   Applies knowledge of phonological and phonemic awareness and strategies for promoting the phonological and phonemic awareness of students with disabilities.

Please refer to skill 8.03

Identify Specific Spelling Instruction

Spelling instruction should include words misspelled in daily writing, generalizing spelling knowledge, and mastering objectives in progressive phases of development. A personal 'dictionary' or 'list' of misspelled words should be in each student's desk, and these specific groups of words can be regularly practiced for mastery. It can easily be added to when a new word error arises.   Students can copy words, use words in sentences, and identify spelling rules for words in order to understand and internalize the spelling.

Below is a full description of the stages of spelling development, which explains what children do and what they are thinking about (Dobler, Johnson & Wolsey, 2013):

1. Pre-Communicative, ages 3–5

- Use scribble writing in the early stage to mimic adults' writing.
- Write some letters, shapes, numbers, possibly mixed together and likely repeated. They understand marks on the page have meaning, but this meaning lies within the writer and marks do not follow left-to-right sequence.
- Do not understand letter/sound connection.
- Show preference to upper case letters, but may mix with lower case.
- Children are enthusiastic about learning the secret written language of adults. They are watching and mimicking whenever possible. Their joyous exuberance for writing is not dissuaded when an adult cannot read what is written.
- An understanding of alphabet letters and their fine motor skills are both developing.
- Young children are eager to put all the physical and mental pieces together, although they are not ready to do this yet.

2. Semi-phonetic, ages 4–6

- Begin to understand letters have sounds, but cannot make a total letter/sound match.
- Use letter names to stand for words (R for are).
- Grasp left to right letter arrangement.
- Know the alphabet letter names and formation.
- Are developing the ability to segment words into sounds (phonemic awareness).
- Can identify beginning sound, ending sound, and strong medial consonants

or surface sounds.

- Children at this stage are putting the pieces together when it comes to the alphabet. They are thinking about using letters to represent words even if their understanding still has some gaps.

3. Phonetic, ages 5–7

- Spell words as they sound by writing a letter for each sound.
- Develop consistent spellings for tricky vowel and consonant combinations
- Phonetic spellings make sense to the speller.
- Use of "child spelling" rather than "adult spelling" is a temporary stage.
- Students at the phonetic stage have grown by leaps and bounds in their thinking. Their use of temporary spelling demonstrates a deepening understanding of how letters and sounds match up to spell a word.
- Others can read their spelling fairly easily, which gives these spellers a boost of confidence to proceed on in their development.

4. Transitional, ages 6–8

- Utilize knowledge from seeing lots of print to include visual patterns in spelling.
- Use a vowel in every syllable.
- Include a vowel in an r-controlled vowel combination.
- Use silent e for many long vowel combinations.
- May use the correct letters to spell a word, but not in the correct order.
- Use paired vowels for long vowel sounds (ea, ee, ai, oo, ui, etc.).
- Include coupling letters (ll, rr, ss, mm).
- Students are thinking about letter combinations seen in print and how these can be used to spell words.
- Their spellings may seem creative but truly reflect sophisticated orthographic knowledge, which is not yet cemented into the speller's understanding.

5. Conventional, ages 9 and older

- Accurately use the English orthographic system for age-appropriate words.
- Show knowledge of word structure (prefixes, suffixes, root words, contraction, compounds, homonyms).
- Continue to develop accuracy with silent vowels and consonants.
- Can think of alternative ways to spell a word if it does not look right.
- Continue to learn tricky patterns (i.e., ie and ei).
- Students have amassed a phenomenal amount of orthographic knowledge compared to a few short years ago.
- They are applying this knowledge with more and more precision.
- Mentally, these spellers are able to put the pieces together, although they still encounter new and tricky words.

Phonemic Awareness

Here are some of the highlights from the evidence-based research on phonemic awareness instruction, according to LINCS (Literacy Information and Communication System) on http://lincs.ed.gov/childhood/phonemicIns.html:

Phonemic awareness can be taught and learned. Effective phonemic awareness instruction teaches children to notice, think about, and work with (manipulate) sounds in spoken language.

Phonemic awareness instruction helps children learn to read. It improves the ability to read words and comprehend what is read.

Phonemic awareness instruction helps children learn to spell. Direct instruction in phonemic awareness, especially in how to segment words into phonemes, helps children relate the sounds to letters as they spell words.

Phonemic awareness instruction is most effective when children are taught to manipulate phonemes by using the letters of the alphabet. Such instruction makes a stronger contribution to the improvement of reading and spelling when children are taught to use letters as they manipulate phonemes rather than when instruction is limited to phonemes alone.

Phonemic awareness instruction is most effective when it focuses on only one or two types of phoneme manipulation, rather than several types. A focus on teaching children to blend and segment phonemes in words, especially, is likely to produce greater benefits to reading ability than teaching several types of manipulation.

Phonemic awareness instruction can help all types of students learn to read, including preschoolers, kindergartners, first graders who are just starting to read, and older, less able readers.

Approximately 20 hours of class time over the school year should suffice for phonemic awareness instruction.

In general, small group instruction is more effective when helping students acquire phonemic awareness and learn to read, compared to individual or whole class instruction.

Instructional Strategies for Teaching Phonological and Phonemic Awareness

Early reading success is reliant upon achieving a certain level of phonological awareness during early developmental stages. Teaching phonological awareness is beneficial for children but the degree of instruction should vary according to each learner's acquired skill sets. There are several strategies one can use to teach phonological awareness. Conducting a brief assessment prior to teaching, such as the Comprehensive Test of Phonological Processing (CTOPP) or the Phonological Awareness Test 2 (PAT 2), will help determine a student's level of functioning so goals can be established.

To establish early developmental phonemic awareness, a teacher may encourage students to rhyme, count syllables, match sounds, and identify phonemes in a word (first or last). One a baseline level is recognized, students may add or subtract the initial, final, or medial/middle sounds in words. They can continue to count phonemes in a word but the words can be longer with more syllables. Students may eventually identify, understand, and manipulate prefixes and suffixes for multisyllabic words

Multisensory Considerations

Make sure the student is counting the sounds rather than the letters in a word. Visual or tactile learners may need to visually represent words, syllables, or phonemes with a manipulative (e.g., tokens, blocks, etc.). A kinesthetic learner may benefit from tapping, jumping, moving hands together (for blending) and moving them apart for (segmenting).

Start lessons with the level(s) a student has demonstrated mastery in. This allows for reteach or review, and builds student confidence. Then a new concept can be introduced. The student should move at their own pace and model teacher examples. The lesson may end with a new or novel phonological task such as a board or card game, experimentation with nonsense words, or a computer game. A few minutes with phonemic software, which may come with the district program, may serve as a closing activity or reward (or both). A student may also close the lesson with a separate computer game that is not connected to district-purchased software, such as *Reader Rabbit*, SIPPS, or a website game hub, such as *Starfall* or *ABCMouse*.

Skill 8.05   **Applies knowledge of the alphabetic principle and word analysis skills (e.g., decoding, structural analysis, sight word vocabulary), and knows how to provide students with disabilities with systematic instruction that promotes their ability to apply the alphabetic principle and word analysis and decoding skills.**

Please refer to skill 8.02

Alphabetic Principle

The alphabetic principle is made up of two parts, alphabetic understanding and phonological recoding. Alphabetic understanding refers to how words are made up of letters that represent sounds. Phonological recoding uses methodical relationships between letters and phonemes to obtain the pronunciation of an unfamiliar printed string or to spell words. Phonological recoding is made up of three elements: regular word reading, irregular word reading, and advanced word analysis. Detailed information regarding this skill can be accessed on the University of Oregon's Center on Teaching and Learning website: http://reading.uoregon.edu/big_ideas/au/au_what.php

Regular Word Reading

Beginning decoding is being able to read from left to right, read simple, unknown regular words, produce the sounds for all letters, and blend sounds into identifiable words.

Beginning spelling is being able to translate speech to print using phonemic awareness (knowledge of each phoneme) and familiarity of letter sounds.

Word reading is crucial because the English language is alphabetic and decoding is a primary way of identifying words. There are too many words in the English language to utilize memorizations as a key word identification technique. The following table is derived from the website referenced above, from the University of Oregon. It demonstrates the types of regular words students encounter, the reason for it ease or difficulty, and specific examples.

Word Type	Reason for Relative Ease/Difficulty	Examples
VC and CVC words that begin with continuous sounds	Words begin with a continuous sound	it, fan
VCC and CVCC words that begin with a continuous sound	Words are longer and end with a consonant blend	lamp, ask
CVC words that begin with a stop sound	Words begin with a stop sound	cup, tin
CVCC words that begin with a stop sound	Words begin with a stop sound and end with a consonant blend	dust, hand
CCVC	Words begin with a consonant blend	crib, blend, snap, flat
CCVCC, CCCVC, and CCCVCC	Words are longer	clamp, spent, scrap, scrimp

Irregular Word Reading

Decoding is an extremely reliable technique for the vast majority of words; however, some irregular words in the English language do not conform to word-analysis instruction (e.g., said, right, was). An irregular word is a word that cannot be decoded because the sounds of the letters do not follow standard rules of pronunciation.

To strengthen students' reliance on the decoding strategy and communicate the utility of this strategy, it is recommended that irregular words are not initially introduced until students can decode words at a rate of one letter-sound per second. Then, irregular words may be introduced.

The teacher must consider how many irregular words to introduce and then decide upon how many to review. Identifying these words as 'sight' words or 'irregular' words, or even 'red' words, is common practice among many reading programs.

Advanced Word Analysis

Advanced word analysis skills are a crucial component to student growth, in both their knowledge of the alphabetic writing system and their ability to read fluently. When advanced, the student has an understanding of letter combinations, consonant-vowel dynamics, Latin and Greek word parts (prefixes, suffixes, roots), and word derivatives.

When teaching the Alphabetic Principle, teachers should begin with letter-sound associations. This entails ensuring that students know the sound that each letter makes. The next step is sound blending, which involves blending the sound of the letters to create a word. The teacher should focus on segmenting and ensuring the student knows what sounds they hear in individual words. Then the student should learn how to manipulate letter-sound correspondences in words. An example of this would be to ask what word you would have if you changed the /r/ in 'ran' to /c/. Students should then be able to read pseudo or nonsense words, such as vas.

Alphabetic principle skills can be assessed using standardized methods. One method used to assess whether are not students understand the Alphabetic Principle is called Dynamic Indicators of Basic Early Literacy Skills (DIBELS). DIBELS is a system in which students are given nonsense words such as 'vij' or 'wex' and are asked to sound out or read each nonsense word to determine if the student knows letter sound correspondences.

Using nonsense words has been debated for years, but has proven to be effective time and time again. The National Right to Read Foundation released an article by Dr. Patrick Groff in 2003 entitled, "The Usefulness of Pseudowords." Dr. Groff describes the usefulness of using such nonsense words. It can be accessed on the NRRF website, on http://www.nrrf.org/essay_pseudowords.htm

Skill 8.06	Applies knowledge of reading fluency and the relationship between reading fluency and reading comprehension, and knows how to provide students with disabilities with systematic instruction that promotes their reading fluency.

During the preschool years, children acquire the cognitive skills in oral language that they apply later on to reading comprehension. Reading aloud to young children is one of the most important things that an adult can do because they are teaching children how to monitor, question, predict, and confirm what they hear in the stories. Reid (1988, p165) describes four metalinguistic abilities that which young children acquire through early involvement in reading activities:

Word Consciousness- Children who have access to books first can tell the story from the pictures. Gradually, they begin to realize the connection between the spoken words and the printed words. Letter and word discrimination begins in the early years.

Language and Conventions of Print- During this stage, children learn how to hold books, where to begin reading, the left to right motion, and how to continue from one line to another.

Functions of Print- Children discover that print can be used for a variety of purposes and functions, including entertainment and information.

Fluency- Through listening to adult models, children learn read in phrases and use intonation.

Mercer and Mercer (p412) divide the reading experience into two basic processes: word recognition and word and idea comprehension. Reading programs may differ in how and when these skills are presented.

WORD RECOGNITION	WORD AND IDEA COMPREHENSION
Configuration	Vocabulary Development
Content analysis	Literal Comprehension
Sight words	Inferential Comprehension
Phonics Analysis	Evaluation or Critical Reading
Syllabication	Appreciation
Structural Analysis	
Dictionary	

Characteristics of Good Readers

Research on reading development has yielded information on the behaviors and habits of good readers versus poor readers. Some of the characteristics of good readers are:

- Before reading, good readers establish a purpose for reading, select possible text structure, choose a reading strategy, and make predictions about what will be in the reading.
- They think about the information that they will read in the text, formulate questions that they predict will be answered in the text, and confirm those predictions the information in the text.
- As they read, good readers continually test and confirm their predictions, go back when something does not make sense, and make new predictions.
- When faced with unfamiliar words, they attempt to pronounce them using analogies to familiar words.

The Fluent and the Non-fluent Reader

Students with learning disabilities, particularly dyslexia, often lack text fluency because they do not automatically recognize words as they read them. The table below summarizes the characteristics of fluent versus non-fluent readers and provides recommendations for strategies to improve reading fluency. It has been shortened to fit page parameters, but can be accessed in its entirety in the book Dyslexia and Reading Difficulties: Research and Resource Guide for Working with All Struggling Readers, by C.A. Spafford and G.S. Grosser, 2005 edition, p. 208-209, or on the website: http://www.education.com/reference/article/fluent-versus-nonfluent-readers/

Fluent Readers	Why	Non-fluent Readers	What to Do
Decode effortlessly, with automaticity and with average reading rates or better for age and/or grade level.	Fluent readers read more, more extensively, and with a variety of printed materials.	Decode laboriously, without automaticity and with lower than expected reading rates for age/or grade level.	Provide many meaningful opportunities to read and reread (repeated readings method) a variety of leveled books and other materials chosen by the student. Provide intensive library support two- to three-hour literacy blocks.
Place a reading emphasis on comprehending words within the context of phrases, sentences, and paragraphs.	Fluent readers have acquired a variety of word recognition strategies that make word reading for the most part effortless.	Place a reading emphasis on identifying or decoding words in isolation before discerning meaning because of word recognition difficulties.	Provide intensive word study support within the context of meaningful text as part of a reading workshop or activity within an intensive literacy block.
Have extensive sight vocabularies.	Fluent readers have more exposure to print and reading practice.	Have limited sight vocabularies as compared to fluent readers of similar age or developmental level.	Practice learning frequently encountered reading words as sight words. Oral reading activities (choral reading, radio reading, paired reading, NIM or Neurological Impress Method, echo reading, readers' theatre, reading aloud).
Are able to effectively handle miscues or errors in word reading.	Fluent readers have acquired a variety of strategies for fixing miscues or errors in word reading.	Often rely on one or two "fix-it" strategies when problem-solving during word-recognition.	Model and explicitly teach a variety of word strategies to use when encountering unfamiliar or new words. Word strategy bookmarks cue the reader and should be consistently used until fluency is adequate or satisfactory.

Can effectively decode and comprehend text simultaneously.	Fluent readers effectively key in on main ideas and important information when reading; they can accurately summarize or paraphrase readings; they are able to self-monitor comprehension and organize information learned from reading as needed.	Experience a diminished ability to comprehend text because more cognitive energies are spent on decoding and identifying words.	Choose a segment of text to reread until it sounds like "people talking." Provide story grammar frameworks. Use marginal notes. Use graphic organizers before/after readings. Routinely request story or text retellings. Practice summarizing/paraphrasing sections of text.
Adjust reading rates according to reading demands.	With frequent and extensive reading practice and feedback, fluent readers become flexible readers, adjusting reading rates as needed.	Have difficulty adjusting reading rates according to reading purpose and text difficulty.	Model various ways to adjust reading rate and link to the reading purpose and text difficulty including scanning, skimming, text mastery, memorizing.

Skill 8.07 **Knows the importance of comprehension in reading, and knows how to provide students with disabilities with instruction in the use of skills and strategies (e.g., critical/creative thinking) to promote their reading comprehension.**

Constructing Meaning from Text

The purpose of reading is to convert visual images (letters and words) into a message. Pronouncing the words is not enough; the reader must be able to extract the meaning from the text. When people read, they utilize four sources of background information to comprehend the meaning behind the literal text (Reid, p 166-171).

Word Knowledge: Information about words and letters. One's knowledge of word meanings is *lexical knowledge*—a sort of dictionary. Knowledge about spelling patterns and pronunciations is *orthographic knowledge*. Poor readers do not develop the level of automaticity in using orthographic knowledge to identify words and decode unfamiliar words.

Syntax and Contextual Information: When children encounter unknown words in a sentence, they rely on their background knowledge to choose a word that makes sense. Errors of younger children therefore are often substitutions of words in the same syntactic class. Poor readers often fail to make use of context clues to help them identify words or activate the background knowledge that would help them with comprehension. Poor readers also process sentences word by word, instead of "chunking" phrases and clauses, resulting in a slow pace that focuses on the decoding rather than comprehension. They also have problems answering who, what, where, when, or why questions, because of their problems with syntax.

Semantic Knowledge: This includes the reader's background about a topic, which is combined with text information as the reader tries to comprehend the material. New information is compared to the background information and incorporated into the reader's schema. Poor readers have problems with using their background knowledge, especially with passages that require inference or cause and effect.

Text Organization: Good readers are able to differentiate types of text structure, e.g. story narrative, exposition, compare-contrast, or time sequence. They use knowledge of text to build expectations and construct a framework of ideas and details on which to build meaning. Poor readers may not be able to differentiate between types of text and often miss important ideas. They may also miss important ideas and details by concentrating on lesser or irrelevant details.

Skill 8.08 **Knows how to provide students with disabilities with systematic instruction to develop skills in writing conventions and competence in written communication.**

Development of Written Expression Skills

Composition should be taught as a process rather than a product. The first step in learning composition is having access to literature and writing materials. When adults read aloud to children, the children learn genres of literature and the function of print and pictures in a book. Having access to paper and writing materials give children opportunities to experiment with drawing and writing. When children enter school, they can learn to write notes, label pictures, and keep journals.

Most of the writing children do at school is transactional writing. Transactional writing includes expository (explaining subjects or procedures), descriptive (helps the reader visualize the topic), or persuasive (explaining a point of view). Students may also write expressively or in a narrative style. Poetic and creative writing is also explored, which requires knowledge of formal literary techniques such as metaphors, similes, personification, and so forth.

Initially, students may be resistant to writing, especially expressive writing, because they may be afraid to show their feelings or make mistakes. Journals are especially helpful to encourage students to practice expressive writing. Free writing will help reduce writing anxiety. Having children participate in journals and free writing will help build confidence. Writing should be integrated in all subject areas, and the atmosphere should be positive. Children's writing should be shared with others for feedback and enjoyment. Writing is truly a vehicle of expression, and can be quite freeing, imaginative, and even healing.

Each phase of the writing process has strategies that help the student develop metacognitive skills and proficiency. Instruction should not just focus on the mechanics (grammar, punctuation, spelling) of writing, but also on developing fluency and positive feelings about the process.

Prewriting: The planning phase. During prewriting, the student must decide on a purpose, find a topic, establish an audience, decide how the paper will be organized, and experiment with ideas. Strategies for generating ideas can be done individually or as a group activity and include:

- Listing
- Brainstorming—gathering ideas about the topic
- Interest inventories
- Free writing

Organizing Content: includes graphic approaches that represent the relationships of ideas visually

- Mapping
- Webbing
- Clustering

Drafting: In this phase, ideas are developed and the writer makes connections between the ideas. During this phase, mechanics should not be considered, and the student should not spend too much time in this phase. Learner activities include:

- Focus on the ideas, not the content.
- Consult the teacher or peer about the content.
- Read the piece or a portion to defocus and generate new ideas.

Revising: After the drafts have been written, the student may reorganize ideas, select ideas for further development, and edit the paper for mistakes in grammar and spelling. Sections of the paper may be removed or reorganized. Strategies include:

- Putting the paper aside for a day or two.
- Asking the teacher or a peer for feedback.
- Use scissors and tape to reorganize sections of the paper.
- Use the computer to aid in revision.

Final Draft: The writer gives the paper a final editing, reads the paper to see that everything makes sense, and makes last corrections before turning the paper in. Some of the things that a student can do to prepare the final draft are:

- Use a checklist to check the final copy for errors.
- Read the story into a tape-recorder and play it back with a written copy to listen. For grammatical errors and pauses where punctuation marks should be.

- Read the paper one sentence at a time to identify sentence fragments.

The Use of Graphic Organizers

Students with expressive or written language disorders, learning disabilities, or who are simply not comfortable writing, will benefit from the use of graphic organizers. Graphic organizers are essentially templates for writing. They can be as simple as a central circle (theme) drawn in the center of a page, with lines coming outward (details related to the theme) from the circle. Other graphic organizers can be more complex, such as a flow chart, with several arrows pointing to steps that need to be taken in a process.

Graphic organizers give students a chance to jot their thoughts on paper and think in terms of the written word. Graphic organizers are often pictorial, thus, they have a welcoming, novel appearance. They incorporate symbols, drawings, pictures, and shapes.

An excellent resource of tens of graphic organizers can be found on the following website by Holt: http://my.hrw.com/nsmedia/intgos/html/igo.htm

Skill 8.09   **Knows the relationship between learning and effective study, critical-thinking, and inquiry skills, and knows how to use various methods and strategies to teach students with disabilities to apply study, critical-thinking, and inquiry skills.**

Most educators recognize that comprehension covers a wide continuum of lower-to-higher level thinking skills. The following is one way of displaying the continuum, beginning on the low side of the spectrum:

1. **Literal** indicates an understanding of the primary, direct (literal) meaning of words, sentences, or passages.
2. **Inferential** involves an understanding of the deeper meanings that are not literally stated in a phrase, sentence, or passage.
3. **Evaluation** signifies a judgment made by comparing ideas or information presented in the written passage with other experiences, knowledge, or values.
4. **Appreciation** involves an emotional response to the written selection.

Using *Barrett's Taxonomy of Cognitive and Affective Dimensions of Reading Comprehension[1],* the teacher can determine the student's level of comprehension and stimulate thinking across a continuum of comprehension levels, by asking questions similar to these about the story of *The Three Bears.*

Literal Comprehension focuses on ideas and information that are explicitly stated in the selection.

Recognition requires the student to locate or identify ideas or information explicitly stated in the reading selection.

1. Recognition of details. Where did the three bears live?
2. Recognition of main ideas. Why did the three bears go out for a walk?
3. Recognition of sequence. Whose porridge was too hot? Whose porridge did Goldilocks taste first?
4. Recognition of comparisons. Whose porridge was too hot? Too cold? Just right?
5. Recognition of cause-and-effect relationships. Why didn't Papa Bear and Mama Bear's chair break into pieces like Baby Bear's chair?
6. Recognition of character traits. Which words can you find to describe Goldilocks?

In any of the above cases, the teacher may provide the answers or may state the answer without the question and have the child show in the pictures, or read in the text, the part of the story pertaining to the statement. The objective is to test the child's literal comprehension and not his or her memory.

Inferential comprehension is demonstrated by the student when he or she "uses the ideas and information explicitly stated in the selection, his/her intuition and personal experiences as a basis for conjectures and hypotheses," according to Barrett (cited in Ekwall & Shanker, 1983, p. 67).

1. Inferring supporting details. Why do you think Goldilocks found Baby Bear's things to be just right?
2. Inferring main ideas. What did the bear family learn about leaving their house unlocked?
3. Inferring sequence. At what point did the bears discover that someone was in their house?
4. Inferring comparisons. Compare the furniture mentioned in the story. Which was adult size and which was a child's size?
5. Inferring cause-and-effect relationships. What made the bears suspect that someone was in their house?
6. Inferring character traits. Which of the bears was the most irritated by Goldilocks' intrusion?
7. Predicting outcomes. Do you think Goldilocks ever went back to visit the bears' house again?
8. Interpreting figurative language. What did the author mean when he wrote, "The trees in the deep forest howled a sad song in the wind?"

Evaluation requires the student to make a judgment by comparing ideas presented in the selection with external criteria provided by the teacher, or by some other external source, or with internal criteria provided by the student himself/herself.

1. Judgment of reality or fantasy. Do you suppose that the story of *The Three Bears* really happened? Why or why not?
2. Judgment of fact or opinion. Judge whether Baby Bear's furniture really was just right for Goldilocks. Why or Why not?

3. Judgment of adequacy and validity. Give your opinion as to whether it was a good idea for the bears to take a walk while their porridge cooled.
4. Judgment of appropriateness. Do you think it was safe for Goldilocks to enter an empty house?
5. Judgment of worth, desirability, and acceptability. Was Goldilocks a guest or an intruder in the bears' home?

Appreciation deals with the psychological and aesthetic impact of the selection on the reader.

1. Emotional response to the content. How did you feel when the three bears found Goldilocks asleep in Baby Bear's bed?
2. Identification with characters or incidents. How do you suppose Goldilocks felt when she awakened and saw the three bears?
3. Reaction to the author's use of language. Why do you think the author called the bears Papa, Mama, and Baby instead of Mr. Bear, Mrs. Bear, and Jimmy Bear?

Skill 8.10   Knows skills for interpreting, analyzing, evaluating, and providing visual images and messages, and knows how to provide systematic instruction that helps students with disabilities learn to interpret, analyze, evaluate, and create visual images and messages in various media and technologies.

In order to facilitate instructions for students with disabilities via visual images and messages, teachers should ensure that learning is visible and explicit. Key information and learning objectives should be highlighted. Tasks and activities should be broken down into steps. Learning games can be used to provide practice of concepts. Numerous methods should be utilized for students to show what they have learned. Students can produce news releases, comic strips, collages, advertisement, websites, maps, dioramas, computer-generated montages and videos, or other visual tasks to demonstrate learning of instructional objectives.

Teachers should plan for modifications of the lessons to appeal to the visual learner. They should access a variety of resources and collaborate with other teachers and professionals. Teachers should make sure they know their students so they can adapt the lesson to target various students' learning styles. The integration of technology, such as computers, Internet, multimedia displays, audio video equipment, art and visual equipment, computer assisted instruction is important when creating visual images.

When modifying the curriculum, teachers should take into account the students' literacy levels and needs. Teachers should use clear, easy instructions and provide students with numerous opportunities to respond and participate in the lesson.

The pacing of the lesson should be adjusted based on the feedback received from the students.

One method of making learning visual to the student is to provide a written list of steps and ensure that students monitor their own work as they finish each step. This list can easily serve as a checklist for students to use to navigate given steps of a task. Auditory instructions should be supported with visual and tactile cues. Teachers should visually model how to complete tasks.

Students should be given ample opportunity to use and incorporate visual technologies into assignments and activities. The use of multi-media technology, graphics, video, sound, computer technology, Internet, CD-Rom, and computer software should be reflected in classroom lessons.

COMPETENCY 009   **THE SPECIAL EDUCATION TEACHER PROMOTES STUDENTS' PERFORMANCE IN MATHEMATICS**

Skill 9.01   **Knows how to provide mathematics instruction that is based on principles of children's learning and development and that reflects recognition of common misconceptions and sources of error in mathematics.**

The Sequential Development of Mathematics Skills and Concepts

According to an article written for Inside Higher Ed by Mitch Smith in 2012, "Officials from all 50 Texas community colleges have endorsed a multiyear project designed to fundamentally change remedial math. In Texas, students referred to developmental classes are 50 percent less likely than their peers to earn a credential or transfer to a four-year college. Math is often their biggest hurdle, and students are steered into algebra-based remediation regardless of their majors." It is imperative that special education teachers and general education teachers alike, tackle the sequential development of mathematics skills head on. Laying the foundations of math principles and numeracy as early as possible can significantly alter the current state of math competency in Texas. Please access the article at:
http://www.insidehighered.com/news/2012/05/09/texas-community-colleges-reinvent-developmental-math

Mathematics instruction proceeds through a sequential development of skills and concepts. For each concept, instruction should proceed from concrete to semi-concrete before moving on to the abstract level of understanding. This section discusses the skills development of mathematics instruction.

Counting and 1:1 Correspondence

From as early as age two, children are expected to be able to count. Counting is a progression of numbers, and can be expressed concretely by using 1:1 correspondence. This entails holding an object, such as a block, and calling it 'one' as it is placed on the table. The following object picked up is therefore 'two,' then the next is 'three' and so forth. Understanding a number represents a quantifiable amount of objects is truly the underpinning of our number system. The concept of zero, or nothing, should also be expressed as well.

Place Value

Students need to know that the position of a given number, or its place value, determines its value in our number system. Students need to know the grouping process, the relationship between place and value of a number that each number to the left is a multiple of 10, and that there is only one digit per position in our number system.

Place Value Chart

Hundred Billions	Ten Billions	Billions	Hundred Millions	Ten Millions	Millions	Hundred Thousands	Ten Thousands	Thousands	Hundreds	Tens	Ones	Tenths	Hundredths	Thousandths	Ten Thousandths	Hundred Thousandths
2	1	0,	9	8	7,	6	5	4,	3	2	1.	2	3	4	5	6

This Chart shows the place value of the number 210,987,654,321.23456

This is how you say it.

Two hundred ten billion, nine hundred eighty seven million, six hundred fifty four thousand, three hundred twenty one, and twenty three thousand four hundred fifty six hundred thousandths.

Math-Aids.Com

Addition and Subtraction

Addition and subtraction are the first mathematical concepts that students are expected to learn. Addition is conceptualized as the union of two sets.

Subtraction is more difficult because it has three different interpretations:

  a. **Taking away:** Taking one quantity away from another. (Zoe has 10 stickers. She gives 5 away to her friend Jamie. How any stickers does Zoe have left?)
  b. **Comparison:** How much more one quantity is than another is. (Ricardo and Matt are selling chocolate bars for the school band, Tom sold 136 chocolate bars and Matt sold 97. How many more chocolate bars has Ricardo sold than Matt?)
  c. **Missing Addend:** How much more of a quantity is needed. (Jeff is saving his money to buy a video game. The game costs $35.99 on sale. Jeff has $29.50 so far. How much more does he need to buy the video game?)

Multiplication and Division

Students need a mastery of addition and subtraction facts in order to do well in multiplication and division, which are extensions of these operations. In fact, multiplication is essentially 'skip counting.' The division algorithm is the most difficult for students to learn.

Multiplication may be viewed in five different ways:

a. **Repeated addition or Skip counting:** 7 x 5 could be viewed as 7 + 7 + 7 + 7 + 7 = 35

b. **Arrays:** 7 x 5 is depicted as 7 rows of 5 objects or 5 rows of 7 objects, like rows of seats in a classroom.

c. **Cartesian product of two sets:** This interpretation is used with problems such as " "Maria goes to Baskin Robbins for an ice cream cone. She decided to buy a two-scoop cone and has 25 flavors to choose from. How many possible combinations can Maria make?" There are 50 possible combinations because 25 choices x 2 scoops of ice cream = 50 combinations.

d. **Linear Prototypes :** The problem 7 x 5 can be shown on number line by starting with 0, and skipping 5 spaces 7 times, stopping on 35.

e. **Multiple sets:** 12 x 6 can be described in a problem like this: Jamal is buying pencils for himself and his two brothers. He buys six packages of pencils. How many pencils did Jamal buy? (12 x 6 = 72.)

Division can be conceptualized in two ways for a problem 32 divided by 8 = 4:

a. **Measurement:** The problem may be seen as 8 groups of 4. A sample problem could read, "Michelle has a 32-inch piece of yarn. She needs an 8-inch piece for her string art project. How many pieces can she cut from the yarn? (The yarn is measured into equal parts.

b. **Partition:** The problem may be seen as 8 dots in each of 4 groups. A sample problem could read, "32 students go on a field trip to a museum. They are assigned to 4 tour guides for the guided tour. If the tour guides each have an equal number of students in their groups, how many students are there in each group? (The large group of 32 is divided into 4 equal groups of 8).

Just as in addition or subtraction, manipulatives and objects can be used in order for special education students to grapple the multiplication or division concept at hand. Grids, tables, number lines, and other visual devices should be employed when necessary. Drawing pictures and changing the pictures, depending upon the operations performed, can also be an useful strategy to covey concepts to students who are having a hard time with the abstraction of the operation. Reality-based examples are always ideal, i.e., 3 x 4 = 12 can be described as three cars in a parking lot, each with four wheels.

Fractions

Fractions represent a piece of a set, and may be interpreted as:

1. **A part of a whole:** (probably the most familiar) Stacey is sharing a pizza with 3 friends. If everyone gets an equal share, what part of the pizza will each girl get? Answer: ¼, 1 divided by 4.

2. **Subset of a parent set:** John's dog has 8 puppies. 3 puppies are white, with

spots. What fraction of the puppies is white, with spots? Answer: 3/8, 3 divided by 8.

3. **A ratio:** Examples of ratios- 2 girls for every 3 boys in a class is also 2 out of 3, or 2:3, or 2/3.

4. **Decimal Conversions:** .7 is also expressed as 7/10 based upon place value principles.

Didactic, hands-on materials are helpful for special education students to understand fractions. Folding paper, using fractional pieces, or sharing a snack may help solidify the notion of fractions by making it concrete and succinct, as well as multisensory.

Problem Solving

The skills of analysis and interpretation are necessary for problem solving. Students with learning disabilities find problem solving difficult, with the result that they often avoid problem solving activities, particularly word problems and those with multiple steps involved. Skills necessary for problem solving include:

a. **Identification of the main idea:** What is the problem about?
b. **Main question of the problem:** What is the problem asking for?
c. **Identify important facts:** What information is necessary to solve the problem?
d. **Choose a strategy and an operation:** How will the student solve the problem and with what operation?
e. **Solve the problem:** Perform the computation.
f. **Check accuracy of computation and compare the answer to the main question:** Does the answer sound reasonable?
g. **If solution is not correct:** Repeat the steps.

It is helpful to supply students with an attack plan for problem solving, or at the very least, arm them with a highlighter so they may highlight the important, critical information. The attack plan can be in the form of a graphic organizer, as used in the previous section for English and writing. Here is an example:

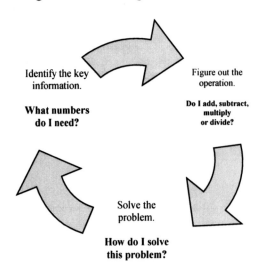

Identify the key information.

What numbers do I need?

Figure out the operation.

Do I add, subtract, multiply or divide?

Solve the problem.

How do I solve this problem?

It is also helpful to provide visual boundaries, such as determined boxes on the paper or folded areas of the paper, so students with visual-spatial integration issues may determine where they can show their work and problem solve on the paper. Some students may also benefit from the use of graphing paper, to allow them to line up calculations, decimals points, and numbers in proper place value order, to decrease the chance of making a mistake.

Secondary Mathematics

Other topics in mathematics that are important to develop, especially as the student enters the higher grades, are spatial relationships, measurements, and patterns. Instruction in these areas allows students to discover relationships and properties of three-dimensional objects, explore the logical nature of mathematics, and build a foundation for algebra and geometry. Secondary students also need instruction in consumer mathematics (ratio, proportion, interest, percent, and consumer credit) because students will need to balance checkbooks, calculate best buys, apply for credit, compare interest rates, and budget their money. Students need to know the mathematics involved in loans, credit cards, mortgages and taxes.

An example of a progression of secondary mathematics in graphic organizer forms can be viewed below, as extracted from the Broad Run High School in Virginia website, http://www.lcps.org/Page/6127

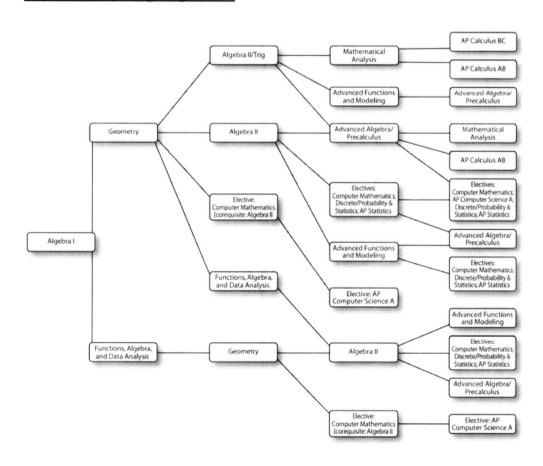

Skill 9.02   Knows how individuals learn and develop mathematical skills, procedures, and concepts.

Reid, 1985, describes four processes that are directly related to an understanding of numbers. Children typically begin learning these processes in early childhood through the opportunities provided by their caretakers. Children who do not get these opportunities have difficulties when they enter school.

1. **Describing:** Characterizing objects, sets or events in terms of their attributes such as calling all cats "kitties" whether they are tigers or house cats.
2. **Classifying:** Sorting objects, sets or events in terms of one or more criterion such as color, size or shape, e.g. black cats versus white cats versus tabby cats.
3. **Comparing:** Determining whether two objects, sets or events are similar or different on the basis of a specified attribute, such as differentiating quadrilaterals from triangles on the basis of the number of sides.
4. **Ordering:** Comparing two or more objects, sets or events, such as ordering children in a family on the basis of age, or on the basis of height.

Children usually begin learning these concepts during early childhood:

1. **Equalizing:** Making two or more objects or sets alike on an attribute, such as putting more milk into a glass so that it matches the amount of milk in another glass.
2. **Joining**: Putting together two or more sets with a common attribute to make one set, such as buying packets of X-Men trading cards to create a complete series.
3. **Separating**: Dividing an object or set into two or more sets, such as passing out cookies from a bag to a group of children so that each child gets three cookies.
4. **Measuring**: Attaching a number to an attribute, such as three cups of flour, or ten gallons of gas.
5. **Patterns:** Recognizing, developing, and repeating patterns, such as secret code messages, designs in a carpet or tile floor.

Most children are not developmentally ready to understand these concepts before they enter school:

1. **Understanding and Working with Numbers Larger than Ten:** The child may be able to recite larger numbers, but is not able to compare or add them, for example.
2. **Part-whole Concept:** The idea of one number as being a part of another number.
3. **Numerical Notation:** Place value, additive system, and zero symbol.

Children with learning problems often have difficulty with these concepts after they enter public school because they have either had not had many experiences with developing these concepts or they are not developmentally ready to understand such concepts.

Sequence of Mathematics Understanding

The understanding of mathematical concepts proceeds in a developmental context from concrete to semi-concrete to abstract. Children with learning difficulties may still be at the semi-concrete level when their peers are ready to work at the abstract level. This developmental sequence has implication for remedial instruction because the teacher will need to incorporate concrete and/or semi-concrete/representational methodologies into lessons for students who did not master these stages of development in their mathematics background. These levels may be explained as follows:

1. **Concrete:** An example of concrete understanding would be demonstrating 3 + 4 = 7 by using sets of addends (3 and 4) with items, such as buttons, and physically bringing them together to demonstrate the sum (7).
2. **Semi-concrete or representational:** An example of semi-concrete understanding would be using pictures of three buttons and four buttons to illustrate 3 + 4 = 7.
3. **Abstract:** The student solves 3 + 4 = 7 without using manipulatives or pictures.

In summary, the levels of mathematics content involve:

Concepts such as the understanding of numbers and terms.
Development of mathematical relationships.
Development of mathematical skills such as computation and measuring.
Development of problem-solving ability.

Skill 9.03   Understands numbers, number systems and their structure, operations and algorithms, and quantitative reasoning, and uses various instructional strategies and resources, including technology, to help students with disabilities understand and apply related content and skills.

Number sense refers to a student's fluidity and flexibility with numbers, the sense of what numbers mean, and an ability to perform mental mathematics and to look at the world and make comparisons.

Students with good number sense can invent their own procedures for performing numerical operations. They can represent the same number in numerous ways depending on the context and reason for this representation. They can identify numbers and number patterns, especially ones that come from the deep structure of the number system. They understand numerical magnitude and can recognize gross numerical errors, or errors that are off by an order of magnitude. Finally, they can think or talk in a sensible way about the general properties of a numerical problem or expression, without doing any precise computation.

Number sense leads to automatic use of math information, but also is a key ingredient in the ability to solve basic math problems. Students must memorize more than 100 basic addition facts in order to fully develop their math problem solving skills.

Number sense is attained through environmental circumstances. Most of the environmental conditions focus on informal teaching by parents, siblings or other relatives. Students from a middle to high-class backgrounds are more likely to have a good number sense when compared to students from low socioeconomic backgrounds. This is based on the fact that well-educated middle class homes tend to have more informal instruction about numbers and things linked to numbers. Number sense in the home is derived from clocks (digital and analog), kitchen timers (microwave and oven), various quantifiable objects on display (pictures along a hallway corridor, fruit in a basket on a table, etc.), the use of a piggy bank or small amounts of money, number magnets on a fridge, recipes cooked with a parent involving measurements, etc. These subtle appearances of math create a subconscious foundation for the subject matter to come when the student arrives to school.

Beginning math instructions should focus on building number sense, especially in students with disabilities. According to special education researchers Pellegrino and Goldman (1987), simultaneously integrating number sense activities with increased number fact memorization rather than teaching these skills sequentially appears to be vital for both reduction of difficulties in math for the general population and for instruction of students with learning disabilities. It is also likely that some students who are drilled on number facts and then taught various algorithms for computations may never fully develop well-rounded number sense.

Pellegrino and Goldman (1987) concluded that the focus of mathematics remediation for students with learning disabilities should involve extended practice on math facts for which the student still relied on counting procedures. Pellegrino and Goldman stated that extended practice would lead to development of a degree of automatic retention that enables students to participate in higher-order aspects of the task.

Many students with learning disabilities have procedural knowledge of basic math facts (i.e., they can correctly calculate the sum of 7 + 6), but they need to input these facts in their memory in a manner that allows for quick, errorless retrieval.

Technology also has a place in assisting students in making memorization of math facts automatic. Drill and practice software can provide individual daily practice. The software provides immediate feedback on incorrect responses and a large amount of practice. The key to using computer programs is to facilitate a practice environment whereby target facts are consistently given until the student is able to retrieve the answer from memory automatically as opposed to counting on his/her fingers. The use of computer-aided instruction has been found to be effective in increasing the rate of memorization of key math facts.

With the proper classroom environment, seemingly mundane computation exercises can be fascinating to children. Arithmetic facts represent strategy-based problems for low performers (both children with learning disabilities and those at risk for school failure). These low performers need systematic instruction in strategy use that others may not.

Skill 9.04 **Applies knowledge of methods, strategies, and resources for teaching students with disabilities to engage in mathematical reasoning and problem solving, apply mathematics in a variety of contexts, and communicate mathematically.**

Effective Teaching Methods for Developing Math Skills in Problem Solving

One of the main reasons for studying mathematics is to acquire the ability to perform problem-solving skills. Problem solving is the process of applying previously acquired knowledge to new and novel situations. Mathematical problem solving is generally thought of as solving word problems; however, there are more skills involved in problem solving than merely reading word problems, deciding on correct conceptual procedures, and performing the computations. Problem solving skills involve posing questions; analyzing situations; hypothesizing, translating, and illustrating results; drawing diagrams, and using trial and error. When solving mathematical problems, students need to be able to apply logic; and thus, determine which facts are relevant.

Problem solving has proven to be the primary area of mathematical difficulty for students. The following methods for developing problem solving skills have been recommended.

1. Allot time for the development of successful problem solving skills. It is a complex process and needs to be taught in a systematic way.
2. Be sure prerequisite skills have been adequately developed. The ability to perform the operations of addition, subtraction, multiplication, and division are necessary sub-skills.
3. Use error analysis to diagnose areas of difficulty. One error in procedure or choice of mathematical operation, once corrected, will eliminate subsequent mistakes following the initial error like the domino effect. Look for patterns of similar mistakes to prevent a series of identical errors. Instruct children on the usage of error analysis to perform self-appraisal of their own work.
4. Teach students appropriate terminology. Many words have a different meaning when used in a mathematical context than in everyday life. For example "set" in mathematics refers to a grouping of objects, but it may be used as a verb, such as in "set the table." Other words that should be defined include "order," "base," "power," and "root."
5. Have students estimate answers. Teach them how to check their computed answer, to determine how reasonable it is. For example, Teddy is asked how many hours he spent doing his homework. If he worked on it two hours before dinner and one hour after dinner, and his answer came out to be 21, Teddy should be able to conclude that 21 hours is the greater part of a day, and is far too large to be reasonable.

Communication in Mathematics: Math Vocabulary

Many students with learning disabilities, specifically with math disorders, may have a problem connecting terminology with symbolism in mathematics. For example, multiplication means to multiply or grow larger, and is represented by a multiplication sign, 'x,' when a student is in elementary school. As he or she progresses into higher math courses, the multiplication sign may take on the form of a dot, and eventually fade. Numbers next to one another, such as 5(4) will soon indicate multiplication. It is helpful to explain symbols and their relation to math vocabulary words, not only to explain the underpinnings of problems solving, but also to assist word problem translation. For example, if a word problem asks for the sum of cookies, it is asking the student to add. Vocabulary is a critical component of math, and often needs clarification.

Skill 9.05   Understands patterns, relations, functions, and algebraic reasoning and analysis, and uses various instructional strategies and resources, including technology, to help students with disabilities understand and apply related content and skills.

Conditional statements are frequently written in **"if-then"** form. The "if" clause of the conditional is known as the **hypothesis**, and the "then" clause is called the **conclusion**. In a proof, the hypothesis is the information that is assumed to be true, while the conclusion is what is to be proven true. A conditional is considered to be of the form:

If p, then q
p is the hypothesis. q is the conclusion.

Conditional statements can be diagrammed using a **Venn diagram**. A diagram can be drawn with one circle inside another circle. The inner circle represents the hypothesis. The outer circle represents the conclusion. If the hypothesis is taken to be true, then you are located inside the inner circle. If you are located in the inner circle then you are also inside the outer circle, so that proves the conclusion is true.

Example:
If an angle has a measure of 90 degrees, then it is a right angle.

In this statement "an angle has a measure of 90 degrees" is the hypothesis.
In this statement "it is a right angle" is the conclusion.

Example:
If you are in Pittsburgh, then you are in Pennsylvania.

In this statement "you are in Pittsburgh" is the hypothesis.
In this statement "you are in Pennsylvania" is the conclusion.

Conditional: If p, then q
p is the hypothesis. q is the conclusion.

Inverse: If ⊔ p, then ⊔ q.
Negate both the hypothesis (If not p, then not q) and the conclusion from the original conditional.

Converse : If q, then p.
Reverse the 2 clauses.
The original hypothesis becomes the conclusion.
The original conclusion then becomes the new hypothesis.

Contrapositive: If ⊔ q, then ⊔ p.
Reverse the 2 clauses. The If not q, then not p original hypothesis becomes the conclusion.
The original conclusion then becomes the new hypothesis.
THEN negate both the new hypothesis and the new conclusion.

Example: Given the **conditional**: If an angle has 60°, then it is an acute angle.

Its **inverse**, in the form "If ⊔ p, then ⊔ q", would be:

If an angle doesn't have 60°, then it is not an acute angle.

NOTICE that the inverse is not true, even though the conditional statement was true.

Its **converse**, in the form "If q, then p", would be:

If an angle is an acute angle, then it has 60°.

NOTICE that the converse is not true, even though the conditional statement was true.

Its **contrapositive**, in the form "If q, then p", would be:

If an angle isn't an acute angle, then it doesn't have 60°.

NOTICE that the contrapositive is true, assuming original conditional statement was true.

TIP: If you are asked to pick a statement that is logically equivalent to a given conditional, look for the contrapositive. The inverse and converse are not always logically equivalent to every conditional. The contra-positive is ALWAYS logically equivalent.

Find the inverse, converse and contrapositive of the following conditional statement. Also determine if each of the 4 statements is true or false.

Conditional: If $x = 5$, then $x^2 - 25 = 0$.   TRUE
Inverse: If $x \neq 5$, then $x^2 - 25 \neq 0$.   FALSE, x could be ⁻5

Converse: If $x^2 - 25 = 0$, then $x = 5$. FALSE, x could be $^-5$
Contrapositive: If $x^2 - 25 \neq 0$, then $x \neq 5$. TRUE

Conditional: If $x = 5$, then $6x = 30$.   TRUE
Inverse: If $x \neq 5$, then $6x \neq 30$.   TRUE
Converse: If $6x = 30$, then $x = 5$.   TRUE
Contrapositive: If $6x \neq 30$, then $x \neq 5$. TRUE

Sometimes, as in this example, all 4 statements can be logically equivalent; however, the only statement that will always be logically equivalent to the original conditional is the contrapositive.

Calculators

Calculators are important tools. They should be encouraged in the classroom and at home. Calculators do not replace basic knowledge, but they can relieve the tedium of mathematical computations, allowing students to explore more challenging mathematical directions. Students need to always check their work by estimating. Texas Instruments has a line of calculators to fit every need of a math student along the continuum of content, from a basic TI-30 calculator to the more advanced scientific calculator (TI-91, for example). The goal of mathematics is to prepare the child to survive in the real world. Technology is a reality in today's society.

Skill 9.06   Understands geometry, spatial reasoning, and measurement concepts and principles, and uses various instructional strategies and resources, including technology, to help students with disabilities understand and apply related content and skills.

Geometric Models

Symmetry is exact similarity between two parts or halves, as if one were a mirror image of the other.

A **Tessellation** is an arrangement of closed shapes that completely covers the plane without overlapping or leaving gaps. Unlike **tiles**, tessellations do not require the use of regular polygons. In art the term is used to refer to pictures or tiles mostly in the form of animals and other life forms, which cover the surface of a plane in a symmetrical way without overlapping or leaving gaps. M. C. Escher is known as the "Father" of modern tessellations. Tessellations are used for tiling, mosaics, quilts and art.

If you look at a completed tessellation, you will see the original motif repeats in a pattern. There are 17 possible ways that a pattern can be used to tile a flat surface or "wallpaper."

There are four basic transformational symmetries that can be used in tessellations: **translation, rotation, reflection,** and **glide reflection**. The transformation of an object is called its image. If the original object was labeled with letters, such as *ABCD*, the image may be labeled with the same letters followed by a prime symbol, *A'B'C'D'*.

A **translation** is a transformation that "slides" an object a fixed distance in a given direction. The original object and its translation have the same shape and size, and they face in the same direction.

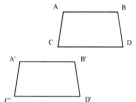

An example of a translation in architecture would be stadium seating. The seats are the same size and the same shape and face in the same direction.

A **rotation** is a transformation that turns a figure about a fixed point called the center of rotation. An object and its rotation are the same shape and size, but the figures may be turned in different directions. Rotations can occur in either a clockwise or a counterclockwise direction.

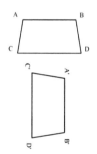

Rotations can be seen in wallpaper and art. A Ferris wheel is an example of rotation.
An object and its **reflection** have the same shape and size, but the figures face in opposite directions.

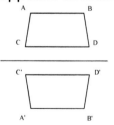

The line (where a mirror may be placed) is called the **line of reflection**. The distance from a point to the line of reflection is the same as the distance from the point's image to the line of reflection.

A **glide reflection** is a combination of a reflection and a translation.

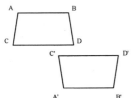

The tessellation below is a combination of the four types of transformational symmetry we have discussed:

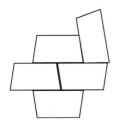

Generating Three Dimensional Figures From Two Dimensional Shapes

Three-dimensional figures in geometry are known as **solids**. A solid is the union of all points on a simple closed surface and all points in its interior. A **polyhedron** is a simple closed surface formed from planar polygonal regions. Each polygonal region is called a **face** of the polyhedron. The vertices and edges of the polygonal regions are called the **vertices** and **edges** of the polyhedron.

A cube is formed from three congruent squares. However, if we tried to put four squares about a single vertex, their interior angle measures would add up to 360°; i.e., four edge-to-edge squares with a common vertex lie in a common plane and therefore cannot form a corner figure of a regular polyhedron.

There are five ways to form corner figures with congruent regular polygons:

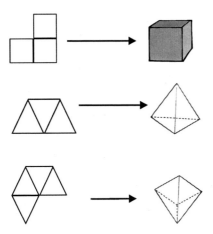

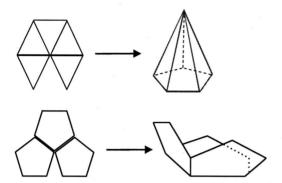

When creating a three-dimensional figure, if any two values of the vertices, faces, and edges are known, the remaining value can be found by using **Euler's Formula**: $V + F = E + 2$.

For example:

To create a pentagonal pyramid, knowing it has six vertices and six faces, using Euler's Formula, would be computed as:

$$V + F = E + 2$$
$$6 + 6 = E + 2$$
$$12 = E + 2$$
$$10 = E$$

Thus, our figure should have 10 edges.

Representing Two- and Three-Dimensional Geometric Figures in the Coordinate Plane.

Any two-dimensional geometric figure can be represented in the **Cartesian** or **Rectangular Coordinate System**. The Cartesian or Rectangular Coordinate System is formed by two perpendicular axes (coordinate axes): the X-axis and the Y-axis. If the dimensions of a two-dimensional, or planar, figure are known, this coordinate system can be used to visualize the shape of the figure.

Example: Represent an isosceles triangle with two sides of length 4.

Draw the two sides along the x- and y- axes and connect the points (vertices).

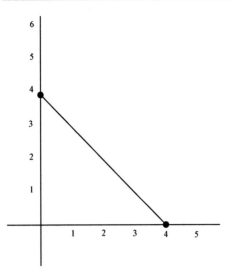

In order to represent three-dimensional figures, three coordinate axes (X, Y, and Z), which are all mutually perpendicular to each other are needed. Since three mutually perpendicular axes cannot be drawn on a two-dimensional surface, we use oblique representations.

Example: Represent a cube with sides of 2.

Once again, three sides are drawn along the three axes to make things easier.

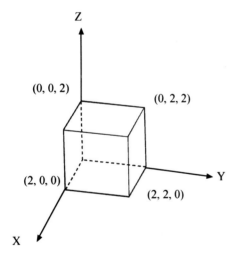

Each point has three coordinates (x, y, z).

Nets

The union of all points on a simple closed surface and all points in its interior form a space figure called a **solid**. The five regular solids, or **polyhedra**, are the cube, tetrahedron, octahedron, icosahedron, and dodecahedron. A **net** is a two-dimensional figure that can be cut out and folded up to make a three-dimensional solid. Below are models of the five regular solids with their corresponding face polygons and nets.

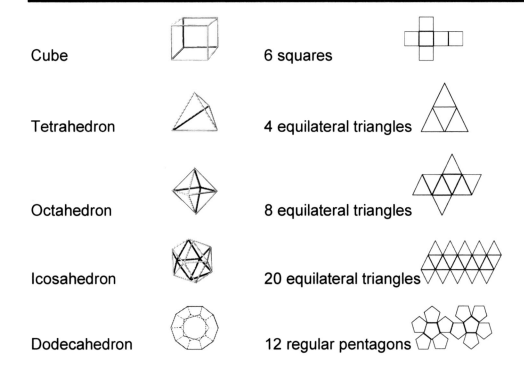

Cube		6 squares
Tetrahedron		4 equilateral triangles
Octahedron		8 equilateral triangles
Icosahedron		20 equilateral triangles
Dodecahedron		12 regular pentagons

Other Examples of Solids:

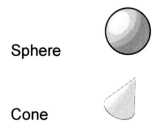

Sphere

Cone

Standard Units of Measurement

"When you can measure what you are speaking about and express it in numbers, you know something about it; but when you cannot measure it, when you cannot express it in numbers, your knowledge is of a meager and unsatisfactory kind." Lord Kelvin

Non-standard units are sometimes used when standard instruments might not be available. For example, students might measure the length of a room by their arm-spans. An inch originated as the length of three barley grains placed end to end. Seeds or stones might be used for measuring weight. In fact, our current "carat," used for measuring precious gems, was derived from carob seeds. In ancient times, baskets, jars and bowls were used to measure capacity.

To estimate measurement of familiar objects, it is first necessary to determine the units to be used.

Examples:

Length
1. The coastline of Florida   miles or kilometers
2. The width of a ribbon   inches or millimeters
3. The thickness of a book   inches or centimeters
4. The length of a football field yards or meters
5. The depth of water in a pool feet or meters

Weight or Mass
1. A bag of sugar   pounds or grams
2. A school bus   tons or kilograms
3. A dime   ounces or grams

Capacity
1. Paint to paint a bedroom   gallons or liters
2. Glass of milk   cups or liters
3. Bottle of soda   quarts or liters
4. Medicine for child   ounces or milliliters

It is necessary to be familiar with the metric and customary system in order to estimate measurements.

Some common equivalents include:

ITEM	APPROXIMATELY EQUAL TO	
	METRIC	IMPERIAL
large paper clip	1 gram	1 ounce
1 quart	1 liter	
average sized man	75 kilograms	170 pounds
1 yard	1 meter	
math textbook	1 kilogram	2 pounds
1 mile	1 kilometer	
1 foot	30 centimeters	
thickness of a dime	1 millimeter	0.1 inches

Estimate the measurement of the following items:

The length of an adult cow = _____ meters
The thickness of a compact disc = _____ millimeters
Your height = _____ meters
length of your nose = _____ centimeters
weight of your math textbook = _____ kilograms
weight of an automobile = _____ kilograms
weight of an aspirin = _____ grams

The units of **length** in the customary system are inches, feet, yards and miles.

> 12 inches (in.) = 1 foot (ft.)
> 36 in. = 1 yard (yd.)
> 3 ft. = 1 yd.
> 5280 ft. = 1 mile (mi.)
> 1760 yd. = 1 mi.

To change from a **larger unit to a smaller unit, multiply**.
To change from a **smaller unit to a larger unit, divide**.

Example:

$\quad$ 4 mi. = _____ yd.
Since 1760 yd. = 1 mile, multiply $4 \times 1760 = 7040$ yd.

Example:

$\quad$ 21 in. = _____ ft.
$21 \div 12 = 1\frac{3}{4}$ ft.

The units of **weight** are ounces, pounds and tons.

> 16 ounces (oz.) = 1 pound (lb.)
> 2,000 lb. = 1 ton (T.)

Example: $2\frac{3}{4}$ T. = _____ lb
$2\frac{3}{4} \times 2,000 = 5,500$ lb.

The units of **capacity** are fluid ounces, cups, pints, quarts, and gallons.

> 8 fluid ounces (fl. oz.) = 1 cup (c.)
> 2 c. = 1 pint (pt.)
> 4 c. = 1 quart (qt.)
> 2 pt. = 1 qt.
> 4 qt. = 1 gallon (gal.)

Example1: 3 gal. = _____ qt.
$\quad 3 \times 4 = 12$ qt.

Example: $1\frac{1}{4}$ cups = _____ oz.
$\quad 1\frac{1}{4} \times 8 = 10$ oz.

<u>Example:</u> 7 c. = _____ pt.

$$7 \div 2 = 3\tfrac{1}{2} \text{ pt.}$$

Square Units can be derived with knowledge of basic units of length by squaring the equivalent measurements.

1 square foot (sq. ft.) = 144 sq. in.
1 sq. yd. = 9 sq. ft.
1 sq. yd. = 1296 sq. in.

<u>Example:</u> 14 sq. yd. = _____ sq. ft.

$$14 \times 9 = 126 \text{ sq. ft.}$$

METRIC UNITS

The metric system is based on multiples of <u>ten</u>. Conversions are made by simply moving the decimal point to the left or right.

kilo-	1000	thousands
hecto-	100	hundreds
deca-	10	tens
deci-	.1	tenths
centi-	.01	hundredths
milli-	.001	thousandths

The basic unit for **length** is the meter. One meter is approximately one yard.

The basic unit for **weight** or mass is the gram. A paper clip weighs about one gram.

The basic unit for **volume** is the liter. One liter is approximately a quart.

The most commonly used units:

1 m = 100 cm	1000 mL= 1 L	
1000 mg = 1 g		
1 m = 1000 mm	1 kL = 1000 L	1 kg = 1000 g
1 cm = 10 mm		
1000 m = 1 km		

The prefixes are commonly listed from left to right for ease in conversion.

K H D U D C M

<u>Example:</u>   63 km = _____ m
Since there are 3 steps from <u>K</u>ilo to <u>U</u>nit, move the decimal point 3 places to the right.
       63 km = 63,000 m

<u>Example:</u>   14 mL = _____ L
Since there are 3 steps from <u>M</u>illi to <u>U</u>nit, move the decimal point 3 places to the left.
       14 mL = 0.014 L

<u>Example:</u>   56.4 cm = _____ mm
       56.4 cm = 564 mm

<u>Example:</u>   9.1 m = _____ km
       9.1 m = 0.0091 km

<u>Example 5</u>:   75 kg = _____ m
       75 kg = 75,000,000 m

The distance around a circle is the **Circumference**. The ratio of the circumference to the diameter is represented by the Greek letter pi. $\Pi \sim 3.14 \sim \frac{22}{7}$.

The circumference of a circle is found by the formula $C = 2\Pi r$ or $C = \Pi d$ where r is the radius of the circle and d is the diameter.

The **Area** of a circle is found by the formula $A = \Pi r^2$.

<u>Example:</u> Find the circumference and area of a circle whose radius is 7 meters.

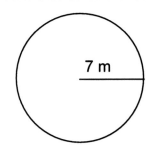

       7 m

C = 2Πr   A = Πr²
   = 2(3.14)(7)   = 3.14(7)(7)
   = 43.96 m   = 153.86 m²

Compute the area remaining when sections are cut out of a given figure composed of triangles, squares, rectangles, parallelograms, trapezoids, or circles.

The strategy for solving problems of this nature should be to identify the given shapes and choose the correct formulas. Subtract the smaller cut out shape from the larger shape.

Sample problems:

1. Find the area of one side of the metal in the circular flat washer shown below:

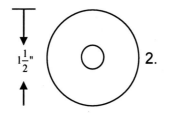

the shapes are both circles.

2. use the formula A = πr^2 for both.

(Inside diameter is $3/8"$**)**

Area of larger circle   Area of smaller circle

A = πr^2 A = πr^2
A = $\pi(.75^2)$ A = $\pi(.1875^2)$
A = 1.76625 in^2 A = .1104466 in^2

Area of metal washer = larger area - smaller area
= 1.76625 in^2 − .1104466 in^2
= 1.6558034 in^2

Skill 9.07   Understands principles and applications of probability and statistics, and uses various instructional strategies and resources, including technology, to help students with disabilities understand and apply related content and skills.

Formulating and Designing Statistical Experiments to Collect, Analyze, and Interpret Data

The Addition Principle of Counting states:
If A and B are events, $n(A or B) = n(A) + n(B) - n(A \cap B).$

Example:

In how many ways can you select a black card or a Jack from an ordinary deck of playing cards?

Let B denote the set of black cards and let J denote the set of Jacks. Then, $n(B) = 26, n(J) = 4, n(B \cap J) = 2$ and

$n(B or J) = n(B) + n(J) - n(B \cap A)$
$= 26 + 4 - 2$
$= 28.$

The Addition Principle of Counting for Mutually Exclusive Events states:

If A and B are mutually exclusive events, $n(A or B) = n(A) + n(B)$.

Example:

A travel agency offers 40 possible trips: 14 to Asia, 16 to Europe and 10 to South America. In how many ways can you select a trip to Asia or Europe through this agency?

Let A denote trips to Asia and let E denote trips to Europe. Then, $A \cap E = \varnothing$ and $n(A or E) = 14 + 16 = 30$.

Therefore, the number of ways you can select a trip to Asia or Europe is 30.

The Multiplication Principle of Counting for Dependent Events states:

Let A be a set of outcomes of Stage 1 and B a set of outcomes of Stage 2. Then the number of ways $n(A and B)$, that A and B can occur in a two-stage experiment is given by:

$n(A and B) = n(A)n(B|A)$, where $n(B|A)$ denotes the number of ways B can occur given that A has already occurred.

Example:

How many ways from an ordinary deck of 52 cards can two Jacks be drawn in succession if the first card is drawn but not replaced in the deck and then the second card is drawn?

This is a two-stage experiment for which we wish to compute $n(A and B)$, where A is the set of outcomes for which a Jack is obtained on the first draw and B is the set of outcomes for which a Jack is obtained on the second draw.

If the first card drawn is a Jack, then there are only three remaining Jacks left to choose from on the second draw. Thus, drawing two cards without replacement means the events A and B are dependent.

$n(A and B) = n(A)n(B|A) = 4 \cdot 3 = 12$

The Multiplication Principle of Counting for Independent Events states:

Let A be a set of outcomes of Stage 1 and B a set of outcomes of Stage 2. If A and B are independent events then the number of ways $n(A and B)$, that A and B can occur in a two-stage experiment is given by: $n(A and B) = n(A)n(B)$.

Example:

How many six-letter code "words" can be formed if repetition of letters is not allowed?

Since these are code words, a word does not have to look like a word; for example, *abcdef* could be a code word. Since we must choose a first letter and a second letter and a third letter and a fourth letter and a fifth letter and a sixth letter, this experiment has six stages.

Since repetition is not allowed there are 26 choices for the first letter; 25 for the second; 24 for the third; 23 for the fourth; 22 for the fifth; and 21 for the sixth. Therefore, we have:

n(six-letter code words without repetition of letters)

$$= 26 \cdot 25 \cdot 24 \cdot 23 \cdot 22 \cdot 21$$
$$= 165,765,600$$

Patterns and Trends in Data and Making Predictions Based on Those Trends

The absolute probability of some events cannot be determined. For instance, one cannot assume the probability of winning a tennis match is ½ because, in general, winning and losing are not equally likely. In such cases, past results of similar events can be used to help predict future outcomes. The **relative frequency** of an event is the number of times an event has occurred divided by the number of attempts.

Relative frequency = $\dfrac{\text{number of successful trials}}{\text{total number of trials}}$

For example, if a weighted coin flipped 50 times lands on heads 40 times and tails 10 times, the relative frequency of heads is 40/50 = 4/5. Thus, one can predict that if the coin is flipped 100 times, it will land on heads 80 times.

Example:

Two tennis players, John and David, have played each other 20 times. John has won 15 of the previous matches and David has won 5.
(a) Estimate the probability that David will win the next match.
(b) Estimate the probability that John will win the next 3 matches.

Solution:
(a) David has won 5 out of 20 matches. Thus, the relative frequency of David winning is 5/20 or ¼. We can estimate that the probability of David winning the next match is ¼.

(b) John has won 15 out of 20 matches. The relative frequency of John winning is 15/20 or ¾. We can estimate that the probability of John winning a future match is ¾. Thus, the probability that John will win the next three matches is ¾ x ¾ x ¾ = 27/64.

Skill 9.08   Applies knowledge of methods, strategies, and resources for teaching students with disabilities to engage in mathematical reasoning and problem solving ,apply mathematics in a variety of contexts, and communicate mathematically

Please refer to skill 9.04

DOMAIN IV.   **FOUNDATIONS AND PROFESSIONAL ROLES AND RESPONSIBILITIES**

COMPETENCY 010   **THE SPECIAL EDUCATION TEACHER UNDERSTANDS THE PHILOSOPHICAL, HISTORICAL, AND LEGAL FOUNDATIONS OF SPECIAL EDUCATION**

Skill 10.01   **Knows the historical foundations of special education, major contributors to the literature, major legislation relevant to knowledge and practice in the education of individuals with disabilities, and current issues and trends in special education.**

Background.   The U.S. Constitution does not specify protection for education. However, all states provide education, and thus individuals are guaranteed protection and due process under the 14th Amendment. The basic source of law for special education is the Individuals Disabilities Education Act (IDEA) and its accompanying regulations. IDEA represents the latest phase in the philosophy of educating children with disabilities. Initially, children with disabilities often did not go to school. When they did, they were segregated into special classes in order to avoid disrupting the regular class. Their education usually consisted of simple academics and later, training for manual jobs.

By the mid-1900s, advocates for children with special needs argued that segregation was inherently unequal. By the time of P.L. 94-142, about half of the estimated 8 million children with special needs in the U.S. were either not being appropriately served in school or were excluded from schooling altogether. There was a disproportionate number of minority children placed in special programs. Identification and placement practices and procedures were inconsistent, and parental involvement was generally not encouraged. After segregation on the basis of race was declared unconstitutional in Brown v, Board of Education, parents and other advocates filed similar lawsuits on behalf of children with special needs. The culmination of their efforts resulted in P.L. 94-142. This section is a brief summary of that law and other major legislation, which affect the manner in which special education services are delivered to children in need of those services.

Significant Legislation and Supreme Court Cases with an Impact on Exceptional Student Education

Brown v. Board of Education (1954): While this case specifically addressed the inequality of "separate but equal" facilities on the basis of race, the concept that segregation was inherently unequal, even if equal facilities were provided, was later applied to handicapping conditions.

The Cooperative Research Act (1954): This act passed the first designation of general funds for the use of students with disabilities.

Public Law 85-926 (1958): Provided grants to intuitions of higher learning and to state education agencies for training professional personnel who would, in turn, train teachers of students with mental retardation.

Elementary and Secondary Education Act (1965): Provided funds for the education of children who were disadvantaged and disabled (Public Law 89-10).

Educational Consolidation and Improvement Act -State Operated Programs PL 89-313 (1965): Provided funds for children with disabilities who are or have been in state-operated or state-supported schools.

Public Law 89-750 (1966): Authorized the establishment of the Bureau Education for the Handicapped (BEH) and a National Advisory Committee on the Handicapped.

Hanson v. Hobson (1967): Ruled that ability grouping (tracking) based on student performance on standardized tests is unconstitutional.

Handicapped Children's Early Education Assistance Act PL 90-538 (1968): Funded model demonstration programs for preschool students with disabilities.

Public law 90-247 (1968): Included provisions for deaf-blind centers, resource centers and expansion of media services for students with disabilities.

Public Law 90-576 (1968): Specified that ten percent of vocational education funds be earmarked for youth with disabilities.

Public Law 91-230 (Amendments to Public Law 89-10) (1969): Previous enactment relating to children with disabilities was consolidated into one act: Education of the Handicapped.

Pennsylvania Association for Retarded Citizens (PARC) v. Commonwealth of Pennsylvania (1972): Special Education was guaranteed to children with mental retardation. The victory in this case sparked other court cases for children with other disabilities.

Mills v. Board of Education of the District of Columbia (1972): The right to special education was extended to all children with disabilities, not just mentally retarded children. Judgments in PARC and Mills paved the way for P.L. 94-142.

Section 504, Rehabilitation Act of 1973: Section 504 expands an older law by extending its protection to other areas that receive federal assistance, such as education. Protected individuals must (a) have a physical or mental impairment that substantially limits one or more major life activities, such as self-care, walking, seeing, breathing, working, and learning and (b) have a record of such an impairment, or (c) be regarded as having such an impairment. A disability in itself is not sufficient grounds for a complaint of discrimination. The person must be otherwise qualified, or able to meet, the requirements of the program in question.

Goss v. Lopez (1975): Ruled that the state could not deny a student education without following due process. While this decision is not based on a special education issue, the process of school suspension and expulsion is obviously critical in assuring an appropriate public education to children with disabilities.

Education for All Handicapped Children Act - P.L. 94-142 (1975): The philosophy behind this piece of legislation is that education is to be provided to all children who meet eligibility requirements. All children are assumed capable of benefiting from education. For children with severe or profound disabilities, "education" may be interpreted to include training in basic self-help skills and vocational training as well as academics.

Larry P. v. Riles (1979): Ordered the reevaluation of black students enrolled in classes for educable mental retardation (EMR) and enjoined the California State department of Education from the use of intelligence tests in subsequent EMR placement decisions.

Parents in Action on Special Education (PASE) v. Hannon (1980): Ruled that IQ tests are necessarily biased against ethnic and racial subcultures.

Board of Education v. Rowley (1982): Amy Rowley was a deaf elementary school student whose parents rejected their school district's proposal to provide a tutor and speech therapy services to supplement their daughter's instruction in the regular classroom. Her parents insisted on an interpreter, even though Amy was making satisfactory social, academic, and educational progress without one. In deciding in favor of the school district, the Supreme Court ruled that school districts must provide those services that permit a student with disabilities to benefit from instruction. Essentially, the court ruled that the states are obligated to provide a "basic floor of opportunity" that is reasonable to allow the child to benefit from social education.

Irving Independent School District v. Tatro (1984): IDEA lists health services as one of the "related services" that schools are mandated to provide to exceptional students. Amber Tatro, who had spina bifida, required the insertion of a catheter on a regular schedule in order to empty her bladder. The issue was specifically over the classification of clean, intermittent catheterization (CIC) as a medical service (not covered under IDEA) or a "related health service", which would be covered. In this instance, the catheterization was not declared a medical service, but a "related service" necessary for the student to have in order to benefit from special education. The school district was obliged to provide the service. The Tatro case has implications for students with other medical impairments who may need services to allow them to attend classes at the school.

Smith v. Robinson, (1984): Concerned reimbursement of attorney's fees for parents who win litigation under IDEA. At the time of this case, IDEA did not provide for such reimbursement. Following this ruling, Congress passed a law awarding attorney's fees to parents who win their litigation.

Honig v. Doe, (1988): Essentially, students may not be denied education or exclusion from school when their misbehavior is related to their disability. The "stay put" provision of IDEA allows students to remain in their current educational setting pending the outcome of administrative or judicial hearings. In the case of behavior which is a danger to the student or others, the court allows school districts to apply their normal procedures for dealing with dangerous behavior, such as time-out, loss of privileges, detention, or study carrels. Where the student has presented an immediate threat to others, that student may be temporarily suspended for up to ten school days to give the school and the parents time to review the IEP and discuss possible alternatives to the current placement.

P.L. 99-457 (1986): Beginning with the 1991-1992 school year, special education programs were required for children ages three to five, with most states offering outreach programs to identify children with special needs from birth to age 3. In place of, or in addition to an annual IEP, the entire family's needs are addressed by an Individual Family Service Plan (IFSP), which is reviewed with the family every six months.

Americans with Disabilities Act (ADA) 1990: Bars discrimination in employment, transportation, public accommodations, and telecommunications in all aspects of life, not just those receiving federal funding. Title II and Title III are applicable to special education because they cover the private sector (such as private schools) and require access to public accommodations. New and remodeled public buildings, transportation vehicles, and telephone systems now must be accessible to the handicapped. ADA also protects individuals with contagious diseases, such as AIDS, from discrimination.

IDEA P.L. 101-476 (1990): The principles of IDEA also incorporate the concept of "normalization." Within this concept, persons with disabilities are allowed access to everyday patterns and conditions of life that are as close as possible or equal to their nondisabled peers. There are seven fundamental provisions of IDEA.

1. **Free Appropriate Public Education (FAPE).** Special Education services are to be provided at no cost to students or their families. The federal and state governments share any additional costs. FAPE also requires that education be appropriate to the individual needs of the students.

2. **Notification and Procedural Rights for Parents.** These include:
   a. The right to examine records and obtain independent evaluations.
   b. The right to receive a clearly written notice that states the results of the school's evaluation of their child and whether the child meets eligibility requirements for placement or continuation of special services. Parents who disagree with the school's decision may request a **due process** hearing and a **judicial hearing** if they do not receive satisfaction through due process.

3. **Identification and Services to All Children:** States must conduct public outreach programs to seek out and identify children who may need services.

4. **Necessary Related Services:** Developmental, corrective, and other support services that make it possible for a student to benefit from special education services must be provided. These may include related services such as speech therapy, occupational therapy, or physical therapy.

5. **Individualized Assessments:** Evaluations and tests must be nondiscriminatory and individualized.

6. **Individualized Education Plans:** Each student receiving special education services must have an **individualized education plan** developed at a meeting that is attended by a qualified representative of the local education agency (LEA). Others who should attend would be the proposed special education teachers, mainstream teachers, parents, and, when appropriate, the student.

7. **Least Restrictive Environment (LRE):** LRE means that the student is placed in an environment, which is not dangerous or overly controlling or intrusive. The student should be given opportunities to experience what other peers of similar mental or chronological age are doing. LRE should be the environment that is the most integrated and normalized for the student's strengths and weaknesses.

Florence County School Dist Four v. Shannon Carter (1993): Established that when a school district does not provide FAPE for a student with disability, the parents may seek reimbursement for private schooling. This decision has encouraged districts to be more inclusive of students with Autism who receive ABA/Lovaas therapy.

Reauthorization of IDEA. P.L 105-17 (1997): In 1997, IDEA was revised and reauthorized as Public Law 105-17 as progressive legislation for the benefit of school age children with special needs, their parents and those who work with these children. The 1997 reauthorization of IDEA made major changes in the areas of the evaluation procedures, parent rights, transition and, discipline.

The evaluation process was amended to require members of the evaluation team to look at previously collected data, tests, and information and to use it when it is deemed appropriate. Previous to IDEA 97 an entire re-evaluation had to be conducted every three years in relation to determine if the child continued to be a "child with a disability." This was changed to allow existing information/ evaluations to be considered which would prevent unnecessary assessment of students and reduce the cost of evaluations.

Parent participation was not a requirement under the previous IDEA for an evaluation team to make decisions regarding a student's eligibility for special education and related services. Under IDEA 97, parents were specifically included as members of the group making the eligibility decision.

The IEP was modified under IDEA 97 to emphasize the involvement of students with special needs in a general education classroom setting, with the services and modifications deemed necessary by the evaluation team.

The **Present Levels of Educational Performance (PLEP)** was changed to require a statement of how the child's disability affects his/her involvement and progress in the general curriculum. IDEA 97 established that there must be a connection between the special education and general education curriculum. For this reason, the PLEP was required to include an explanation of the extent to which the student will *not* be participating with nondisabled children in the general education class and in extracurricular and non-academic activities.

The IEP now had an established connection to the general education setting and had to provide the needed test accommodations that would be provided on all state and district wide assessments of the student with special needs. IDEA 97's emphasis on raising the standards of those in special education placed an additional requirement of a definitive reason why a standard general education assessment would not be deemed appropriate for a child, and how the child should then be assessed.

IDEA 97 looked at how parents were receiving annual evaluations on their child's IEP goals and determined that parents were not receiving sufficient feedback. IDEA 97 required schools to make reports to parents on the progress of their child at least as frequently as the progress of nondisabled peers was reported.

The IEP was also modified to include a review of the student's transitional needs and services specifically:

- Beginning when a student is 14 (later changed to age 16), and annually thereafter, the student's IEP must contain a statement of his/her transition service needs under the various components of that IEP that focus upon the student's courses of study (e.g., vocational education or advanced placement); and

- Beginning at least one year before the student reaches the age of majority under state law, the IEP must contain a statement that the student has been informed of the rights under the law that will transfer to him/ her upon reaching the age of majority.

Discipline

IDEA 97 broadened the schools' right to take a disciplinary action with children who have been classified as needing special education services with those students that knowingly possess or use illegal drugs or sell or solicit the sale of a controlled substance while at school or school functions.

Manifest Determination Review

Under IDEA 97, suspensions/disciplinary consequences could result in an alternative educational placement. This possibility was to be weighed by a Manifest Determination Review (MDR), which is held by an ARD committee. MDRs must occur no more than ten days after the disciplinary action. The MDR must determine:

1. Does the child's disability impair his/her ability to understand the impact and consequences of the behavior under disciplinary action?
2. Did the child's disability impair his/her ability to control the behavior subject to discipline?

Determination of a relationship between the student's disability and the behavior in question could allow the student to remain in his/her current placement. When no relationship between the behavior and the disability is established, IDEA 97 utilized FAPE to allow relevant disciplinary procedures to be applied to the child in the same manner in which they would be applied to children without disabilities,

Functional Behavioral Assessments (FBAs) and Behavior Intervention Plans (BIPs) now became a requirement in many situations for schools to both modify and provide disciplinary consequences.

No Child Left Behind Act (NCLB), (2002). No Child Left Behind, Public Law 107-110, was signed on January 8, 2002. NCLB addresses accountability of school personnel for student achievement with the expectation that every child will demonstrate proficiency in reading, math, and science. As students progress through the school system, testing will show if an individual teacher has effectively met the needs of his/her students. Through testing, each student's adequate yearly progress or lack thereof will be tracked. NCLB affects regular and special education students, gifted students and slow learners, and children of every ethnicity, culture and environment. NCLB is a document that encompasses every American educator and student in the public school system.

Elementary teachers (K-3) are responsible for teaching reading and using different, scientific-based approaches as needed. Elementary teachers of upper grades teach reading, math and science. Middle and high school teacher teach to new, higher standards. Sometimes teachers may have to provide remediation for students who did not have adequate instruction in earlier grades.

Special educators are responsible for teaching students to a level of proficiency comparable to their non-disabled peers. This raises the bar of academic expectations throughout the grades. For some students with disabilities, the criteria for getting a diploma is more difficult than in the past. Although a small percentage of students with disabilities will need alternate assessment, they still need to meet grade appropriate goals.

In order for special education teachers to meet the professional criteria of this act, they must be *highly qualified*, that is certified or licensed in their area of special education and show proof of a specific level of professional development in the core subjects that they teach. As special education teachers receive specific education in the core subjects they teach, they will be better prepared to teach to the same level of learning standards as the general education teacher.

M.L. v. Federal Way School District, State of Washington (2004): The Ninth Circuit Court of Appeals ruled that absence of a regular education teacher on an IEP team was a serious procedural error.

Reauthorization of IDEA, (2004): Required all secondary level special education teachers to be no less qualified than other teachers of the same subject areas.

The second revision of IDEA occurred in 2004, IDEA was re-authorized as the Individuals with Disabilities Education Improvement Act of 2004 (IDEIA 2004), commonly referred to as IDEA 2004, became effective July 1, 2005.

It was the intention to improve IDEA by adding the philosophy/understanding that special education students need preparation for further study beyond the high school setting by teaching compensatory methods. Accordingly, IDEA 2004 provided a close tie to PL 89-10, the Elementary and Special Education Act of 1965, and stated that students with special needs should have maximum access to the general curriculum. This was defined as the amount needed for an individual student to reach his fullest potential. Full inclusion was stated not to be the only option by which to achieve this, and specified that compensatory should be taught to students for whom inclusion was not the best setting.

IDEA 2004 added a new requirement for special education teachers on the secondary level enforcing NCLBs "Highly Qualified" requirements in the subject area of their curriculum. The rewording in this part of IDEA states that they shall be "no less qualified" than teachers in the core areas.

Free and Appropriate Public Education (FAPE), was revised by mandating that students have maximum access to appropriate general education. Additionally, LRE placement for those students with disabilities must have the same school placement rights as those students who are not disabled. IDEA 2004 recognizes that due to the nature of some disabilities, appropriate education may vary in the amount of participation/placement in the general education setting. For some students, FAPE will mean a choice as to the type of educational institution they attend (private school for example), any of which must provide the special education services deemed necessary for the student through the IEP.

Skill 10.02 Applies knowledge of models, theories, and philosophies that provide the basis for special education practice.

Special education is precisely what the term denotes: education of a special nature for students who have special needs. The academic and behavioral techniques that are used today in special education are a culmination of "best practices" and evolved from a number of disciplines (e.g. medicine, psychology, sociology, language, ophthalmology, otology) to include education. Each of these disciplines contributed uniquely to their field so that the needs of special students might be better met in the educational arena.

Unfortunately, during the earlier part of the 1900s and mid-1950s, too many educators placed in positions of responsibility, refused to recognize their professional obligation for assuring that all children receive a free, appropriate, public education. Specific mandates are now stated in national laws, state regulations, and local policies. These mandates, the result of many years of successful litigation and political advocacy, govern the delivery of special education.

What special educators do is one thing; how services are delivered is yet another. The concept of **inclusion** stresses the need for educators to rethink the continuum of services, which was designed by Evelyn Deno and has been in existence since the early 1970s. Many school districts developed educational placement sites, which contain options listed on this continuum. These traditional options extend from the least restrictive to the most restrictive special education settings. The least restrictive environment is the regular education classroom. The present trend is to team special education and regular classroom teachers in regular classrooms. This avoids pulling out students for resource room services, and provides services by specialists for students who may be showing difficulties similar to those of special education students.

Although the origin of special education services for youngsters with disabilities is relatively recent, the history of public attitude toward people with disabling conditions was recorded as early as 1552. The Spartans practiced infanticide, the killing of abandonment of malformed or sickly babies. The ancient Greeks and Romans thought people with disabilities were cursed and forced them to beg for food and shelter. Those who could who could not fend for themselves were allowed to perish. Some with mental disabilities were employed as fools for the entertainment of the Roman royalty.

During the Middle Ages, persons with disabilities were viewed within the aura of the unknown, and were treated with a mixture of fear and reverence. Some were wandering beggars, while others were used as jesters in the courts. The Reformation brought about a change of attitude, however. Individuals with disabilities were accused of being possessed by the devil, and exorcism flourished. Many innocent people were put in chains and cast into dungeons.

The early seventeenth century was marked by a softening of public attitude toward persons with disabilities. Hospitals began to provide treatment for those with emotional disturbances and mental retardation. A manual alphabet for those with deafness was developed, and John Locke became the first person to differentiate between persons who had mental retardation and those who had emotional disturbance.

In America, the colonists treated people with severe mental disorders as criminals, while those who were harmless were left to beg or were treated as paupers. At one time, it was common practice to place them with the person who would provide for them at the least cost to the public.

The Nineteenth Century: The Beginning of Training

In 1799, Jean Marc Itard, a French physician, found a 12-year old boy who had been abandoned in the woods of Averyron, France. His attempts to civilized and educate the boy, Victor, established many of the educational principles presently in use in the field of special education, including developmental and multisensory approaches, sequencing of tasks, individualized instruction, and a curriculum geared toward functional life skills.

Itard's work had an enormous impact upon public attitude toward individuals with disabilities. During the late 1700s, rudimentary procedures were devised by which those with sensory impairments (i.e. deaf, blind) could be taught, closely followed in the early 1800s by attempts to teach students with mild intellectual disabilities and emotional disorders (i.e. at that time to as the "idiotic" and "insane"). Throughout Europe, schools for students with visual and hearing impairments were erected, paralleled by the founding of similar institutions in the United States. In 1817, Thomas Hopkins Gallaudet founded the first American school for students who were deaf, known today as Gallaudet University in Washington, D.C., one of the world's best institutions of higher learning for those with deafness. Gallaudet's work was followed closely by that of Samuel Gridley Howe, who was instrumental in the founding of the Perkins Institute for students who were blind in 1829.

The mid-1800s saw the further development of Itard's philosophy of education of students with mental disabilities. Around that time, Itard's student, Edward Seguin, immigrated to the United States, where he established his philosophy of education for persons with mental retardation in a publication entitled *Idiocy and Its Treatment by the Physiological Method* in 1866. Seguin was instrumental in the establishment of the first residential school for individuals with mental retardation in the United States.

State legislatures began to assume the responsibility for housing people with physical and mental disabilities. The institutional care was largely custodial. Institutions were often referred to as warehouses due to the deplorable conditions of many. Humanitarians like Dorthea Dix helped to relieve anguish and suffering to institutions for persons with mental illnesses.

1900 - 1919: Specific Programs

The early twentieth century saw the publication of the first standardized test of intelligence by Alfred Binet of France. The test was designed to identify educationally sub-standard children, but by 1916, the test was revised by an American Louis Terman, and the concept of the intelligence quotient (IQ) was introduced. Since then the IQ test has come to be used as a predictor of both retarded (delayed) and advanced intellectual development.

At approximately the same time, Italian physician Maria Montessori was concerned with the development of effective techniques for early childhood education. Although she is known primarily for her contributions to this field, her work included methods of education for children with mental retardation as well, and the approach she developed is used in preschool programs today.

Ironically, it was the advancement of science and the scientific method that led special education to its worst setback in modern times. In 1912, psychologist Henry Goddard published a study based on the Killikak family, in which he traced five generations of the descendants of a man who had one legitimate child and one illegitimate child. Among the descendants of the legitimate child were numerous mental defectives and social deviates. This led Goddard to conclude that mental retardation and social deviation were inherited traits, and therefore that mental and social deviates were a threat to society, an observation that he called the Eugenics Theory. Reinforcing the concept of retardation as hereditary was a popular philosophy called positivism. Falling by the wayside was seen as the natural, scientific outcome for the defective person in society. Consequently, during this time, mass institutionalization and sterilization of persons with mental retardation and criminals were practiced.

Public school programs for persons with mental retardation gradually increased during this same period. The first college programs for the preparation of special education teachers were established between 1900 and 1920.

1919 - 1949: Professional and Expansion of Services

Awareness of the need for medical and mental health treatment in the community was evidenced during the 1920s. Halfway houses became a means for monitoring the transition from institution to community living; outpatient clinics were established to provide increased medical care. Social workers and other support personnel were dispensed into the community to coordinate services for the needy. The thrust toward humane treatment within the community came to an abrupt halt during the 1930s and 1940s, primarily due to economic depression and widespread dissatisfaction toward the recently enacted social programs.

There are two factors related to World War I and II that helped to improve public opinion toward persons with disabilities. First was the intensive screening of the population of young men with physical and mental disabilities that were in the United States. Second, patriotism caused people to regard the enormous number of young men who returned from the wars with physical and emotional disabilities in a different light than they would have been regarded before that time. People became more sensitive to the problems of the veterans with disabilities, and this acceptance generalized to other groups in the special needs population. With increased public concern for people with disabilities came new research. John B. Watson introduced behaviorism, which shifted the treatment emphasis from psychoanalysis to learned behavior. In 1920, Watson theorized that maladaptive (or abnormal) behavior was learned by through conditioning.

B.F. Skinner followed with a book entitled the *Behavior of Organisms,* which outlined principles of operant behavior (i.e. voluntary) behavior.

In 1922, the Council for Exceptional Children (first called the International Council for Exceptional Children) was founded. During the 1920s, many comprehensive statewide programs were initiated. The number of special education programs in public schools increased at a rapid rate until the 1930s, when the push for humane and effective treatment of people with disabilities began to diminish once again. The period of the Depression was marked by large-scale institutionalization and lack of treatment. Part of the cause was inadequately planned programs and poorly trained teachers. WWII did much to swing the pendulum back in the other direction, however, and inaugurated the most active period in the history of the development of special education.

1950 - 1969: The Parents, the Legislators, and the Courts Become Involved

The first two decades of the second half of this century was characterized by increased federal involvement in general education, gradually extending to special education. In 1950, came the establishment of the National Association of Retarded Children, later renamed the National Association of Retarded Citizens (NARC). NARC was the result of the efforts among concerned parents who felt the need of an appropriated public education. Increased media coverage exposed the miserable conditions in some of the institutions devoted to caring for people with disabilities, especially those with intellectual and emotional disabilities, and treatment consequently became more humane.

It was at about this time that parents of children with disabilities discovered the federal courts as a powerful agent on behalf of their children. The 1954 decision in the Brown v. the Topeka Board of Education case guaranteed equal opportunity rights to a free public education for all citizens, and the parents of children and youth with disabilities insisted that their children be included in that decision. From this point on, the court cases and public laws enacted as a result of court decisions, are too numerous to include in their entirety. Only those few, which had the greatest impact on the development of special education as we know it today, are listed. Collectively, they are part of a movement in U.S. Supreme Court history known as the Doctrine of Selective Incorporation, under which the states are compelled to honor various substantive rights under procedural authority of the 14th Amendment.

History of Dyslexia

Though there is truly a long, arduous past for those with visible special needs and mental challenges, the history of dyslexia is a bit more scientifically driven from the very beginnings of the disorder's naming. Dyslexics were not cast away per se, but were not readily identified until the nineteenth century. This is perhaps due to the high illiteracy rate among much of humankind throughout the world up until the point of the industrial revolution, when suddenly, reading became a marketable skill for those who wanted to become lawyers, doctors, businessmen, and the like.

Prior to this, writing or scribing, as well as reading, were highly specific skills. Priests and trained scholars were readers and writer: not the majority of the population by any means. It was not common place for the average working man, and especially the woman, to ever need the skill of reading, or even writing. Early school houses served rudimentary curriculums for students who were not required to show up to class regularly for any set amount of years or skill levels. The job market was simply different prior to the nineteenth century. Many people were self-reliant, and reading was not necessary to be a farmer or a homesteader, or an indentured servant. Education was for the elite, the upper-class, and nobility, for centuries upon centuries.

Dyslexia's identification dates back to 1869 when Sir Francis Galton, a psychologist, started to look into the individual differences in children's learning abilities. At that time, educators and psychologists were not investigating the causes of childhood learning difficulties. In fact, public schools were just barely beginning to form in the United States at that point, as America slowly shifted from the one room, multi-aged school house model. Medical professionals were the people who treated learning difficulties, if at all, because learning problems were considered a medical condition.

By 1878. Adolph Kussmaul, a German neurologist, began the first recorded study of people with reading difficulties. He felt there was an underlying neurological impairment. He noted his patients wrote and read words 'in the wrong order' and he used the term 'word blindness' to label the problem.

In 1891, Dr. Dejerne wrote an article in the Lancet journal and reported a story of one his patients, who suffered brain injury after being struck in the head by a crowbar. Dr. Dejerne claimed his patient could no longer read, and the patient also lost other language functions as well. It was now believed that people with difficulty reading had some form of brain damage or brain injury.

In the 1930s, dyslexia appeared often in professional literature and by 1967, the Orton Dyslexia Society began. The main goal of the Society was to raise public awareness and describe the remedial needs of dyslexics.

The US Department of Education recognized dyslexia as a disorder or disability in 1994. Professionals still used the term 'dyslexia' and 'specific learning difficulties' although dyslexia was now specifically acknowledged. In 1997 the Orton Dyslexia Society changed its name to the International Dyslexia Association because they dealt with dyslexia across the globe and not just in the US.

Skill 10.03 **Applies current educational terminology and definitions regarding individuals with disabilities, including professionally accepted classification systems and current incidence and prevalence figures.**

Please refer to skill 2.04 for definitions regarding individuals with disabilities

Eligibility for special education services is based on a student having one of the disabilities identified in IDEA and demonstration of educational need through professional evaluation. Often a student with a disability will fall into more than one of the characteristics listed in IDEA 2004. For example, a student with a hearing impairment may also have a specific learning disability, or a student on the autism spectrum may also demonstrate a language impairment. In fact, language impairment is inherent in autism. Sometimes the eligibility is defined as a multiple disabilities (with one listed as a primary eligibility on the IEP and the others listed as secondary). Sometimes there are overlapping needs that are not necessarily listed as a secondary disability.

Teachers of special education students should be aware of the similarities between areas of disabilities as well as differences. Students with disabilities (in all areas) may demonstrate difficulty with social skills. For a student with hearing impairment, social skills may be difficult because of not hearing social language. The student with an emotional disturbance may have difficulty with social skills because of a special type of psychological disturbance. A student with autism, might be unaware of the social cues given with voice, facial expression, and body language. Each of these students would need social skill instruction, but in a different way.

Special educators should be knowledgeable of the cause and severity of the disability and its manifestations in the specific student when planning an appropriate special education program. Because of the unique needs of the child, such programs are documented in the child's IEP – Individualized Education Plan.

The following estimates of the prevalence of specific disabilities were given in IDEA 2004 Public law 108-446 and have been published over the past three decades.

Area of Exceptionality	Percent of School Population
Speech Impairment	3.7
Mentally Retardation	2.3
Emotionally Disturbance	2.0
Learning Disability	
Hearing Impairment	0.6
Deaf-Blind and other Multi-Disabilities	0.6
Orthopedic Impairment/Other Health Impairment	0.5
Visually Impairment	0.1
Total:	11.6

Source: U.S. Department of Education, Office of Special Education Programs, Data Analysis Systems (DANS).

Child Count

Reports containing the numbers and percentages of children and youth receiving special education and related services have been published by the U.S. Department of Education since school year 1976-1977. These reported statistics are based upon child count data received from the states and territories across the nation. These data have assisted in determining the extent to which children with disabilities across the nation are receiving services in accordance with the law.

The following table displays the reported numbers of students served in special education along with the corresponding percent for each exceptionality category for school years 2002-2003. Perusal of the data reveals the increase in total number served by exceptionality category. Decreases in some categories have been offset by increases in others.

Number and Percentages of Students Served Under IDEA, Part B and Number and Percentage, School Year 2004

Exceptionality Category	Number Served	Percent
Specific Learning Disabled	2,848,016	45.5
Speech or Language Impairments	1,317,422	21.0
Mental Retardation	579,130	9.3
Serious Emotional Disturbance	487,907	7.8
Multiple Disabilities	137,421	2.2
Hearing Impairments	75,800	1.2
Orthopedic Impairments	68,972	1.1
Other Health Impairments	518,343	8.2
Visual Impairments	27,409	0.4
Deaf-Blindness	1,423	0
Autism	178,244	2.9
Traumatic Brain Injury	23,722	0.4
All Disabilities	6,264,202	100.0

Source: U.S. Department of Education, Office of Special Education Programs, Data Analysis System (DANS), "Report of children with disabilities receiving special education under Part B of the Individuals with Disabilities Education Act," 2004. Data updated as of July 30, 2005.

Special Education Students, Broken into Categories

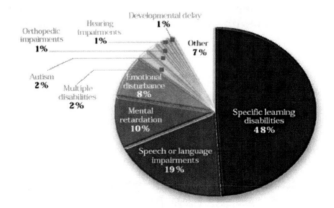

SOURCE: Education Week analysis of data from the U.S. Department of Education, Office of Special Education Programs, Data Analysis System, 2002-03.

Skill 10.04   Analyzes issues relating to definition and identification procedures for individuals with disabilities, including individuals from culturally and/or linguistically diverse backgrounds.

People with disabilities from diverse cultures are considerably disadvantaged in attaining complete participation in all areas of society. The obstacles that people from diverse cultures have to withstand include the lack of culturally appropriate outreach, language and communication barriers, attitudinal barriers, and the lack of individuals from diverse cultures in the disability services profession.

Individuals from diverse backgrounds are at a disadvantage when it comes to receiving services related to their disability and even being diagnosed with a disability. This is compounded by not having a significant number of teachers and other professional from diverse cultures, so the communication barriers continue to exist.

In fact, this issue is evident particularly in Texas, where the number of minority students in general, including those with special needs and disabilities, is growing at an exponential rate. Hispanic students made up more than 48 percent of the enrollment in Texas schools in the 2008-09 school year (Stutz, 2010). And the rate is increasing each year. Two out of three Texas teachers in the past school year were white, a proportion that has changed only slightly in recent years. The teacher pool was 22 percent Hispanic (Stutz, 2010).

Special education teachers should be aware that although students across disabilities may demonstrate difficulty in similar ways, the causes may be very different. For example, some disabilities are due to specific sensory impairments (hearing or vision), some due to cognitive ability (mental retardation), and some due to neurological impairment (autism or some learning disabilities). The reason for the difficulty should be a consideration when planning the program of special education intervention.

Additionally, Special Education Teachers should be aware that each area of disability has a range of involvement. Some students may have minimal disability and require no services. Others may need only a few accommodations and have 504 plan. Some may need an IEP that outlines a specific special education program which might be implemented in an inclusion/resource program, self-contained program, or in a residential setting.

Skill 10.05   Understands factors that influence the overrepresentation of culturally and/or linguistically diverse students in programs for individuals with disabilities.

The following has been extracted from an online article written by Dr. John Hosp for the RTI Action Network, 2013, accessible on:
http://www.rtinetwork.org/learn/diversity/disproportionaterepresentation

History of Disproportionate Representation in Special Education

In 1968, the U.S. Department of Education's Office of Civil Rights (OCR) began conducting a biennial survey of elementary and secondary schools in the United States (see Donovan & Cross, 2002, for a more detailed description). One focus of the data in these surveys has been placement in special education programs disaggregated by various student characteristics (e.g., sex, race/ethnicity, receipt of free/reduced price lunch, language proficiency). The patterns of disproportionality have remained relatively stable at the national level for the past 40 years (Chinn & Hughes, 1987; Donovan & Cross, 2002; Finn, 1982; Hosp & Reschly, 2004; MacMillan & Reschly, 1998; Oswald, Coutinho, Best, & Singh, 1999).

Most research on disproportionate representation has focused on the number of students identified for services or within specific programs or placements; however, calls have recently increased for shifting the focus away from documentation of disproportionality and directing it instead to the generation of solutions (e.g., Donovan & Cross, 2002; Markowitz, Garcia, & Eichelberger, 1997; Serna, Forness, & Nielsen, 1998). Researchers are stepping up to the challenge by examining additional factors that might be important for addressing students' needs, such as restrictiveness of placements (i.e., the percentage of time a student spends with his or her typical peers— a lower percentage indicating a more restrictive placement; Hosp & Reschly, 2002; Skiba, Poloni-Staudinger, Gallini, Simmons, & Feggins-Azziz, 2006); eligibility for multiple services, including special education and English language learner services (de Valenzuela, Copeland, Qi, & Park, 2006; Zehler, Fleishman, Hopstock, Pendzick, & Stephenson, 2003); and linking disproportionality to the achievement gap (Hosp & Reschly, 2004). These considerations, coupled with some of the core principles of RTI, show promise for addressing the issue of disproportionality.

However, there is first another important point about disproportionality to consider. Why is disproportionate representation of culturally and linguistically diverse students in special education services problematic? If every child is provided opportunity and services that are perceived as positive and effective on the basis of his or her needs, disproportionality is not a problem in and of itself (although it could be a reflection of broader social problems). Therein lies the heart of the concern. Special education programs and services are often not perceived as positive or effective; in addition, the processes for identifying and delivering services is not always applied equally or fairly. These are some of the reasons that RTI is being viewed as a promising way to address the underlying problems illuminated by disproportionality patterns.

| Skill 10.06 | Recognizes various perspectives (e.g., medical, psychological, behavioral, educational) regarding definitions and etiologies of disabilities. |

Please refer to skill 1.01

Skill 10.07   Understands cultural variations in beliefs, traditions, and values and their effects on the relationships among child, family, and school.

The student's capacity and potential for academic success within the overall educational experience are products of his/her total environment: classroom and school system, home and family, and neighborhood and community in general. All of these segments are interrelated and can be supportive, one of the other, or divisive, one against the other. As a matter of course, the teacher will become familiar with all aspects of the system, the school and the classroom pertinent to the students' educational experience. This would include not only process and protocols, but also the availability of resources provided to meet the academic, health, and welfare needs of students. It is incumbent upon the teacher to look beyond the boundaries of the school system to identify additional resources as well as issues and situations which will effect (directly or indirectly) a student's ability to succeed in the classroom.

Examples of Resources

- Libraries, museums, zoos, planetariums, etc.
- Clubs, societies and civic organizations, community outreach programs of private businesses, corporations, and government agencies.
- Departments of social services within the local community.

Initial contacts for resources outside of the school system will usually come from within the system itself: from administration, teacher organizations, department heads, and other colleagues.

Examples of Issues/Situations

Students from Multicultural Backgrounds: Curriculum objectives and instructional strategies may be inappropriate and unsuccessful when presented in a single format which relies on the student's understanding and acceptance of the values and common attributes of a specific culture which is not his/her own.

Parental/Family Influences: Attitude, resources and encouragement available in the home environment may be attributes for success or failure.

Families with higher incomes are able to provide increased opportunities for students. Students from lower income families will need to depend on the resources available from the school system and the community. This should be orchestrated by the classroom teacher in cooperation with school administrators and educational advocates in the community.

Family members with higher levels of education often serve as models for students, and have high expectations for academic success. And families with specific aspirations for children (often, regardless of their own educational background) encourage students to achieve academic success, and are most often active participants in the process.

A family in crisis (caused by economic difficulties, divorce, substance abuse, physical abuse, etc.) creates a negative environment which may profoundly impact all aspects of a student's life, and particularly his/her ability to function academically. The situation may require professional intervention. It is often the classroom teacher who will recognize a family in crisis situation and instigate an intervention by reporting on this to school or civil authorities.

Regardless of the positive or negative impacts on the students' education from outside sources, it is the teacher's responsibility to ensure that all students in the classroom have an equal opportunity for academic success. This begins with the teacher's statement of high expectations for every student, and develops through planning, delivery and evaluation of instruction which provides for inclusion and ensures that all students have equal access to the resources necessary for successful acquisition of the academic skills being taught and measured in the classroom.

Effects of Cultural and Environmental Influences on Students and Families

When minority or culturally diverse children are being screened for language problems, learning disabilities, or other exceptional student programs, the tests and assessment procedures must be non-discriminatory. Furthermore, testing should be done in the child's native language; however, if school instruction has not been in the native language, there may appear to be a problem because assessments typically measure school language. Even with native English-speaking children, there are differences between the language that is functional at home and in the community, and the language requirements of school.

Cultural and societal attitudes towards gender change over time. While attitudes towards younger boys playing with dolls or girls preferring sports to dolls have relaxed, children eventually are expected as adults to conform to the expected behaviors for males and females.

Other factors that influence students with disabilities and their families include abuse, neglect, and substance abuse.

Abuse

Whether abuse is to the child or to a parent, the effect transcends the immediate situation to interaction with others in the home, school, and community. If the child with a disability is the one who is abused, that child may be distrustful of others, and may continue the cycle of behavior by acting out in abusive ways towards others.

If a parent of the child with a disability is being abused, the child may feel responsible, and may be actively trying to protect the abused parent. At the least, the child will carry emotional and possibly psychological effects of living in a home where abuse happens. A parent who is being abused will be less likely to be able to attend to the needs of the child with a disability. Parents in this situation tend to be secretive about the fact that the abuse even occurs. Unfortunately, having a child with a disability puts excessive strain on a marriage. Abusive tendencies may be exaggerated.

Neglect

If a child with a disability is neglected physically or emotionally, he or she may exhibit a number of behaviors. The neglected child will most likely be distrustful of adults in general. The child may horde classroom materials, snacks, etc. At the very least he or she may be unfocused on school work. In the instances of abuse and neglect (or suspected instances), the special educator (as all educators) is a mandated reporter to the appropriate agency (such as Child Protective Services).

Substance Abuse

If a child with a disability or a parent is involved in substance abuse, that abuse will have a negative effect in the areas of finances, health, productivity, and safety. It is important for the special education teacher to be aware of signs of substance abuse. The teacher should also be proactive in teaching drug awareness. She should also know the appropriate school channels for getting help for the student as well as community agencies that can help parents involved in substance abuse.

Skill 10.08   Applies knowledge of the continuum of placement and services for individuals with disabilities.

Please refer to skill 3.06.

The following table represents the types of services on the continuum, with the most restrictive at the bottom of the table.

LOCATION OF SERVICE	DESCRIPTION
Regular Classroom	Student functions in the regular classroom with no special assistance or services.
Itinerant Teacher or Consultation in Regular Education	Student receives consultation or assistance from a special education teacher who comes to the general education classroom
Resource Room	Student remains in the regular classroom most of the time, but goes to a special education class for certain subjects or blocks of time.
Partially Self-Contained Special Education Class	Student attends some regular education classes and some special education classes, depending on the IEP.

Self-contained Special Education Class	Minimal attendance in regular education classes; majority of time spent in special education classes
Center School	Student attends a school designed to service a specific type of disability. May or may not be located in the student's neighborhood. May or may not be residential. May be a public school or a private school supported by the state.
Other Placements Outside the School Setting	Includes residential hospital (i.e. psychiatric or substance abuse) facilities, homebound placement, and services in juvenile correctional facilities or programs.

COMPETENCY 011   THE SPECIAL EDUCATION TEACHER APPLIES KNOWLEDGE OF PROFESSIONAL ROLES AND RESPONSIBILITIES AND ADHERES TO LEGAL AND ETHICAL REQUIREMENTS OF THE PROFESSION

Skill 11.01   **Knows how to exercise objective professional judgment, maintain a high level of competence and integrity in professional practice, and participate in professional activities and organizations that may benefit individuals with disabilities, their parents/guardians, and/or colleagues.**

The special education teacher comes to the job with past experiences as well as personal opinions and beliefs. It is vital that the teacher not let those personal persuasions guide him/her professionally. Objective professional judgment is important in all areas of the teacher's role.

Objective professional judgment should be exercised when considering the cultural, religious, and sexual orientations of the special educator's students and their families. An unbiased approach to communication maintains positive interaction and increased cooperation between home and school. The result is a better educational program that will meet the individual student's needs.

Objectivity should also be exercised when considering assessment of possible disability. Educator preference for a particular assessment should be secondary to matching the needs of the child with a specific instrument. Assessment tools should be researched-based and determined to be appropriate for the needs of the specific student.

When establishing the special education program, the specific student's IEP must be followed. If the special educator determines that the goals and objectives of the IEP no longer fit the child's needs, an ARD meeting should be called to review and possibly revise the document. Again, the revision of the IEP should be based on the needs of the child as determined objectively and not the personal preference of the teacher for a particular type of program or schedule. This objectivity should include: materials, scheduling, activities, and evaluation.

The student's IEP should also be focused on the learning standards established by the state. In particular, learning activities should be employed that provide measurable outcomes. Such data provides objective evaluation of student progress and mastery of the targeted standards.

Professional objectivity is crucial in communication with administration for representation of students' needs for placement, programming, materials, scheduling, and staffing needs. When documented, data-driven information is presented, optimum decisions are made for students with disabilities and for the school community in general.

A note regarding email communication: it is all recorded, documented, written evidence. Emails are a convenient way to communicate with parents as well as colleagues today, but beware of hastily sending email containing information regarding students. Emails can be beneficial for all parties; meetings can be scheduled quickly, recaps of meetings can be read quickly, documents can be attached with ease, etc. Teachers can use email to inform parents of recent grades, though a phone call is often preferred. Teachers can help their children make up missing assignments and/or prepare for upcoming quizzes and exams. In many ways the digital sharing of information, newsletters, assignments and class documents can be more effective than giving hard copies, since they can be accessed often and at any time, and have less of a risk of getting lost.

Skill 11.02 Knows consumer and professional organizations, publications, and journals relevant to individuals with disabilities, and knows how to access information on cognitive, communicative, physical, cultural, social, and emotional characteristics and needs of individuals with disabilities.

Various divisional organizations of the Council for Exceptional Children publish professional journals in their area of exceptionality. These journals and their corresponding organizations are listed, along with addresses from which journals may be ordered. Other journals are published by related fields such as rehabilitation, mental health, and occupational guidance. Below is a partial list of important professional organizations and publications which special education teachers should be familiar with:

1. American Association for Health, Physical Education, Recreation and Dance for the Handicapped
   1201 16th Street, N.W.
   Washington, D.C. 20005

2. Behavioral Disorders
   Council for Children with Behavioral Disorders (CCBD)
   1920 Association Drive
   Reston, VA 22091-1589

3. Career Development for Exceptional Individuals
   Division on Career Development (DCD)
   1920 Association Drive
   Reston, VA 22091-1589

4. Diagnostique
   Council for Educational Diagnostic Services (CEDS)
   1920 Association Drive
   Reston, VA 22091-1589

5. Education and Training of the Mentally Retarded
   Division on Mental Retardation (CEC-MR)
   1920 Association Drive
   Reston, VA 22091-1589

6. Journal of Childhood Communication Disorders
   Division for Children with Communication Disorders (DCCD)
   1920 Association Drive
   Reston, VA 22091-1589

7. Journal of the Division for Early Childhood
   Division for Early Childhood (DEC)
   1920 Association Drive
   Reston, VA 22091-1589

8. Journal for the Education of the Gifted
   The Association for the Gifted (TAG)
   JEG, Wayne State University Press
   5959 Woodward Avenue
   Detroit, MI 48202

9. Journal of Special Education Technology
   Technology and Media Division (TAM)
   JSET, UMC 68
   Utah State University
   Logan, UT 84322

10. Learning Disabilities Focus
    Learning Disabilities Research
    Division for Learning Disabilities
    1920 Association Drive
    Reston, VA 22091-1589

11. National Down Syndrome Society
    666 Broadway
    New York, NY 10011

12. Teacher Education and Special Education
    Teacher Education Division (TED)
    Special Press
    P.O. Box 2524, Dept. CEC
    Columbus, OH 43216

13. Teaching Exceptional Children
    1920 Association Drive
    Reston, VA 22091-1589

14. Technology and Learning
    600 Harrison Street
    San Francisco, CA 94107

15. Word of Mouth
    Hammill Institute on Disabilities
    8700 Shoal Creek Blvd.
    Austin, TX 78757-6897

Professional Organizations of Interest to Special Educators

The professional associations representing the spectrum of services for individuals with disabilities are listed here. Some of these organizations date from the pioneer times of special education and are still in active service.

Organization	Members	Mission
Alexander Graham Bell Association for the Deaf and Hard of Hearing 3417 Volta Place, N.W. Washington, D.C. 20007 Phone: (202) 337-5220 Fax: (202) 337-8314 Email: info@agbell.org http://listeningandspokenlanguage.org/	Teachers of the deaf, speech-language pathologists, audiologists, physicians, hearing aid dealers	To promote the teaching of speech, lip reading, and use of residual hearing to persons who are deaf; encourage research; and work to further better education of persons who are deaf.
Alliance for Technology Access 1119 Old Humboldt Road Jackson, TN 38305 Phone (800) 914-3017 Fax (731) 554-5283 TTY (731) 554-5284 Email:atainfo@ataccess.org http://www.Ataccess.org	People with disabilities, family members, and professionals in related fields, and organizations with work in their own communities and ways to support the mission.	To increase the use of technology by children and adults with disabilities and functional limitations.
American Council of the Blind 2200 Wilson Boulevard Suite 650 Arlington, VA 22201-3354 Phone: (202) 467-5081 (800) 424-8666 Fax: (703) 465-5085 Email: info@acb.org http://Acb.org	People with visual impairments or blindness, family members, and professionals, and people who want to become leaders or members of ACB chapters in their own communities.	To improve the well-being of all blind and visually impaired people by: serving as a representative national organization of blind people and conducting a public education program to promote greater understanding of blindness and the capabilities of blind people.

Organization	Members	Mission
American Council on Rural Special Education (ACRES) West Virginia University 509 Allen Hall, Box 6122 Morgantown, WV 26506 Phone: (304) 293-3450 Email: acres-sped@mail.wvu.edu http://acres-sped.org	Open to anyone interested in supporting their mission	To provide leadership and support that will enhance services for individuals with exceptional needs, their families, and the professionals who work with them, and for the rural communities in which they live
American Psychological Association 750 First Street, NE, Washington, DC 20002-4242 Phone: (800) 374-2721 Fax: (202) 336-5500 TTY: (202) 336-6123 http://www.apa.org	Psychologists and Professors of Psychology	Scientific and professional society working to improve mental health services and to advocate for legislation and programs that will promote mental health; facilitate research and professional development.
American Society for Deaf Children 800 Florida Avenue NE Washington, CD 20002 Phone: (800) 942-2732 Email: asdc@deafchildren.org http://www.deafchildren.org	Open to all who support the mission of the association	To provide support, encouragement and information to families raising children who are deaf or hard of hearing.
American Speech-Language-Hearing Association 2200 Research Boulevard Rockville, MD 20850 Phone: (301) 296-5700 http://www.asha.org	Specialists in speech-language pathology and audiology	To advocate for provision of speech-language and hearing services in school and clinic settings; advocate for legislation relative to the profession; and work to promote effective services and development of the profession.
The Arc of the United States 1825 K Street NW, Suite 1200 Washington, DC 20002 Phone: (800) 433-5255 http://www.thearc.org	Parents, professionals, and others interested in individuals with mental retardation	Work on local, state, and national levels to promote treatment, research, public understanding, and legislation for persons with mental retardation; provide counseling for parents of students with mental retardation.

Organization	Members	Mission
Asperger Syndrome Education Network (ASPEN) 9 Aspen Circle Edison, NJ 08820 Phone: (732) 321-0880 http://www.aspennj.org		Provides families and individuals whose lives are affected by Autism Spectrum Disorders and Nonverbal Learning Disabilities with education, support and advocacy.
Association for Children and Adults with Learning Disabilities 4900 Girard Road Pittsburgh, PA 15227 Phone: (412) 81-2253 http://www.acldonline.org	Parents of children with learning disabilities and interested professionals	Advance the education and general well-being of children with adequate intelligence who have learning disabilities arising from perceptual, conceptual, or subtle coordinative problems, sometimes accompanied by behavior difficulties.
Attention Deficit Disorder Association 15000 Commerce Pkwy, Suite C Mount Laurel, NJ 08054 Phone: (856) 439-9099 FAX: (856) 439-0525 Email: membership@add.org http://www.add.org	Open to all who support the mission of ADDA	Provide information, resources and networking to adults with AD/HD and to the professionals who work with them.
Autism Society of America 4340 East-West Hwy, Suite 350 Bethesda, MD 20814 Phone: (800) 328-8476 http://www.autism-society.org	Open to all who support the mission of ASA	To increase public awareness about autism and the day-to-day issues faced by individuals with autism, their families and the professionals with whom they interact. The Society and its chapters share a common mission of providing information and education, and supporting research and advocating for programs and services for the autism community.

Organization	Members	Mission
Brain Injury Association of America 8201 Greensboro Drive Suite 611 McLean, VA 22102 Phone: (703) 761-0750 http://www.biausa.org	Open to all	Provide information, education and support to assist the 5.3 million Americans currently living with traumatic brain injury and their families.
Formerly Child and Adolescent Bipolar Association (CABF), Now The Balanced Mind Parent Network 730 N. Franklin Street, Suite 501 Chicago, IL 60654-7225 Phone: (847) 492-8510 http://www.bpkids.org	Physicians, scientific researchers, and allied professionals who provide services to children and adolescents with bipolar disorder or depression, as well as parents and students.	Educate families, professionals, and the public about pediatric bipolar disorder; connects families with resources and support; advocates for and empowers affected families; and supports research on pediatric bipolar disorder and its cure.
Children and Adults with Attention Deficit/ Hyperactive Disorder (CHADD) 4601 Presidents Drive Suite 300 Lanham, MD 20706 Phone: (301) 306-7070 Fax: (301) 306-7090 http://www.chadd.org	Open to all	Provide resources and encouragement to parents, educators and professionals on a grassroots level through CHADD chapters.
Council for Exceptional Children (CEC) 2900 Crystal Drive, Suite 1000 Arlington, VA 22202 Phone: (888) 232-7733 TTY: (866) 915-5000 FAX: (703) 264-9494 http://www.cec.sped.org	Teachers, administrators, teacher educators, and related service personnel	Advocate for services for individuals with disabilities and gifted individuals. A professional organization that addresses service, training, and research relative to exceptional persons.

Organization	Members	Mission
Council for Educational Diagnostic Services 2900 Crystal Drive, Suite 1000 Arlington, VA 22202 Phone: (888) 232-7733 http://community.cec.sped.org/CEDS/home/	Members of the Council for Exceptional Children who are school psychologists, educational diagnosticians, [and] social workers who are involved in diagnosing educational difficulties	Promote the most appropriate education of children and youth through appraisal, diagnosis, educational intervention, implementation, and evaluation of a prescribed educational program. Work to facilitate the professional development of those who assess students. Work to further development of better diagnostic techniques and procedures.
Council of Administrators of Special Education 101 Katelyn Circle, Suite E Warner Robins, GA 31088 Phone: (478) 333-6892 Fax: (478) 333-2453 Email: lpurcell@casecec.org http://www.casecec.org	Members of the Council for Exceptional Children who are administrators, directors, coordinators, or supervisors of programs, schools, or classes for exceptional children; college faculty who train administrators	Promote professional leadership; provide opportunities for the study of problems common to its members; communicate through discussion and publications information that will facilitate improved services for children with exceptional needs.
Division for Communicative Disabilities and Deafness 2900 Crystal Drive, Suite 1000 Arlington, VA 22202 http://www.dcdd.us	Members of the Council for Exceptional Children who are speech-language pathologists, audiologists, teachers of children with communication disorders, or educators of professionals who plan to work with children who have communication disorders	Promote the education of children with communication disorders. Promote professional growth and research.

Organization	Members	Mission
Division for Early Childhood 3415 S. Sepulveda Blvd. Suite 1100, Unit 1127 Los Angeles, CA 90034 Phone: (310) 428-7209 Fax: (855) 678-1989 Email: dec@dec-sped.org http://www.dec-sped.org	Members of the Council for Exceptional Children who teach preschool children and infants or educate teachers to work with young children	Promote effective education for young children and infants. Promote professional development of those who work with young children and infants. Promote legislation and research.
Division for Physical, ~~and~~ Health and Multiple Disabilities 2900 Crystal Drive, Suite 1000 Arlington, VA 22202 Phone: (888) 232-7733 http://community.cec.sped.org/DPHMD/Home/	Members of the Council for Exceptional Children who work with individuals who have physical disabilities or educate professionals to work with those individuals	Promote closer relationships among educators of students who have physical impairments or are homebound. Facilitate research and encourage development of new ideas, practices, and techniques through professional meetings, workshops, and publications.
Division on Visual Impairments 2900 Crystal Drive, Suite 1000 Arlington, VA 22202 http://www.cecdvi.org	Members of the Council for Exceptional Children who work with individuals who have visual disabilities or educate professionals to work with those individuals	Work to advance the education and training of individuals with visual impairments. Work to bring about better understanding of educational, emotional, or other problems associated with visual impairment. Facilitate research and development of new techniques or ideas in education and training of individuals with visual problems.
Division on Career Development and Transition Two Ballston Plaza 1110 N. Glebe Road Arlington, VA 22201 2900 Crystal Drive, Suite 1000 Arlington, VA 22202 http://www.dcdt.org	Members of the Council for Exceptional Children who teach or in other ways work toward career development and vocational education of exceptional children	Promote and encourage professional growth of all those concerned with career development and vocational education. Promote research, legislation, information dissemination, and technical assistance relevant to career development and vocational education.

Organization	Members	Mission
Epilepsy Foundation of America (EFA) 8301 Professional Place Landover, MD 20785 Phone: (800) 332-1000 Fax: (301) 577-2684 http://www.epilepsyfoundation.org	A non-membership organization	Work to ensure that people with seizures are able to participate in all life experiences; and to prevent, control and cure epilepsy through research, education, advocacy and services.
Family Center on Technology and Disability (FCTD) 1825 Connecticut Avenue, NW 7th Floor Washington, DC 20009 Phone: (202) 884-8068 Fax: (202) 884-8441 Email: fctd@fhi360.org http://www.fctd.info	Non member association	Designed to support organizations and programs that work with families of children and youth with disabilities.
Hands and Voices P.O. Box Denver CO 80237 Phone: (866) 422-0422 http://www.handsandvoices.org	Families, professionals, other organizations, pre-service students, and deaf and hard of hearing adults who are all working towards ensuring successful outcomes for children who are deaf and hard of hearing.	Support families and their children who are deaf or hard of hearing, as well as the professionals who serve them.
The International Dyslexia Association 40 York Road, 4th floor Baltimore, Maryland 21204 Phone: (410) 296-0232 Fax: (410) 321-5069 http://www.interdys.org	Anyone interested in IDA and its mission can become a member	Provide information and referral services, research, advocacy and direct services to professionals in the field of learning disabilities.

Organization	Members	Mission
Learning Disabilities Association of America (LDA) 4156 Library Road Pittsburgh, PA 15234 Phone: (412) 341-1515 Fax: (412) 344-0224 http://www.ldanatl.org	Anyone interested in LDA and its mission can become a member	Provide cutting edge information on learning disabilities, practical solutions, and a comprehensive network of resources. Provides support to people with learning disabilities, their families, teachers and other professionals.
National Association of Special Education Teachers (NASET) 1250 Connecticut Avenue, N.W. Suite 200 Washington D.C. 20036 Phone and Fax: 800-754-4421 contactus@naset.org	All special education teachers in America; provides individual or group/district membership	The mission is to render all possible support and assistance to professionals who teach children with special needs. **NASET** promotes innovation in special education research, practice, and policy in order to foster exceptional teaching for exceptional children.
National Association of the Deaf (NAD) 8630 Fenton Street, Suite 820, Silver Spring, MD Phone: (209) 210-3819 TTY: (301) 587-1789, , FAX: (301) 587-1791 http://nad.org	Anyone interested in NAD and its mission can become a member	Promote, protect, and preserve the rights and quality of life of deaf and hard of hearing individuals in the United States of America.
National Mental Health 1 Choke Cherry Road Rockville, MD 20857 Phone: (877) SAMSA-7 www.samhsa.gov	Government Agency	Developed for users of mental health services and their families, the general public, policy makers, providers, and the media.

Organization	Members	Mission
TASH **(Formerly The Association for Persons with Severe Handicaps)** 1001 Connecticut Avenue, NW, Suite 235 Washington, DC 20036 Phone: (202) 540-9020 Fax: (202) 540-9019 http:// www.tash.org	Anyone interested in TASH and its mission can become a member	Create change and build capacity so that all people, no matter their perceived level of disability, are included in all aspects of society.
US Department of Education Office of Special Education and Rehabilitative Services 400 Maryland Avenue, SW Washington, D.C. 20202 Phone: (800) USA-LEARN http://www.ed.gov/about/offices/list/osers/index.html	Government Resource	Committed to improving results and outcomes for people with disabilities of all ages.
Wrights Law http://wrightslaw.com	Non-membership organization	Provide parent advocacy training and updates on the law throughout the country.
National Association for the Education of Young Children 1313 L St. N.W. Suite 500, Washington DC 20005 Phone: (800) 424-2460 http://www.naeyc.org		Promote service and action on behalf of the needs and rights of young children, with emphasis on provision of educational services and resources.
National Easter Seal Society 233 South Wacker Drive, Suite 2400 Chicago, IL 60606 Phone: (800) 221-6827 TTY: (312) 726-1494 http://www.easterseals.com	State units (49) and local societies (951); no individual members	Establish and run programs for individuals with physical impairments, usually including diagnostic services, speech therapy, preschool services, physical therapy, and occupational therapy.

Skill 11.03 **Applies skills for participating effectively in identifying, diagnosing, placing, and developing programming for students with disabilities, including using advocacy skills and competencies to support the education of students in least restrictive environments.**

Refer to Skill 2.04, Skill 3.04 and Skill 7.01 for further detail.

IEP Development

The ARD committee convenes to discuss the child's current functional level along with assessment results and information gathered from the committee. From that information, the committee agrees on the goals the child should be working toward. The committee then discusses the supports and services and modifications that the child needs to reach those goals. Finally, the ARD committee determines where those special education services will be provided (location and placement). The location where services will be provided and the student's placement must be in the student's least restrictive environment.

Special education services occur at a variety of levels, some more restrictive than others. The largest number of students (i.e. mild disabilities) is served in settings closest to normal educational placements. Service delivery in more restrictive settings is limited to students with severe or profound disabilities, who comprise a smaller population within special education. The exception is correctional facilities, which serve a limited and restricted populace.

Dismissal

A student may be dismissed from special education services is he or she no longer qualifies as having one of the disability categories identified in IDEA, or if he or she no longer exhibits a need for special education services. The student must be reevaluated prior to dismissal. Every three years, a triennial or reevaluation is held, to reassess the student's overall development, IEP structure and current psychoeducational testing. Dismissal may coincide with such meetings, or at an IEP meeting. Results from testing may indicate a student is ready to be released from various services.

Advocating for Students with Disabilities and the Special Education Program

Because of the unique needs of each student with disabilities, special education teachers are frequently advocates for their students and the special education program in general. In order to be an effective advocate, the teacher must be knowledgeable in a number of areas. First, the special educator must understand the general education program that is the counterpart of his or her program. Factors such as student expectations (learning standards), materials used, and teacher training and in-service provide a starting point. If the special educator is familiar with the goals and overall program for all students at a particular grade level, the teacher will have a clear picture of the direction he or she should take in working with the students with disabilities.

The special educator should also have a clear understanding of each student's strengths and needs. The special educator must consider how each student can participate in the general education curriculum to the extent that it is beneficial for that student (IDEA 2004).

In addition, special educators should have an understanding of alternate materials that would be useful or necessary and what resources for materials are available.

It is imperative that the special education teacher has a working knowledge of IDEA and NCLB in order to be familiar with the laws governing the delivery of special education services

Often advocacy happens between general and special education teachers. A special educator may see modification or accommodation possibilities that could take place in the general education classroom. It is the responsibility of the special educator to advocate for those possibilities to occur. The special education teacher may also offer to make supplementary materials or to work with a group of students in the general education setting. When students with disabilities are in an inclusion classroom, give and take on the part of both teachers as a team is crucial.

The special education teacher may need to be an advocate for the special education program or the needs of an individual student with the administration. Although success for all students is important to administration, often the teacher must explain the need for items such as comparable materials written at the different reading level, the need for assistance in the classroom, or the offering of specific classes or therapies.

AIM Targets – Consider the LRE (Least Restrictive Environment)

According to SAISD (San Antonio Independent School District, 2014, www.saisd.net), there are five areas designated as priorities in Special Education known as the Analyze, Improve, and Measure (AIM) targets. They are as follows:

1. **Initial Assessment- Must be completed in 60 days**
   - It determines whether a student has a disability and needs special education services
   - It provides instructional information, helps determine the individualized education program, and the goals in the Admission, Review, and Dismissal (ARD) committee meeting.
2. **Least Restrictive Environment (LRE)**
   - The general education instructional setting must be considered first.
   - There must be a continuum of services available.
   - Include non-academic and extracurricular activities with non-disabled peers.

3. Related Services

- Support goals in the Individual Education Plan (IEP)
- Are based on assessment and educational needs.
- Can be delivered in a variety of ways and locations.

4. Reevaluation

- Students must be considered for reevaluation every three years.
- Reevaluation determines whether a student is still eligible.
- Focuses on how to meet specific educational needs.
- The ARD will meet to review existing data and determine the scope of reevaluation

5. Transition

- On or before the age of 14, transition services must be discussed and a course of study planned.
- On or before the age of 16, an Individual Transition Plan (ITP) must be written.
- The ITP must be incorporated into the student's IEP.
- The student participates in the development of the ITP.
- Outside agencies may be involved in the meetings.
- 30 days' notice required to ITP meetings for agency participation.

Skill 11.04 **Applies knowledge of assurances and due process rights related to assessment, eligibility, and placement, and knows the rights and responsibilities of parents/guardians, students, teachers, other professionals, and schools.**

The Family Educational Rights and Privacy Act 1974 (FERPA), also known as the Buckley Amendment, assures confidentiality of student records. Parents are afforded the right to examine, review, request changes in information deemed inaccurate, and stipulate persons who might access their child's records.

"Due process is a set of procedures designed to ensure the fairness of educational decisions and the accountability of both professionals and parents in making these decisions" (Kirk and Gallagher, 1986, p. 24). These procedures serve as a mechanism by which the child and his family can voice their opinions or concerns, and sometimes dissents. Due process safeguards exist in all matters pertaining to identification, evaluation, and educational placement.

Due process occurs in two realms, substantive and procedural. Substantive due process is the content of the law (e.g. appropriate placement for special education students). Procedural due process is the form through which substantive due process is carried out (e.g. parental permission for testing). Public Law 101-476 contains many items of both substantive and procedural due process.

1. A due process hearing may be initiated by parents or the Local Education Agency (LEA) as an impartial forum for challenging decisions about identification, evaluation, or placement. Either party may present evidence, cross-examine witnesses, obtain a record of the hearing, and be advised by counsel or by individuals having expertise in the education of individuals with disabilities. Findings may be appealed to the state education agency (SEA) and if still dissatisfied, either party may bring civil action in a state of federal district court. Hearing timelines are set by legislation.

2. Parents may obtain an independent evaluation if there is disagreement about the education evaluation performed by the LEA. The results of such an evaluation: (1) must be considered in any decision made with respect to the provision of a free, appropriate public education for the child, and (2) may be presented as evidence at a hearing. Further, the parents may request this evaluation at public expense: (1) if a hearing officer requests an independent educational evaluation, (2) if the decision from a due process hearing is that the LEA's evaluation was inappropriate. If the final decision holds that, the evaluation performed is appropriate, the parent still has the right to an independent educational evaluation, but not as public expense.

3. Written notice must be provided to parents prior to a proposal or refusal to initiate or make a change in the child's identification, evaluation, or educational placement. The notice must include:

   a. A listing of parental due process safeguards.
   b. A description and a rationale for the chosen action.
   c. A detailed listing of components (e.g. tests, records, reports) which was the basis for the decision.
   d. Assurance that the language and content of notices were understood by the parents.

4. Parental consent must be obtained before evaluation procedures can occur, unless there is a state law specifying otherwise.

5. Sometimes parents or guardians cannot be identified to function in the due process role. When this occurs, a suitable person must be assigned to act as a surrogate. This is done by the LEA in full accordance with legislation.

Do not hesitate in becoming familiar with Wrightslaw. Special education teachers attend several meetings each year which pertain to this very crux of special education laws. The Wrightslaw website has a wealth of information regarding all facets of this skill. There is even a You Tube channel for Wrightslaw. The website for reviewing all the Wrightslaw details is: http://www.wrightslaw.com/

Skill 11.05   Knows legal and ethical issues (e.g., liability) relevant to working with individuals with disabilities, and knows how to conduct instructional and other professional activities consistent with the requirements of laws, rules and regulations, and local district policies and procedures, including complying with local, state, and federal monitoring and evaluation requirements

Please refer to skills 10.01 and 10.02

Despite challenges to the principles underlying PL 94-142 in the early 1980s, total federal funding for the concept increased as new amendments were passed throughout the decade. These amendments expanded services to infants, preschoolers, and secondary students. (Rothstein, 1995).

Following public hearings, Congress voted in 1990 not to include Attention Deficit Disorders (ADD) as a new exceptionality area. Determining factors included the alleged ambiguity of the definition and eligibility criteria for students with ADD, the large number of students who might be identified if it became a service delivery area, the subsequent cost of serving such a large population, and the fact that many of these students are already served in the exceptionality areas of learning disabilities and behavior disorders.

The revision of the original law that we now call IDEA included some other changes. These changes were primarily in language (terminology), procedures (especially transition), and addition of new categories (autism and traumatic brain injury).

Despite challenges to federal services and mandates in special education as an extension of the Fourteenth Amendment since 1980, there has actually been growth in mandated categories and net funding. The Doctrine of Selective Incorporation is the name for one major set of challenges to this process. While the 1994 conservative turnover in the Congress might seem to undercut the force of PL 94-132, three decades of recent history show strong bi-partisan support for special education, and consequently, IDEA, or a joint federal-state replacement, will most likely remain strong. Lobbyists and activists representing coalition and advocacy groups for those with disabilities have combined with bi-partisan congressional support to avert the proposed changes, which would have meant drastic setbacks in services for persons with disabilities.

There presently remain several philosophical controversies in special education. The need for labels for categories continues to be questioned. Many states are serving special needs students by severity level rather than by the exceptionality category.

Presently, special educators are faced with possible changes in what is considered to be the least restrictive environment (LRE) for educating students with special needs. Following upon the heels of the regular education initiative, the concept of inclusion has come to the forefront. Both of these movements were, and are, an attempt to educate special needs students in the mainstream of the regular classroom. Both limit pulling out students from regular classroom instructional activities, and both incorporate the services of special education teachers in the regular classroom in collaboration with general classroom teachers

Skill 11.06 **Knows the roles of and relationships among federal, state, and local entities with regard to the regulation and provision of special education and related services, including specialized health care services.**

Irving Independent School District v. Tatro 1984. IDEA lists health services as one of the "related services" that schools are mandated to provide to exceptional students. Amber Tatro, who had Spina Bifida, a developmental congenital disorder, required the insertion of a catheter on a regular schedule in order to empty her bladder. The issue was specifically over the classification of clean, intermittent catheterization as a medical service (not covered under IDEA) or a "related health service", which would be covered. In this instance, the catheterization was not declared a medical service, but a "related service" necessary for the student to have in order to benefit from special education. The school district was obliged to provide the service. The Tatro case has implications for students with other medical impairments who may need services to allow them to attend classes at the school.

School Board of Nassau County v. Arline, 1987. Established that contagious diseases are a disability under Section 504 of the Rehabilitation Act and that people with such disabilities are protected from discrimination, if otherwise qualified.

Skill 11.07 **Applies knowledge of practices that conform to standards and policies of the profession, including the Code of Ethics and Standard Practices for Texas Educators and the Council for Exceptional Children (CEC) Code of Ethics.**

The special educator is expected to use accepted teaching practices with measurable outcomes. The special educator is expected to use professionalism and confidentiality in his/her role as a teacher. Professional organizations provide a structure for understanding those expectations.

The *Council for Exceptional Children (CEC)* is a national professional organization (with state chapters) that encompasses teaching in of all areas of disability. The CEC has established a *Code of Ethics for Educators of Persons with Exceptionalities.* In brief, the code charges educators with continuing to learn best practices in the education of students with disabilities, providing a quality educational program that will best meet the needs of their students and their families, and abiding by legal and ethical guidelines of the profession.

The CEC has a number of *Special Interest Divisions,* such as the Council for Children with Behavioral Disorders (CCBD) and the Division for Culturally and Linguistically Diverse Exceptional Learners (DDEL).

In addition to the CEC, there are other organizations specific to particular disabilities. The *Learning Disabilities Association of American (LDA)* and the *National Center for Learning Disabilities (NCLD)* provide guidance in best practices and conduct for teachers of students with learning disabilities.

The *American Speech and Hearing Association (ASHA)* is one of the professional organizations for speech pathologists. The *Council on the Education of the Deaf* (CED) is a professional organization for educators of deaf children.

The *National Institute of Mental Health* also provides information on emotional disabilities, autism, and ADD/ADHD.

Membership in a reputable organization for educators of children with disabilities (such as the above examples) provides ongoing education through workshops and conventions, professional literature and communication with other professionals in the field. It is the educator's checkpoint for implementation of professional standards and policies.

Revised Code of Ethics and Standard Practices for Texas Educators (effective Sept. 1, 2002)

Statement of Purpose

The Texas educator shall comply with standard practices and ethical conduct toward students, professional colleagues, school officials, parents, and members of the community and shall safeguard academic freedom. The Texas educator, in maintaining the dignity of the profession, shall respect and obey the law, demonstrate personal integrity, and exemplify honesty. The Texas educator, in exemplifying ethical relations with colleagues, shall extend just and equitable treatment to all members of the profession. The Texas educator, in accepting a position of public trust, shall measure success by the progress of each student toward realization of his/her potential as an effective citizen. The Texas educator, in fulfilling responsibilities in the community, shall cooperate with parents and others to improve the public schools of the community.

Enforceable Standards

I. Professional Ethical Conduct, Practices, and Performance.

Standard 1.1. The educator shall not knowingly engage in deceptive practices regarding official policies of the school district or educational institution.

Standard 1.2. The educator shall not knowingly misappropriate, divert, or use monies, personnel, property or equipment committed to his/her charge for personal gain or advantage.

Standard 1.3. The educator shall not submit fraudulent requests for reimbursement, expenses, or pay.

Standard 1.4. The educator shall not use institutional or professional privileges for personal or partisan advantage.

Standard 1.5. The educator shall neither accept nor offer gratuities, gifts, or favors that impair professional judgment or to obtain special advantage. This standard shall not restrict the acceptance of gifts or tokens offered and accepted openly from students, parents or other persons or organizations in recognition or appreciation of service.

Standard 1.6. The educator shall not falsify records, or direct or coerce others to do so.

Standard 1.7. The educator shall comply with state regulations, written local school board policies and other applicable state and federal laws.

Standard 1.8. The educator shall apply for, accept, offer, or assign a position or a responsibility on the basis of professional qualifications.

II. Ethical Conduct Toward Professional Colleagues.

Standard 2.1. The educator shall not reveal confidential health or personnel information concerning colleagues unless disclosure serves lawful professional purposes or is required by law.

Standard 2.2. The educator shall not harm others by knowingly making false statements about a colleague or the school system.

Standard 2.3. The educator shall adhere to written local school board policies and state and federal laws regarding the hiring, evaluation, and dismissal of personnel.

Standard 2.4. The educator shall not interfere with a colleague's exercise of political, professional or citizenship rights and responsibilities.

Standard 2.5. The educator shall not discriminate against or coerce a colleague on the basis of race, color, religion, national origin, age, sex, disability, or family status.

Standard 2.6. The educator shall not use coercive means or promise of special treatment in order to influence professional decisions or colleagues.

Standard 2.7. The educator shall not retaliate against any individual who has filed a complaint with the SBEC under this chapter.

III. Ethical Conduct Toward Students.

Standard 3.1. The educator shall not reveal confidential information concerning students unless disclosure serves lawful professional purposes or is required by law.

Standard 3.2. The educator shall not knowingly treat a student in a manner that adversely affects the student's learning, physical health, mental health, or safety.

Standard 3.3. The educator shall not deliberately or knowingly misrepresent facts regarding a student.

Standard 3.4. The educator shall not exclude a student from participation in a program, deny benefits to a student, or grant an advantage to a student on the basis of race, color, sex, disability, national origin, religion, or family status.

Standard 3.5. The educator shall not engage in physical mistreatment of a student.

Standard 3.6. The educator shall not solicit or engage in sexual conduct or a romantic relationship with a student.

Standard 3.7. The educator shall not furnish alcohol or illegal/unauthorized drugs to any student or knowingly allow any student to consume alcohol or illegal/unauthorized drugs in the presence of the educator.

CEC Code of Ethics for Educators of Persons with Exceptionalities

We declare the following principles to be the Code of Ethics for educators of persons with exceptionalities. Members of the special education profession are responsible for upholding and advancing these principles. Members of The Council for Exceptional Children agree to judge and be judged by them in accordance with the spirit and provisions of this Code.

1. Special education professionals are committed to developing the highest educational and quality of life potential of individuals with exceptionalities.

2. Special education professionals promote and maintain a high level of competence and integrity in practicing their profession.

3. Special education professionals engage in professional activities which benefit individuals with exceptionalities, their families, other colleagues, students, or research subjects.

4. Special education professionals exercise objective professional judgment in the practice of their profession.

5. Special education professionals strive to advance their knowledge and skills regarding the education of individuals with exceptionalities.

6. Special education professionals work within the standards and policies of their profession.

7. Special education professionals seek to uphold and improve where necessary the laws, regulations, and policies governing the delivery of special education and related services and the practice of their profession.

8. Special education professionals do not condone or participate in unethical or illegal acts, nor violate professional standards adopted by the Delegate Assembly of CEC.

The Council for Exceptional Children. (1993). CEC Policy Manual, Section Three, part 2 (p. 4). Reston, VA: Author.

Originally adopted by the Delegate Assembly of The Council for Exceptional Children in April 1983.

Skill 11.08   Demonstrates awareness of personal cultural biases and differences that may affect one's teaching, and knows how to demonstrate respect for the culture, gender, and personal beliefs of individual students.

The role of the special education teacher is to advocate for the most appropriate education for students with disabilities and to guide them in discovering new knowledge and developing new skills to the best of their potential. According to IDEA 2004, the special educator is to prepare students for future, purposeful work in society with the possibility of post-secondary education or training.

Although each special educator is also a person with a set of experiences, opinions and beliefs, it is important the special educator remain unbiased and positive in his/her professional role with students, parents, administration, and the community. Differences in culture, religion, gender, or sexual orientation should not influence the teacher's approach to instruction, student goals or expectations, or advocacy.

In order to remain unbiased, the special educator should take advantage of opportunities to learn about various cultures, religions, genders, and sexual orientations. This can be accomplished through reading, classroom awareness activities as appropriate, and teacher in-service.

Reading to increase awareness and acceptance of cultural differences may be done through professional, adult literature as well as through books to be read with the class. Exposure to multicultural literature is an effective way of becoming familiar with other cultures. This familiarity breeds comfort and respect. Cultural activities in the classroom are especially well received as foods, dress, and games are easily added to curriculum and often address learning standards.

The teacher's reaction to differences with students and their families models the commonly taught character education trait of respect. When the teacher demonstrates respect for all individuals, it is likely that respect will also be practiced by students, parents, and administration.

Skill 11.09   Applies procedures for safeguarding confidentiality with regard to students with disabilities (e.g. by maintaining the confidentiality of electronic correspondence and records, ensuring the confidentiality of conversations), and recognizes the importance of respecting students' privacy.

One of the most important professional practices a teacher must maintain is student confidentiality. This extends far beyond paper records, and goes into the realm of oral discussions. Teachers are expected not to mention the names of students and often the specifics of their character in conversations with those who are not directly involved with them, inside and outside of school.

In the school environment, teacher record keeping comes in three main formats with specific confidentiality rules. All of the records stated below should be kept in a locked place within the classroom or an office within the school:

1. *Teacher's personal notes on a student.*

   When a teacher takes notes on a student's actions including behaviors and/or grade performance that are not intended to be placed in a school recorded format, such as a report card, the teacher may keep this information private and confidential to his/her own files. Teachers may elect to share this information or not.

2. *Teacher daily recorded grades and attendance of the student.*

   Teacher's grade books and attendance records are to be open to the parent/guardian of that child who wishes to check on their child. Only that child's information may be shared, not that of others.

3. *Teacher recorded/notation on records that appear in the student cumulative file.*

   There are specific rules regarding the sharing of the cumulative records of students.

   a. Cumulative files will follow a student that transfers within the school district, from school to school.

   b. All information placed in a cumulative file may be examined by a parent at any time it is requested. If a parent requests to review their child's cumulative file, the file should be shown as it is in its current state, including IEPs.

   c. When information from a cumulative file is requested by another person/entity outside of the parent/guardian, the information may not be released without the express written consent of the parent/guardian. The parental consent must specify which records may be shared with the other party of interest.

If a parent/guardian has expresses intent to enroll their child in another school, that school may receive the student's educational record without parental consent. However, according to FERPA, the school sending the information must make a reasonable attempt to notify the parent/guardian of the request.

Today's world is quickly becoming a digital environment. Teachers now communicate often with email and are keeping records in digital formats, often within a district mandated program. Teachers should keep in mind that emails and other electronic formats can be forwarded. When writing emails, teachers should maintain a professional decorum just as when they are writing their own records. Emails for public employees such as teachers may have a mandated storage time of up to ten years.

Skill 11.10 **Knows laws, regulations, and policies related to the provision of specialized health care in the educational setting.**

Please refer to Skills 10.01, 10.02 and I 11.06

COMPETENCY 012   THE SPECIAL EDUCATION TEACHER KNOWS HOW TO COMMUNICATE AND COLLABORATE EFFECTIVELY IN A VARIETY OF PROFESSIONAL SETTINGS.

Skill 12.01   Understands the collaborative roles of students, parents/ guardians, teachers, and other school and community personnel in planning and implementing an individualized program, and applies effective strategies for working collaboratively in various contexts.

The roles of the special education teacher and the general education teacher require that they work together to ensure that students with disabilities are able to attain their educational objectives in the least restrictive environment. Some students are best served in the general education setting with additional accommodations, while other students may be best served in the special education setting. The educators must work together to decide what educational program is best suited for the student and where the student can best meet his goals and objectives.

These decisions should be made during the student's ARD meeting. It is important that the special education teacher, the general education teacher, and other interested professionals, such as the speech pathologist, are in attendance at the meeting so they can discuss and collaborate on their role in helping the student.

Students with disabilities often experience insufficient access to and a lack of success in the general education curriculum. To promote improved access to the general curriculum for all learners, information should be presented in various formats using a variety of media forms; students should be given numerous methods to express and demonstrate what they have learned; and students should be provided with multiple entry points to engage their interest and motivate their learning.

Printed reading materials can be challenging to individuals with disabilities. Technology can help alleviate some of these difficulties by providing a change from printed text to electronic text that can be modified, enhanced, programmed, linked, and searched.

Text styles and font sizes can be changed as required by readers with visual disabilities. Text can be read aloud with computer-based text-to-speech translators and combined with illustrations, videos, and audio. Electronic text provides alternative formats for reading materials that can be tailored to match learner needs, and structured in ways that enhance the learning process and expand both physical and cognitive access.

Lesson Plan Collaboration

According to Walther-Thomas et al (2000), *Collaboration for Inclusive Education*, ongoing professional development that provides teachers with opportunities to create effective instructional practice is vital and necessary, "A comprehensive approach to professional development is perhaps the most critical dimension of sustained support for successful program implementation." The inclusive approach incorporates learning programs that include all stakeholders in defining and developing high quality programs for students. Figure 1 below shows how an integrated approach of stakeholders can provide the optimal learning opportunity for all students.

Figure 1-Integrated Approach to Learning

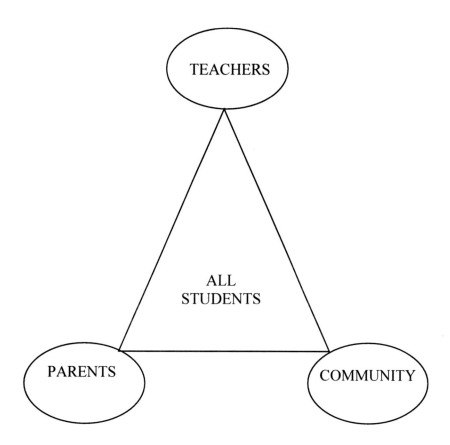

In the integrated approach to learning, teachers, parents, and community support become the integral apexes to student learning. The focus and central core of the school community is triangular as a representation of how effective collaboration can work in creating success for student learners. The goal of student learning and achievement now become the heart of the school community. The direction of teacher professional development in constructing effective instruction is clearly articulated in a greater understanding of facilitating learning strategies that develop skills and education equity for students.

Research has shown that educators who collaborate become more diversified and effective in implementation of curriculum and assessment of effective instructional practices. The ability to gain additional insight into how students learn and modalities of differing learning styles can increase a teacher's capacity to develop proactive instructional methods. Teachers who team teach or have daily networking opportunities can create a portfolio of curriculum articulation and inclusion for students.

People in business are always encouraged to network in order to further their careers. The same can be said for teaching. If teachers get together and discuss what is going on in their classrooms, those discussions make the "whole" much stronger than the parts. Even if there are not formal opportunities for such networking, it is wise for schools or even individual teachers to develop them and seek them out.

Skill 12.02   Applies knowledge of factors that promote effective communication and collaboration with students, parents/ guardians, teachers, paraprofessionals, and other school and community personnel.

Effective communication must occur between teacher and students, as well as among students. Clarity of expression as well as appropriate feedback is essential to successful teaching.

The special educator needs to be able to teach students who require varying techniques and approaches. She must be able to recognize specific needs, must possess diagnostic capabilities, and must make the necessary environment and instruction adaptations, all on an individual basis.

Teachers must be able to diagnose individual learning styles because the way in which students learn differs just as abilities vary. Learning can be affected by environmental elements like sound, room arrangement, and physical elements such as time of day, mobility. Coupled with the concern for learning styles is the use of sensory channels such as visual, auditory, and kinesthetic. The teacher of students with special needs must identify modality channels through which students process information most proficiently.

Special techniques are needed in order to teach basic skills, students vary in their rate of learning, need for routine, and ability to memorize or retain what they learn, reasoning skills, and ability to generalize newly acquired concepts. Students must be able to learn from simple to more complex levels within a task hierarchy in order to experience success, and become independent learners.

The teacher must be able to observe non-verbal cues given by students that signal confusion, boredom, or general restlessness. The teacher might decide, based on student reaction or body language, that too much material is being covered. A teacher may need to shorten the lesson and incorporate several personalized questions or examples to increase student involvement and attention.

Not all communication is delivered in a verbal manner. Indeed, words spoken are not always true indicators of what a person means and feels. Non-verbal communication, such as body language, facial expression, tone of voice, and speaking patterns, are all clues to the underlying message the student is attempting to deliver. The teacher demonstrates her willingness to listen by sitting close, leaning forward, making eye-to-eye contact, and showing understanding by nodding or smiling. By so doing, the teacher is sending the message that he or she cares, is concerned about the student's feelings, and will take the time necessary to understand what is really being communicated.

To facilitate further communication, the teacher must become an active listener. This involves much more than just restating what the person has said. The teacher's responses must reflect the other person's feelings rather than the spoken language. It is essential that the teacher say back what she understands the student's message to mean, as well as the feelings perceived, and ask for correctness of interpretation. Often, teachers enter into active listening, with body language conveying a willingness to listen, but respond in such a way that judgment or disapproval of the underlying message is conveyed. Evaluative responses from the listener will decrease attempts to communicate. Encouragement toward communicative efforts is enhanced by use of statements rather than questions, spoken in the present tense and with use of personal pronouns, reflective of current feelings about the situation, and offering self-disclosure of similar experiences or feelings if the teacher feels inclined to do so.

Response to the child's feelings is particularly important since the student's message may not convey what he or she actually feels. For example, a student who has failed a test may feel inadequate and have the need to blame someone else, such as the teacher, for the failure. The student might say to the teacher, "You didn't tell me that you were including all the words from the last six weeks on the spelling test." The teacher, if responding solely to the spoken message might say, "I know I told you that you would be tested over the entire unit. You just weren't listening!" The intuitive, sensitive teacher would look beyond the spoken words by saying, "You're telling me that it feels bad to fail a test." By responding to the child's feelings, the teacher lets the student know that he/she understands his personal crisis, and the student is encouraged to communicate further.

SUPPORT AND PROFESSIONAL SERVICES

When making eligibility, program, and placement decisions about a student, the special education teacher serves as a member of a multidisciplinary team. Teachers are involved in every aspect regarding the education of individual students; therefore, they need to be knowledgeable not only about teaching and instructional techniques, but also know about support services. These services will need to be coordinated, and teachers must be able to work in a collaborative manner.

Close contact and communication must be established and maintained between the school district staff, each base school, and the various specialists (or consultants) providing related services. These persons often serve special needs students in auxiliary (i.e., providing help) and supplementary (i.e., in addition to) ways. The principles and methods of special education must be shared with regular educators, and tenets and practices of regular education must be conveyed to special educators. Job roles and unique responsibilities and duties of support specialists like speech/language pathologists, physical and occupational therapists, social workers, school psychologists, nurses, and others need to be known by all teachers.

The services which can be provided by community resources, and the support that can be given by parents and professional organizations, must be known to all in order for maximum education for exceptional students to occur. Professional services are offered on a local, state, and national level for most areas of disability. Teachers are able to stay abreast of most current practices and changes by reading professional journals, attending professional conferences, and maintaining membership in professional organizations.

Identifying Principles and Analyzing Factors Related to the Coordination of Efforts

When professionals work together to provide services for students with disabilities, it is important that they work as a cohesive team using information sharing systems and proper scheduling procedures.

A system should be put into place for sharing program materials, tracking student's mastery of goals and objectives, and supporting the various requirements of administrative and teaching staff. Because of the variety of learning objectives and the need to make the special education curriculum appropriate for each student, information sharing is critical. It is not uncommon for a teacher in one part of the school to be completely unaware of what another teacher is doing. Two teachers may have similar students with similar intensive needs, and by sharing information, lesson plans, and behavior modification strategies, the workload is shared and students benefit from a more cohesive program.

Professionals also need to work together to ensure that students with disabilities are receiving the services outlined in the IEP. The speech pathologist, the occupational therapist, the general education teacher, and the special education teacher may all be providing services to one student. In order to ensure that the proper time is allotted for each service, the professionals involved will have to work together to develop a schedule for the student to ensure that nothing is left out and all areas outlined in the IEP are addressed. This will also help when ensuring the student's with disabilities that can be taught in groups are grouped with other students that may have the same requirements. This can only be effectively done when professional share schedules, student information and student requirements. If they work together, they can accomplish a lot more then when working independently.

Assuring that Students with Disabilities Receive Services as Specified in Their IEPs

The student's IEP must state the special education and related services and supplementary aids and services to be provided to the student. A statement of the program modifications or supports for school personnel that will allow the student to become involved in and progress in the general curriculum, should also be included in the IEP. In the past, students with disabilities were sometimes placed in the regular education classroom for the sake of inclusion without any help or support. IDEA '97 required that supplementary aids and services, accommodations, modifications, and supports play a more important role in a student's education.

The IEP should specify supports for school personnel. The decisions as to which supplementary aids and services, accommodations, modifications or supports are appropriate for a particular student are to be made on an individualized basis by the ARD committee.

The approach should be to create from the beginning a curriculum with built-in supports for diverse learners, rather than to fit in supplementary aids and services, accommodations, modifications, or supports after the fact.

The IEP should include ways for the parent and the teacher to objectively measure the student's progress or lack of progress in the special education program. If the student is not receiving the services specified in the IEP, then they may not be able to meet the goals outlined in their IEP. Careful monitoring and reporting of goals and objectives on the same schedule as progress is reported for students in general education should help ensure that student's receive the services to which they are entitled.

If the student is entitled to additional services from a speech pathologist, occupational therapist, or other specialist, the teacher should ensure that the specified services outlined in the IEP are being provided to the students. This can be done by working with the principal or other administrators and discussing how much time has been allotted for the additional services and ensuring that each student receives the time allotted and spelled out in his/her IEP.

The Roles of Community Personnel in Providing Services to Students with Special Needs, Including Transition Services.

Community personnel contribute valuable services and expertise in their respective areas. A team approach between district ancillary services and local school-based staff is essential.

Educational Diagnostician or Licensed Specialist in School Psychology (LSSP). The diagnostician participates in the referral, identification, and program planning processes. The diagnostician contributes to the multidisciplinary team by adding important observations, data, and inferences about the student's performance. The person in this role conducts an evaluation, by observing the student in the classroom environment, taking a case history, and administers a battery of formal and informal individual tests. The diagnostician is involved as a member of a professional team throughout the stages of referral, assessment, placement, and program planning.

Physical Therapist (PT). The PT works with disorders of bones, joints, muscles, and nerves following medical assessment. Physical therapy includes the use of adaptive equipment, and prosthetic and orthotic devices to facilitate independent movement. This type of therapy helps individuals with disabilities to develop or recover their physical strength and endurance.

Occupational Therapist (OT). The OT is trained in helping students develop self-help skills (e.g., self-care, motor, perceptual, and vocational skills). The students are actively involved in the treatment process to quicken recovery and rehabilitation. Fine motor, as well as gross motor skills are often focal points of remediation.

Speech and Language Pathologist (SLP). The SLP assists in the identification and diagnosis of children with speech or language disorders.

School Nurse. The school nurse offers valuable information about diagnostic and treatment services. She is knowledgeable about diets, medications, therapeutic services, health-related services, and care needed for specific medical conditions.

Paraprofessionals and General Education Teachers. Paraprofessionals and general education teachers are important collaborators with teachers of exceptional students. Although they may have daily exposure to exceptional students, they may not have the theoretical or experience to assure their effective interaction with such students. They do bring valuable perspective to, and opportunities for breadth and variety in, an exceptional child's educational experience. General education teachers also offer curriculum and subject matter expertise and a high level of professional support, while paraprofessionals may provide insights born of their particular familiarity with individual students. CEC suggests that teachers can best collaborate with general education teachers and paraprofessionals by:

- Offering information about the characteristics and needs of children with exceptional learning needs.
- Discussing and brainstorming ways to integrate children with exceptionalities into various settings within the school community.
- Modeling best practices and instructional techniques and accommodations, and coaching others in their use.
- Keeping communication about children with exceptional learning needs and their families confidential.
- Consulting with these colleagues in the assessment of individuals with exceptional learning needs.
- Engaging them in group problem-solving and in developing, executing, and assessing collaborative activities.
- Offering support to paraprofessionals by observing their work with students, and offering feedback and suggestions.

Related Service Providers and Administrators. Related service providers and administrators offer specialized skills and abilities that are critical to a exceptional education teacher's ability to advocate for his or her student and meet a school's legal obligations to the student and his/her family. Related service providers, such as speech, occupational and language therapists, and psychologists, offer expertise and resources unparalleled in meeting a child's developmental needs. Parents may also have a tutor for the student, perhaps to work on a particular content area which presents difficulty for the student. Administrators are often experts in the resources available at the school and local education agency levels, the culture and politics of a school system, and can be powerful partners in meeting the needs of exceptional education teachers and students.

A teacher's most effective approach to collaborating with these professional includes:

- Confirming mutual understanding of the accepted goals and objectives of the student with exceptional learning needs as documented in his/her IEP.
- Soliciting input about ways to support related service goals in classroom settings.
- Understanding the needs and motivations of each and acting in support whenever possible; facilitating respectful and beneficial relationships between families and professionals.
- Regularly and accurately communicating observations and data about the child's progress or challenges.

Skill 12.03 Knows how to foster respectful and beneficial relationships between families and professionals in the school and community.

One of the responsibilities of the special education teacher is to be the contact point for parents. The students' parents expect the special education teacher to be the unique professional that understands their child better than anyone else in the building. The parents expect the teacher to make and maintain contact with others in the educational setting who will interact with their child.

When parents/guardians know that they can talk to one teacher and that teacher will share the information that will benefit their child throughout the educational setting, they are confident in the ability of the teacher and learn to respect him/her at a higher level. The special education teacher should utilize his or her knowledge to discover community resources that may prove beneficial to the parents/guardians during and after their child's time in the public educational setting.

There are various reasons parents may not be happy with the school. Sometimes they may feel their child is not receiving the services specified on the IEP. Some may not be happy with the least restrictive environment enacted. A professional manner in addressing these situations will foster confidence that the school is providing the best placement for their child. Sometimes a parent need to "vent" their anger because they too become frustrated and are looking for how best to help their child at home.

Effective teaching and learning for students begins with teachers who can demonstrate sensitivity for diversity in teaching and relationships within school communities. Student portfolios include work that has a multicultural perspective and inclusion where students share cultural and ethnic life experiences in their learning. Teachers are responsive to including cultural and diverse resources in their curriculum and instructional practices.

Exposing students to culturally sensitive room decorations and posters that show positive and inclusive messages is one way to demonstrate inclusion of multiple cultures. Teachers should also continuously make cultural connections that are relevant and empowering for all students and communicate academic and behavioral expectations. Cultural sensitivity is communicated beyond the classroom with parents and community members to establish and maintain relationships.

Diversity can be further defined as the following:

- Differences among learners, classroom settings and academic outcomes
- Biological, sociological, ethnicity, socioeconomic status psychological needs, learning modalities and styles among learners
- Differences in classroom settings that promote learning opportunities such as collaborative, participatory, and individualized learning groupings
- Expected learning outcomes that are theoretical, affective and cognitive for students

The target of diversity allows teachers a variety of opportunities to expand their experiences with students, staff, community members and parents from culturally diverse backgrounds, so that their experiences can be proactively applied in promoting cultural diversity inclusion in the classroom. Teachers are able to engage and challenge students to develop and incorporate their own diversity skills in building character and relationships with cultures beyond their own. In changing the thinking patterns of students to become more cultural inclusive in the 21st century, teachers are addressing the globalization of our world.

Skill 12.04   Knows typical concerns of families of individuals with disabilities and appropriate strategies to support families in dealing with these concerns.

All parents share some basic goals for their children. They want their children to grow up to be healthy, happy members of society who lead independent lives with productive employment. Parents of students with disabilities are no different, although the path that their children take may have additional turns and obstacles along the way.

Health: Many children with disabilities have associated health problems or are at risk for health problems. Many also take medication(s) routinely for health or behavioral conditions. Parents of students with disabilities are concerned with their child's long range health, the cost of health care (as children as later as adults), and the effects of medication on their child's behavior, health, and school work.

Happiness: The quality of life for more severely disabled children is different from that of the general population. Even students with less severe physical conditions (for example, a learning disability) may have lower self-esteem because they feel "stupid" or "different" because they leave the inclusion classroom for some special education services. Students with disabilities often have difficulty making friends which can also impact happiness.

Parents of students with disabilities feel the emotional impact of the disability on their children. Parents are anxious to help their children feel good about themselves and fit in to the general population of their peers.

Social goals may be included on the IEP. Some students, (particularly those on the autism spectrum) may have a specified time on the IEP to meet with a speech and language pathologist to work on social language. Other students may meet regularly with the school counselor or psychologist to discuss situations from the classroom or general school setting.

Independence: Initially, parents of students with disabilities may be somewhat overprotective of their child. Soon after, however, parents begin to focus on ways to help their child function independently.

Young children with disabilities may be working on self-care types of independence such as dressing, feeding, and toilet use. Elementary students may be working on asking for assistance as needed, completing work, being prepared for class with materials (books, papers, etc.) High school students may be working on driving, future job skills, or preparation for post-secondary education.

Job Training: IDEA 2004 addresses the need for students with a disability to be prepared for a job or post-secondary education in order to be independent, productive members of society.

Job training goals and objectives for the student with a disability may be vocational such as food service, mechanical, carpentry, etc. Job training goals for other students may include appropriate high school coursework to prepare for a college program.

Productivity: Ultimately, the goal of parent and school is for the student to become a productive member of society who can support himself financially and live independently. This type of productivity happens when the student becomes an adult with a measure of good health, positive self-esteem and ability to interact positively with others, independent personal and work skills, and job training.

Particular Stages of Concern: Parents of students with special needs deal with increased concern at times when the child is going into a new stage of development or age. Some of these times include: when the child is first identified as having a disability, entrance into an early childhood special education program, kindergarten (when it is evident that the disability remains despite services received thus far), third grade (when the student is expected to use more skills independently), junior high school, and entrance into high school.

Additional IEP goals and objectives may be warranted at these times as the student is expected to use a new set of skills or may be entering a new educational setting.

It should be noted that parents are often more concerned when a younger, nondisabled sibling surpasses the child with the disability in some skill (such as feeding or reading). Previously, the parents may not have fully been aware of what most children can do at a particular age.

Skill 12.05 **Applies knowledge of strategies for encouraging and assisting parents/guardians in their role as active participants in their children's education, and applies procedures for planning and conducting collaborative conferences with parents/ guardians.**

Strategies for Parent-Teacher Conferences

Parent-teacher conferences are scheduled at regular intervals throughout the school year. These conferences provide excellent opportunities to discuss their children's progress, what they are learning and how it may relate to future plans for their academic growth

Before the Conference:

1. Be Prepared! The parents/guardians may be interested in seeing their children's records. You should be ready to share your student's portfolios, assessments, and other pertinent information. Make sure your preparation for these meetings allows for you to share grades of the individual child without sharing the information of another.
2. Check to see if there are any possible mistakes in your record keeping.
3. Write down at least three positive comments you would like to share with the parent. This is a way to declare the positives if you have a need to discuss negatives.
4. Schedule a set amount of time for each conference. Don't overbook your schedule! Remember that some conferences should be allotted more time than others.
5. Anticipating parents' questions will also provide you with the opportunity to appear professional when they are asked.
6. Remember the goal of the conference goes beyond simple communication; it is to forge an alliance to work together for the betterment of their child.
7. Ask your mentor for suggestions in preparing for the conference.

During the Conference:

1. Maintain a professional decorum! Remember the student's needs come first!
2. Remember this is your opportunity to learn about the student from his/her parents. You must show that you value their information.

3. Don't monopolize the time. While you may things you consider important to share, parents need opportunities to voice their own concerns.
4. Be an active listener! If you must take notes, let the parents know why you have chosen to do this.
5. Remember to ask for suggestions. Get the "inside information" on the strategies that work with the parents. This enables you to show a united front.
6. Closure: Orally summarize the conference at the end. Schedule another conference if needed.

After the Conference:

1. Review your notes. This will help you prepare a course of action.
2. Follow through! If you and the parent agreed upon a strategy or something that needed to be done on your part make sure you follow through.
3. Share any pertinent information with others who work with the student.
4. Commit yourself to maintaining the strength of the parent school connection.
5. Document the time, place, and participants for future reference.

The best resource a teacher has in reaching a student is having contact with his/her parents/guardians. Good teaching recognizes this fact and seeks to strengthen this bound through communication.

The first contact a teacher has with parents should be before the school year starts. While the teacher may be required to send a letter out stating the required supplies for the class, this does not count as an initial contact.

Parents are accustomed to hearing that their child has done something bad/wrong when they receive a phone call from a teacher. Parents should be contacted whenever possible to give positive feedback. When the teacher calls John's mother and says, "John got an A on the test today," the teacher has just encouraged the parent to maintain open communication lines. A good rule of thumb is to give three positive calls for every negative call.

Modern technology has opened two additional avenues for communicating with parents. School/ classroom websites are written with the intent of sharing regularly with parents/guardians. Many teachers now post their plans for the marking period and provide extra-credit/homework from these websites. Email is now one of the main modes of communication in the world today. Most parents now have email and are more than willing to give the teacher their email address to be kept appraised of their child's academic and behavioral needs.

Skill 12.06 **Applies knowledge of effective communication in various professional contexts, and knows ethical practices for confidential communication regarding individuals with disabilities.**

Parents and Families

Families know students better than almost anyone, and are a valuable resource for teachers of exceptional students. Often, an insight or observation from a family member, or his/her reinforcement of school standards or activities, mean the difference between success and frustration in a teacher's work with children. Suggestions for relationship building and collaboration with parents and families include:

- Using laypersons' terms when communicating with families, and making the communication available in the language of the home.
- Searching out and engaging family members' knowledge and skills in providing services, educational and therapeutic, to student.
- Exploring and discussing the concerns of families and helping them find tactics for addressing those concerns.
- Planning collaborative meetings with children and their families, and assisting them to become active contributors to their educational team.
- Ensuring that communications with and about families is confidential and conducted with respect for their privacy.
- Offering parents accurate and professionally presented information about the pedagogical and therapeutic work being done with their child.
- Keeping parents abreast of their rights, of the kinds of practices that might violate them, and of available recourse if needed.
- Acknowledging and respect cultural differences.

Skill 12.07 **Knows the types of information generally available from parents/guardians, school officials, the legal system, and community service agencies.**

Knowing where to find information is an essential part of being a teacher. Parents, school officials, the legal system, and community agencies are places the special education teacher can learn more to assist students.

Parents generally have the most information. They know what happens from the moment a child wakes to the time he or she goes to bed. They have seen the child grow, fail, and succeed. The information provided by the parent can assist the teacher in developing strategies to reach the student. Parents can provide information on their child's social interactions, intellectual interests, and their emotional and physical health.

Questions to ask the parents include:

- How does your son/daughter communicate with others at home? With his/her peers? Does he/she relate well to adults?
- Does your child have need help following directions at home?
- Can the student sense the feelings of others?
- Does your child take medication? What is the medication?
- What are your son/daughters hobbies? What are your child's study habits?

School officials such as principals and special education administrators also have information to share. They are often the people who have seen the student in a variety of situations and contexts through the years he or she has been in the school, and often are the ones that the student can claim as the one constant in their time in school. They often will share information on past behaviors, home life, academics, and what strategies they know work best with the student. Attendance clerks can also provide information.

There are times that the legal system is involved with one of your students. Parole officers or child protective social workers may provide information and seek information as well. When this happens, it is best to check with the school administration about procedural guidelines

Skill 12.08   Applies knowledge of the collaborative and consultative roles of special education teachers, paraprofessionals, and other school personnel in integrating individuals with disabilities into general educational settings.

Please refer to skills 12.01 and 12.02

Skill 12.09   Knows how to collaborate with teachers in the general educational setting and other school and community personnel to integrate individuals with disabilities into various learning environments.

Parent and Professional Advocacy Activity and Parent Organization

There have always been, and will always be, exceptional children with special needs, but special education services have not always been in existence to provide for these needs. Private school and state institutions were primary sources of education for individuals with retardation in earlier years. The 9th and 10th amendments to the U.S. Constitution leave education as an unstated power, and therefore vested in the states. As was the practice in Europe, government funds in America were first appropriated to experimental schools to determine whether students with disabilities actually could be educated. During the mid-twentieth century, legislators and governors in control of funds, faced with evidence of need and the efficacy of special education programs, refused to expend funds adequately, thus creating the ultimate need for federal guidelines in PL 94-142 to mandate flow-through money. Concurrently, due process rights and procedures were outlined, based on litigation and legislation enacted by parents of children with disabilities, parent organizations, and professional advocacy groups. "Public support in the form of legislation and appropriation of funds has been achieved and sustained only by the most arduous and persevering efforts of individuals who advocate for exceptional children." (Hallahan & Kauffman, 1986, p. 26).

Parents, professionals, and other members of advocacy groups and organizations finally succeeded in bringing to the attention of legislators astounding data about the population of youth with disabilities in our country. Among the findings revealed, Congress noted that: (1) there were more than eight million children with disabilities in the United States, and more than half were not receiving an appropriate education; (2) more than one million children with disabilities were excluded from the educational system, and many other children with disabilities were enrolled in regular education classes where they were not benefiting from the educational services provided because of their undetected conditions; and (3) due to inadequate educational services within the public school systems, families were forced to seek services outside the public realm. Years of advocacy effort resulted in the current laws and court decisions mandating special education at a federal level.

Teachers of students with disabilities are expected to manage many roles and responsibilities, not only as concern their students, but also with respect to students' caregivers and other involved educational, medical, therapeutic, and administrative professionals. Because the needs of exceptional students are by definition multidisciplinary, a teacher of exceptional children often serves as the hub of a many-pronged wheel, communicating, consulting, and collaborating with the various stakeholders in a child's educational life. Managing these relationships effectively can be a challenge, but is central to successful work in exceptional education.

Skill 12.10   Knows how to serve as a resource person for families, general education teachers, administrators, and other school personnel regarding the characteristics and needs of individuals with disabilities.

Special education teachers are to serve as a resource for families and other professionals that may be involved with students with special needs. In order to be an effective resource the teacher must possess the following:

1. Great communication skills.
2. Knowledge of current laws relating to special education.
3. Knowledge of the child's IEP.
4. Knowledge of available resources and professional publications related to special education.

Each of these issues have been discussed thoroughly throughout this study guide. Please refer to previous skills for each topic.

Texas Special Education EC-12 (161) Test Framework

The remainder of this text contains a sample test, followed by an answer key and rationale for each question. There are 135 questions in total on this exam, as well as the real exam, though students will only be scored on 120 of the questions. There are fifteen questions that are used for studies and for future exams, but these fifteen questions are not identified.

The questions range in difficulty, and include easy, average, and rigorous types. Domain 1 comprises approximately 13% of the test, and the typical number of scorable multiple choice items is about 16. Domain II and Domain III are each represented in the test, and cover 33% of the content respectively, for a total of 66%, or approximately 80 questions in these two domains. Domain IV entails 20% of the exam, or roughly 24-25 questions.

The test taker will receive one point for each correct response and zero points for each incorrect response. The score range is 100-300, with a passing score of 240. Further information about scoring is available on www.texes.ets.org

Sample Test

Directions: Read each item and select the best response

1. **Which is an educational characteristic common to students with mild intellectual learning and behavioral disabilities?**
(Skill 1.01) (Easy)

   A. Show interest in schoolwork

   B. Have intact listening skills

   C. Require modification in classroom instruction

   D. Respond better to passive than to active learning tasks

2. **Individuals with mental retardation can be characterized as:**
(Skill 1.01) (Rigorous)

   A. Often indistinguishable from normal developing children at an early age

   B. Having a higher than normal rate of motor activity

   C. Displaying significant discrepancies in ability levels

   D. Uneducable in academic skills

3. **All of the following EXCEPT which one are characteristics of a student who has an emotional disturbance?**
(Skill 1.01) (Average)

   A. Socially accepted by peers.

   B. Highly disruptive to the classroom environment.

   C. Academic difficulties.

   D. Areas of talent overlooked by a teacher

4. **Echolalia is a characteristic of which disability?**
(Skill 1.01) (Average)

   A. Autism

   B. Mental Retardation

   C. Social Pragmatic Disorder

   D. ADHD

5. Michael's teacher complains that he is constantly out of his seat. She also reports that he has trouble paying attention to what is going on in class for more than a couple of minutes at a time. He appears to be trying, but his writing is often illegible, containing many reversals. Although he seems to want to please, he is very impulsive and stays in trouble with his teacher. He is failing reading, and his math grades, though somewhat better, are still below average. Michael's Full and Individual Evaluation (FIE) should include assessment for:
(Skill 1.01) (Average)

A. Mild mental retardation

B. Specific learning disabilities

C. Mild behavior disorders

D. Hearing impairment

6. Autism is a disorder characterized by:
(Skill 1.01) (Easy)

A. Distorted relationships with others

B. Perceptual anomalies

C. Self-stimulation

D. All or the above

7. As a separate exceptionality category in IDEA, autism:
(Skill 1.01) (Average)

A. Includes emotional/behavioral disorders as defined in federal regulations

B. Adversely affects educational performance

C. Is thought to be a form of mental illness

D. Is a developmental disability that affects verbal and non-verbal communication

8. The definition for "Other Health Impaired (OHI)" in IDEA:
(Skill 1.04) (Average)

A. Is the definition that accepts heart conditions.

B. Includes deafness, blindness or profound mental retardation

C. includes Autism and PDD

D. Includes cochlear implants

9. Which of the following is a possible side-effect of an Anti-depressant? *(Skill 1.07) (Rigorous)*

A. Anxiety

B. Aggression

C. Tremors

D. Restlessness

10. Mrs. Stokes has been teaching her third-grade students about mammals during a recent science unit. Which of the following would be true of a criterion-referenced test she might administer at the conclusion of the unit?
(Skill 2.01) (Average)

   A. It will be based on unit objectives

   B. Derived scores will be used to rank student achievement.

   C. Standardized scores are effective of national performance samples

   D. All of the above

11. For which of the following purposes is a norm-referenced test least appropriate? *(Skill 2.01) (Average)*

   A. Screening

   B. Individual program planning

   C. Program evaluation

   D. Making placement decisions

12. The extent to which a test measures what its authors or users claim that it measures is called its:
(Skill 2.01) (Rigorous)

   A. Validity

   B. Reliability

   C. Normality

   D. Acculturation

13. Safeguards against bias and discrimination in the assessment of children include:
(Skill 2.02) (Easy)

   A. The testing of a child in Standard English

   B. The requirement for the use of one standardized test

   C. The use of evaluative materials in the child's native language or other mode of communication

   D. All testing performed by a certified, licensed psychologist, LSSP, or educational diagnostician.

14. Which of the following is an example of an Alternative Assessment?
(Skill 2.05) (Rigorous)

   A. Testing skills in a "real world" setting in several settings.

   B. Pre-test of student knowledge of fractions before beginning Wood Shop.

   C. Answering an essay question that allows for creative thought.

   D. A compilation of a series of tests in a portfolio.

15. Which of the following is an example of tactile perception?
(Skill 2.08) (Average)

   A. Making an angel in the snow with one's body

   B. Running a specified course

   C. Identifying a rough surface with eyes closed

   D. Demonstrating aerobic exercises

16. Which of the following activities best exemplifies a kinesthetic exercise in developing body awareness?
(Skill 2.08) (Average)

   A. Touching materials of different textures

   B. Singing with motions "Head, Shoulders, Knees and Toes."

   C. Identifying geometric shapes being drawn on one's back

   D. Making a shadow-box project

17. Which of the following teaching activities is least likely to enhance observational learning in students with special needs?
(Skill 2.08) (Rigorous)

A. A verbal description of the task to be performed, followed by having the children immediately attempt to perform the instructed behavior

B. A demonstration of the behavior, followed by an immediate opportunity for the children to imitate the behavior

C. A simultaneous demonstration and explanation of the behavior, followed by ample opportunity for the children to rehearse the instructed behavior

D. Physically guiding the children through the behavior to be imitated, while verbally explaining the behavior

18. The most important steps in writing a Functional Behavioral Assessment (FBA) is:
(Skill 2.09) (Rigorous)

A. Establish a replacement behavior

B. Establish levels of interventions.

C. Establish antecedents related or causative to the behavior.

D. Establish assessment periods of FBA effectiveness.

19. A good method to teach ethical understanding to those in the functional curriculum is:
(Skill 3.02) (Rigorous)

A. Modeling

B. The unfinished Story.

C. Handouts

D. Questionnaire

20. What components of the IEP are required by law?
    (Skill 3.04) (Average)

    A. Present level of academic and functional performance; statement of how the disability affects the student's involvement and progress; evaluation criteria and timeliness for instructional objective achievement; modifications of accommodations

    B. Projected dates for services initiation with anticipated frequency, location and duration; statement of when parent will be notified; statement of annual goals

    C. Extent to which child will not participate in regular education program; transitional needs for students age 16

    D. All of the above.

21. ARD meetings are held for different reasons. Which of the following would be a reason to hold an ARD meeting?
    (Skill 3.04) (Average)

    A. Moving from one school to another within the school district

    B. Temporary placement in inclusion

    C. A teacher requests a child to be removed from his/her class

    D. Transition to post-secondary school life

22. The greatest number of students receiving special services are enrolled primarily in:
    (Skill 3.06) (Average)

    A. The regular classroom

    B. The resource room

    C. Self-contained classrooms

    D. Special schools

23. The most restrictive environment in which an individual might be placed and receive instruction is that of:
(Skill 3.06) (Easy)

   A. Institutional setting

   B. Homebound instruction

   C. Special schools

   D. Self-contained special classes

24. Which of the following questions most directly evaluates the utility of instructional material?
(Skill 3.07) (Rigorous)

   A. Is the cost within budgetary means?

   B. Can the materials withstand handling by students?

   C. Are the materials organized in a useful manner?

   D. Are the needs of the students met by the use of the materials?

25. Which of the following is a good example of a generalization?
(Skill 3.09) (Average)

   A. Jim has learned to add and is now ready to subtract

   B. Sarah adds sets of units to obtain a product

   C. Bill recognizes a vocabulary word on a billboard when traveling

   D. Jane can spell the word "net" backwards to get the word "ten"

26. In which of the following ways does an effective teacher utilize pacing as a means of matching a student's rate of learning?
(Skill 4.02) (Rigorous)

   A. Selected content is presented based upon prerequisite skills, then presented in modified measures of time.

   B. Tasks are presented during optimum time segments

   C. Special needs students always require smaller steps and learning segments regardless of the activity or content

   D. Teacher utilizes tier assessment after presenting materials

27. In establishing your behavior management plan with the students, it is best to:
(Skill 4.04) (Average)

A. Have rules written and in place on day one

B. To hand out a copy of the rules to the students on day one

C. Have separate rules for each class on day one

D. Have students involved in creating the rules on day one

28. A life space interview is used for?
(Skill 4.04) (Rigorous)

A. Transition to exit Interview

B. Analysis of proficiency levels

C. Maintenance of acceptable behavior

D. To create awareness of distorted perceptions

29. Which electronic device enables persons with hearing impairments to make and receive phone calls?
(Skill 4.06) (Average)

A. Personal companion

B. Telecommunication Device for the Deaf (TDD)

C. Deafnet

D. Hearing aids

30. What can you do to make create a good working environment with a classroom assistant?
(Skill 4.09) (Rigorous)

A. Plan lessons with the assistant

B. Write a contract that clearly defines his/her responsibilities in the classroom

C. Remove previously given responsibilities

D. All of the above

31. Alan has failed repeatedly in his academic work. He needs continuous feedback in order to experience small, incremental achievements. What type of instructional material would best meet this need?
    (Skill 4.09) (Rigorous)

    A. Programmed materials

    B. Audiotapes

    C. Materials with no writing required

    D. Worksheets

32. After purchasing what seemed to be a very attractive new math kit for use with her students who have learning disabilities, Ms. Davis discovered her students could not use the kit unless she read the math problems and instructions to them, as the readability level was higher than the majority of the students' functional reading capabilities. Which criterion of the materials selection did Ms. Davis most likely fail to consider when selecting this math kit?
    (Skill 4.09) (Average)

    A. Durability

    B. Relevance

    C. Component Parts

    D. Price

33. Acculturation refers to the individual's:
    (Skill 5.01) (Rigorous)

    A. Gender

    B. Experiential background

    C. Social class

    D. Ethnic background

34. Some environmental elements which influence learning styles include all except:
(Skill 5.02) (Rigorous)

A. Light

B. Temperature

C. Design

D. Motivation

35. When teaching a student, who is predominantly auditory, to read, it is best to:
(Skill 5.04) (Rigorous)

A. Stress sight vocabulary

B. Stress phonetic analysis

C. Stress the shape and configuration of the word

D. Stress rapid reading

36. The effective teacher varies her instructional presentations and response requirements depending upon:
(Skill 5.04) (Easy)

A. Student needs

B. The task at hand

C. The learning situation

D. All of the above

37. Which is NOT a step teachers use to establish cooperative learning groups in the classroom? The teacher:
(Skill 5.04) (Rigorous)

A. Select members of each learning group

B. Directly teach cooperative group skills

C. Assign cooperative group skills

D. Have students self-evaluate group efforts

38. Joey is in a mainstreamed preschool program. One of the means his teacher uses in determining growth in adaptive skills is that of observation. Some questions about Joey's behavior that she might ask include:
(Skill 5.06) (Average)

A. Is he able to hold a cup?

B. Can he call the name of any of his toys?

C. Can he reach for an object and grasp it?

D. All of the above

39. Vocational training programs are based on all of the following ideas except:
(Skill 5.08) (Average)

   A. Students obtain career training from elementary through high school

   B. Students acquire specific training in job skills prior to exiting school

   C. Students need specific training and supervision in applying skills learned in school to requirements in job situations

   D. Students obtain needed instruction and field-based experiences that help them to be able to work in specific occupations

40. In career education specific training and preparation required for the world of work occurs during the phase of:
(Skill 5.08) (Average)

   A. Career Awareness

   B. Career Exploration

   C. Career Preparation

   D. Daily Living and Personal-Social Interaction

41. The social skills of students in programs for children with mental retardation are likely to be appropriate for children of their mental age, rather than chronological age. This means that the teacher will need to do all of the following except:
(Skill 5.08) (Easy)

   A. Model desired behavior

   B. Provide clear instructions

   C. Expect age appropriate behaviors

   D. Adjust the physical environment when necessary

42. Janiay requires Occupational Therapy and Speech Therapy services. She is your student. What must you do to assure her services are met?
(Skill 5.10) (Rigorous)

   A. Watch the services being rendered.

   B. Schedule collaboratively.

   C. Ask for services to be given in a push-in model.

   D. Ask them to train you to give the service.

43. Cognitive learning strategies include:
(Skill 5.12) (Rigorous)

A. Reinforcing appropriate behavior

B. Teaching students how to manage their own behavior in school

C. Heavily structuring the learning environment

D. Generalizing learning from one setting to another

44. Which of the following must be provided in a written notice to parents when proposing a child's educational placement?
(Skill 6.03) (Easy)

A. A list of parental due process safeguards

B. A list of current test scores

C. A list of persons responsible for the child's education

D. A list of academic subjects the child has passed

45. What determines whether a person is entitled to protection under Section 504?
(Skill 6.03) (Average)

A. The individual must meet the definition of a person with a disability

B. The person must be able to meet the requirements of a particular program in spite of his or her disability

C. The school, business or other facility must be the recipient of federal funding assistance

D. All of the above

46. Free Appropriate Public Education (FAPE) describes special education and related services as?
(Skill 6.03) (Easy)

A. Public expenditure and standard to the state educational agency

B. Provided in conformity with each student's individualized education program, if the program is developed to meet requirements of the law.

C. Include preschool, elementary and/or secondary education in the state involved

D. All of the above.

47. Strategies specifically designed to move the learner from dependence to independence include: *(Skill 6.04) (Rigorous)*

    A. Assessment, planning, implementation, and reevaluation

    B. Demonstration, imitation, assistance, prompting, and verbal instruction

    C. Cognitive modeling and self-guidance through overt, faded overt and covert stages

    D. B and C

48. Target behaviors must be: *(Skill 6.04) (Rigorous)*

    A. Observable

    B. Measurable

    C. Definable

    D. All of the above

49. Which tangible reinforcer would Mr. Whiting find to be most effective with teenagers? *(Skill 6.05) (Easy)*

    A. Plastic whistle

    B. Winnie-the-Pooh book

    C. Free Homework Pass

    D. Toy ring

50. Charise comes into your room and seems to know every button to push to get you upset with her. What would be a good intervention? *(Skill 6.05) (Rigorous)*

    A. Nonverbal Interactions

    B. Self-monitoring

    C. Proximity Control

    D. Planned Ignoring

51. Children with disabilities are least likely to improve their social-interpersonal skills by: *(Skill 6.06) (Rigorous)*

    A. Developing sensitivity to other people

    B. Making behavioral choices in social situations

    C. Developing social maturity

    D. Talking with their sister or brother.

52. Modeling is an essential component of which self-training approach? *(Skill 6.08) (Rigorous)*

    A. Self-instructional training

    B. Self-monitoring

    C. Self-reinforcing

    D. Self-punishing

53. A functional curriculum includes:
(Skill 6.10) (Average)

A. A specific commercial curriculum

B. Life skills

C. Remedial academics

D. Vocational placement.

54. A Behavioral Intervention Plan (BIP):
(Skill 6.10) (Rigorous)

A. Should be written by a team.

B. Should be reviewed annually.

C. Should be written by the teacher who is primarily responsible for the student.

D. Should consider placement.

55. IEPs continue to have multiple sections; one section, present levels now addresses what?
(Skill 6.10) (Easy)

A. Academic achievement and functional performance

B. English as a second language

C. Functional performance

D. Academic achievement

56. What can a teacher plan that will allow him/her to avoid adverse situations with students?
(Skill 6.11) (Rigorous)

A. Lessons

B. Recess

C. Environment

D. Class schedule

57. What TWO student behaviors are indicative of a possible crisis?
(Skill 6.11) (Average)

A. Bullying and socially active.

B. Uncontrolled and intermittent periods of laughter and rage.

C. High academic performance and gang activity

D. Victim of violence and uncontrolled anger

58. Students with autistic tendencies can be more successful academically when the teacher:
(Skill 7.02) (Average)

A. Ignores inappropriate behaviors.

B. Allows them to go out of the room during instruction.

C. Keeps a calendar on the board of expected transitions.

D. Asks the ARD committee for a 1:1 aide.

59. One of the most important goals of the special education teacher is to foster and create with the student:
(Skill 7.02) (Easy)

A. Handwriting skills.

B. Self-Advocacy

C. An increased level of reading

D. Logical reasoning

60. Children are engaged in a game of charades. Which type of social-interpersonal skill is the teacher most likely attempting to develop?
(Skill 7.04) (Rigorous)

A. Sensitivity to others

B. Making behavioral choices in social situations

C. Social maturity

D. All of the above

61. Students who receive special services in a regular classroom with consultation, generally have academic and/or social-interpersonal performance deficits at which level of severity?
(Skill 7.04) (Easy)

A. Mild

B. Moderate

C. Severe

D. Profound

62. Social maturity may be evidenced by the student's: *(Skill 7.04) (Easy)*

   A. Recognition of rights and responsibilities (his own and others)

   B. Display of respect for legitimate authority figures

   C. Formulation of a valid moral judgment

   D. Demonstration of all of the above

63. Five-year-old Tom continues to substitute the /w/ sound for the /r/ sound when pronouncing words; therefore, he often distorts words e.g., "wabbit" for "rabbit" and "wat" for "rat." His articulation disorder is basically a problem in: *(Skill 8.01) (Average)*

   A. Phonology

   B. Morphology

   C. Syntax

   D. Semantics

64. Which of the following is untrue about the ending "er"? *(Skill 8.01) (Rigorous)*

   A. It is an example of a free morpheme

   B. It represents one of the smallest units of meaning within a word

   C. It is called an inflectional ending

   D. When added to a word, it connotes a comparative status

65. Which component of language involves language content rather than the form of language? *(Skill 8.01) (Average)*

   A. Phonology

   B. Morphology

   C. Semantics

   D. Syntax

66. How many major categories do most reading programs conceptually separate the reading process into? *(Skill 8.02) (Easy)*

   A. One

   B. Two

   C. Three

   D. Four

67. Daniela is a first grade student who is misspelling words such as 'again,' 'some,' and 'were.' She would most benefit from explicit instruction and reinforcement in which facet of the reading process?
(Skill 8.02) (Average)

   A. Sight Words

   B. Reading Comprehension

   C. Fluency

   D. Word Attack Skills

68. Comprehension categories should be classified by which of the following?
(Skill 8.02) (Average)

   A. Literal Meaning

   B. Reorganization

   C. Inference

   D. All of the above

69. What is a major approach for teaching beginning reading skills?
(Skill 8.03) (Average)

   A. Linguistic Emphasis

   B. Meaning Emphasis

   C. Code Emphasis

   D. B and C

70. Which of the following is an example of a whole language, or whole-word, reading program?
(Skill 8.03) (Average)

   A. Merrill Linguistic Reading

   B. Edmark Reading

   C. Orton-Gillingham

   D. DISTAR

71. Maribel is a fifth grader who reads on grade level. She readily generates the purposes for reading a selection, forms questions, and then reads her selection. Maribel is exhibiting which variation of the directed reading method?
(Skill 8.03) (Rigorous)

   A. Language Experience Approach

   B. Individualized Reading Approach

   C. Direct-Reading Thinking Activity

   D. Pre-Reading Strategies

72. Using word families, such as the *-un* family, including words like *fun, sun*, and *run*, is an advantageous approach when teaching beginning reading because:
(Skill 8.03) (Average)

A. Students recognize similar spelling patterns

B. Vocabulary is highly controlled

C. There is an emphasis on auditory memory skills

D. Nonsense words are used

73. In which stage of spelling development does a child typically grasp left to right letter arrangement?
(Skill 8.04) (Average)

A. Pre-Communicative Stage

B. Semi-phonetic Stage

C. Phonetic Stage

D. Transitional Stage

74. Which activity most specifically promotes phonemic awareness development, and helps students relate the sounds to letters as they spell words?
(Skill 8.04) (Average)

A. Direct Instruction

B. Word Dictation

C. Syllabication

D. Segmenting Words into Phonemes

75. The CTOPP and the PAT 2 are two examples of:
(Skill 8.04) (Rigorous)

A. Reading evaluations

B. Phonological assessments

C. Fluency assessments

D. Sight Word evaluations

76. When learning blending and segmenting of sounds, a kinesthetic learner may prefer to:
(Skill 8.04) (Average)

A. Move hands together and apart

B. Use computer software

C. Draw diagrams

D. Listen to sounds

77. Name the two parts which make up the alphabetic principle.
(Skill 8.05) (Average)

   A. Alphabetic understanding and word analysis

   B. Decoding skills and phonological recoding

   C. Alphabetic understanding and phonological recoding

   D. Phonological recoding and spelling skills

78. What is an example of a CVCC word?
(Skill 8.05) (Easy)

   A. bat

   B. bait

   C. bake

   D. belt

79. Irregular words do not conform to word analysis instruction. Which word below is irregular?
(Skill 8.05) (Easy)

   A. was

   B. hand

   C. tale

   D. yet

80. Which system is used to assess the alphabetic principle?
(Skill 8.05) (Average)

   A. DIBELS

   B. PAT 2

   C. WISC

   D. LEP

81. What is a metalinguistic ability a young child acquires through early involvement in reading activities?
(Skill 8.06) (Average)

   A. Word consciousness

   B. Functions of print

   C. Fluency

   D. All of the above

82. Mrs. Sanchez is constructing a checklist for her reading group students. The list includes several traits of good readers. Which of the following may appear on this list?
(Skill 8.06) (Average)

   A. Skim and scan unfamiliar words

   B. Establish a purpose for reading, before reading

   C. Make predictions and formulate questions

   D. B and C

83. Bryon is a ninth grader with dyslexia. He was tested and diagnosed in sixth grade. He does not read fluently, particularly when reading narrative texts for English class. His teacher is reading *Romeo and Juliet* with the class and has asked Bryon's consultant teacher for strategies to help Bryon read more fluently when reading his lines. Which of the following strategies is most effective?
(*Skill 8.06*) (*Average*)

A. Provide round robin reading activities

B. Choose a segment of the text to reread until it sounds like "people talking"

C. Copy the text into a journal

D. None of the above

84. When students read, they utilize four sources of background information to comprehend the meaning behind the literal text. The four sources include word knowledge, syntax and contextual information, semantic knowledge, and:
(*Skill 8.07*) (*Rigorous*)

A. Vocabulary Lexicon

B. Fluency

C. Text Organization

D. Sentence Variety

85. What do students rely on in order to understand an unknown word they encounter in a text?
(*Skill 8.07*) (*Average*)

A. Background Information

B. Substitution

C. Selective Omission

D. Syntax

86. Knowledge of spelling patterns and pronunciations is called:
(*Skill 8.07*) (*Rigorous*)

A. Orthographic knowledge

B. Lexical Knowledge

C. Semantic Knowledge

D. Decoding Knowledge

87. _____is a skill that teachers help students develop to sustain learning throughout life
(*Skill 8.07*) (*Rigorous*)

A. Work ethic

B. Basic Math Computation

C. Reading

D. Critical thinking

88. During which written composition stage are students encouraged to read their stories aloud to others? *(Skill 8.08) (Average)*

A. Planning

B. Drafting

C. Revising/editing

D. Sharing/publication

89. Which of the following is an example of cross-modal perception involving integrating visual stimuli to an auditory verbal process? *(Skill 8.10) (Rigorous)*

A. Following spoken directions

B. Describing a picture

C. Finding certain objects in pictures

D. B and C

90. Math instruction should move in a sequential manner, from: *(Skill 9.01) (Average)*

A. Abstract to Semi-concrete to Concrete

B. Concrete to Semi-Concrete to Abstract

C. Semi-concrete to Concrete to Abstract

D. Abstract to Concrete to Semi-Concrete

91. What is 1:1 correspondence? *(Skill 9.01) (Average)*

A. Using objects to represent quantities

B. Using manipulatives to show patterns

C. Recognizing numbers in order

D. Recognizing number patterns

92. The position of a number, or its _____, determines its value in the number system. *(Skill 9.01) (Easy)*

A. Quantity

B. Place Value

C. Order

D. Face Value

93. Subtraction has three different interpretations. These include taking away, missing addend, and: *(Skill 9.01) (Average)*

A. Determined Order

B. Missing Quotient

C. Dividend

D. Comparison

94. Which is an example of repeated addition? *(Skill 9.01)* *(Easy)*

   A. 9 + 9 + 9 = 27

   B. 27 + 9 = 36

   C. 9 + 8 + 7 = 24

   D. 9 + 9 – 9 = 9

95. Manipulatives, or the use of tactile objects, are useful to utilize with students for which operation? *(Skill 9.01)* *(Average)*

   A. Addition

   B. Subtraction

   C. Multiplication

   D. All of the above

96. Which is an example of a fraction? *(Skill 9.01)* *(Average)*

   A. Quotient

   B. Ratio

   C. Decimal Conversion

   D. B and C

97. A special education teacher has asked a fifth grader, Raul, to use a highlighter to determine important information in math word problems. The highlighter is a tool to help Raul: *(Skill 9.01)* *(Rigorous)*

   A. Identify important facts

   B. Check computation

   C. Find the main idea

   D. None of the above.

98. Students with visual or spatial integration problems may benefit from the use of _____ paper when problem solving to increase accuracy. *(Skill 9.01)* *(Average)*

   A. Blank

   B. Graph

   C. Cut

   D. Colored

99. Classifying in math includes: *(Skill 9.02)* *(Average)*

   A. Sorting by characteristic

   B. Lining up

   C. Describing

   D. All of the above

100. The idea of one number as being a part of another number is the: *(Skill 9.02) (Average)*

    A. Numerical Notation

    B. Comparing Quantities

    C. Pattern Identification

    D. Part-Whole Concept

101. A student's fluidity and flexibility with numbers is called: *(Skill 9.03) (Average)*

    A. Number Sense

    B. Computational Skill

    C. Memorization

    D. 1:1 Correspondence

102. Where is number sense derived? *(Skill 9.03) (Rigorous)*

    A. Home

    B. School

    C. Siblings

    D. All of the above

103. Technology can enhance students' understanding of math. Which of the following is a technologically-driven math tool? *(Skill 9.03) (Easy)*

    A. Math computer program

    B. Dry erase board

    C. Notebook

    D. Manipulatives

104. Most children entering school are not developmentally ready to understand concepts such as? *(Skill 9.03) (Rigorous)*

    A. Zero symbol

    B. Equalizing.

    C. Joining

    D. Patterns

105. The No Child Left Behind Act (NCLB) affected students with Limited English Proficiency (LEP) by :
(Skill 10.01) (Rigorous)

A. Requiring these students to demonstrate English Language Proficiency before a high school diploma is granted.

B. Providing allowances for schools not to require them to take and pass state reading exams (TAKS) if the students were enrolled in US schools for less than a year.

C. Providing allowances for these students to opt out of state math tests if the student was enrolled in a US school for less than one year.

D. Both B and C

106. The opportunity for a student with a disability to attend a class as close to the normal as possible describes:
(Skill 10.01) (Easy)

A. Least Restrictive Environment

B. Normalization

C. Mainstreaming

D. Deinstitutionalization

107. Included in data brought to the attention of Congress regarding the evaluation procedures for education of students with disabilities was the fact that?
(Skill 10.01) (Average)

A. There were a large number of children and youths with disabilities in the United States

B. Many children with disabilities were not receiving an appropriate education

C. Many parents of children with disabilities were forced to seek services outside of the public realm

D. All of the above

108. The Individuals with Disabilities Education Act (IDEA) was signed into law in and later reauthorized to its current in what years?
(Skill 10.01) (Easy)

A. 1975 and 2004

B. 1980 and 1990

C. 1990 and 2004

D. 1995 and 2001

109. How was the training of special education teachers changed by the No Child Left Behind Act of 2002?
(Skill 10.01) (Average)

A. Required all special education teachers to be certified in reading and math

B. Required all special education teachers to take the same coursework as general education teachers

C. If a special education teacher is teaching a core subject, he or she must meet the standard of a highly qualified teacher in that subject.

D. All of the above

110. Which component changed with the reauthorization of the Education for all Handicapped Children Act of 1975 (EHA) 1990 EHA Amendment?
(Skill 10.01) (Average)

A. Specific terminology

B. Due process protections

C. Non-discriminatory reevaluation procedures

D. Individual Education Plans

111. Which is untrue about the Americans with Disabilities Act (ADA)?
(Skill 10.01) (Easy)

A. It was signed into law the same year as IDEA by President Bush

B. It reauthorized the discretionary programs of EHA

C. It gives protection to all people on the basis of race, sex, national origin, and religion

D. It guarantees equal opportunities to persons with disabilities in employment, public accommodations, transportation, government services, and telecommunications.

112. Legislation in Public Law 94 – 142 attempts to:
(Skill 10.01) (Rigorous)

A. Match the child's educational needs with appropriate educational services

B. Include parents in the decisions made about their child's education

C. Establish a means by which parents can provide input

D. All of the above

113. **Which legislation has forced public and private facilities to accommodate those who are physically disabled?**
(Skill 10.01) (Easy)

    A. ADA

    B. IDEA

    C. 504 Plan

    D. PL 105-17

114. **Bob shows behavior problems such as lack of attention, out of seat and talking out. His teacher has kept data on these behaviors and has found that Bob is showing much better self-control since he has been self-managing himself through a behavior modification program. The most appropriate placement recommendation for Bob at this time is probably:**
(Skill 10.02) (Average)

    A. Any available part-time special education program

    B. The regular classroom solely

    C. A social behavior class for one period a day

    D. A resource room for one period a day

115. **Which of the following examples would be considered of highest priority when determining the need for the delivery of appropriate special education and related services?**
(Skill 10.06) (Rigorous)

    A. A ten-year-old girl with profound mental retardation who is receiving education services in a state institution.

    B. A six-year-old girl who has been diagnosed with autism is placed in a special education class within the local school. Her mother wants her to attend residential school next year, even though the girl is showing progress.

    C. An eight-year-old boy is repeating first grade for the second time and exhibits problems with toileting, gross motor functions, and remembering number and letter symbols. His regular classroom teacher claims the referral forms are too time-consuming and refuses to complete them. He also refuses to make accommodations because he feels every child should be treated alike.

D. A twelve-year-old boy with mild disabilities who was placed in a behavior disorders program, but displays obvious perceptual deficits (e.g. reversal of letters and symbols, and inability to discriminate sounds). He was originally thought to have a learning disability, but did not meet state criteria for this exceptionality category, based on results of standard scores. He has always had problems with attending to a task, and is now beginning to get into trouble during seatwork time. His teacher feels that he will eventually become a real behavior problem. He receives social skills training in the resource room one period a day.

116. **You note that a child in your class is expressing discomfort when placing his back against a chair. You ask him if he is OK, and he says its nothing. You notice what appears to be a belt mark on his shoulder. What is the first thing you should do?**
(Skill 10.07) (Rigorous)

A. Send the child to the nurse

B. Contact an administrator

C. Call Child Protective Services

D. Follow the school policy

117. **You are monitoring the cafeteria and you noticed Joshua stuffing his pockets with food. Not just snack food, but lunch items as well. You suspect:**
(Skill 10.07) (Average)

A. Joshua may not be getting fed at home.

B. Joshua has Obsessive Compulsive Disorder (OCD).

C. Joshua is just an average growing boy.

D. Joshua is trying to be funny.

118. **In order for a student to function independently in the learning environment, which of the following must be true?**
(Skill 10.08) (Average)

A. The learner must understand the nature of the content

B. The student must be able to do the assigned task

C. The teacher must communicate the task to the learner

D. The student must complete the task.

119. Jane is a third grader. Mrs. Smith, her teacher, noted that Jane was having difficulty with math and reading assignments. The results from recent diagnostic tests showed a strong sight vocabulary, strength in computational skills, but a weakness in comprehending what she read. This weakness was apparent in mathematical word problems as well. The multi-disciplinary team recommended placement in a special education resource room for two periods each school day. For the remainder of the school day, her placement will be:
(Skill 10.08) (Average)

A. In the regular classroom

B. At a special school

C. In a self-contained classroom

D. In a resource room

120. A mother is upset that her child is not being helped and asks you about the difference between the 504 Plan and an IEP. What is the difference?
(Skill 11.01) (Rigorous)

A. 504 plan requires classification, IEP requires labeling.

B. 504 plan provides no services, only adaptations.

C. 504 plan is better for children who have ADHD.

D. 504 plan provides little interventions/services, while an IEP is more intensive providing more services, such as a special class.

121. Which of the following is a specific change of language in IDEA?
(Skill 11.05) (Average)

A. The term "Disorder" changed to "Disability"

B. The term "Children" changed to "Children and Youth"

C. The term "Handicapped" changed to "Impairments"

D. The term "Handicapped" changed to "With Disabilities"

122. **Which is a less than ideal example of collaboration in successful inclusion?**
(Skill 12.01) (Rigorous)

   A. Special education teachers are part of the instructional team in a regular classroom

   B. Special education teachers are informed of the lesson before hand and assist regular education teachers in the classroom

   C. Teaming approaches are used for problem solving and program implementation

   D. Regular teachers, special education teachers, and other specialists or support teachers co-teach

123. **The best resource a teacher can have to reach a student is?**
(Skill 12.01) (Rigorous)

   A. Contact with the parents/guardians.

   B. A successful behavior modification Exam.

   C. A listening ear.

   D. Gathered scaffold approach to teaching.

124. **A paraprofessional has been assigned to assist you in the classroom. What action on the part of the teacher would lead to a poor working relationship?**
(Skill 12.02) (Average)

   A. Having the paraprofessional lead a small group.

   B. Telling the paraprofessional what you expect him/her to do.

   C. Defining classroom behavior management as your responsibility alone.

   D. Taking an active role in his/her evaluation.

125. **Mrs. Freud is a consultant teacher. She has two students with Mr. Ricardo. Mrs. Freud should:**
(Skill 12.02) (Average)

   A. Co-Teach

   B. Spend two days a week in the classroom helping out.

   C. Discuss lessons with the teacher and suggest modifications before class.

   D. Pull her students out for instructional modifications.

126. If a student is predominantly a visual learner, he may learn more effectively by:
(Skill 12.02) (Easy)

   A. Reading aloud while studying

   B. Listening to a cassette tape

   C. Watching a DVD

   D. Using body movement

127. Presentation of tasks can be altered to match the student's rate of learning by:
(Skill 12.02) (Rigorous)

   A. Describing how much of a topic is presented in one day and how much practice is assigned, according to the student's abilities and learning style

   B. Using task analysis, assign a certain number of skills to be mastered in a specific amount of time

   C. Introducing a new task only when the student has demonstrated mastery of the previous task in the learning hierarchy

   D. Using standardized assessments to measure skills

128. All of the following are suggestions for altering the presentation of tasks to match the student's rate of learning except:
(Skill 12.02) (Average)

   A. Teach in several shorter segments of time rather than a single lengthy session

   B. Continue to teach a task until the lesson is completed in order to provide more time on task

   C. Watch for nonverbal cues that indicate students are becoming confused, bored, or restless

   D. Avoid giving students an inappropriate amount of written work

129. You should prepare for a parent-teacher conference by:
(Skill 12.02) (Average)

   A. Memorizing student progress/grades.

   B. Anticipating questions.

   C. Scheduling the meetings during your lunch time.

   D. Planning a tour of the school.

130. Lotzie is not labeled as needing special education services and appears unable to function on grade level in both academics and socially. He is in 9th grade reading picture books, and consistently displays immature behavior that can be misinterpreted. You have already observed these behaviors. What should be done first?
(Skill 12.02) (Rigorous)

A. Establish a rapport with the parents.

B. Initiate a special education referral

C. Plan and discuss possible interventions with the teacher.

D. Address the class about acceptance.

131. Television, movies, radio, and newspapers contribute to the public's poor understanding of disabilities by:
(Skill 12.04) (Average)

A. Only portraying those who look normal.

B. Portraying the person with the disability as one with incredible abilities.

C. Showing emotionally disturbed children

D. Portraying all people in wheel chairs as independent.

132. An individual with disabilities in need of employability training, as well a job, should be referred to what governmental agency for assistance?
(Skill 12.04) (Average)

A. Office of Mental Retardation and Developmental Disabilities (OMRDD)

B. Vocational and Educational Services for Individuals with Disabilities (VESID)

C. Social Services

D. ARC

133. **What do the 9th and 10th Amendments to the U.S. Constitution state about education?**
(Skill 12.09) (Rigorous)

   A. That education belongs to the people

   B. That education is an unstated power vested in the states

   C. That elected officials mandate education

   D. That education is free

134. **Manifest Determination Review (MDR) ARD committees should first:**
(Skill 12.10) (Average)

   A. Make a decision on whether to return the student to placement

   B. Determine if the disability was a cause of the behavior.

   C. Evaluate the placement for possible needed change.

   D. Examine past behaviors.

135. **A Pre-IEP team coordinates and participates in due diligence through what process?**
(Skill 12.10) (Rigorous)

   A. Child study team meets first time without parents

   B. Teachers take child learning concerns to the school counselor

   C. School personnel initiate Response to Intervention (RTI)

   D. All of the above

Answer Key

1.	C	45.	D	89.	B	133.	A
2.	A	46.	D	90.	B	134.	B
3.	A	47.	D	91.	A	135.	D
4.	A	48.	D	92.	B		
5.	B	49.	C	93.	D		
6.	D	50.	D	94.	A		
7.	D	51.	D	95.	D		
8.	A	52.	A	96.	D		
9.	C	53.	B	97.	A		
10.	A	54.	A	98.	B		
11.	B	55.	A	99.	A		
12.	A	56.	C	100.	D		
13.	C	57.	D	101.	A		
14.	A	58.	C	102.	D		
15.	C	59.	B	103.	A		
16.	B	60.	A	104.	A		
17.	A	61.	A	105.	A		
18.	C	62.	D	106.	B		
19.	B	63.	A	107.	D		
20.	D	64.	A	108.	C		
21.	D	65.	C	109.	C		
22.	A	66.	C	110.	A		
23.	A	67.	A	111.	B		
24.	C	68.	D	112.	D		
25.	C	69.	D	113.	A		
26.	A	70.	B	114.	B		
27.	D	71.	C	115.	C		
28.	D	72.	A	116.	D		
29.	B	73.	B	117.	A		
29.	A	74.	D	118.	B		
30.	A	75.	B	119.	A		
31.	B	76.	A	120.	D		
32.	B	77.	C	121.	D		
33.	D	78.	D	122.	B		
35.	B	79.	A	123.	A		
36.	D	80.	A	124.	C		
37.	D	81.	D	125.	C		
38.	D	82.	D	126.	C		
39.	A	83.	B	127.	C		
40.	C	84.	C	128.	B		
41.	C	85.	A	129.	B		
42.	B	86.	A	130.	A		
43.	B	87.	D	131.	B		
44.	A	88.	C	132.	B		

Rationales for Sample Test

1. **Which is an educational characteristic common to students with mild intellectual learning and behavioral disabilities?**
   (Skill 1.01) (Easy)

   A. Show interest in schoolwork

   B. Have intact listening skills

   C. Require modification in classroom instruction

   D. Respond better to passive than to active learning tasks

Answer: C. Require modification in classroom instruction

Some of the characteristics of students with mild learning and behavioral disabilities are as follows: Lack of interest in schoolwork; prefer concrete rather than abstract lessons; weak listening skills; low achievement; limited verbal and/or writing skills; respond better to active rather than passive learning tasks. Have areas of talent or ability often overlooked by teachers; prefer to receive special help in regular classroom; higher dropout rate than regular education students; achieve in accordance with teacher expectations; require modification in classroom instruction; and are easily distracted.

2. **Individuals with mental retardation can be characterized as:**
   (Skill 1.01) (Rigorous)

A. Often indistinguishable from normal developing children at an early age

B. Having a higher than normal rate of motor activity

C. Displaying significant discrepancies in ability levels

D. Uneducable in academic skills

Answer: A. Often indistinguishable from normal developing children at an early age.

Some characteristics of individual with mental retardation or intellectual disabilities:

- IQ of 70 or below
- Limited cognitive ability; delayed academic achievement, particularly in language-related subjects
- Deficits in memory which often relate to poor initial perception, or inability to apply stored information to relevant situations
- Impaired formulation of learning strategies
- Difficulty in attending to relevant aspects of stimuli: slowness in reaction time or in employing alternate strategies

3. **All of the following EXCEPT which one are characteristics of a student who has an emotional disturbance?**
   (Skill 1.01) (Average)

A. Socially accepted by peers.

B. Highly disruptive to the classroom environment.

C. Academic difficulties.

D. Areas of talent overlooked by a teacher

Answer: A. Socially accepted by peers.

While a child may be socially accepted by peers, children who are emotionally disturbed tend to alienate those around them, and are often ostracized.

4.   Echolalia is a characteristic of which disability?
(Skill 1.01) (Average)

A.   Autism

B.   Mental Retardation

C.   Social Pragmatic Disorder

D.   ADHD

Answer: A. Autism

Echolalia is echoing/repeating the speech of others, which is a characteristic of autism.

5. Michael's teacher complains that he is constantly out of his seat. She also reports that he has trouble paying attention to what is going on in class for more than a couple of minutes at a time. He appears to be trying, but his writing is often illegible, containing many reversals. Although he seems to want to please, he is very impulsive and stays in trouble with his teacher. He is failing reading, and his math grades, though somewhat better, are still below average. Michael's Full and Individual Evaluation (FIE) should include assessment for: *(Skill 1.01) (Average)*

A. Mild mental retardation

B. Specific learning disabilities

C. Mild behavior disorders

D. Hearing impairment

Answer: B. Specific learning disabilities

Some of the characteristics of persons with learning disabilities:

- Hyperactivity: A rate of motor activity higher than normal
- Perceptual difficulties: Visual, auditory, and hap tic perceptual problems
- Perceptual-motor impairments: Poor integration of visual and motor systems, often affecting fine motor coordination.
- Disorders of memory and thinking: Memory deficits, trouble with problem-solving, concept formation and association, poor awareness of own metacognitive skills (learning strategies)
- Impulsiveness: Acts before considering consequences, poor impulse control, often followed by remorselessness.
- Academic problems in reading, math, writing or spelling; significant discrepancies in ability levels.

6.   **Autism is a disorder characterized by:**
     (Skill 1.01) (Easy)

A.   Distorted relationships with others

B.   Perceptual anomalies

C.   Self-stimulation

D.   All or the above

Answer: D. All or the above

In IDEA, the 1990 Amendment to the Education for All Handicapped Children Act, autism was classified as a separate exceptionality category. Thought to be caused by a neurological or biochemical dysfunction, autism generally becomes evident before age 3. The condition occurs in about one of every 500 persons. Smith and Luckasson, 1992, describe it as a severe language disorder which affects thinking, communication, and behavior. They list the following characteristics:

- **Absent or distorted relationships with people:** Inability to relate with people except as objects, inability to express affection, or ability to build and maintain only distant, suspicious or bizarre relationships.
- **Extreme or peculiar problems in communication:** Absence of verbal language or language that is not functional such as echolalia (parroting what one hears), misuse of pronouns (e.g. he for you or I for her), neologisms (made-up meaningless words or sentences), talk that bears little or no resemblance to reality.
- **Self-stimulation:** Repetitive stereo-typed behavior that seems to have no purposes other than providing sensory stimulation. this may take a wide variety of forms, such as swishing saliva, twirling objects, patting one's cheeks, flapping one's arms, staring,…etc.
- **Self-injury:** Repeated physical self-abuse, such as biting, scratching, or poking oneself, head banging, …etc
- **Perceptual anomalies:** Unusual responses or absence of response to stimuli that seem to indicate sensory impairment or unusual sensitivity.

7.   **As a separate exceptionality category in IDEA, autism:**
      (Skill 1.01) (Average)

A.   Includes emotional/behavioral disorders as defined in federal regulations

B.   Adversely affects educational performance

C.   Is thought to be a form of mental illness

D.   Is a developmental disability that affects verbal and non-verbal communication

Answer: D. Is a developmental disability that affects verbal and non-verbal communication

Autism affects interacting with others, because communication is moderately to profoundly impaired.

8.   **The definition for "Other Health Impaired (OHI)" in IDEA:**
      (Skill 1.04) (Average)

A.   Is the definition that accepts heart conditions.

B.   Includes deafness, blindness or profound mental retardation

C.   includes Autism and PDD.

D.   Includes cochlear implants.

Answer: A. Is the definition that accepts heart conditions.

OHI includes a variety of reasons and diagnoses including heart conditions.

9.   **Which of the following is a possible side-effect of an Anti-depressant?** *(Skill 1.07) (Rigorous)*

A.   Anxiety

B.   Aggression

C.   Tremors

D.   Restlessness

Answer: C. Tremors

Tremors is one indicator of a possible side-effect of an anti-depressant,

10. **Mrs. Stokes has been teaching her third-grade students about mammals during a recent science unit. Which of the following would be true of a criterion-referenced test she might administer at the conclusion of the unit?**
     (Skill 2.01) (Average)

A.   It will be based on unit objectives

B.   Derived scores will be used to rank student achievement.

C.   Standardized scores are effective of national performance samples

D.   All of the above

Answer: A. It will be based on unit objectives

Criterion-referenced tests measure the progress made by individuals in mastering specific skills. The content is based on a specific set of objectives rather than on the general curriculum. Criterion-referenced tests provide measurements pertaining to the information a given student needs to know and the skills that student needs to master.

11. **For which of the following purposes is a norm-referenced test least appropriate?** *(Skill 2.01) (Average)*

A. Screening

B. Individual program planning

C. Program evaluation

D. Making placement decisions

Answer: B. Individual program planning

Norm-referenced tests have a large advantage over criterion-referenced tests when used for screening or program evaluation. Norm-referenced tests provide a means of comparing a student's performance to the performance typically expected of others of his age.

12. **The extent to which a test measures what its authors or users claim that it measures is called its:**
    (Skill 2.01) (Rigorous)

A. Validity

B. Reliability

C. Normality

D. Acculturation

Answer: A. Validity

Validity is the degree or extent to which a test measures what it was designed or intended to measure. Reliability is the extent to which a test is consistent in its measurements.

13. **Safeguards against bias and discrimination in the assessment of children include:**
(Skill 2.02) (Easy)

A. The testing of a child in Standard English

B. The requirement for the use of one standardized test

C. The use of evaluative materials in the child's native language or other mode of communication

D. All testing performed by a certified, licensed psychologist, LSSP, or educational diagnostician

Answer: C. The use of evaluative materials in the child's native language or other mode of communication

The law requires that the child be evaluated in his native language, or mode of communication. The idea that a licensed psychologist evaluates the child does not meet the criteria if it is not done in the child's normal mode of communication.

14. **Which of the following is an example of an Alternative Assessment?**
(Skill 2.05) (Rigorous)

A. Testing skills in a "real world" setting in several settings.

B. Pre-test of student knowledge of fractions before beginning Wood Shop.

C. Answering an essay question that allows for creative thought.

D. A compilation of a series of tests in a portfolio.

Answer: A. Testing skills in a "real world" setting in several settings.

Naturalistic Assessment is a form of alternative assessment that requires testing in actual application settings of life skills. The skill of using money correctly could be correctly assessed in this method by taking the student shopping in different settings.

15. **Which of the following is an example of tactile perception?**
(Skill 2.08) (Average)

A. Making an angel in the snow with one's body

B. Running a specified course

C. Identifying a rough surface with eyes closed

D. Demonstrating aerobic exercises

Answer: C. Identifying a rough surface with eyes closed

Tactile: Having to do with touch.

16. **Which of the following activities best exemplifies a kinesthetic exercise in developing body awareness?**
(Skill 2.08) (Average)

A. Touching materials of different textures

B. Singing with motions "Head, Shoulders, Knees and Toes."

C. Identifying geometric shapes being drawn on one's back

D. Making a shadow-box project

Answer: B. Singing with motions "Head, Shoulders, Knees and Toes."

Kinesthetic: Having to do with body movement.

17. **Which of the following teaching activities is least likely to enhance observational learning in students with special needs?**
   (Skill 2.08) (Rigorous)

A. A verbal description of the task to be performed, followed by having the children immediately attempt to perform the instructed behavior

B. A demonstration of the behavior, followed by an immediate opportunity for the children to imitate the behavior

C. A simultaneous demonstration and explanation of the behavior, followed by ample opportunity for the children to rehearse the instructed behavior

D. Physically guiding the children through the behavior to be imitated, while verbally explaining the behavior

Answer: A. A verbal description of the task to be performed, followed by having the children immediately attempt to perform the instructed behavior

Children with disabilities need to be given a chance to observe, or see, the behavior so that they can imitate it. Simply hearing a verbal description of a task is not generally preferred for students with disabilities. Students need demonstration, modeling, and physical guidance to internalize what is expected.

18. **The most important steps in writing a Functional Behavioral Assessment (FBA) is:**
   (Skill 2.09) (Rigorous)

A. Establish a replacement behavior

B. Establish levels of interventions.

C. Establish antecedents related or causative to the behavior.

D. Establish assessment periods of FBA effectiveness.

Answer: C. Establish antecedents related or causative to the behavior.

An FBA will only be successful if antecedents are recognized. Avoidance of situations, and training/cultivating of replacement behaviors then become possible.

19. **A good method to teach ethical understanding to those in the functional curriculum is:**
    (Skill 3.02) (Rigorous)

A.   Modeling

B.   The unfinished Story.

C.   Handouts

D.   Questionnaire

Answer: B. The unfinished Story.

The unfinished story ends where an ethical judgment should take place and allows for the students to discuss what the right choice should be.

20. **What components of the IEP are required by law?**
    (Skill 3.04) (Average)

A.   Present level of academic and functional performance; statement of how the disability affects the student's involvement and progress; evaluation criteria and timeliness for instructional objective achievement; modifications of accommodations

B.   Projected dates for services initiation with anticipated frequency, location and duration; statement of when parent will be notified; statement of annual goals

C.   Extent to which child will not participate in regular education program; transitional needs for students age 16

D.   All of the above.

Answer: D. All of the above.

IEPs state 14 elements that are required, review them in Skill 1.3 under IEP. Educators must keep themselves apprised of the changes and amendments to laws such as IDEA 2004 with addendums released in October of 2006.

21. **ARD committee meetings are held for different reasons. Which of the following would be a reason to hold an ARD meeting?**
    (Skill 3.04) (Average)

A.   Moving from one school to another within the school district.

B.   Temporary placement in inclusion.

C.   A teacher requests a child to be removed from his/her class.

D.   Transition to post-secondary school life.

Answer: D. Transition to post-secondary school life.

Post-school transition is one of the most important ARD committee meetings held. It discusses services the student may/will need to be successful in the post-school environment.

22. **The greatest number of students receiving special services are enrolled primarily in:**
    (Skill 3.06) (Average)

A.   The regular classroom

B.   The resource room

C.   Self-contained classrooms

D.   Special schools

Answer: A. The regular classroom

With the implementation of least restrictive environment, the majority of students are currently serviced and spend most of their time in the regular education classroom.

23. **The most restrictive environment in which an individual might be placed and receive instruction is that of:**
    (Skill 3.06) (Easy)

A.   Institutional setting

B.   Homebound instruction

C.   Special schools

D.   Self-contained special classes

Answer: A. Institutional setting

Individuals who require significantly modified environments for care treatment and accommodation may be educated in an institutional setting. These individuals usually have profound/multiple disorders.

24. **Which of the following questions most directly evaluates the utility of instructional material?**
    (Skill 3.07) (Rigorous)

A.   Is the cost within budgetary means?

B.   Can the materials withstand handling by students?

C.   Are the materials organized in a useful manner?

D.   Are the needs of the students met by the use of the materials?

Answer: C. Are the materials organized in a useful manner?

The organization and facility of use of the materials addressed the utility of the materials.

25. Which of the following is a good example of a generalization? (Skill 3.09) (Average)

A. Jim has learned to add and is now ready to subtract

B. Sarah adds sets of units to obtain a product

C. Bill recognizes a vocabulary word on a billboard when traveling

D. Jane can spell the word "net" backwards to get the word "ten"

Answer: C. Bill recognizes a vocabulary word on a billboard when traveling

Generalization is the occurrence of a learned behavior in the presence of a stimulus other than the one that produced the initial response. It is the expansion of a student's performance beyond the initial setting. Students must be able to expand or transfer what is learned to other settings (e.g., reading to math word problems, resource room to regular classroom). Generalization may be enhanced by the following:

- Use many examples in teaching to deepen application of learned skills
- Use consistency in initial teaching situations, and later introduce variety in format, procedure and use of examples
- Have the same information presented by different teachers, in different settings, and under varying conditions
- Include a continuous reinforcement schedule at first, later changing to delayed and intermittent schedules as instruction progresses
- Teach students to record instances of generalization and to reward themselves at that time
- Associate naturally occurring stimuli when possible

26. **In which of the following ways does an effective teacher utilize pacing as a means of matching a student's rate of learning?**
(Skill 4.02) (Rigorous)

A.   Selected content is presented based upon prerequisite skills, then presented in modified measures of time.

B.   Tasks are presented during optimum time segments

C.   Special needs students always require smaller steps and learning segments regardless of the activity or content

D.   Teacher utilizes tier assessment after presenting materials

Answer: A. Selected content is presented based upon prerequisite skills, then presented in modified measures of time.

Pacing utilizes a scaffold approach to teaching with modified time periods of presentation of new material.

27. **In establishing your behavior management plan with the students it is best to:**
(Skill 4.04) (Average)

A.   Have rules written and in place on day one.

B.   To hand out a copy of the rules to the students on day one.

C.   Have separate rules for each class on day one.

D.   Have students involved in creating the rules on day one.

Answer: D. Have students involved in creating the rules on day one.

Rules are easier to follow when students not only know the reason they are in place, but took part in creating them. It may be good to already to have a few rules pre-written and then to discuss if they cover all the rules the students have created.

28. **A life space interview is used for?**
(Skill 4.04) (Rigorous)

A. Transition to exit interview.

B. Analysis of proficiency levels.

C. Maintenance of acceptable behavior.

D. To create awareness of distorted perceptions.

Answer: D. To create awareness of distorted perceptions.

Life space interviews are given in a here-and-now fashion. Often they employ role plays to increase awareness of misunderstandings, and can be used to prepare a student for mediation.

29. **Which electronic device enables persons with hearing impairments to make and receive phone calls?**
(Skill 4.06) (Average)

A. Personal companion

B. Telecommunication Device for the Deaf (TDD)

C. Deafnet

D. Hearing aids

Answer: B. Telecommunication Device for the Deaf (TDD)

TDDs are available throughout the world today. Many public telephones now carry this feature in a small box under the phone.

30. **What can you do to make create a good working environment with a classroom assistant?**
    (Skill 4.09)(Rigorous)

A.   Plan lessons with the assistant

B.   Write a contract that clearly defines his/her responsibilities in the classroom

C.   Remove previously given responsibilities

D.   All of the above

Answer: A. Plan lessons with the assistant.

Planning with your classroom assistant shows that you respect his/her input , and allows you to see the areas in which he/she feels confident.

31. **Alan has failed repeatedly in his academic work. He needs continuous feedback in order to experience small, incremental achievements. What type of instructional material would best meet this need?**
    (Skill 4.09)(Rigorous)

A.   Programmed materials

B.   Audiotapes

C.   Materials with no writing required

D.   Worksheets

Answer: A. Programmed materials

Programmed materials are best suited as Alan would be able to chart his progress as he achieves each goal. He can monitor himself and take responsibility for his successes.

32. After purchasing what seemed to be a very attractive new math kit for use with her students who have learning disabilities, Ms. Davis discovered her students could not use the kit unless she read the math problems and instructions to them, as the readability level was higher than the majority of the students' functional reading capabilities. Which criterion of the materials selection did Ms. Davis most likely fail to consider when selecting this math kit?
(Skill 4.09)(Average)

A. Durability

B. Relevance

C. Component Parts

D. Price

Answer: B. Relevance

Relevance was the criterion she most likely failed to consider, due to the fact that the students had learning disabilities and would not be able to read at the level required by the math kit.

33. Acculturation refers to the individual's:
(Skill 5.01)(Rigorous)

A. Gender

B. Experiential background

C. Social class

D. Ethnic background

Answer: B. Experiential background

A person is the product of his experiences.

34. **Some environmental elements which influence learning styles include all except:**
   (Skill 5.02) (Rigorous)

   A.   Light

   B.   Temperature

   C.   Design

   D.   Motivation

Answer: D. Motivation

Individual learning styles are influenced by environmental, emotional, sociological, and physical elements. Environmental include sound, light, temperature and design. Emotional elements include such as motivation, persistence, responsibility and structure. Motivation is not an environmental element.

35. **When teaching a student, who is predominantly auditory, to read, it is best to:**
   (Skill 5.04) (Rigorous)

   A.   Stress sight vocabulary

   B.   Stress phonetic analysis

   C.   Stress the shape and configuration of the word

   D.   Stress rapid reading

Answer: B. Stress phonetic analysis

Sensory modalities are one of the physical elements that affect learning style. Some students learn best through their visual sense (sight), others through their auditory sense (hearing) and still others by doing, touching and moving (tactile-kinesthetic). Auditory learners generally listen to people, follow verbal directions, and enjoy hearing records, cassette tapes, and stories. Phonics has to do with sound, an auditory stimulus.

36.   **The effective teacher varies her instructional presentations and response requirements depending upon:**
       (Skill 5.04) (Easy)

A.   Student needs

B.   The task at hand

C.   The learning situation

D.   All of the above

Answer: D. All of the above

Differentiated instruction, and meeting the needs of the group as a whole must cater to the student's mode of learning to be successful.

37.   **Which is NOT a step teachers use to establish cooperative learning groups in the classroom? The teacher:**
       (Skill 5.04) (Rigorous)

A.   Select members of each learning group

B.   Directly teach cooperative group skills

C.   Assign cooperative group skills

D.   Have students self-evaluate group efforts

Answer: D. Have students self-evaluate group efforts

According to Henley et al, there are four steps to establishing cooperative learning groups:
1. The teacher selects members of each learning group.
2. The teacher directly teaches cooperative group skills.
3. The teacher assigns cooperative group activities.
4. The teacher evaluates group efforts.

38. **Joey is in a mainstreamed preschool program. One of the means his teacher uses in determining growth in adaptive skills is that of observation. Some questions about Joey's behavior that she might ask include:**
(Skill 5.06) (Average)

A. Is he able to hold a cup?

B. Can he call the name of any of his toys?

C. Can he reach for an object and grasp it?

D. All of the above

Answer: D. All of the above

Some characteristics of individual with mental retardation or intellectual disabilities:

- IQ of 70 or below
- Limited cognitive ability; delayed academic achievement, particularly in language-related subjects
- Deficits in memory which often relate to poor initial perception, or inability to apply stored information to relevant situations
- Impaired formulation of learning strategies
- Difficulty in attending to relevant aspects of stimuli: slowness in reaction time or in employing alternate strategies.

39. **Vocational training programs are based on all of the following ideas except:**
(Skill 5.08) (Average)

A.   Students obtain career training from elementary through high school

B.   Students acquire specific training in job skills prior to exiting school

C.   Students need specific training and supervision in applying skills learned in school to requirements in job situations

D.   Students obtain needed instruction and field-based experiences that help them to be able to work in specific occupations

Answer: A. Students obtain career training from elementary through high school

Vocational education programs or transition programs prepare students for entry into the labor force. They are usually incorporated into the work-study at the high school or post-secondary levels. They are usually focused on job skills, job opportunities, and skill requirements for specific jobs, personal qualifications in relation to job requirements, work habits, money management, and academic skills needed for specific jobs.

40. **In career education specific training and preparation required for the world of work occurs during the phase of:**
(Skill 5.08) (Average)

A.   Career Awareness

B.   Career Exploration

C.   Career Preparation

D.   Daily Living and Personal-Social Interaction

Answer: C. Career Preparation

Curricular aspects of Career Education include:

- Career Awareness: Diversity of available jobs
- Career Exploration: Skills needed for occupational groups
- Career Preparation: Specific training and preparation required for the world of work

41. The social skills of students in programs for children with mental retardation are likely to be appropriate for children of their mental age, rather than chronological age. This means that the teacher will need to do all of the following except:
(Skill 5.08) (Easy)

A. Model desired behavior

B. Provide clear instructions

C. Expect age appropriate behaviors

D. Adjust the physical environment when necessary

Answer: C. Expect age appropriate behaviors

Students with mental retardation will exhibit social behaviors appropriate for their mental, rather than chronological ages.

42. Janiay requires Occupational Therapy and Speech Therapy services. She is your student. What must you do to assure her services are met?
(Skill 5.10) (Rigorous)

A. Watch the services being rendered.

B. Schedule collaboratively.

C. Ask for services to be given in a push-in model.

D. Ask them to train you to give the service.

Answer: B. Schedule collaboratively.

Collaborative scheduling of students to receive services is both your responsibility and that of the service provider. Scheduling together allows for both your convenience and that of the service provider. It also will provide you with an opportunity to make sure the student does not miss important information.

43. **Cognitive learning strategies include:**
     (Skill 5.12) (Rigorous)

A.   Reinforcing appropriate behavior

B.   Teaching students how to manage their own behavior in school

C.   Heavily structuring the learning environment

D.   Generalizing learning from one setting to another

Answer: B. Teaching students how to manage their own behavior in school

Engaging students as participants in learning is an example of creating metacognitive learning.

44. **Which of the following must be provided in a written notice to parents when proposing a child's educational placement?**
     (Skill 6.03) (Easy)

A.   A list of parental due process safeguards

B.   A list of current test scores

C.   A list of persons responsible for the child's education

D.   A list of academic subjects the child has passed

Answer: A. A list of parental due process safeguards

Written notice must be provided to parents prior to a proposal or refusal or refusal to initiate or make a change in the child's identification, evaluation or educational placement. Notices must contain:

- A listing of parental due process safeguards.
- A description and a rationale for the chosen action.
- A detailed listing of components (e.g. tests, records, reports) which were
- The basis for the decision.
- Assurance that the language and content of the notices were understood by the parents.

45.   **What determines whether a person is entitled to protection under Section 504?**
      (Skill 6.03) (Average)

A.   The individual must meet the definition of a person with a disability

B.   The person must be able to meet the requirements of a particular program in spite of his or her disability

C.   The school, business or other facility must be the recipient of federal funding assistance

D.   All of the above

Answer: D. All of the above

To be entitled to protection under Section 504, an individual must meet the definition of a person with a disability, which is: any person who (i) has a physical or mental impairment which substantially limits one or more of that person's major life activities, (ii) has a record of such impairment, or (iii) is regarded as having such an impairment. Major life activities are: caring for oneself, performing manual tasks, walking, seeing, hearing, speaking, breathing, learning, and working. The person must also be "otherwise qualified," which means that the person must be able to meet the requirements of a particular program in spite of the disability. The person must also be afforded "reasonable accommodations" by recipients of federal financial assistance.

46. **Free Appropriate Public Education (FAPE) describes special education and related services as?**
    (Skill 6.03) (Easy)

A. Public expenditure and standard to the state educational agency

B. Provided in conformity with each student's individualized education program, if the program is developed to meet requirements of the law.

C. Include preschool, elementary and/or secondary education in the state involved

D. All of the above.

Answer: D. All of the above.

FAPE states that special education and related services are provided at public expense; meet the standards of the state educational agency; include preschool, elementary and/or secondary education in the state involved; and are provided in conformity with each student's IEP.

47. **Strategies specifically designed to move the learner from dependence to independence include:**
    (Skill 6.04) (Rigorous)

A. Assessment, planning, implementation, and reevaluation

B. Demonstration, imitation, assistance, prompting, and verbal instruction

C. Cognitive modeling and self-guidance through overt, faded overt and covert stages

D. B and C

Answer: D. B and C

Both are correct, as demonstration is a form of modeling.

48. **Target behaviors must be:**
    (Skill 6.04) (Rigorous)

A.   Observable

B.   Measurable

C.   Definable

D.   All of the above

Answer: D. All of the above

Behaviors must be observable, measurable and definable in order to be assessed and changed.

49. **Which tangible reinforcer would Mr. Whiting find to be most effective with teenagers?**
    (Skill 6.05) (Easy)

A.   Plastic whistle

B.   Winnie-the-Pooh book

C.   Free Homework Pass

D.   Toy ring

Answer: C. Free Homework Pass

Students in their teens often want something that will assist their grades. Tangible rewards such as the homework pass are appropriate for this age level.

50. **Charise comes into your room and seems to know every button to push to get you upset with her. What would be a good intervention?** *(Skill 6.05) (Rigorous)*

A. Nonverbal Interactions

B. Self-monitoring

C. Proximity Control

D. Planned Ignoring

Answer: D. Planned Ignoring

Planned Ignoring takes control from the student and tends to reduce the irritating behaviors as they do not draw the attention they were employed to receive.

51. **Children with disabilities are least likely to improve their social-interpersonal skills by:** *(Skill 6.06) (Rigorous)*

A. Developing sensitivity to other people

B. Making behavioral choices in social situations

C. Developing social maturity

D. Talking with their sister or brother.

Answer: D. Talking with their sister or brother.

The social skills of the child are known in the family, and seen as "normal" for him/her. Regular conversation with a family member would be the least conducive to improving social skills. Remember, the purpose in building social-interpersonal skills is to improve a person's ability to maintain interdependent relationships between persons.

52. **Modeling is an essential component of which self-training approach?**
(Skill 6.08) (Rigorous)

A. Self-instructional training

B. Self-monitoring

C. Self-reinforcing

D. Self-punishing

Answer: A. Self-instructional training

Cognitive modeling: The adult model performs a task while verbally instructing himself

Self-instruction: The child performs the task while instructing himself, silently or overtly

Self-monitoring: Refers to procedures by which the learner records whether or not he is engaging in certain behaviors, particularly those that would lead to increased academic achievement and/or social behavior

53. **A functional curriculum includes:**
(Skill 6.10) (Average)

A. A specific commercial curriculum

B. Life skills

C. Remedial academics

D. Vocational placement.

Answer: B. Life skills

While a, c and, d may be utilized in the functional curriculum, the curriculum may not be considered functional without addressing life skills.

54. **A Behavioral Intervention Plan (BIP):**
(Skill 6.10) (Rigorous)

A. Should be written by a team.

B. Should be reviewed annually.

C. Should be written by the teacher who is primarily responsible for the student.

D. Should consider placement.

Answer: A. Should be written by a team.

IDEA 2004, establishes that the BIP is a team intervention.

55. **IEPs continue to have multiple sections; one section, present levels now addresses what?**
(Skill 6.10) (Easy)

A. Academic achievement and functional performance

B. English as a second language

C. Functional performance

D. Academic achievement

Answer: A. Academic achievement and functional performance

The student's present level of academic achievement and functional performance is a required component of the IEP and essential to developing appropriate goals and objectives for the student.

56. **What can a teacher plan that will allow him/her to avoid adverse situations with students?**
(Skill 6.11) (Rigorous)

A. Lessons

B. Recess

C. Environment

D. Class schedule

Answer: C. Environment

The only preventative control over adverse situations is that which a teacher has over his/her room. Simple things, such as moving desk assignments to moving distractions and creating time-out areas, are environmental issues teachers can control.

57. **What TWO student behaviors are indicative of a possible crisis?**
(Skill 6.11) (Average)

A. Bullying and socially active.

B. Uncontrolled and intermittent periods of laughter and rage.

C. High academic performance and gang activity

D. Victim of violence and uncontrolled anger

Answer: D. Victim of violence and uncontrolled anger

While a student may display one behavior indicating he/she maybe be entering a crisis state for the school to be concerned about, often two or more signs are displayed. Victims of violence that display uncontrolled rage may be seen as a crisis waiting to happen.

58. **Students with autistic tendencies can be more successful academically when the teacher:**
(Skill 7.02) (Average)

A.   Ignores inappropriate behaviors.

B.   Allows them to go out of the room during instruction.

C.   Keeps a calendar on the board of expected transitions.

D.   Asks the ARD committee for a 1:1 aide.

Answer: C. Keeps a calendar on the board of expected transitions.

Students with autism tend to exhibit a resistance to transition unless that transition is already expected. Placing calendars and schedule where they can be seen are important to easing the stress associated with transitions.

59. **One of the most important goals of the special education teacher is to foster and create with the student:**
(Skill 7.02) (Easy)

A.   Handwriting skills.

B.   Self-Advocacy

C.   An increased level of reading

D.   Logical reasoning

Answer: B. Self-Advocacy

When a student achieves the ability to recognize his/her deficits and knows how to correctly advocate for his/her needs, the child has learned one of the most important skills of his/her life.

60.   **Children are engaged in a game of charades. Which type of social-interpersonal skill is the teacher most likely attempting to develop? (Skill 7.04) (Rigorous)**

A.   Sensitivity to others

B.   Making behavioral choices in social situations

C.   Social maturity

D.   All of the above

Answer: A. Sensitivity to others

Children with disabilities often perceive facial expressions and gestures differently to their nondisabled peers, due to their impairment. The game of charades, a guessing game, would help them develop sensitivity to others.

61.   **Students who receive special services in a regular classroom with consultation, generally have academic and/or social-interpersonal performance deficits at which level of severity? (Skill 7.04) (Easy)**

A.   Mild

B.   Moderate

C.   Severe

D.   Profound

Answer: A. Mild

The majority of students receiving special services are enrolled primarily in regular classes. Those with mild learning and behavior problems exhibit academic and/or social interpersonal deficits that are often evident only in a school-related setting. Physically, these students appear no different than their peers.

62. **Social maturity may be evidenced by the student's:**
(Skill 7.04) (Easy)

A. Recognition of rights and responsibilities (his own and others)

B. Display of respect for legitimate authority figures

C. Formulation of a valid moral judgment

D. Demonstration of all of the above

Answer: D. Demonstration of all of the above

Some additional evidence of social maturity:

- The ability to cooperate
- Following procedures formulated by an outside party
- Achieving appropriate levels of independence

63. **Five-year-old Tom continues to substitute the "w" sound for the "r" sound when pronouncing words; therefore, he often distorts words e.g., "wabbit" for "rabbit" and "wat" for "rat." His articulation disorder is basically a problem in:**
(Skill 8.01) (Average)

A. Phonology

B. Morphology

C. Syntax

D. Semantics

Answer: A. Phonology

Phonology is the system of rules about sounds and sound combinations for a language. A phoneme is the smallest unit of sound that combines with other sounds to make words.

64. **Which of the following is untrue about the ending "er?"**
   (Skill 8.01) (Rigorous)

A. It is an example of a free morpheme

B. It represents one of the smallest units of meaning within a word

C. It is called an inflectional ending

D. When added to a word, it connotes a comparative status

Answer: A. It is an example of a free morpheme

Morpheme: the smallest unit of meaningful language. "Er" on its own, has no meaning.

65. **Which component of language involves language content rather than the form of language?** *(Skill 8.01) (Average)*

A. Phonology

B. Morphology

C. Semantics

D. Syntax

Answer: C. Semantics

Semantics involves specifics regarding word usage.

66. How many major categories do most reading programs conceptually separate the reading process into? *(Skill 8.02) (Easy)*

A. One

B. Two

C. Three

D. Four

Answer: C. Three

Most reading programs conceptually separate the reading process into three major categories: sight word vocabulary, word attack skills, and reading comprehension.

67. Daniela is a first grade student who is misspelling words such as 'again,' 'some,' and 'were.' She would most benefit from explicit instruction and reinforcement in which facet of the reading process? *(Skill 8.02) (Average)*

A. Sight Words

B. Reading Comprehension

C. Fluency

D. Word Attack Skills

Answer: A. Sight Words

Sight words are high-frequency words that are easily identified by a learner. Primary age students will use word lists composed of high-frequency words such as the Dolch Sight Words.

68. **Comprehension categories should be classified by which of the following?** *(Skill 8.02) (Average)*

A. Literal Meaning

B. Reorganization

C. Inference

D. All of the above

Answer: D. All of the above

Thomas Barrett suggests that comprehension categories should be classified as: literal meaning, reorganization, inference, evaluation, and appreciation.

69. **What is a major approach for teaching beginning reading skills?** *(Skill 8.03) (Average)*

A. Linguistic Emphasis

B. Meaning Emphasis

C. Code Emphasis

D. B and C

Answer: D. B and C

Methods of teaching beginning reading skills may be divided into two major approaches: code emphasis and meaning emphasis.

70. **Which of the following is an example of a whole language, or whole-word, reading program?** *(Skill 8.03)(Average)*

A. Merrill Linguistic Reading

B. Edmark Reading

C. Orton-Gillingham

D. DISTAR

Answer: B. Edmark Reading

Edmark Reading Program is a whole-word approach to reading. It is not phonetically-based, and includes the use of sight words and whole word methods for teaching reading.

71. **Maribel is a fifth grader who reads on grade level. She readily generates the purposes for reading a selection, forms questions, and then reads her selection. Maribel is exhibiting which variation of the directed reading method?** *(Skill 8.03)(Rigorous)*

A. Language Experience Approach

B. Individualized Reading Approach

C. Direct-Reading Thinking Activity

D. Pre-Reading Strategies

Answer: C. Direct-Reading Thinking Activity

A variation of the direct reading method is the DRTA, or Direct-Reading Thinking Activity. This is where the student must generate the purpose for reading the selection, form questions, and read the selection.

72. **Using word families, such as the –un family, including words like fun, sun, and run, is an advantageous approach when teaching beginning reading because: (Skill 8.03) (Average)**

A. Students recognize similar spelling patterns

B. Vocabulary is highly controlled

C. There is an emphasis on auditory memory skills

D. Nonsense words are used

Answer: A. Students recognize similar spelling patterns.

Some advantages sees the consistent spelling patterns of the lessons, which guide the students to understand and recognize similar word endings, spelling features, and rhyming sounds.

73. **In which stage of spelling development does a child typically grasp left to right letter arrangement? (Skill 8.04) (Average)**

A.   Pre-Communicative Stage

B. Semi-phonetic Stage

C. Phonetic Stage

D. Transitional Stage

Answer: B. Semi-phonetic Stage

Semi-phonetic Stage of Spelling, ages 4–6

• Begin to understand letters have sounds, but cannot make a total letter/sound match.
• Use letter names to stand for words (R for are).
• Grasp left to right letter arrangement.
• Know the alphabet letter names and formation.
• Are developing the ability to segment words into sounds (phonemic awareness).
• Can identify beginning sound, ending sound, and strong medial consonants or surface sounds.
• Children at this stage are putting the pieces together when it comes to the alphabet. They are thinking about using letters to represent words even if their understanding still has some gaps.

74. **Which activity most specifically promotes phonemic awareness development, and helps students relate the sounds to letters as they spell words?** *(Skill 8.04) (Average)*

A. Direct Instruction

B. Word Dictation

C. Syllabication

D. Segmenting Words into Phonemes

Answer: D. Segmenting Words into Phonemes

This directly impacts a child's ability to spell. Direct instruction in phonemic awareness, especially in how to segment words into phonemes, helps children relate the sounds of letters as they spell words.

75. **The CTOPP and the PAT 2 are two examples of:** *(Skill 8.04) (Rigorous)*

A. Reading evaluations

B. Phonological assessments

C. Fluency assessments

D. Sight Word evaluations

Answer: B. Phonological Assessments

These two tests help determine a student's level of phonological functioning so goals can be established.

76. **When learning blending and segmenting of sounds, a kinesthetic learner may prefer to:** *(Skill 8.04) (Average)*

A.   Move hands together and apart

B.   Use computer software

C.   Draw diagrams

D.   Listen to sounds

Answer: A.   Move hands together and apart

Kinesthetic learners prefer to learn with movement incorporated into their lessons and activities. This multisensory methodology allows kinesthetic pathways to be highlighted at the learner is acquiring information, in their preferred learning style, and is likely to be more effective.

77. **Name the two parts which make up the alphabetic principle.** *(Skill 8.05) (Average)*

A.   Alphabetic understanding and word analysis

B.   Decoding skills and phonological recoding

C.   Alphabetic understanding and phonological recoding

D.   Phonological recoding and spelling skills

Answer: C.   Alphabetic understanding and phonological decoding

The alphabetic principle is made up of two parts: alphabetic understanding and phonological decoding.

78.   **What is an example of a CVCC word?** *(Skill 8.05) (Easy)*

A.   bat

B.   bait

C.   bake

D.   belt

Answer: D. belt

CVCC words begin with a consonant, followed by a vowel which makes the short sound, then two consonants which make a consonant blend.

79.   **Irregular words do not conform to word analysis instruction. Which word below is irregular?** *(Skill 8.05) (Easy)*

A.   was

B.   hand

C.   tale

D.   yet

Answer: A. was

The word 'was' is phonetically spelled 'wuz' and therefore, does not conform to word analysis. It is an irregular word which can be taught as a sight word for memorization.

80. **Which system is used to assess the alphabetic principle?** *(Skill 8.05) (Average)*

A. DIBELS

B. PAT 2

C. WISC

D. LEP

Answer: A. DIBELS

DIBELS is a system in which students are given nonsense words such as 'ot' and 'yog' and are asked to sound out or read each nonsense word to determine if the student knows the letter sound correspondence.

81. **What is a metalinguistic ability a young child acquires through early involvement in reading activities?** *(Skill 8.06) (Average)*

A. Word consciousness

B. Functions of print

C. Fluency

D. All of the above

Answer: D. All of the above

A child acquires all three due to early involvement with reading activities. He or she also gains language and conventions of print.

82.   Mrs. Sanchez is constructing a checklist for her reading group students. The list includes several traits of good readers. Which of the following may appear on this list? (*Skill 8.06*) (*Average*)

A.   Skim and scan unfamiliar words

B.   Establish a purpose for reading, before reading

C.   Make predictions and formulate questions

D.   B and C

Answer: D. B and C

Research on reading development has yielded information on the behaviors and habits of good readers versus poor readers. Some of the characteristics of good readers are:

- Before reading, good readers establish a purpose for reading, select possible text structure, choose a reading strategy, and make predictions about what will be in the reading.
- They think about the information that they will read in the text, formulate questions that they predict will be answered in the text, and confirm those predictions the information in the text.
- As they read, good readers continually test and confirm their predictions, go back when something does not make sense, and make new predictions.
- When faced with unfamiliar words, they attempt to pronounce them using analogies to familiar words.

83.   Bryon is a ninth grader with dyslexia. He was tested and diagnosed in sixth grade. He does not read fluently, particularly when reading narrative texts for English class. His teacher is reading *Romeo and Juliet* with the class and has asked Bryon's consultant teacher for strategies to help Bryon read more fluently when reading his lines. Which of the following strategies is most effective? *(Skill 8.06) (Average)*

A.   Provide round robin reading activities

B.   Choose a segment of the text to reread until it sounds like "people talking"

C.   Copy the text into a journal

D.   None of the above

Answer: B. Choose a segment of the text to reread until it sounds like 'people talking.'

Other ways to boost fluency include providing short play and story frameworks, using marginal notes, and providing intensive word study in conjunction with the text selection.

84.   When students read, they utilize four sources of background information to comprehend the meaning behind the literal text. The four sources include word knowledge, syntax and contextual information, semantic knowledge, and: *(Skill 8.07) (Rigorous)*

A.   Vocabulary Lexicon

B.   Fluency

C.   Text Organization

D.   Sentence Variety

Answer: C. Text Organization

Good readers are able to differentiate types of text structure, e.g. story narrative, exposition, compare-contrast, or time sequence. They use knowledge of text to build expectations and construct a framework of ideas and details on which to build meaning. Poor readers may not be able to differentiate between types of text and often miss important ideas. They may also miss important ideas and details by concentrating on lesser or irrelevant details.

85. **What do students rely on in order to understand an unknown word they encounter in a text?** *(Skill 8.07) (Average)*

A.   Background Information

B.   Substitution

C.   Selective Omission

D.   Syntax

Answer: A. Background Information

When children encounter unknown words in a sentence, they rely on their background knowledge to choose a word that makes sense. Errors of younger children therefore are often substitutions of words in the same syntactic class. Poor readers often fail to make use of context clues to help them identify words or activate the background knowledge that would help them with comprehension. Poor readers also process sentences word by word, instead of "chunking" phrases and clauses, resulting in a slow pace that focuses on the decoding rather than comprehension. They also have problems answering who, what, where, when, or why questions, because of their problems with syntax.

86. **Knowledge of spelling patterns and pronunciations is called:** *(Skill 8.07) (Rigorous)*

A.   Orthographic Knowledge

B.   Lexical Knowledge

C.   Semantic Knowledge

D.   Decoding Knowledge

Answer: A. Orthographic Knowledge

Orthographic knowledge is important for readers to acquire so they know how to spell, identify words, and decode.

87. _____ is a skill that teachers help students develop to sustain learning throughout life
(Skill 8.07) (Rigorous)

A.   Work ethic

B.   Basic Math Computation

C.   Reading

D.   Critical thinking

Answer: D. Critical thinking

Critical thinking sustains the ability of a person to learn from life, books, and experience.

88. During which written composition stage are students encouraged to read their stories aloud to others?
(Skill 8.08) (Average)

A.   Planning

B.   Drafting

C.   Revising/editing

D.   Sharing/publication

Answer: C. Revising/editing

Reading stories to others is encouraged at this stage as both the child and the audience will distinguish errors and make corrections. The child also learns to accept constructive criticism.

89. **Which of the following is an example of cross-modal perception involving integrating visual stimuli to an auditory verbal process?** *(Skill 8.10) (Rigorous)*

A. Following spoken directions

B. Describing a picture

C. Finding certain objects in pictures

D. B and C

Answer: B. Describing a picture

We see (visual modality) the picture and use words (auditory modality) to describe it.

90. **Math instruction should move in a sequential manner, from:** *(Skill 9.01) (Average)*

A. Abstract to Semi-concrete to Concrete

B. Concrete to Semi-Concrete to Abstract

C. Semi-concrete to Concrete to Abstract

D. Abstract to Concrete to Semi-Concrete

Answer: B. Concrete to Semi-Concrete to Abstract

Concrete instruction is very literal, basic, and utilizes objects and manipulatives as well as several didactic tools. It is important to begin with concrete concepts first, so a student may then move to semi-concrete and then abstract concepts in math.

91.   **What is 1:1 correspondence?** *(Skill 9.01) (Average)*

A.   Using objects to represent quantities

B.   Using manipulatives to show patterns

C.   Recognizing numbers in order

D.   Recognizing number patterns

Answer: A.   Using objects to represent quantities

From as early as age two, children are expected to be able to count. Counting is a progression of numbers, and can be expressed concretely by using 1:1 correspondence. This entails holding an object, such as a block, and calling it 'one' as it is placed on the table. The following object picked up is therefore 'two,' then the next is 'three' and so forth. Understanding a number represents a quantifiable amount of objects is truly the underpinning of our number system.

92.   **The position of a number, or its _____, determines its value in the number system.** *(Skill 9.01) (Easy)*

A.   Quantity

B.   Place Value

C.   Order

D.   Face Value

Answer: B.   Place Value

Students need to know the given position of a number in order to understand its true value, or place value, alone or in the context of a larger or multi-digit number, before or after the decimal.

93. **Subtraction has three different interpretations. These include taking away, missing addend, and:** *(Skill 9.01) (Average)*

A.   Determined Order

B.   Missing Quotient

C.   Dividend

D.   Comparison

Answer: D. Comparison

Subtraction has three different interpretations. Comparison is important since it allows students to identify how much more one quantity is from another.

94. **Which is an example of repeated addition?** *(Skill 9.01) (Easy)*

A. $9 + 9 + 9 = 27$

B. $27 + 9 = 36$

C. $9 + 8 + 7 = 24$

D. $9 + 9 - 9 = 9$

Answer: A. $9 + 9 + 9 = 27$

Repeated addition also lends itself to skip counting, when a student can infer the next quantity by adding the same number repeatedly.

95. **Manipulatives, or the use of tactile objects, are useful to utilize with students for which operation?** *(Skill 9.01) (Average)*

A.   Addition

B.   Subtraction

C.   Multiplication

D.   All of the above

Answer: D.   All of the above.

Manipulatives and tactile objects allow students to gain a concrete understanding of all operations, as well as division.

96. **Which is an example of a fraction?** *(Skill 9.01) (Average)*

A.   Quotient

B.   Ratio

C.   Decimal Conversion

D.   B and C

Answer: D.   B and C

Ratio and Decimal conversions are examples of the forms fractions can take. Fractions can also be considered parts of a whole, or a subset of a parent set.

97. A special education teacher has asked a fifth grader, Raul, to use a highlighter to determine important information in math word problems. The highlighter is a tool to help Raul: *(Skill 9.01) (Rigorous)*

A. Identify important facts

B. Check computation

C. Find the main idea

D. None of the above.

Answer: A. Identify important facts

By using the highlighter, or even simply underlining and circling important data in a word problem, students can identify the important facts pertaining to the problem.

98. Students with visual or spatial integration problems may benefit from the use of _____ paper when problem solving to increase accuracy. *(Skill 9.01) (Average)*

A. Blank

B. Graph

C. Cut

D. Colored

Answer: B. Graph

Graph paper, as well as lined, or even folded paper, gives spatial parameters for calculations. They all give a framework for working on computation, and allow for organization to occur in math calculations, such as lining up decimals in an addition problem with monetary values.

99. **Classifying in math includes:** *(Skill 9.02) (Average)*

A. Sorting by characteristic

B. Lining up

C. Describing

D. All of the above

Answer: A. Sorting by characteristic

Sorting allows for categorization, whether it be by size, shape, color or other attributes.

100. **The idea of one number as being a part of another number is the:** *(Skill 9.02) (Average)*

A. Numerical Notation

B. Comparing Quantities

C. Pattern Identification

D. Part-Whole Concept

Answer: D. Part-Whole Concept

Most children afre able to understand this concept before entering school. They may also understand working with numbers larger than ten, and basic numerical notation.

101. A student's fluidity and flexibility with numbers is called: *(Skill 9.03) (Average)*

A.   Number Sense

B.   Computational Skill

C.   Memorization

D.   1:1 Correspondence

Answer: A. Number Sense

Number sense is truly the basis for mathematical understanding.

102. Where is number sense derived? *(Skill 9.03) (Rigorous)*

A.   Home

B.   School

C.   Siblings

D.   All of the above

Answer: D. All of the above

Number sense occurs before a child enters school, and continues into adulthood. Children may count objects, bake, cook, measure, and do other skills with parent or relative guidance, well before entering school

103. **Technology can enhance students' understanding of math. Which of the following is a technologically-driven math tool?** *(Skill 9.03) (Easy)*

A.   Math computer program

B.   Dry erase board

C.   Notebook

D.   Manipulatives

Answer: A.   Math computer program

Various games, software, programs, and websites provide additional math instruction to students for a very low cost, if any.

104. **Most children entering school are not developmentally ready to understand concepts such as?**
(Skill 9.03) (Rigorous)

A.   Zero symbol

B.   Equalizing.

C.   Joining

D.   Patterns

Answer: A. Zero symbol

Understanding the concept of zero requires an understanding of place value.

105. **The No Child Left Behind Act (NCLB) affected students with Limited English Proficiency (LEP)by :**
    (Skill 10.01) (Rigorous)

A.   Requiring these students to demonstrate English Language Proficiency before a high school diploma is granted.

B.   Providing allowances for schools not to require them to take and pass state reading exams (TAKS) if the students were enrolled in US schools for less than a year.

C.   Providing allowances for these students to opt out of state math tests if the student was enrolled in a US school for less than one year.

D.   Both B and C

Answer: A. Requiring these students to demonstrate English Language Proficiency before a high school diploma is granted.

NCLB stipulates that students who are classified as LEP must pass an English Language Proficiency assessment, in addition to completing the required number of class credits, before they can graduate from high school.

106. **The opportunity for a student with a disability to attend a class as close to the normal as possible describes:**
(Skill 10.01) (Easy)

A. Least Restrictive Environment

B. Normalization

C. Mainstreaming

D. Deinstitutionalization

Answer: B. Normalization

Normalization is a term coined in the early 1980s to describe a goal of creating conditions of care and environment as close to normal. This description tore down the concept of "institutionalization" in favor of community residence placement.

107. **Included in data brought to the attention of Congress regarding the evaluation procedures for education of students with disabilities was the fact that?**
(Skill 10.01) (Average)

A. There were a large number of children and youths with disabilities in the United States

B. Many children with disabilities were not receiving an appropriate education

C. Many parents of children with disabilities were forced to seek services outside of the public realm

D. All of the above

Answer: D. All of the above

All of the above listed factors were brought to the attention of Congress in an effort to bring about reform in the area of education of students with disabilities.

108. **The Individuals with Disabilities Education Act (IDEA) was signed into law in and later reauthorized to its current in what years?**
(Skill 10.01) (Easy)

A.   1975 and 2004

B.   1980 and 1990

C.   1990 and 2004

D.   1995 and 2001

Answer: C. 1990 and 2004

IDEA, Public Law 101-476 is a consolidation and reauthorization of all prior special education mandates, with amendments. It was signed into law by President Bush on October 30, 1990. Revision of IDEA occurred in 2004, IDEA was re-authorized as the Individuals with Disabilities Education Improvement Act of 2004 (IDEA 2004) is commonly referred to as IDEA 2004. IDEA 2004 became effective on July 1, 2005.

109. **How was the training of special education teachers changed by the No Child Left Behind Act of 2002?**
(Skill 10.01) (Average)

A.   Required all special education teachers to be certified in reading and math

B.   Required all special education teachers to take the same coursework as general education teachers

C.   If a special education teacher is teaching a core subject, he or she must meet the standard of a highly qualified teacher in that subject.

D.   All of the above

Answer: C. If a special education teacher is teaching a core subject, he or she must meet the standard of a highly qualified teacher in that subject.

In order for a special education teacher to be a student's sole teacher of a core subject, the teacher must meet the professional criteria of NCLB. The teacher must be *highly qualified*, that is certified or licensed in his/her area of special education and show proof of a specific level of professional development in the core subjects that he/she teaches. As special education teachers receive specific education in the core subject they teach, they will be better prepared to teach to the same level of learning standards as the general education teacher.

110. **Which component changed with the reauthorization of the Education for all Handicapped Children Act of 1975 (EHA) 1990 EHA Amendment?**
(Skill 10.01) (Average)

A.   Specific terminology

B.   Due process protections

C.   Non-discriminatory reevaluation procedures

D.   Individual Education Plans

Answer: A. Specific terminology

The EHA amendment requires specific terminology as a new component.

111. **Which is untrue about the Americans with Disabilities Act (ADA)?**
(Skill 10.01) (Easy)

A.   It was signed into law the same year as IDEA by President Bush

B.   It reauthorized the discretionary programs of EHA

C.   It gives protection to all people on the basis of race, sex, national origin, and religion

D.   It guarantees equal opportunities to persons with disabilities in employment, public accommodations, transportation, government services, and telecommunications.

Answer: B. It reauthorized the discretionary programs of EHA

EHA is the precursor of IDEA, the Individuals with Disabilities Education Act. ADA, however, is Public Law 101 – 336, the Americans with Disabilities Act, which gives civil rights protection to all individuals with disabilities in private sector employment, all public services, public accommodations, transportation and telecommunications. It was patterned after the Rehabilitation Act of 1973.

112. **Legislation in Public Law 94 – 142 attempts to:**
(Skill 10.01) (Rigorous)

A.   Match the child's educational needs with appropriate educational services

B.   Include parents in the decisions made about their child's education

C.   Establish a means by which parents can provide input

D.   All of the above

Answer: D. All of the above

Much of what was stated in separate court rulings and mandated legislation was brought together into what is now considered to be the "backbone" of special education. Public Law 94 – 142, (education for All Handicapped Children Act) was signed into law by President Ford in 1975. It was the culmination of a great deal of litigation and legislation from the late 1960's to the mid-1970's, that included decisions supporting the need to assure an appropriate education to all persons regardless of race, creed, or disability. In 1990, this law was reauthorized and renamed the Individuals with Disabilities education Act, IDEA.

113. **Which legislation has forced public and private facilities to accommodate those who have physical disabilities?**
(Skill 10.01) (Easy)

A.   ADA

B.   IDEA

C.   504 Plan

D.   PL 105-17

Answer: A. ADA

To date many accommodations to public facilities such as sidewalks, public transit, and public bathrooms have been made because of the expressed needs which were legislated in the American's With Disabilities Act.

114. **Bob shows behavior problems such as lack of attention, out of seat and talking out. His teacher has kept data on these behaviors and has found that Bob is showing much better self-control since he has been self-managing himself through a behavior modification program. The most appropriate placement recommendation for Bob at this time is probably:**
(Skill 10.02) (Average)

A.   Any available part-time special education program

B.   The regular classroom solely

C.   A social behavior class for one period a day

D.   A resource room for one period a day

Answer: B. The regular classroom solely

Bob is able to self-manage himself and is very likely to behave like the other children in the regular classroom. The regular classroom is the least restrictive environment.

115. Which of the following examples would be considered of highest priority when determining the need for the delivery of appropriate special education and related services?
(Skill 10.06) (Rigorous)

A.   A ten-year-old girl with profound mental retardation who is receiving education services in a state institution.

B.   A six-year-old girl who has been diagnosed with autism is placed in a special education class within the local school. Her mother wants her to attend residential school next year, even though the girl is showing progress.

C.   An eight-year-old boy is repeating first grade for the second time and exhibits problems with toileting, gross motor functions, and remembering number and letter symbols. His regular classroom teacher claims the referral forms are too time-consuming and refuses to complete them. He also refuses to make accommodations because he feels every child should be treated alike.

D.   A twelve-year-old boy with mild disabilities who was placed in a behavior disorders program, but displays obvious perceptual deficits (e.g. reversal of letters and symbols, and inability to discriminate sounds). He was originally thought to have a learning disability, but did not meet state criteria for this exceptionality category, based on results of standard scores. He has always had problems with attending to a task, and is now beginning to get into trouble during seatwork time. His teacher feels that he will eventually become a real behavior problem. He receives social skills training in the resource room one period a day.

Answer: C. An eight-year-old boy is repeating first grade for the second time and exhibits problems with toileting, gross motor functions, and remembering number and letter symbols. His regular classroom teacher claims the referral forms are too time-consuming and refuses to complete them. He also refuses to make accommodations because he feels every child should be treated alike.

Although all of the above are important areas of need, the most critical would be the child for whom no modifications are being made.

116. **You note that a child in your class is expressing discomfort when placing his back against a chair. You ask him if he is OK, and he says its nothing. You notice what appears to be a belt mark on his shoulder. What is the first thing you should do?**
     (Skill 10.07) (Rigorous)

A.   Send the child to the nurse.

B.   Contact an administrator.

C.   Call Child Protective Services

D.   Follow the school policy.

Answer: D. Follow the school policy.

You are required to report all suspected abuse and neglect to CPS. Most schools have policies in place regarding this issue, however, the law requires you to report your concerns. Many school policies request giving prior notice to an administrator before calling CPS. This action allows for easier communication between you, CPS, and the school. Depending on the abuse, the child may need to see the nurse immediately. You may also have to judge the child's reaction before requesting him/her to go to the nurse.

117. **You are monitoring the cafeteria and you noticed Joshua stuffing his pockets with food. Not just snack food, but lunch items as well. You suspect:**
     (Skill 10.07) (Average)

A.   Joshua may not be getting fed at home.

B.   Joshua has Obsessive Compulsive Disorder (OCD).

C.   Joshua is just an average growing boy.

D.   Joshua is trying to be funny.

Answer: A. Joshua may not be getting fed at home.

Hording food is a symptom of neglect. The child wants to save the food because he will not have anything to eat after school, or before school. Inform your administrator of your suspicion and collaborate with other professionals to address your concerns.

118. **In order for a student to function independently in the learning environment, which of the following must be true?**
     (Skill 10.08) (Average)

A.   The learner must understand the nature of the content

B.   The student must be able to do the assigned task

C.   The teacher must communicate the task to the learner

D.   The student must complete the task.

Answer: B. The student must be able to do the assigned task

Together with the above, the child must be able to ask for and obtain assistance if necessary.

119. **Jane is a third grader. Mrs. Smith, her teacher, noted that Jane was having difficulty with math and reading assignments. The results from recent diagnostic tests showed a strong sight vocabulary, strength in computational skills, but a weakness in comprehending what she read. This weakness was apparent in mathematical word problems as well. The multi-disciplinary team recommended placement in a special education resource room for two periods each school day. For the remainder of the school day, her placement will be:**
     (Skill 10.08) (Average)

A.   In the regular classroom

B.   At a special school

C.   In a self-contained classroom

D.   In a resource room

Answer: A. In the regular classroom

The resource room is a special room inside the school environment where the child goes to be taught by a teacher who is certified in the area of disability. The remainder of the school day should be with her grade level peers in the general education setting.

120. **A mother is upset that her child is not being helped and asks you about the difference between the 504 Plan and an IEP. What is the difference?**
(Skill 11.01) (Rigorous)

A. 504 plan requires classification, IEP requires labeling.

B. 504 plan provides no services, only adaptations.

C. 504 plan is better for children who have ADHD.

D. 504 plan provides little interventions/services, while an IEP is more intensive providing more services, such as a special class.

Answer: D. 504 plan provides little interventions/services, while an IEP is more intensive providing more services such as a special class.

504 plans provide for only a few services, such as a test modification or the allowance of a child to have a fidget toy. IEPs are needed for to receive modified instruction and more services to assist the student's academic success.

121. **Which of the following is a specific change of language in IDEA?**
(Skill 11.05) (Average)

A. The term "Disorder" changed to "Disability"

B. The term "Children" changed to "Children and Youth"

C. The term "Handicapped" changed to "Impairments"

D. The term "Handicapped" changed to "With Disabilities"

Answer: D. The term "Handicapped" changed to "With Disabilities"

"Children" became "individuals", highlighting the fact that some students with special needs were adolescents not just "children". The word "handicapped" was changed to "with disabilities", denoting the difference between limitations imposed by society, (handicap) and an inability to do certain things (disability). "With disabilities" also demonstrates that the person is thought of first, and the disabling condition is but one of the characteristics of the individual.

122. **Which is a less than ideal example of collaboration in successful inclusion?**
(Skill 12.01) (Rigorous)

A. Special education teachers are part of the instructional team in a regular classroom

B. Special education teachers are informed of the lesson before hand and assist regular education teachers in the classroom

C. Teaming approaches are used for problem solving and program implementation

D. Regular teachers, special education teachers, and other specialists or support teachers co-teach

Answer: B. Special education teachers are informed of the lesson before hand and assist regular education teachers in the classroom

In an inclusive classroom, all students need to see both teachers as equals. The situation described places the special education teacher more in a paraprofessional role. In effective inclusion, both the regular education and the special education teacher take equal responsibility for the class.

123. **The best resource a teacher can have to reach a student is?**
(Skill 12.01) (Rigorous)

A. Contact with the parents/guardians.

B. A successful behavior modification Exam.

C. A listening ear.

D. Gathered scaffold approach to teaching.

Answer: A. Contact with the parents/guardians.

Parents are often the best source of information on their children. They generally know if a behavior management technique will be successful. They also can inform you of influences outside of school that may affect school performance and behavior.

124. A paraprofessional has been assigned to assist you in the classroom. What action on the part of the teacher would lead to a poor working relationship?
(Skill 12.02) (Average)

A.   Having the paraprofessional lead a small group.

B.   Telling the paraprofessional what you expect him/her to do.

C.   Defining classroom behavior management as your responsibility alone.

D.   Taking an active role in his/her evaluation.

Answer: C. Defining classroom behavior management as your responsibility alone.

When you do not allow another adult in the room to enforce the class rules, you create an environment where the other adult is seen as someone not to be respected. No one wants to be in a work environment where they do not feel respected.

125. Mrs. Freud is a consultant teacher. She has two students with Mr. Ricardo. Mrs. Freud should:
(Skill 12.02) (Average)

A.   Co-Teach

B.   Spend two days a week in the classroom helping out.

C.   Discuss lessons with the teacher and suggest modifications before class.

D.   Pull her students out for instructional modifications.

Answer: C. Discuss lessons with the teacher and suggest modifications before class.

Consultant teaching provides the least interventions possible for the academic success of the child. An occasional observation of the dynamics of the classroom may also be helpful to make appropriate suggestions for providing modifications for the student.

126. **If a student is predominantly a visual learner, he may learn more effectively by:**
(Skill 12.02) (Easy)

A.   Reading aloud while studying

B.   Listening to a cassette tape

C.   Watching a DVD

D.   Using body movement

Answer: C. Watching a DVD

Visual learners use their sense of sight, which is the sense being used to watch a DVD.

127. **Presentation of tasks can be altered to match the student's rate of learning by:**
(Skill 12.02) (Rigorous)

A.   Describing how much of a topic is presented in one day and how much practice is assigned, according to the student's abilities and learning style

B.   Using task analysis, assign a certain number of skills to be mastered in a specific amount of time

C.   Introducing a new task only when the student has demonstrated mastery of the previous task in the learning hierarchy

D.   Using standardized assessments to measure skills.

Answer: C. Introducing a new task only when the student has demonstrated mastery of the previous task in the learning hierarchy

Pacing is the term used for altering of tasks to match the student's rate of learning. This can be done in two ways; altering the subject content and the rate at which tasks are presented.

128. **All of the following are suggestions for altering the presentation of tasks to match the student's rate of learning except:**
(Skill 12.02) (Average)

A. Teach in several shorter segments of time rather than a single lengthy session

B. Continue to teach a task until the lesson is completed in order to provide more time on task

C. Watch for nonverbal cues that indicate students are becoming confused, bored, or restless

D. Avoid giving students an inappropriate amount of written work

Answer: B. Continue to teach a task until the lesson is completed in order to provide more time on task

This action taken does not alter the subject content; neither does it alter the rate at which tasks are presented.

129. **You should prepare for a parent-teacher conference by:**
(Skill 12.02) (Average)

A. Memorizing student progress/grades.

B. Anticipating questions.

C. Scheduling the meetings during your lunch time.

D. Planning a tour of the school.

Answer: B. Anticipating questions.

It pays to anticipate parent questions. It makes you more likely to be able to answer them. It is also possible that your anticipating them may be a way for you to plan what to speak to the parent about.

130. **Lotzie is not labeled as needing special education services and appears unable to function on grade level in both academics and socially. He is in 9th grade reading picture books, and consistently displays immature behavior that can be misinterpreted. You have already observed these behaviors. What should be done first?** *(Skill 12.02) (Rigorous)*

A.   Establish a rapport with the parents.

B.   Initiate a special education referral

C.   Plan and discuss possible interventions with the teacher.

D.   Address the class about acceptance.

Answer: A. Establish a rapport with the parents.

When a student enters 9th grade in a poor placement such as this, it is not unusual for the parents to have been opposed to special education. The best way to help the student is to establish a rapport with the parents. You need to help them see why their child would benefit from special education services.

131. **Television, movies, radio, and newspapers contribute to the public's poor understanding of disabilities by:** *(Skill 12.04) (Average)*

A.   Only portraying those who look normal.

B.   Portraying the person with the disability as one with incredible abilities.

C.   Showing emotionally disturbed children

D.   Portraying all people in wheel chairs as independent.

Answer: B. Portraying the person with the disability as one with incredible abilities.

Many movies, TV shows, etc. only show a person with a disability who has "overcome" his/her disability with a talent. The media tends to only show those with incredible talent, and ignore any struggles the person with disabilities may have had.

132. **An individual with disabilities in need of employability training, as well a job, should be referred to what governmental agency for assistance?**
     (Skill 12.04) (Average)

A.   Office of Mental Retardation and Developmental Disabilities (OMRDD)

B.   Vocational and Educational Services for Individuals with Disabilities (VESID)

C.   Social Services

D.   ARC

Answer: B. Vocational and Educational Services for Individuals with Disabilities (VESID)

While the other agencies may also be able to provide services, VESID is the agency that specifically targets vocational services for individuals with disabilities.

133. **What do the 9th and 10th Amendments to the U.S. Constitution state about education?**
     (Skill 12.09) (Rigorous)

A.   That education belongs to the people

B.   That education is an unstated power vested in the states

C.   That elected officials mandate education

D.   That education is free

Answer: A. That education belongs to the people

The concept of unstated power regarding education was instituted. It was felt that some education should be state specific. The refusal of states to provide services for those needing special education services, and a need for financial support encouraged the federal government to take a more involved stance.

134. **Manifest Determination Review (MDR) ARD committees should first:**
(Skill 12.10) (Average)

A. Make a decision on whether to return the student to placement

B. Determine if the disability was a cause of the behavior.

C. Evaluate the placement for possible needed change.

D. Examine past behaviors.

Answer: B. Determine if the disability was a cause of the behavior.

The purpose of the Manifest Determination Review (MDR) ARD committee is to evaluate the behavior in light of the student's disability. IDEA 2004 states that if the behavior was not related to the student's disability, the student should receive the same disciplinary consequence as a student who does not have a disability.

135. **A Pre-IEP team coordinates and participates in due diligence through what process?**
(Skill 12.10) (Rigorous)

A. Child study team meets first time without parents

B. Teachers take child learning concerns to the school counselor

C. School personnel initiate Response to Intervention (RTI)

D. All of the above

Answer: D. All of the above

The Pre-IEP Team coordinates and participates in due diligence through a process that includes teachers or parents concerns about academic or functional development. The school counselor is typically the person who coordinates the Response to Intervention data and referrals for special education assessment.

REFERENCES

AGER, C.L. & COLE, C.L. (1991). A review of cognitive-behavioral interventions for children and adolescents with behavioral disorders. Behavioral Disorders. 16(4), 260-275.

AIKEN, L.R. (1985). Psychological Testing and Assessment (5th ed.) Boston: Allyn and Bacon.

ALBERTO, P.A. & TROUTHMAN, A.C. (1990). Applied Behavior Analysis for Teachers: Influencing Students Performance. Columbus, Ohio: Charles E. Merrill.

ALGOZZINE, B. (1990) Behavior Problem Management. Educator's Resource Service. Gaithersburg, MD: Aspen Publishers.

ALGOZZINE, B., RUHL, K., 7 RAMSEY, R. (1991). Behaviorally Disordered? Assessment for Identification and Instruction CED Mini-library. Renson, VA: The Council for Exceptional Children.

AMBRON, S.R. (1981. Child Development (3rd ed.). New York: Holt, Rinehart and Winston.

ANERSON, V., & BLACK, L. (Eds.). (1987, Winter). National news: U.S. Department of Education releases special report (Editorial). GLRS Journal [Georgia Learning Resources System].

ANGUILI, r. (1987, Winter). The 1986 Amendment to the Education of the Handicapped Act. Confederation [A quarterly publication of the Georgia Federation Council for Exceptional Children].

ASHLOCK, R.B. (1976). Error Patterns in Computation: A Semi-programmed Approach (2nd ed.). Columbus, Ohio: Charles E. Merrill.

ASSOCIATION OF RETARDED CITIZENS OF GEORGIA (1987). 1986-87 Government Report. College Park, GA: Author.

AUSUBEL, D.P. & SULLIVAN, E.V. (1970) Theory and Problems of Child Development. New York: Grune & Stratton.

BANKS, J.A., & McGee Banks, C.A. (1993). Multicultural Education (2nd ed.). Boston: Allyn and Bacon.

BARRETT, T.C. (Ed.). (1967). The Evaluation of Children's Reading Achievement. In Perspectives in Reading No. 8. Newark, Delaware: International Reading Association.

BARTOLI, J.S. (1989). An ecological response to Cole's interactivity alternative. Journal of Learning Disabilities, 22(5). 292-297.

BASILE-JACKSON, J. The Exceptional Child in the Regular Classroom. Augusta, GA: East Georgia Center, Georgia Learning Resources System.

BAUER, A.M., & SHEA, T.M. (1989). Teaching Exceptional Students in Your Classroom. Boston: Allyn and Bacon.

BENTLEY, E.L. Jr. (1980). Questioning Skills [Videocassette & manual series]. Northbrook, IL. Hubbard Scientific Company. (Project STRETCH [Strategies to Train Regular Educators to Teach Children with Handicaps]. Module 1. ISBN 0-8331-1906-0).

BERDINE, W.H. & BLACKHURST, A.E. (1985). An Introduction to Special Education. (2nd ed.) Boston: Little, Brown and Company.

BLAKE, K. (1976). The Mentally Retarded: An Educational Psychology. Englewood Cliff, NJ: Prentice-Hall.

BOHLINE, D.S. (1985). Intellectual and Affective Characteristics of Attention Deficit Disordered Children. Journal of Learning Disabilities. 18 (10). 604-608.

BOONE, R. (1983). Legislation and litigation. In R.E. Schmid, & L. Negata (Eds.). Contemporary Issues in Special Education. New York: McGraw Hill.

BRANTLINGER, E.A., & GUSKIN, S.L. (1988). Implications of social and cultural differences for special education. In Meten, E.L. Vergason, G.A., & Whelan, R.J. Effective Instructional Strategies for Exceptional Children. Denver, CO: Love Publishing.

BREWTON, B. (1990). Preliminary identification of the socially maladjusted. In Georgia Psycho-educational Network, Monograph #1. An Educational Perspective On: Emotional Disturbance and Social Maladjustment. Atlanta, GA Psychoeducational Network.

BROLIN, D.E. & KOKASKA, C.J. (1979). Career Education for Handicapped Children Approach. Renton, VA: The Council for Exceptional Children.

BROLIN, D.E. (Ed). (1989) Life Centered Career Education: A Competency Based Approach. Reston, VA: The Council for Exceptional Children.

BROWN, J.W., LEWIS, R.B., & HARCLEROAD, F.F. (1983). AV instruction: Technology, Media, and Methods (6TH ED.). New York: McGraw-Hill.

BRYAN, T.H., & BRYAN, J.H. (1986). Understanding Learning Disabilities (3rd ed.). Palo Alto, CA: Mayfield.

BRYEN, D.N. (1982). Inquiries Into Child Language. Boston: Allyn & Bacon.

BUCHER, B.D. (1987). Winning Them Over. New York: Times Books.

BUSH, W.L., & WAUGH, K.W. (1982). Diagnosing Learning Problems (3rd ed.) Columbus, OH: Charles E. Merrill.

CAMPBELL, P. (1986). Special Needs Report [Newsletter]. 1(1). 1-3.

CARBO, M., & DUNN, K. (1986). Teaching Students to Read Through Their Individual Learning Styles. Englewood Cliffs, NJ. Prentice Hall.

CARTWRIGHT, G.P. & CARTWRIGHT, C.A., & WARD, M.E. (1984). Educating Special Learners (2nd ed.). Belmont, CA: Wadsworth.

CEJKA, J.M. (Consultant), & NEEDHAM, F. (Senior Editor). (1976). Approaches to Mainstreaming. [Filmstrip and cassette kit, units 1 & 2]. Boston: Teaching Resources Corporation. (Catalog Nos. 09-210 & 09-220).

CHALFANT, J. C. (1985). Identifying Learning Disabled Students: A Summary of the National Task Force Report. Learning Disabilities Focus. 1, 9-20.

CHARLES, C.M. (1976). Individualizing Instructions. St Louis: The C.V. Mosby Company.

CHRISPEELS, J.H. (1991). District Leadership in Parent Involvement - Policies and Actions in Sand Diego. Phi Delta Kappa, 71, 367-371.

CLARIZIO, H.F. (1987). Differentiating Characteristics. In Georgia Psychoeducational Network, Monograph #1, An educational Perspective on: Emotional Disturbance and Social Maladjustment. Atlanta, GA Psychoeducational Network.

CLARIZIO, H.F. & MCCOY, G.F. (1983) Behavior Disorders in Children (3rd ed.). New York: Harper & Row.]

COLES, G.S. (1989). Excerpts from The Learning Mystique: A Critical Look at Disabilities. Journal of Learning Disabilities. 22 (5). 267-278.

COLLINS, E. (1980). Grouping and Special Students. [Videocassette & manual series]. Northbrook, IL: Hubbard Scientific Company. (Project STRETCH [Strategies to Train Regular Educators to Teach Children with Handicaps], Module 17, ISBN 0- 8331-1922-2).

CRAIG, E., & CRAIG, L. (1990). Reading In the Content Areas [Videocassette & manual series]. Northbrook, IL: Hubbard Scientific Company. (Project STRETCH [Strategies to Train Regular Educators to Teach Children with Handicaps].Module 13, ISBN 0-8331-1918-4).

COMPTON, C., (1984). A Guide to 75 Tests for Special Education. Belmont, CA., Pitman Learning.

COUNCIL FOR EXCEPTIONAL CHILDREN. (1976). Introducing P.L. 94-142. [Filmstrip-cassette kit manual]. Reston, VA: Author.

COUNCIL FOR EXCEPTIONAL CHILDREN. (1987). The Council for Exceptional Children's Fall 1987. Catalog of Products and Services. Renton, VA: Author.

COUNCIL FOR EXCEPTIONAL CHILDREN DELEGATE ASSEMBLY. (1983). Council for Exceptional Children Code of Ethics (Adopted April 1983). Reston, VA: Author.

CZAJKA, J.L. (1984). Digest of Data on Person With Disabilities (Mathematics Policy Research, Inc.). Washington, D.C.: U.S. Government Printing Office.

DELL, H.D. (1972). Individualizing Instruction: Materials and Classroom Procedures. Chicago: Science Research Associates.

DEMONBREUN, C., & MORRIS, J. Classroom Management [Videocassette & Manual series]. Northbrook, IL: Hubbard Scientific Company. Project STRETCH (Strategies to Train Regular Educators to Teach Children with Handicaps]. Module 5, ISBN 0-8331-1910-9).

DEPARTMENT OF EDUCATION. Education for the Handicapped Law Reports. Supplement 45 (1981), p. 102: 52. Washington, D.C.: U.S. Government Printing Office.

DEPARTMENT OF HEALTH, EDUCATION AND WELFARE, OFFICE OF EDUCATION. (1977, August 23). Education of Handicapped Children. Federal Register, 42, (163).

DIANA VS. STATE BOARD OF EDUCATION, Civil No. 70-37 R.F.P. (N.D.Cal. January, 1970).

DIGANGI, S.A., PERRYMAN, P., & RUTHERFORD, R.B., Jr. (1990). Juvenile Offenders in the 90's A Descriptive Analysis. Perceptions, 25(4), 5-8.

DIVISION OF EDUCATIONAL SERVICES, SPECIAL EDUCATION PROGRAMS (1986). <u>Fifteenth Annual Report to Congress on Implementation of the Education of the Handicapped Act.</u> Washington, D.C.: U.S. Government Printing Office.

DOYLE, B.A. (1978). <u>Math Readiness Skills.</u> Paper presented at National Association of School Psychologists, New York. K.J. (1978). <u>Teaching Students Through Their Individual Learning Styles</u>.

DUNN, R.S., & DUNN, K.J. (1978). <u>Teaching Students Through Their Individual Learning Styles: A Practical Approach.</u> Reston, VA: Reston.

EPSTEIN, M.H., PATTON, J.R., POLLOWAY, E.A., & FOLEY, R. (1989). Mild retardation: Student characteristics and services. <u>Education and Training of the Mentally Retarded,</u> 24, 7-16.

EKWALL, E.E., & SHANKER, J.L. 1983). <u>Diagnosis and Remediation of the Disabled Reader</u> (2nd ed.) Boston: Allyn and Bacon.

FIRTH, E.E. & REYNOLDS, I. (1983). Slide tape shows: A creative activity for the gifted students. <u>Teaching Exceptional Children.</u> 15(3), 151-153.

FRYMIER, J., & GANSNEDER, B. (1989). <u>The Phi Delta Kappa Study of Students at Risk.</u> Phi Delta Kappa. 71(2) 142-146.

FUCHS, D., & DENO, S.L. 1992). Effects of curriculum within curriculum-based measurement. <u>Exceptional Children 58</u> (232-242).

FUCHS, D., & FUCHS, L.S. (1989). Effects of examiner familiarity on Black, Caucasian, and Hispanic Children. A Meta-Analysis. <u>Exceptional Children.</u> 55, 303-308.

FUCHS, L.S., & SHINN, M.R. (1989). Writing CBM IEP objectives. In M.R. Shinn, <u>Curriculum-based Measurement: Assessing Special Students.</u> New York: Guilford Press.

GAGE, N.L. (1990). <u>Dealing With the Dropout Problems?</u> Phi Delta Kappa. 72(4), 280-285.

GALLAGHER, P.A. (1988). <u>Teaching Students with Behavior Disorders: Techniques and Activities for Classroom Instruction</u> (2nd ed.). Denver, CO: Love Publishing.

GEARHEART, B.R. (1980). <u>Special Education for the 80s.</u> St. Louis, MO: The C.V. Cosby Company.

GEARHART, B.R. & WEISHAHN, M.W. (1986). <u>The Handicapped Student in the Regular Classroom</u> (2nd ed.). St Louis, MO: The C.V. Mosby Company.

GEARHART, B.R. (1985). <u>Learning Disabilities: Educational Strategies</u> (4th ed.). St. Louis: Times Mirror/ Mosby College of Publishing.

GEORGIA DEPARTMENT OF EDUCATION, PROGRAM FOR EXCEPTIONAL CHILDREN. (1986). <u>Mild Mentally Handicapped</u> (Vol. II), Atlanta, GA: Office of Instructional Services, Division of Special Programs, and Program for Exceptional Children. Resource Manuals for Program for Exceptional Children.

GEORGIA DEPARTMENT OF HUMAN RESOURCES, DIVISION OF REHABILITATION SERVICES. (1987, February). Request for Proposal [Memorandum]. Atlanta, GA: Author.

GEORGIA PSYCHOEDUCATIONAL NETWORK (1990). <u>An Educational Perspective on: Emotional Disturbance and Social Maladjustment.</u> Monograph #1. Atlanta, GA Psychoeducational Network.

GEREN, K. (1979). <u>Complete Special Education Handbook.</u> West Nyack, NY: Parker.

GILLET, P.K. (1988). Career Development. Robinson, G.A., Patton, J.R., Polloway, E.A., & Sargent, L.R. (eds.). <u>Best Practices in Mild Mental Disabilities.</u> Reston, VA: The Division on Mental Retardation of the Council for Exceptional Children.

GLEASON, J.B. (1993). <u>The Development of Language</u> (3rd ed.). New York: Macmillan Publishing.

GOOD, T.L., & BROPHY, J.E. (1978). <u>Looking into Classrooms</u> (2nd Ed.). New York: Harper & Row.

HALL, M.A. (1979). Language-Centered Reading: Premises and Recommendations. <u>Language Arts, 56</u> 664-670.

HALLLAHAN, D.P. & KAUFFMAN, J.M. (1988). <u>Exceptional Children: Introduction to Special Education.</u> (4th Ed.). Englewood Cliffs, NJ; Prentice-Hall.

HALLAHAN, D.P. & KAUFFMAN, J.M. (1994). <u>Exceptional Children: Introduction to Special Education</u> 6th ed.). Boston: Allyn and Bacon.

HAMMILL, D.D., & BARTEL, N.R. (1982). <u>Teaching Children With Learning and Behavior Problems</u> (3rd ed.). Boston: Allyn and Bacon.

HAMMILL, D.D., & BARTEL, N.R. (1986). <u>Teaching Students with Learning and Behavior Problems</u> (4th ed.). Boston and Bacon.

HAMILL, D.D., & BROWN, L. & BRYANT, B. (1989) A Consumer's Guide to Tests in Print. Austin, TX: Pro-Ed.

HANEY, J.B. & ULLMER, E.J. ((1970). Educational Media and the Teacher. Dubuque, IA: Wm. C. Brown Company.

HARDMAN, M.L., DREW, C.J., EGAN, M.W., & WOLF, B. (1984). Human Exceptionality: Society, School, and Family. Boston: Allyn and Bacon.

HARDMAN, M.L., DREW, C.J., EGAN, M.W., & WORLF, B. (1990). Human Exceptionality (3rd ed.). Boston: Allyn and Bacon.

HARGROVE, L.J., & POTEET, J.A. (1984). Assessment in Special Education. Englewood Cliffs, NJ: Prentice-Hall.

HARING, N.G., & BATEMAN, B. (1977). Teaching the Learning Disabled Child. Englewood Cliffs, NJ: Prentice-Hall.

HARRIS, K.R., & PRESSLEY, M. (1991). The Nature of Cognitive Strategy Instruction: Interactive strategy instruction. Exceptional Children, 57, 392-401.

HART, T., & CADORA, M.J. (1980). The Exceptional Child: Label the Behavior [Videocassette & manual series], Northbrook, IL: Hubbard Scientific Company. (Project STRETCH [Strategies to Train Regular Educators to Teach Children with Handicaps], Module 12, ISBN 0-8331-1917-6). HART, V. (1981) Mainstreaming Children with Special Needs. New York: Longman.

HENLEY, M., RAMSEY,R.S., & ALGOZZINE, B. (1993). Characteristics of and Strategies for Teaching Students with Mild Disabilities. Boston: Allyn and Bacon.

HEWETT, F.M., & FORNESS, S.R. (1984). Education of Exceptional Learners. (3rd ed.). Boston: Allyn and Bacon.

HOWE, C.E. (1981) Administration of Special Education. Denver: Love.

HUMAN SERVICES RESEARCH INSTITUTE (1985). Summary of Data on Handicapped Children and Youth. (Digest). Washington, D.C.: U.S. Government Printing Office.

JOHNSON, D.W. (1972) Reaching Out: Interpersonal Effectiveness and Self-Actualization. Englewood Cliffs, NJ: Prentice-Hall.

JOHNSON, D.W. (1978) Human Relations and Your Career: A Guide to Interpersonal Skills. Englewood Cliffs, NJ: Prentice-Hall.

JOHNSON, D.W., & JOHNSON, R.T. (1990). Social Skills for Successful Group Work. Educational Leadership. 47 (4) 29-33.

JOHNSON, S.W., & MORASKY, R.L. Learning Disabilities (2nd ed.) Boston: Allyn and Bacon.

JONES, F.H. (1987). Positive Classroom Discipline. New York: McGraw-Hill Book Company.

JONES, V.F., & JONES, L. S. (1986). Comprehensive Classroom Management: Creating Positive Learning Environments. (2nd ed.). Boston: Allyn and Bacon.

JONES, V.F. & JONES, L.S. (1981). Responsible Classroom Discipline: Creating Positive Learning Environments and Solving Problems. Boston: Allyn and Bacon.

KAUFFMAN, J.M. (1981) Characteristics of Children's Behavior Disorders. (2nd ed.). Columbus, OH: Charles E. Merrill.

KAUFFMAN, J.M. (1989). Characteristics of Behavior Disorders of Children and Youth. (4th ed.). Columbus, OH: Merrill Publishing.

KEM, M., & NELSON, M. (1983). Strategies for Managing Behavior Problems in the Classroom. Columbus, OH: Charles E. Merrill.

KERR, M.M., & NELSON, M. (1983) Strategies for Managing Behavior Problems in the Classroom. Columbus, OH: Charles E. Merrill.

KIRK, S.A., & GALLAGHER, J.J. (1986). Educating Exceptional Children (5th ed.). Boston: Houghton Mifflin.

KOHFELDT, J. (1976). Blueprints for construction. Focus on Exceptional Children. 8 (5), 1-14.

KOKASKA, C.J., & BROLIN, D.E. (1985). Career Education for Handicapped Individuals (2nd ed.). Columbus, OH: Charles E. Merrill.

LAMBIE, R.A. (1980). A systematic approach for changing materials, instruction, and assignments to meet individual needs. Focus on Exceptional Children, 13(1), 1-12.

LARSON, S.C., & POPLIN, M.S. (1980). Methods for Educating the Handicapped: An Individualized Education Program Approach. Boston: Allyn and Bacon.

LERNER, J. (1976) Children with Learning Disabilities. (2nd ed.). Boston: Houghton Mifflin.

LERNER, J. (1989). Learning Disabilities,: Theories, Diagnosis and Teaching Strategies (3rd ed.). Boston: Houghton Mifflin.

LEVENKRON, S. (1991). Obsessive-Compulsive Disorders. New York: Warner Books.

LEWIS, R.B., & DOORLAG, D.H. (1991). Teaching Special Students in the Mainstream. (3rd ed.). New York: Merrill.

LINDSLEY, O. R. (1990). Precision Teaching: By Teachers for Children. Teaching Exceptional Children, 22. (3), 10-15.

LINDDBERG, L., & SWEDLOW, R. (1985). Young Children Exploring and Learning. Boston: Allyn and Bacon.

LONG, N.J., MORSE, W.C., & NEWMAN, R.G. (1980). Conflict in the Classroom: The Education of Emotionally Disturbed Children. Belmont, CA: Wadsworth.

LOSEN, S.M., & LOSEN, J.G. (1985). The Special Education Team. Boston: Allyn and Bacon.

LOVITT, T.C. (1989). Introduction to Learning Disabilities. Boston: Allyn and Bacon.

LUND, N.J. * DUCHAN, J.F. (1988)/ Assessing Children's Language in Naturalist Contexts. Englewood Cliffs, NJ: Prentice Hall

MALE, M. (1994) Technology for Inclusion: Meeting the Special Needs of all Children. (2nd ed.). Boston: Allyn and Bacon.

MANDELBAUM, L.H. (1989). Reading. In G.A. Robinson, J.R., Patton, E.A., Polloway, & L.R. Sargent (eds.). Best Practices in Mild Mental Retardation. Reston, VA: The Division of Mental Retardation, Council for Exceptional Children.

MANNIX. D. (1993). Social Skills for Special Children. West Nyack, NY: The Center for Applied Research in Education.

MARSHALL, ET AL, VS. GEORGIA U.S. District court for the Southern District of Georgia. C.V. 482-233. June 28, 1984.

MARSHALL, E.K., KURTZ, P.D., & ASSOCIATES. Interpersonal Helping Skills. San Francisco, CA: Jossey-Bass Publications.

MARSTON, D.B. (1989) A curriculum-based measurement approach to assessing academic performance: What it is and why do it. In M. Shinn (Ed.). Curriculum-Based Measurement: Assessing Special Children. New York: Guilford Press.

MCDOWELL, R.L., ADAMSON, G.W., & WOOD, F.H. (1982). Teaching Emotionally Disturbed Children. Boston: Little, Brown and Company.
MCGINNIS, E., GOLDSTEIN, A.P. (1990). Skill Streaming in Early

Childhood: Teaching Prosocial Skills to the Preschool and Kindergarten Child. Champaign, IL: Research Press.

MCLOUGHLIN, J.A., & LEWIS, R.B. (1986). Assessing Special Students (3rd ed.). Columbus, OH: Charles E. Merrill.

MERCER, C.D. (1987). Students with Learning Disabilities. (3rd. ed.). Merrill Publishing.

MERCER, C.D., & MERCER, A.R. (1985). Teaching Children with Learning Problems (2nd ed.). Columbus, OH: Charles E. Merrill.

MEYEN, E.L., VERGASON, G.A., & WHELAN, R.J. (Eds.). (1988). Effective Instructional Strategies for Exceptional Children. Denver, CO: Love Publishing.

MILLER, L.K. (1980). Principles of Everyday Behavior Analysis (2nd ed.). Monterey, CA: Brooks/Cole Publishing Company.
MILLS VS. THE BOARD OF EDUCATON OF THE DISTRICT OF COLUMBIA, 348F. Supp. 866 (D.C. 1972).

MOPSICK, S.L. & AGARD, J.A. (Eds.) (1980). Cambridge, MA: Abbott Associates.

MORRIS, C.G. (1985). Psychology: An Introduction (5th ed.). Englewood Cliffs, NJ: Prentice-Hall.

MORRIS, J. (1980). Behavior Modification. [Videocassette and manual series]. Northbrook, IL: Hubbard Scientific Company. (Project STRETCH [Strategies to Train Regular Educators to Teach Children with Handicaps,] Module 16, Metropolitan Cooperative Educational Service Agency.).
MORRIS, J. & DEMONBREUN, C. (1980). Learning Styles [Videocassettes & Manual series]. Northbrook, IL: Hubbard Scientific Company. (Project STRETCH [Strategies to Train Regular Educators to Teach Children with Handicaps], Module 15, ISBN 0-8331-1920-6).

MORRIS, R.J. (1985). Behavior Modification with Exceptional Children: Principles and Practices. Glenview, IL: Scott, Foresman and Company.

MORSINK, C.V. (1984). Teaching Special Needs Students in Regular Classrooms. Boston: Little, Brown and Company.

MORSINK, C.V., THOMAS, C.C., & CORREA, V.L. (1991). Interactive Teaming, Consultation and Collaboration in Special Programs. New York: MacMillan Publishing.

MULLSEWHITE, C.R. (1986). Adaptive Play for Special Needs Children: Strategies to Enhance Communication and Learning. San Diego: College Hill Press.

NORTH CENTRAL GEORGIA LEARNING RESOURCES SYSTEM/CHILD SERVE. (1985). Strategies Handbook for Classroom Teachers. Ellijay, GA.

PATTON, J.R., CRONIN, M.E., POLLOWAY, E.A., HUTCHINSON, D., & ROBINSON, G.A. (1988). Curricular considerations: A life skills orientation. In Robinson, G.A., Patton, J.R., Polloway, E.A., & Sargent, L.R. (Eds.). Best Practices in Mental Disabilities. Des Moines, IA: Iowa Department of Education, Bureau of Special Education.

PATTON, J.R., KAUGGMAN, J.M., BLACKBOURN, J.M., & BROWN, B.G. (1991). Exceptional Children in Focus (5th ed.). New York: MacMillan.

PAUL, J.L. (Ed.). (1981). Understanding and Working with parents of Children with Special Needs. New York: Holt, Rinehart and Winston.

PAUL, J.L. & EPANCHIN, B.C. (1991). Educating Emotionally Disturbed Children and Youth: Theories and Practices for Teachers. (2nd ed.). New York: MacMillan. PENNSYLVANIA ASSOCIATION FOR RETARDED CHILDREN VS. COMMONWEALTH OF PENNSYLVANIA, 334 F. Supp. 1257 (E.D., PA., 1971), 343 F. Supp. 279 (L.D. PA., 19972).

PHILLIPS, V., & MCCULLOUGH, L. (1990). Consultation based programming: Instituting the Collaborative Work Ethic. Exceptional Children. 56 (4), 291-304.

PODEMSKI, R.S., PRICE, B.K., SMITH, T.E.C., & MARSH, G.E., IL (1984). Comprehensive Administration of Special Education. Rockville, MD: Aspen Systems Corporation.

POLLOWAY, E.A., & PATTON, J.R. (1989). Strategies for Teaching Learners with Special Needs. (5th ed.). New York: Merrill.

POLLOWAY, E.A., PATTON, J.R., PAYNE, J.S., & PAYNE, R.A. 1989). Strategies for Teaching Learners with Special Needs, 4th ed.). Columbus, OH: Merrill Publishing.

PUGACH, M.C., & JOHNSON, L.J. (1989a). The challenge of implementing collaboration between general and special education. Exceptional Children, 56 (3), 232-235.

PUGACH, M.C., & JOHNSON, L.J. (1989b). Pre-referral interventions: Progress, Problems, and Challenges. Exceptional Children, 56 (3), 217-226.

RADABAUGH, M.T., & YUKISH, J.F. (1982). Curriculum and Methods for the Mildly Handicapped. Boston: Allyn and Bacon.

RAMSEY, R.S. (1981). Perceptions of disturbed and disturbing behavioral characteristics by school personnel. (Doctoral Dissertation, University of Florida) Dissertation Abstracts International, 42(49), DA8203709.

RAMSEY, R.S. (1986). Taking the practicum beyond the public school door. Journal of Adolescence. 21(83), 547-552.

RAMSEY, R.S., (1988). Preparatory Guide for Special Education Teacher competency Tests. Boston: Allyn and Bacon, Inc.

RAMSEY, R.S., DIXON, M.J., & SMITH, G.G.B. (1986) Eyes on the Special Education: Professional Knowledge Teacher Competency Test. Albany, GA: Southwest Georgia Learning Resources System Center.

RAMSEY R.W., & RAMSEY, R.S. (1978). Educating the emotionally handicapped child in the public school setting. Journal of Adolescence. 13(52), 537-541.

REINHEART, H.R. (1980). Children I Conflict: Educational Strategies for the Emotionally Disturbed and Behaviorally Disordered. (2nd ed.). St Louis, MO: The C.V. Mosby Company.

ROBINSON, G.A., PATTON, J.R., POLLOWAY, E.A., & SARGENT, L.R. (Eds.). (1989a). Best Practices in Mental Disabilities. Des Moines, IA Iowa Department of Education, Bureau of Special Education.

ROBINSON, G.A., PATTON, J.R., POLLOWAY, E.A., & SARGENT, L.R. (Eds.). (1989b). Best Practices in Mental Disabilities. Renton, VA: The Division on Mental Retardation of the Council for Exceptional Children.

ROTHSTEIN, L.F. (1995). Special education Law (2nd ed.). New York: Longman Publishers.

SABATINO, D.A., SABATION, A.C., & MANN, L. (1983). Management: A Handbook of Tactics, Strategies, and Programs. Aspen Systems Corporation.

SALVIA, J., & YSSELDYKE, J.E. (1985). Assessment in Special Education (3rd. ed.). Boston: Houghton Mifflin.

SALVIA J., & YSSELDYKE, J.E. (1991). Assessment (5th ed.). Boston: Houghton Mifflin.

SALVIA, J. & YSSELDYKE, J.E. (1995) Assessment (6th ed.). Boston: Houghton Mifflin.

SATTLER, J.M. (1982). Assessment of Children's Intelligence and Special Abilities (2nd ed.). Boston: Allyn and Bacon.

SCHLOSS, P.J., HARRIMAN, N., & PFIEFER, K. (in press). Application of a sequential prompt reduction technique to the independent composition performance of behaviorally disordered youth. Behavioral Disorders.

SCHLOSS, P.J.., & SEDLAK, R.A.(1986). Instructional Methods for Students with Learning and Behavior Problems. Boston: Allyn and Bacon.

SCHMUCK, R.A., & SCHMUCK, P.A. (1971). Group Processes in the Classroom. Dubuque, IA: William C. Brown Company.

SCHUBERT, D.G. (1978). Your teaching - the tape recorder. Reading Improvement, 15(1), 78-80.

SCHULZ, J.B., CARPENTER, C.D., & TURNBULL, A.P. (1991). Mainstreaming Exceptional Students: A Guide for Classroom Teachers. Boston: Allyn and Bacon.

SEMMEL, M.I., ABERNATHY, T.V., BUTERA G., & LESAR, S. (1991). Teacher perception of the regular education initiative. Exceptional Children, 58 (1), 3-23.

SHEA, T.M., & BAUER, A.M. (1985). Parents and Teachers of Exceptional Students: A Handbook for Involvement. Boston: Allyn and Bacon.

SIMEONSSON, R.J. (1986). Psychological and Development Assessment of Special Children. Boston: Allyn and Bacon.

SMITH, C.R. (1991). Learning Disabilities: The Interaction of Learner, Task, and Setting. Boston: Little, Brown, and Company.

SMITH, D.D., & LUCKASSON, R. (1992). Introduction to Special Education: Teaching in an Age of Challenge. Boston: Allyn and Bacon.

SMITH, J.E., & PATTON, J.M. (1989). A Resource Module on Adverse Causes of Mild Mental Retardation. (Prepared for the President's Committee on Mental Retardation).

SMITH, T.E.C., FINN, D.M., & DOWDY, C.A. (1993). <u>Teaching Students With Mild Disabilities.</u> Fort Worth, TX: Harcourt Brace Jovanovich College Publishers.

SMITH-DAVIS, J. (1989a April). <u>A National Perspective on Special Education.</u> Keynote presentation at the GLRS/College/University Forum, Macon, GA.

STEPHENS, T.M. (1976). <u>Directive Teaching of Children with Learning and Behavioral Disorders.</u> Columbus, OH Charles E. Merrill.

STERNBURG, R.J. (1990). <u>Thinking Styles: Key to Understanding Performance.</u> Phi Delta Kappa, 71(5), 366-371.

SULZER, B., & MAYER, G.R. (1972). <u>Behavior Modification Procedures for School Personnel.</u> Hinsdale, IL: Dryden.

TATEYAMA-SNIEZEK, K.M. (1990.) Cooperative Learning: Does it improve the academic achievement of students with handicaps? <u>Exceptional Children, 57</u>(2), 426-427.

THIAGARAJAN, S. (1976). Designing instructional games for handicapped learners. <u>Focus on Exceptional Children.</u> 7(9), 1-11.

THOMAS, O. (1980). <u>Individualized Instruction</u> [Videocassette & manual series]. Northbrook, IL: Hubbard Scientific Company. (Project STRETCH [Strategies to Train Regular Educators to Teach Children with Handicaps]. Module 14, ISBN 0- 8331-1919-2).

THOMAS, O. (1980). <u>Spelling</u> [Videocassette & manual series]. (Project STRETCH [Strategies to Train Regular Educators to Teach Children with Handicaps]. Module 10, ISBN 0-83311915-X).

THORNTON, C.A., TUCKER, B.F., DOSSEY, J.A., & BAZIK, E.F. (1983). <u>Teaching Mathematics to Children with Special Needs.</u> Menlo Park, CA: Addison-Wesley.

TURKEL, S.R., & PODEL, D.M. (1984). Computer-assisted learning for mildly handicapped students. <u>Teaching Exceptional Children.</u> 16(4), 258-262.

TURNBULL, A.P., STRICKLAND, B.B., & BRANTLEY, J.C. (1978). <u>Developing Individualized Education Programs.</u> Columbus, OH: Charles E. Merrill.

U.S. DEPARTMENT OF EDUCATION. (1993). <u>To Assure the Free Appropriate Public Education of all Children with Disabilities. (Fifteenth annual report to Congress on the Implementation of The Individuals with Disabilities Education Act.).</u> Washington, D.C.

WALKER, J.E., & SHEA, T.M. (1991). Behavior Management: A Practical Appoach for Educators. New York: MacMillan.

WALLACE, G., & KAUFFMAN, J.M. (1978). Teaching Children with Learning Problems. Columbus, OH: Charles E. Merrill.

WEHMAN, P., & MCLAUGHLIN, P.J. (1981). Program Development in Special Education. New York: McGraw-Hill.

WEINTRAUB, F.J. (1987, March). [Interview].

WESSON, C.L. (1991). Curriculum-based measurement and two models of follow-up consultation. Exceptional Children. 57(3), 246-256.

WEST, R.P., YOUNG, K.R., & SPOONER, F. (1990). Precision Teaching: An Introduction. Teaching Exceptional Children. 22(3), 4-9.

WHEELER, J. (1987). Transitioning Persons with Moderate and Severe Disabilities from School to Adulthood: What Makes it Work? Materials Development Center, School of Education, and Human Services. University of Wisconsin-Stout.

WHITING, J., & AULTMAN, L. (1990). Workshop for Parents. (Workshop materials). Albany, GA: Southwest Georgia Learning Resources System Center.

WIEDERHOLT, J.L., HAMMILL, D.D., & BROWN, V.L. (1983). The Resource Room Teacher: A Guide to Effective Practices (2nd ed.). Boston: Allyn and Bacon.

WIIG, E.H., & SEMEL, E.M. (1984). Language Assessment and Intervention for the Learning Disabled. (2nd ed.). Columbus, OH: Charles E. Merrill.

WOLFGANG, C.H., & GLICKMAN, C.D.(1986). Solving Discipline Problems: Strategies for Classroom Teachers (2nd ed.). Boston: Allyn and Bacon.

YSSELKYKE, J.E., ALGOZZINE, B., (1990). Introduction to Special Education (2nd ed.). Boston: Houghton Mifflin.

YSSELDYKE, J.E., ALGOZZINE, B., & THURLOW, M.L. (1992). Critical Issues in Special Education (2nd ed.). Boston: Houghton Mifflin Company.

YSSEDLYKE, J.E., THURLOW, M.L., WOTRUBA, J.W., NANIA, PA.A (1990). Instructional arrangements: Perceptions From General Education. Teaching Exceptional Children, 22(4), 4-8.

ZARGONA, N., VAUGHN, S., 7 MCINTOSH, R. (1991). Social Skills Interventions and children with behavior problems: A review. <u>Behavior Disorders, 16</u>(4), 260-275.

ZIGMOND, N., & BAKER, J. (1990). Mainstream experiences for learning disabled students (Project Meld): Preliminary report. <u>Exceptional Children, 57</u>(2), 176-185.

ZIRPOLI, T.J., & MELLOY, K.J. (1993). <u>Behavior Management.</u> New York: Merri

CPSIA information can be obtained at www.ICGtesting.com
Printed in the USA
BVOW04s0020200116

433467BV00020BA/160/P